THE ECONOMICS OF AN AGING SOCIETY

THE ECONOMICS
of an
AGING SOCIETY

Robert L. Clark, Richard V. Burkhauser, Marilyn Moon,
Joseph F. Quinn, and Timothy M. Smeeding

Blackwell
Publishing

350 Main Street, Malden, MA 02148-5020, USA
108 Cowley Road, Oxford OX4 1JF, UK
550 Swanston Street, Carlton South, Melbourne, Victoria 3053, Australia

First published 2004 by Blackwell Publishing Ltd

Library of Congress Cataloging-in-Publication Data

Clark, Robert L.
   The economics of an aging society/by Clark, Robert L. ... [et al.].
      p. cm.
Includes bibliographical references and index.
   ISBN 0–631–22615–X (hardcover: alk. paper) – ISBN 0–631–22616–8 (pbk: alk. paper)
1. Aged – United States – Economic conditions. 2. Retirement income – United States.
I. Clark, Robert L.
   HQ1064.U5E267 2004
   305.26′0973—dc21

                                                           2003006952

A catalogue record for this title is available from the British Library.

Set in 10/12½ Garamond
by Newgen Imaging Systems (P) Ltd, Chennai, India

For further information on
Blackwell Publishing, visit our website:
http://www.blackwellpublishing.com

CONTENTS

LIST OF FIGURES

LIST OF TABLES

ACKNOWLEDGMENTS

Each of the authors of this book has built a career around research on the economics of aging. We have often taught courses in which the topics examined in this book have been a major component. For years, we had discussed the need for a textbook that would be accessible to economists, demographers, policy-makers, sociologists and others interested in the economic implications of aging. Finally, we decided to write our own book. The authors have spent over two years in writing this book. Our efforts have been supported by a number of people who have kept us on the production schedule, improved the quality of the manuscript, and helped shape our ideas on the economics of aging. A special thanks goes to Florence Allen who turned a manuscript into a book. We would also like to thank Krista Dowling, Kim Desmond, Mary Santy, Kati Foley, Martha Bonney, and Kevin Cahill for research and editorial assistance. We would also like to express our appreciation to Elizabeth Wald of Blackwell who guided us through the final production stages of the book.

CHAPTER ONE

Introduction

"All of us are aging." This cliché is often used to try to interest younger Americans in everything from the purchase of life or long-term care insurance to enrolling in a company's pension plan or establishment of a 401K plan to joining the debate about the future of Social Security and Medicare to reading a book on aging issues. And while it may not always be a successful strategy, it is nonetheless true. As a society, we are aging and issues facing older Americans will continue to increase in importance as the demographic tsunami known as the baby boom moves inexorably to age 65. It will become increasingly difficult to ignore aging issues and their implications for our well-being. We will all live longer lives, on average, and these extra years can be seen as a blessing more than a burden. Indeed, one might argue the relevance of considering aging as a "growth industry."

Despite some claims to the contrary, our economic future is not a sure thing. It is not necessary to assume that an aging society will break the public bank as "greedy geezers" demand an unreasonable share of resources. Nor is it necessarily the case that there will be too few resources to meet the legitimate needs of older Americans. Rather, our economic future is predicated on making good policy choices and understanding both the direct and indirect consequences of various actions. What we do in both collective and individual decisions will help shape the future. This book offers a context in which to view the decisions that will be made.

The economics of aging covers a broad range of issues, all of which can make a difference to every one of us. And from a selfish point of view, there are lessons to be learned for our own lives and opportunities to take advantage of when working in this area. For example, we authors have worked for over 125 years on aging issues, and we still have not resolved all these issues!

WHY WRITE A BOOK ON THE ECONOMICS OF AGING?

The decisions we will need to make in the future are too important to face with no context or framework. That is, in principle, we may all agree that we do not like the fact that some older Americans are poor or that some do not have sufficient health insurance. But what next? At the most elementary level, how do we measure poverty and access to health care in ways that can tell us whether the policies we have in place are succeeding? Current official poverty measures are based on many assumptions, each of which, if changed, could substantially change measured poverty. Other countries use a significantly different measure of poverty. Which is the best measure and why? In the case of health care insurance, there is considerable debate on what constitutes an adequate or reasonable benefit package. Deciding when coverage is adequate (and does not spur over-use of health care services) will have substantial consequences on how we evaluate the current Medicare program and what, if anything, should be added to meet our standards.

Once we understand the size of the social problem we are considering, we need to look at various potential remedies and analyze both their direct consequences and whether they create unintended effects that we do not like. If we increase the generosity of public programs like Social Security and Medicare, for example, will we effectively discourage younger Americans from saving or from staying longer in the labor force? If we "privatize" Social Security and Medicare, what will be the consequences on beneficiaries? The primary advantage of allowing consumers choice in a private market is that presumably each one of us knows what's best for him or herself. But will all consumers have enough information to make "rational" choices about their investment? Even if on average the expected returns to such a system are higher, what responsibility should society take for those whose investments turn out to be lower than average? And will individual choices create side effects that will affect what others can receive?

These are questions well suited to economic analysis. In the end, undertaking such analyses will not tell us which alternative policies to choose, but will allow decision-making to be based on information regarding the likely responses to policy initiatives. Good economic analysis recognizes that values and prejudices exist, but it tries to create objective measures that people with different viewpoints can still use to make choices from alternatives. That is, individuals can use their own criteria and values to choose, but ideally they will better understand what the impacts are likely to be if the issues are first studied systematically.

Economic analysis includes refinement of measures, attempting to capture appropriate indicators for a particular issue. For example, the average income of older Americans would not be very helpful in understanding how prevalent poverty is among this group. The average more heavily reflects the impact of those with high incomes. Four people with incomes of $5,000 each and one person with $1,000,000 in income would result in an average income of $204,000 even though four of them would be poor. A direct measure of poverty or other income measures would do a better job of providing the relevant information. But even limiting the set of measures to the "appropriate" ones may still leave a range of conflicting information.

Another economic concept that is important for understanding aging issues is how behavior will change in response to a change in the economic incentives a person faces. Offering a large pension when a person turns age 62, all other things remaining unchanged, will likely encourage that individual to retire. Economic analysis assumes that individuals weigh the costs and benefits of various approaches in making decisions. From studies of how people have responded to changes in incentives in the past, it is possible to predict with considerable accuracy the impact of a future policy change.

People tend to make changes at the "margin" – that is, public programs are reformed, but seldom totally revamped. Individuals make decisions about work and savings, for example, but usually only in small steps. Changes in economic incentives that seek to affect these marginal decisions can have a big impact over time. For example, a small increase in worker productivity will mount up over time and lead to a substantially different financial future. From a practical perspective, this might mean how to encourage twenty-somethings to put just a bit of their salaries into retirement plans, for instance. As will be discussed in this volume, putting aside savings early on can make an enormous difference at retirement.

But, in aging, multiple factors are often at work adding to the complexity of various analyses. Incremental change often means that only one set of incentives is altered at any one time. Public policy can change to encourage workers to stay in the labor force longer – for example, by raising the normal age of retirement under Social Security as is now taking place. But if employers offer incentives to encourage workers to retire early, it is not clear what the ultimate outcome will be because of conflicting incentives.

In addition, other factors are clearly also important, including cultural attitudes about the role of families and government, medical advances that can affect lifespan and quality of life, and how our population will change in response to a different mix of old and young. But one cannot take on all the issues even in a volume of this length. Instead we try to focus our discussions of these issues as they relate to the key social policies and programs – Old-Age, Survivors and Disability Insurance, Medicare and Medicaid, Supplemental Security Income, private pension policy, etc. – that are likely to be changed by them and to have significant effects on current and future older Americans. This is not a theoretical exercise. It is the job of policy-makers to reduce the "cultural lag" between changing social needs brought about by these demographic and cultural changes and the institutions established to meet these needs in our society. This book focuses on some of these social changes and provides the reader with the tools to evaluate the policy choices proposed to address them.

HOW THIS BOOK CAN HELP YOU

One advantage of providing an economic framework for studying aging issues is that the principles remain the same even when circumstances vary. Thus, while the analysis provided here is up to date, many of the circumstances faced by older Americans and those planning for the future will change.

New problems and challenges arise every day. Economic and policy choices by individuals, firms, and nations are made within the context of the models described throughout this book. While the models and the theories on which they are based remain constant, optimal choices depend on the economic and social framework governing policy options. The best choice for tomorrow may differ from what we select today. For example, in the 1990s, early retirement loomed as an appealing prospect to many people in their fifties. Just a few more years of 25 percent increases in assets and they would end up on "easy street." In 2003, after three years of contraction in those assets, many of these same people are now talking about working well into their sixties or even seventies. Privatization of Social Security in which people could control the investment of their tax contributions (and presumably increase their returns in an ever-rising stock market) seemed to many to be an easy fix for the costs of an aging society in the 1990s. But a more conservative, basic floor of retirement income now looks more attractive to people whose investment portfolios have decreased in value by 50 percent or more, or whose companies' economic declines have nearly wiped out the expected benefit of their pension plans.

Americans' life expectancies continue to expand and their age-based impairment and work limitation rates appear to be declining. But as yet, there has been little evidence that this will decrease the enormous burden that health care costs place on seniors themselves and on taxpayers who help support the Medicare and Medicaid programs. State and local governments, which share many of the costs of long-term care with the federal government, are currently in a financial crisis and in the future may find this area of public support difficult to sustain.

There are no easy answers to the challenges we face as every rich society, and most developing ones, age. And indeed, the choices we make will be influenced by our willingness as a society to share resources and to make difficult choices regarding taxation and family responsibility. Some analysts who focus on the public sector, for example, refer to Social Security and Medicare as "unsustainable." But what does that mean? Cuts in these programs could ease burdens on government, but how will individuals and families respond? Will the underlying problems and needs go away simply because we make reductions in government support? Health care and financial needs will likely remain: the key question is how we as a society organize and pay for them. An essential aspect of analyses of aging is recognizing that lifespan questions must also be taken into account – at different points in time we are both taxpayers and seniors who benefit from programs. This adds to the complexity of assessing the fairness of various approaches.

How should we balance accountability and the specific circumstances facing older Americans? Are we willing to promote individual responsibility and then abide by the outcomes? The health and economic status of older Americans represents a lifetime of decisions and choices, but also the impacts of outside forces that are beyond anyone's control. This lifetime perspective makes issues of aging even more complicated than those facing policy for children and younger families.

It is not our intent in this volume to provide definitive answers to all the policy questions that society will face. In fact, we as authors are unlikely to reach consensus on all the choices that will need to be made over time. Rather, we attempt to put the issues in a factual context and to offer the principles of economic analysis that you can use to make those choices for yourself.

THE RANGE OF ISSUES COVERED

This volume starts with an assessment of the current situation in the United States, but we also include explicit references to other countries. We do so because the range of problems we face with respect to our aging society is remarkably similar to those faced by other countries. Yet as we will see, the social policies and institutions established in other countries do not always match ours. This does not suggest that one country's set of solutions is better or worse in solving common problems. International comparisons are interesting and useful, but it is difficult to make direct inferences about the "appropriate" policy for a given country with respect to choices made in other countries because of the many important differences between countries. Even in comparison with Canada and Western European nations, there are significant attitudinal and cultural differences, including, for example, views about the role of government, inequality in incomes and other circumstances, and the value of choice and individuality that must be taken into consideration. Where it can help inform the issues under study in the United States and remind us that we are not unique, we provide international comparisons here and in other sections of the book, but this is not intended to be a fully integrated cross-national comparison of aging policy.

Also in Part I is a chapter on the economic status of older Americans, presenting measures that will appear again in many places in the following chapters. It quickly becomes apparent that different measures of economic well-being yield different results but the basic trends are the same. The economic status of older Americans has improved substantially since World War II, but pockets of poverty remain and the risk of a fall into poverty is much greater for women than for men. Social policy, especially dramatic increases in the breadth and generosity of Social Security benefits, has had a major role in the decline in the risk of poverty at older ages, but a key question is whether Social Security will continue to do so in the future.

Part II addresses retirement policies in the private sector. Individuals' decisions about when to retire depend upon the resources that will be available to them after leaving the labor force, what their current circumstances are, and what incentives employers impose on the decision. Chapter 4, in particular, introduces a number of key economic concepts that will also be discussed in later chapters. Work and retirement issues have become more complicated over time. Even the definition of retirement is hard to pin down as many seniors return to the labor force after initially leaving a job and beginning to draw retirement benefits. Americans are living longer, so should they expect to work longer as well? The fluidity of employer decisions and even whether they will remain in business to meet promises of deferred compensation such as pension payments adds to future uncertainties.

Part III is devoted to the enormous Social Security program that provides nearly universal coverage of retirement and disability benefits. This program is given credit for substantially reducing poverty in the United States among people aged 65 and older. It was intentionally designed to reward work through the benefit formula that establishes what people are paid in retirement. But that formula is also weighted so as to provide higher proportional benefits to those with low wages. Finding an appropriate balance for these two goals of the program are key issues in the debate over reforms in the Social Security program. Further, the generosity of the benefits provided depend upon what role it is intended to play in the incomes of retirees. Should Social Security be viewed as a floor or the major source of retirement income? A full chapter is also devoted to disability policy. While often given less attention than the retirement and survivor portion of Social Security, disability issues are an important part of aging, particularly since many disability beneficiaries are older.

Part IV turns to health care issues. Health care is a separate and crucial concern for older Americans, and it also has important consequences on their economic well-being. Older Americans face substantially higher health care costs than the young, and although the Medicare program provides nearly universal coverage to this population, its benefits are limited, leaving substantial financing burdens to seniors. This also results in a complicated health care system where most seniors purchase or qualify for additional supplemental coverage. The high and rising costs of health care have made it a particular focus of reforms – both adopted and still under consideration. Many policy-makers are alarmed about the projected future costs of Medicare. Although coverage for acute care services such as hospitalization and physician services is not fully adequate, coverage for long-term care is even more problematic. Long-term care needs are largely supportive in nature – including nursing care and help for normal activities of daily living. Either because of chronic health conditions or simply the frailty of the very old, many older Americans rely on help from others, either at home or in institutions. This care tends to be very expensive and public help is largely limited to those with low incomes and assets.

Our primary objective in writing this book was to provide students with a balanced overview of the economic and policy implications of individual and population aging. Three goals emerged in preparing the manuscript. First, the chapters should present the most recent data on important aspects of our aging population, provide detailed discussion of the major government programs for the elderly, describe the complex nature of employer retirement policies, and assess the economic status of older Americans, in order to make the reader a more informed citizen with respect to key issues in aging public policy debates. Second, the analysis in the chapters should provide students with sufficient economic concepts to compare and contrast alternative policy choices and examine the trade-offs involved in developing appropriate public policies. Most importantly, there is "no such thing as a free lunch." The desirable social aims of providing more generous retirement benefits or better health care must be paid for by someone. The payment can be in the form of higher taxes paid by some to provide benefits to others or it might create "unintended consequences" that lead to saving or work behavior that is socially counter-productive and wasteful. Third, discussion should be provocative and personally interesting to our readers. It is for you to judge if we have achieved these three goals by making you think about your own retirement, plan your future better, and become more involved in developing a national retirement policy for the twenty-first century.

PART ONE

Population Aging and the
Income of the Elderly

CHAPTER TWO

The Graying of America and the World

INTRODUCTION

This book examines the economics of individual and population aging. Most of us are familiar with the importance of an individual aging throughout his or her lifetime. There are significant phases of life that individuals move through such as early childhood, elementary and secondary schooling, entering the labor force, and building a career. If we do not die early, we reach old age and enter a period of retirement. These steps associated with individual aging are easily understood, in part, because we can observe aging in ourselves, our spouses, our parents, and our children. While the analysis presented in this book includes some discussion of the earlier stages of life, the examination of individual aging concentrates on retirement decisions and life in retirement.

Populations, societies, and organizations also age. Population aging is reflected in the increasing average age of a nation's population or an increase in the proportion of the population represented by those above certain ages such as the proportion of the population over age 60 or over age 65. Fewer people understand the aging of populations and its implications. This chapter seeks to provide a basic understanding of the dynamics of population change and then to present data on the aging of America and other countries of the world. Similarly, organizations like a company's labor force can also age. The rate of aging of a workforce is influenced by the human resource policies of the employer. The analysis in this chapter will focus primarily on population aging but will also examine the aging of the national labor force and other organizations.

How widespread and how pervasive is population aging? Why should you and government policy-makers be concerned about the effects of population aging on the national economy and on society? The answers to these questions are at the heart of both the national and global interest in the topic of population aging. In this chapter, we examine the global phenomenon of aging both from a population and from an individual point of view. The objective is to provide an understanding of the causes and consequences of population aging in developed and developing countries.

The world and its population are undergoing significant changes in fertility, mortality and life expectancy, and age structure. These demographic changes have altered the length and the importance of various stages of life. In the twenty-first century, reaching age 60 signifies the attainment of a relatively new stage of life. For many people, reaching this age leads to retirement from a lifetime of work. Retirement can last for well over 20 years for many people in developed countries and individuals must carefully plan for their financial needs in retirement if they are to continue their living standards during this time. Financing a lengthening retirement necessitates greater savings either through national retirement plans, company pension plans, or private savings.

The demographic transformation to an aging society is very far advanced in the United States, in Europe, and in other developed countries. In addition, population aging is now occurring in many developing countries. Population aging will have profound effects on the economics of everyday life, on family arrangements, on how we spend our time, social security programs, and national health systems. This chapter provides information central to understanding the demographics of population aging.

POPULATION MATHEMATICS

Demographers have developed mathematical models to project how populations change size and age structure over time. These models are based on an initial population of a certain size and age structure. The analyst then makes assumptions about the future of various transition rates such as age-specific fertility rates, mortality rates, and immigration rates. If immigration is ignored and fertility and mortality are held constant, repeated annual simulations ultimately produce a population growing (or declining) at a constant rate with a stable age distribution. By stable age distribution, we mean that the age structure of the population does not change over time. For example, the percentage of the population age 65 and older would be the same in all years.

These models can also be applied to organizations such as an individual company. In this case, the transition rates would be new hires, quits, and retirements. In both cases, the transition rates are to some degree endogenous. National governments can influence fertility through the use of subsidies for children while mortality rates can be altered by increases in research budgets for medical technology. Of course, immigration is directly influenced by national policies. Companies can determine their size and age structure by using alternative human resource policies such as hiring only young workers, retirement plans and the incentives that they provide, lifetime employment policies, and layoffs.

National populations

The size and age structure of a population are determined by the national experience in deaths, births, and net immigration. Age-specific mortality rates reflect the proportion of people at each age that die during the year. Using mortality rates, the average life expectancy for a country can be calculated. Reductions in mortality lead to increases in life expectancy. Other factors being constant, reductions in mortality will increase the average age of the population and produce population aging. This is especially true when the declines in mortality are at the older ages. Death rates do not exhibit linear improvements over time. Wars, epidemics such as AIDS in Africa, famines, and medical innovations can result in significant changes in population size and age structure in relatively short periods of time.

The number of births per 1,000 women at each age produces an age-specific fertility rate. These data can then be used to derive a total fertility rate for the nation. The total fertility rate indicates the number of children an average woman would have during her lifetime. Excluding immigration, a total fertility rate of about 2.1 yields enough births over time to keep the population at about the same size. In other words, a fertility rate of 2.1 would result in a population exhibiting zero population growth. Fertility rates in excess of 2.1 are associated with an increasing population while lower fertility rates ultimately will produce declining populations. In general, growing populations with high fertility rates have more children and relatively fewer older persons. In contrast, populations with lower fertility rates will have a higher percentage of older persons and relatively few children.

Net positive immigration increases the population size while net negative immigration will reduce the number of people in any society. The impact of immigration on population age structure depends on the age of the migrants and their mortality and fertility patterns. National immigration policies influence the size and age structure of populations. Countries differ widely in such policies. Among the developed countries, Australia, New Zealand, and the United States have long been countries built on immigrant populations while Japan has a very restrictive immigration policy. Many developing countries have faced substantial outmigration as workers leave for better working opportunities in other countries. Immigrants leaving developing countries are typically younger persons of working age and are often male. Significant outmigration of persons of specific ages will alter the age distribution of a national population.

The impact of mortality, fertility, and immigration on population size and its age structure can easily be shown using mathematical models. These models start with an initial population size and age structure. One method of analysis is to assume that the country is not affected by immigration (a zero immigration policy). Thus, the population will only be influenced by fertility and mortality rates. Now assume that age-specific mortality rates and fertility rates remain constant into the future. The future population can be simulated using these assumptions. The modeler can develop alternative scenarios by assuming higher or lower mortality and fertility rates.

These simulations illustrate that declines in fertility produce more slowly growing or even declining populations that are characterized by a higher proportion of older persons. Declines in mortality also increase population size; however, the impact of these declines on a population's age structure depends on whether the mortality improvements are at younger or older ages. Declines in infant mortality act much the same as increases in fertility and will tend to make the population younger. Declines in mortality at older ages result in more persons in the older age categories and, hence, produce an older population. Population projections are important for national economic planning and play a central role in evaluating the future cost of social security programs. Most developed countries make regular evaluations of the future cost of their social security programs that use long-range population projections to determine expected benefits payments.

One demographic tool often used to assess the age structure of a population and its economic impact is the dependency ratio. Dependency ratios measure the number of people below a certain age compared to the population of working age (the youth dependency ratio) or the number of persons above a certain age to those of working age (the old age dependency ratio). Adding these two ratios together, one could examine the total dependency ratio (young plus old compared to the working age population). As would be expected, populations with high fertility rates have high youth dependency ratios. Examples of countries with high youth dependency ratios include many of the nations of Africa and Latin America. Countries with lower fertility rates will have higher old age dependency ratios, for example, Japan, France, and Germany.

The ages used to determine young and old dependents are influenced by the wealth of a society and its economic and social institutions. For example, in developing countries, young people may leave school at a very young age to enter the labor force and retirement is only a dream. Thus, the upper age for young dependency might be as low as 12 and a relatively old age should be used to determine the old age dependency ratio. In more developed countries, age 18 might be more appropriate for the upper limit on the youth dependency ratio while the tendency toward early retirement might suggest that the old age dependency ratio begins at 60. Box 2.1 illustrates the impact of alternative mortality and fertility assumptions on population age structure and the dependency rates.

Box 2.1 *Demographic History*

Demographers and economists use dependency ratios to illustrate the ratio of persons in the traditional dependent ages to the number of people of working ages. These ratios are often thought to impact on national savings rates and the rate of economic growth. They certainly have implications for financing programs for the dependent populations such as schools for children and retirement plans for older persons. Table 2.1 illustrates the changes in the dependency ratios that are occurring around the world. While the more developed regions are currently much older and well advanced in the aging process, during the next 50 years, the less developed regions will also be aging very rapidly.

Table 2.1 Dependency rates by region, 1970–2050

Region	1970	1998	2025	2050
Total dependency ratio				
World	75	59	52	55
More developed regions	56	49	58	72
Less developed regions	84	62	51	53
Least developed regions	90	86	64	47
Old age dependency ratio				
World	10	11	15	23
More developed regions	15	21	32	42
Less developed regions	7	8	12	21
Least developed regions	6	6	6	11

Source: United Nations, 1997. The youth population ratio is based on persons under age 15 and the old age population ratio is those age 65 and over. Thus, the total population ratio indicates the number of persons aged 0–14 plus those 65 and older expressed as a percentage of the number of persons aged 15–64.

Table 2.2 Actual and projected total fertility rates by country, 1990–2025

Region or country	1990	2000	2025
World	3.4	2.8	2.3
More developed regions	1.9	1.6	1.7
Less developed regions	3.7	3.1	2.4
China	2.2	1.8	1.7
France	1.8	1.8	1.4
Germany	1.5	1.4	1.3
Italy	n/a	1.2	1.3
India	3.8	3.1	2.2
Japan	1.5	1.4	1.6
Sweden	2.1	1.5	1.5
United Kingdom	n/a	1.7	1.4
United States	2.1	2.1	2.2

Sources: US Census Bureau, International Aging Database (2000) and Kinsella and Velkoff (2001, figure 2.5).

The demographic history of the past 50 years in virtually all developed countries includes a post-World War II baby boom followed by steady declines in fertility rates. Fertility rates in many European countries and in Japan are now below 1.5 births per woman (see table 2.2). Without substantial net immigration, these countries will begin to decline in absolute size in the coming years. In fact, Japan is facing the prospect of population decline in this decade and projections indicate that the population in 2030 will be almost 10 percent smaller than the 2000 Japanese population. Projections also indicate that the populations of Italy and Germany will begin to decline during the next quarter century. National populations in all of these countries and in the United States are becoming much older. Without a considerable increase in fertility rates, all of these countries must begin to develop national policies based on the prospect of having 20 percent or more of their populations over age 65.

Rapid improvements in medical technology and declines in mortality at the older ages are accelerating the population aging process. Fewer people dying means more people surviving into the next older age group. In addition to increasing the number of people over, say, age 65, declines in mortality are rapidly increasing the number of people at much older ages, such as the proportion of the population over age 80 (see table 2.3). The increase in the very old population also presents society and individuals with new and unique challenges and opportunities concerning the quality of life during these additional years of life. Key issues include how to provide adequate health at the very old ages and how to finance and increase number of years in retirement.

Significant declines in the fertility rates are also occurring in many developing countries. Declines in fertility are sharply curtailing the rate of population growth in these countries. Based on recent changes in fertility in the developing countries, world population projections have substantially reduced the expected size of the

Table 2.3 Oldest-old in national populations

Countries	Percent of population 80 and over			80 and older as percent of 65 plus		
	1975	2000	2030	1975	2000	2030
China	0.6	0.9	2.9	12.5	13.1	18.3
France	2.5	3.7	7.5	18.3	23.3	31.2
Germany	2.2	3.5	7.2	14.6	21.6	28.1
Italy	1.9	4.0	9.0	16.0	22.2	32.1
India	0.3	0.6	1.4	8.1	13.1	15.7
Japan	1.1	3.7	11.1	13.5	21.7	39.3
Sweden	2.7	5.0	8.6	17.8	29.2	34.3
United Kingdom	2.4	4.0	7.0	17.0	25.5	29.7
United States	2.1	3.3	5.3	20.4	26.5	26.4

Source: Kinsella and Velkoff (2001, table 1).

Table 2.4 Pace of population aging: years required for population aged 65 and over to rise from 7 to 14 percent of national population

Country	Aging period	Number of years required
Developed Countries		
France	1865–1980	115
Sweden	1890–1975	85
United States	1944–2013	69
United Kingdom	1930–1975	45
Spain	1947–1992	45
Japan	1970–1996	26
Developing Countries		
China	2000–2027	27
Singapore	2001–2028	27
Chile	2000–2025	25
Thailand	2003–2025	22
Brazil	2011–2032	21
Colombia	2017–2037	20

Source: West and Kinsella (1998).

future world population and increased the anticipated rate of population aging. The number of older persons in developing countries is expanding rapidly as is the proportion of the population in the older ages. The pace of population aging is especially rapid in some of the Asian countries such as Japan, Singapore, Korea, Taiwan, and Malaysia. Table 2.4 shows the number of years required for the population aged 65 and older to double from 7 percent of the total population to 14 percent of the population in selected developed and developing countries. Compared to the older, more developed western countries, the Asian nations must develop policies and economies to deal with population aging in a much faster time frame.

Organizations aging

Organizations also can age. For example, we could consider the national labor force of a country. As the population ages, the labor force also tends to age; however, the aging of the labor force depends on any changes in age-specific participation rates. For example, declines in the labor force participation rates of older persons will dampen the aging of the labor force compared to the aging of the population. In most developed countries, the participation rates of men 65 and older declined rapidly for much of the twentieth century. Few older men working meant that the labor force did not age as rapidly as the population. The US labor force will age more rapidly in the coming decade. The proportion of the labor force composed of persons 55 and older increased from 11.9 percent in 1990 to 12.9 percent in 2000 and is projected to rise to 16.9 percent in 2010. The median age of the labor force has risen from approximately 36 years in 1990 to a projected 41 years in 2010. The economic effects of the aging of national labor forces are explored in other chapters.

The labor force of individual companies also reflects the aging of the population and labor force; however, the age structure of a firm is dependent on its own human resource policies and the demand for its product. Rapidly growing firms tend to hire relatively more among younger workers and have fewer older workers. This results in a rather young labor force. More mature firms that have been in business for many years tend to be older. Firms that have long-term declines in the demand for their product can become old very quickly. If a firm stops employing new workers, its current labor force ages in place and the workforce becomes older each year. Of course, companies could also decide to reduce the number of workers on their payrolls through early retirement plans. In such cases, older workers may be the first ones to leave. It is easily shown that the resulting age structure is dependent on how the firms react to fluctuations in the demand for their product. Human resource policies directly influence entrance and exit rates and, thus, the age structure of the firm. Understanding these choices by firms is important when assessing implications of the economics of aging in the labor market.

IMPROVING LIFE EXPECTANCY IN AMERICA

Along with the other developed countries, America has undergone a significant demographic transition during the past 100 years. The twentieth century was truly historic in terms of the improvement in the average lifespan of Americans. Table 2.5 summarizes changes in life expectancy during this 100-year period. The increasing life expectancy at older ages along with rising per capita wealth has created

Table 2.5 The change in American life expectancies during the twentieth century

	1900	2000
Life expectancy at birth	48	77
Average Remaining Life at Age 20	43.0	58.0
Average Remaining Life at Age 65	10.4	18.5

The 2000 numbers are based on projections from the 1990 Census. In 1990, the life expectancy at birth was 75.37 years, at 20 it was 56.63 years and at 65 it was 17.28 years.
Source: Lee (1997).

an increasing period of retirement for most Americans. In sum, Americans are living longer but retiring earlier than their parents and grandparents. As a result, retirement years have increased in number for the average person and time in retirement has increased as a portion of total lifespan.

Life expectancy at birth rose by 29 years or by roughly 60 percent between 1900 and 2000. A boy born today can expect to live to 74 years of age and a newly born female has a life expectancy of 80 years of age. Thus, the average life expectancy for all babies born in 2000 is about 77 years. During this period, there has been a dramatic improvement in infant mortality; however, mortality rates declined at all ages. In the early part of the twentieth century, declines in infant mortality and child-hood disease produced most of the gains in average life expectancy. In the latter half of the century, most of the gains in longevity took place explicitly at older ages.

At the dawn of the twentieth century, a 20 year old could expect to live another 43 years. One hundred years later, a 20 year old could expect to live an average of an additional 58 years. Much of the focus in this study of the economics of population aging is concerned with these extra 15 years of average adult life. Table 2.5 also shows that the remaining life expectancy of 65 year olds increased by eight years over the twentieth century, for an average rate of improvement of one month per year, or roughly one added life year every 12 years. Today, life expectancy is increasing at about one year per decade: that is slightly faster than during the early part of the twentieth century.

Based on these mortality rates, a 20 year old in 1900 had about a 52 percent chance of reaching age 65 and then could expect to live another 11.7 years. In contrast, a 20 year old in 2000 had better than an 83 percent chance of reaching age 65 after which another 17.5 years of life could be expected! Many analysts believe that mortality improvements at older ages will continue to occur. Life expectancy of 65 year olds could reach 25 years by the end of the twenty-first century, thus further expanding the retirement years. In one century, a whole new stage of life was added to the life cycle for individuals. Retirement became a significant component of the expected life for most Americans as life expectancy increased and labor force participation fell dramatically for older men. The result was that the retirement period increased in duration so the average American now spends almost one-third of their adult life in retirement.

Although much improved, life expectancy in the United States remains well below that of many other developed countries. Japan has the highest life expectancy in the world with life expectancy at birth now reaching almost 81. Most of the European countries along with Australia, Canada, New Zealand, and Singapore have an average life expectancy exceeding that of the US by one to three years.

Increased life expectancies require careful consideration and planning by both individuals and society at large. Social norms about the expected age of retirement and eligibility ages for Social Security and Medicare benefits need to be reconsidered. Extra years of life in old age and retirement require reflection on the quality of life during these additional years. Increasing life expectancy and its economic and policy implications are central themes in understanding the economics of aging.

While life expectancy has been increasing, fertility has been declining. Over the same 1900–2000 period, fertility rates declined as women delayed childbearing and, on average, gave birth to fewer children. The combined effect of declining infant mortality, longer lives, and lower fertility rates has created an aging society. In 1900, only 4 percent of Americans were 65 or older. Today, nearly 13 percent of Americans are 65 and older. By 2030, an estimated 20 percent or one in five Americans will be age 65 or older. Projections indicate that there will be over 70 million people 65 and over.

The growth in the number of older persons and the aging of the population are the primary causes of the projected social security deficit and the rapid escalation of projected expenditures for health services. Thus, we can see that individual aging and increasing life expectancy require each of us to reconsider our lifetime plans for work and retirement along with consumption and savings decisions. At the macro-level, population aging requires that national retirement and health policies be reformed.

Aging in America

Population aging in America was one of the dominant cultural and economic events of the twentieth century. Expected changes in mortality and fertility imply that further aging will occur. To better understand the continued aging of society, this section provides a graphical depiction of demographic changes in America. The cumulative effects of past and projected demographic changes have created a new population age structure for society. This changing age structure can be clearly shown using a graphical analysis favored by many demographers. The analysis presents the population age structure in a graph that has the percent of population on the horizontal axis separately for men and women. The vertical axis lists age cohorts in chronological order. In 1900, the population of America took the form of a pyramid with large numbers of children at the bottom and very few aged individuals at the top. This structure also characterized most of the nations of the world at that time.

Over the past century, the population age structure of America has shifted from the pyramid that characterized the age structure of the early twentieth century to something more like a rectangle with all generations more equally represented.

Box 2.2 *Trends in Older Workers: Prevalence of Work Limitations and Impairments*

As this chapter shows, the risk of death at all ages has declined and the life expectancy of Americans has substantially increased over time. But are Americans also leading healthier lives or are they merely adding years of life filled with serious impairments and work limitations? The answer to this question is more controversial because the data necessary to answer it are weaker. Yet it is critical to know the answer. If each succeeding generation of older workers not only is likely to live longer but also healthier and more productive lives, then they have the option of staying in the workforce longer to support their added years of life. They will also require fewer medical services as they age.

On the other hand, if their added years of life are ones of poorer health, with serious impairments that limit their ability to work and require greater medical services, then this will require much greater saving on their part while younger or substantial increases on the part of the younger and healthier population to support them in old age. These two very different scenarios have dramatically different implications for the Social Security Old-Age, Survivors and Disability Insurance Program and for future Medicare and Medicaid Program expenses that are more fully discussed in later chapters.

There is some room for optimism. Manton et al. (1997) report declines in the trends in self-reported chronic disabilities among those over age 65 between 1982 and 1994. Crimmins et al. (1999) report significant improvements in the ability of men and women in their sixties to work between 1982 and 1993, again based on self-reports. But critics of these data argue that self-reported information on impairments or ability to work is subject to substantial reporting error and that no consistently collected objective information exists on impairments and work disabilities.

Table 2.6 was developed by Andrew Houtenville for this book using Current Population Survey (CPS) and National Health Interview Survey (NHIS) data that show self-reported responses by men and women of different ages to questions about their ability to work (whether they have a work limitation) and about their impairments. Reports of a work limitation increase with age in both data sets. A sub-sample of CPS respondents were asked the same question one year later. While the percentage of persons who report "longer-term" work limitations is much smaller than the percentage who report a work limitation at any given time, the prevalence of such self-reports also rises with age. The prevalence of a work limitation among those at younger ages is quite small in all years and even at ages 55–61 is only 16.1 percent in 2000. Those aged 55–61 with longer-term work limitations are even fewer, 11.3 percent in 2000. Most workers approaching retirement age do not have work limitations. These data, which cover the period 1981 through 2000, seem to show no real trends in single period work limitation reports but a slight increase in longer-term self-reported work limitation reports among those aged 55–61 in the later part of the 1990s. Trends in self-reported impairments also seem to rise between 1981 and 1995, the last year that consistent questions on impairments were asked in the NHIS.

Table 2.6 Prevalence of work limitation and impairment by age, 1981–2000

	Current Population Survey								National Health Interview Survey							
	Work limitation				Two-period work limitation				Work limitation				Impairment			
	Age group				Age group				Age group				Age group			
Survey Year	25–34	35–44	45–54	55–61	25–34	35–44	45–54	55–61	25–34	35–44	45–54	55–61	25–34	35–44	45–54	55–61
1981	4.0	5.9	10.3	16.8	na	na	na	na	na	na	na	na	na	na	na	na
1982	3.9	5.9	10.4	17.4	1.7	3.0	6.0	8.3	na	na	na	na	na	na	na	na
1983	3.8	5.7	9.7	16.7	1.8	2.7	5.6	9.9	5.8	8.8	14.2	22.0	14.3	19.9	22.7	29.6
1984	4.1	5.6	9.8	17.1	2.0	2.9	5.0	8.8	5.6	8.6	13.5	22.1	16.4	20.0	24.6	30.3
1985	4.1	6.0	10.2	17.5	1.9	2.7	5.7	9.4	5.4	8.5	13.1	22.7	16.5	21.7	27.4	31.3
1986	4.4	6.0	9.8	17.2	na	na	na	na	5.3	8.6	13.2	21.7	16.3	20.7	25.6	28.5
1987	4.4	6.2	9.5	17.0	3.3	5.7	10.7	9.7	5.1	7.8	12.8	19.8	17.3	20.5	22.8	29.3
1988	4.4	5.9	8.6	15.6	2.9	4.6	9.4	9.1	5.6	8.0	12.7	20.0	16.3	20.4	25.9	28.9
1989	4.0	6.3	9.0	16.0	2.9	3.9	9.0	8.8	5.8	8.9	12.7	21.1	17.0	20.3	22.7	26.2
1990	4.2	6.0	9.5	16.6	3.1	5.4	10.4	9.9	5.3	8.5	13.0	18.8	16.7	20.0	24.1	29.7
1991	4.4	6.3	9.4	15.8	2.8	5.0	9.7	9.4	5.5	8.8	13.3	19.9	16.1	21.1	25.8	29.1
1992	4.6	6.4	9.7	15.9	3.1	5.1	9.5	9.5	6.4	9.8	13.7	20.8	17.4	22.4	26.3	31.2
1993	4.8	6.5	9.7	15.6	3.5	5.8	9.7	9.9	6.7	9.8	14.5	22.5	17.5	21.7	25.0	29.2
1994	5.1	7.0	10.7	17.1	3.5	6.2	9.3	9.9	6.7	9.8	14.1	20.6	18.4	20.8	24.9	28.9
1995	4.7	7.3	10.6	16.7	4.1	5.3	10.5	11.5	6.3	9.4	14.4	21.0	15.3	19.5	24.1	32.6
1996	4.5	7.3	10.5	16.8	na	na	na	na	6.1	9.4	13.5	20.0	15.9	16.7	24.3	30.0
1997	4.3	7.1	10.6	16.9	2.2	3.8	5.7	11.2	na	na	na	na	na	na	na	na
1998	3.6	7.0	10.5	16.5	2.2	4.5	6.4	10.6	na	na	na	na	na	na	na	na
1999	3.8	6.7	10.0	16.2	2.2	3.7	6.5	11.3	na	na	na	na	na	na	na	na
2000	3.8	6.7	9.8	16.1	2.3	3.8	5.8	11.3	na	na	na	na	na	na	na	na

na refers to not available.

Source: Created by Andrew Houtenville from March Current Population Survey and National Health Interview Survey. See Burkhauser et al. (2002) for a fuller discussion of these data and how they were developed.

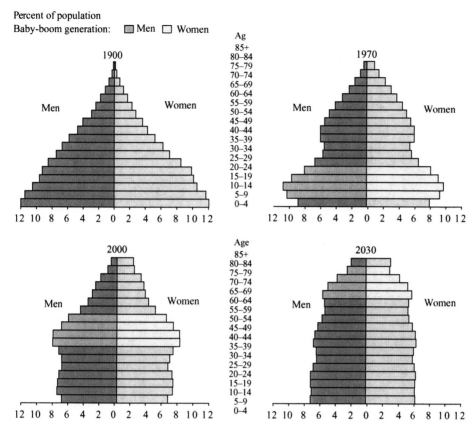

Percent of population
Baby-boom generation: ■ Men □ Women

Figure 2.1 US population by age and sex, 1900, 1970, 2000, and 2030
http://www.prb.org/Content/NavigationMenu/PRB/AboutPRB/Population_Bulletin2/Elderly_Americans.htm
U.S. population in 1990 does not include Alaska or Hawaii. The baby-boom generation includes persons
born between 1946 and 1964.
Source: Himes 2002 Figure1.

Figure 2.1, taken from Himes (2001), shows how this transformation took place
by presenting the actual population age structure for 1900, 1970, and 2000 along
with a projected age structure for 2030. The United States has seen its elderly
population, defined as persons age 65 or older, grow more than tenfold during
the twentieth century. There were just over 3 million Americans age 65 or older in
1900 compared to nearly 35 million in 2000. This expansion in the number of older
persons explains the increase at the top of the graph while reduced fertility is
responsible for the shrinking size of the base of the pyramid.

At the turn of the twentieth century, three demographic trends (high fertility, declining infant and child mortality, and high rates of international immigration) were act-
ing together to keep the US population young. The age distribution of the US
population at the beginning of the twentieth century was heavily skewed toward
younger ages. This distribution is represented by the broad base of the population

age–sex pyramid for 1900 as shown in figure 2.1. The pyramid also reveals that the elderly made up a tiny share of the US population in 1900. Only 4 percent of Americans were age 65 or older, while more that one half of the population (54 percent) was under age 25. At that time, America was primarily an agrarian nation, with large family farms dominating the economic and social landscape. Social insurance was not yet invented, and retirement usually occurred when one could no longer work and death soon followed. Almost all of the aged lived with their children.

Both child and adult health improved and fertility fell during the first half of the century. The inflow of international immigrants slowed considerably after 1920. The Great Depression of the 1930s saw birthrates plummet as well. These trends caused some initial start of population aging in America. The trend was, however, interrupted after World War II by the baby boom that continued for almost two decades. A huge surge in births between 1946 and 1964 resulted from a decline in childlessness (more women had at least one child) combined with larger family sizes (many more women had three or more children). The sustained increase in birth rates during this period fueled a rapid increase in the child population.

By 1970, these baby boomers had moved into their teens and young adult years, creating a bulge in that year's age-sex pyramid shown in figure 2.1 (shaded). The pyramid in 1970 therefore looks like the 1900 pyramid, except for the people in their thirties (who were the Great Depression generation) and for children under age 5, where the first signs of the "baby bust" can be seen.

The large decline in fertility continued and produced something of a baby bust. Young American women reaching adulthood in the late 1960s and 1970s were slower to marry and start families than their older counterparts. Unlike their mothers, they were more likely to have permanent attachments to the labor force (owing to their greater levels of education and to greater job opportunities in the growing service sector of the American economy). They were more likely to divorce if they married. US fertility sank to an all-time low and has not really recovered. The average age of the population started to climb as the large baby-boom generation moved into adulthood, and was replaced by the much smaller baby-bust cohort. By 2000, the baby-boom bulge had moved up to the middle adult ages. The aging of this cohort resulted in a shrinking of the bottom of the traditional population pyramid. These demographic changes took place in the face of the rapid population immigration during the 1980s and 1990s that increased the size of the cohorts in the pyramid under age 60 for 2000. The population's age structure at younger and older ages became more evenly distributed as added life years at the oldest ages increased.

By 2030, the large baby-boom cohorts will be age 65 and older. At that time, the US Census Bureau and the Social Security Administration both predict that the American population will be relatively evenly distributed across age groups, as figure 2.1 shows. All persons age 30 and over were already born when this chart was drawn, and demographers see no evidence of increasing birth rates over the next 30 years. Immigration is not expected to have a major influence on younger generations. These demographic changes will continue to alter the shape of the population pyramid toward that shown for 2030. The most rapid growth for any age group will be in the fraction of persons age 65 and over.

Changes in demographic composition: age, gender, and race

The demographic transition of the twentieth century produced a slowing of population growth and the aging of the population. The discussion above provided a general overview of the demographic changes. Within the context of the general population aging, there are several additional demographic changes that must be considered. Simply observing that the proportion of the population age 65 and over has increased misses the changing age structure among the elderly. We now consider some of these important changes in the composition of the elderly population including the growth in the oldest old, increasing number of women, a growth in the number of nonwhite elderly, health status of the elderly, and regional aging.

The fraction of the population age 85 and older has been rising rapidly. In 2000, 1 in 8 of those over 65 were also over 85, compared to only 1 in 20 in 1950. Among persons age 65 or older, the "oldest-old" are the fastest-growing segment of the elderly population. While those 85 or older made up only about 1.5 percent of the total US population in 2000, they constituted about 12 percent of all elderly. More than 4 million people in the United States were 85 or older in the 2000 Census. By 2050, there are projected to be 19 million to 29 million Americans age 85 or older. The rate of growth of the oldest old will depend on medical progress against cancer and cardiovascular diseases. These oldest-old will make up 5 to 8 percent of the total population in 2050. At this time, more than 20 percent of all elderly Americans will be over age 85. This group is of special interest to planners because those 85 or older are more likely to require medical attention, long-term care services, and other special needs.

Another important facet of population aging is the gender composition of the old. In 2000, there were an estimated three women for every two men age 65 or older. The sex ratio is even more skewed among the oldest-old. In 2000, the number of men per 100 women was 82 among persons aged 65 to 74, 65 among those aged 75 to 84, and there were only 41 men per 100 women among persons aged 85 and older. The sex composition of the elderly population is due to the fact that women have higher life expectancies than men at every age (table 2.7). The preponderance of women among the elderly reflects the higher death rates for men than for women at every age. Since most women marry men who are older than they are, the majority of elderly women today will outlive their spouses by many years. Thus, many women will face the challenges of living for a number of years as widows. These older widows have very high poverty rates. The differential mortality rates and the resulting lengthy period of widowhood require carefully planning by families and a reassessment of national retirement policies. Discussion in the later chapters highlights the importance of national retirement policies and their treatment of women.

Other gender-related issues are also emerging. By 2020, the proportion of women age 62 and over who will be divorced or never married is expected to reach 25 percent compared to just over 12 percent in 1991. Older women who are widowed or divorced are also less likely than older men to remarry. As a result, older

Table 2.7 Life expectancy at birth and at age 65 in years, by sex, 1900, 1950, and 2000

	At birth			At age 65		
	Total	Male	Female	Total	Male	Female
1900	47.3	46.3	50.3	11.9	11.5	12.2
1950	68.2	65.6	71.1	13.9	12.8	15.0
2000	76.9	74.1	79.5	17.9	16.3	19.2

Sources: National Center for Health Statistics (2001, table 28); and Minino and Smith (2001, table 6).

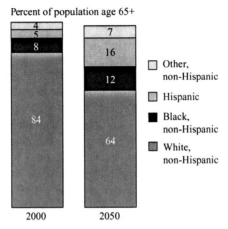

Figure 2.2 Elderly Americans by race and ethnicity, 2000 and 2050
The 2000 figures refer to residents who identified with one race. About 2 percent of Americans identified with more than one race in the 2000 Census.
Source: Himes 2002 Figure 4.

women are more likely than older men to be poor, to live alone, to enter nursing homes, and to depend on people other than their spouses for care. Many of the difficulties of growing older are compounded by past discrimination that disadvantaged women in the workplace and now threatens their economic security. Because high divorce rates and declining rates of marriage for baby-boom women will mean higher proportions of low-income older women in coming decades, social policy has to change to accommodate these trends or the high poverty rates amongst this group will continue.

A third important aspect of population aging in America will be its changing racial and ethnic composition. The US elderly population is becoming more racially and ethnically diverse. Today, about 84 percent of the elderly population are non-Hispanic white compared with about 69 percent of the total US population. By 2050, the proportion of elderly who are non-Hispanic white is projected to drop to 64 percent as the growing minority populations move into old age (see figure 2.2).

Although Hispanics made up only about 5 percent of the elderly population in 2000, 16 percent of the elderly population in 2050 is projected to be Hispanic. Similarly, blacks accounted for 8 percent of the elderly population in 2000, but are expected to make up 12 percent of elderly Americans in 2050. Since most African Americans and Latinos are less wealthy than their counterparts, there will again be pressure for elderly poverty rates to increase as the new century moves forward.

Major racial and ethnic groups age at different rates, depending upon fertility, mortality, and immigration within these groups. Immigration can also have a significant influence on the age structure of racial and ethnic minority groups. This is especially true among Hispanics in America. Although most immigrants tend to be in their young adult ages, when people are most likely and willing to assume the risks of moving to a new country, US immigration policy also favors the entry of parents and other family members of these young immigrants. Other countries generally do not follow this policy. Hence, the number of immigrants age 65 or older is more rapidly increasing in the United States, as more foreign-born elderly move to the United States from Latin America, Asia, or Africa to join their children.

Finally, healthy life expectancy, the number of years over age 65 that a person can expect to be in good health, has also increased. While health status still declines at older ages, the age at which this phenomenon takes place has also increased. Increasingly, people in their sixties and seventies report that their health status has improved and that their limitations in the activities they can accomplish have declined. While dementia and loss of memory continue at high rates for persons in their eighties and beyond, the general trend is toward declining disability at older ages. Thus, we can expect both added longevity and higher quality of life at older ages.

Population aging also varies considerably by geographical regions or across states. Among the states, Florida has the highest proportion of older persons with 17.6 percent of its 2000 population being age 65 or older compared to only 12.4 percent for the national average. The concentration of older persons in Florida is typically explained by high rates of in-migration among the elderly seeking a warmer climate. However, states with relatively high concentrations of older persons include Pennsylvania (15.6 percent), West Virginia (15.3 percent), Iowa (14.9 percent), and North Dakota (14.7 percent). These states do not have the more temperate climates of sunny Florida. The aging of these states is primarily the result of high out-migration of younger persons. Regional aging can occur for many reasons including economic fluctuations. The rapid aging of state and local population can create economic and policy challenges for these governmental units.

Promises and challenges of population aging

The new demographic realities of the twenty-first century are posing new challenges for individuals, families, and political institutions. It seems clear that America has not completed its demographic transition and further changes will continue.

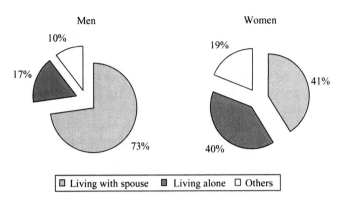

Figure 2.3 Living arrangements of persons, 65+: 2000
Source: US Census Bureau, 2002.

Mortality rates are expected to continue to decline, particularly for those in higher age groups, thus increasing the life expectancy of 65-year olds. However, major uncertainty surrounds the future fertility of American women. The demographic future of America will be very different if fertility rates drop from their current level of about 2.1 to 1.5 or below. These lower fertility rates that are now prevailing in Europe and in Japan will ultimately produce declining populations with approximately 30 percent of the population age 65 and older.

One type of economic challenge presented by population aging is the effect it will have on living arrangements and on housing. Most elderly persons live alone or with their spouse (see figure 2.3). Increased Social Security benefits, better health status, and the changing delivery of care giving from institutions (nursing homes) to the community have all produced increasing physical, as well as fiscal independence among the aged. Increasingly, the elderly demand housing that is designed explicitly for their needs with fewer stairs, larger doorways and other age-specific technological improvements.

In 2000, less than 20 percent of women aged 65 and older lived with someone other than their spouse. And for those aged 75 and over, this proportion increased only to 22 percent. Moreover, the proportion of elders living in nursing homes has actually declined from 5.1 percent in 1950 to 4.5 percent in 2000. Among those 85 and over, the drop in institutionalization was from 24.5 to 18.2 percent. These trends reveal the importance of developing adequate housing suitable for the elderly who may have some physical disability.

The increase in years of remaining life should not be viewed as a burden on society but as an opportunity for enhancing the quality of life. Society must plan for and adopt appropriate policies to deal creatively with population aging and the differing needs of older persons. A better understanding of these issues and the economic forces they produce should stimulate the design of policies that can deal more effectively with aging societies to the benefit of all citizens, young and old.

INTERNATIONAL AGING

Population aging is not a phenomenon occurring only in the United States. Most countries of the world are now aging and the population of the world at large is aging very rapidly. The United Nations (2002) reports:

1. Population ageing is unprecedented, without parallel in the history of humanity. Increases in the proportions of older persons (60 years or older) are being accompanied by declines in the proportions of the young (under age 15). By 2050, the number of older persons in the world will exceed the number of young for the first time in history. Moreover, by 1998 this historic reversal in relative proportions of young and old had already taken place in the more developed regions.

2. Population ageing is pervasive, a global phenomenon affecting every man, woman and child. The steady increase of older age groups in national populations, both in absolute numbers and in relation to the working-age population, has a direct bearing on the intergenerational and intragenerational equity and solidarity that are the foundations of society.

Population aging has been underway in the developed countries for decades. However, in the future, population aging will occur even more rapidly in the developing countries. The number of older persons in developing countries is growing extremely rapidly. Both China and India have more persons age 60 and over than the United States does today. Because of the absolute sizes of their populations, the number of elderly persons in these countries will continue to be among the largest in the world.

The projected aging of the various regions of the world is shown in table 2.8. The developed regions of Europe and North America already have 13 to 16 percent of their populations aged 65 and older and the population is projected to increase to 20 to 24 percent by 2030. In contrast, the elderly population currently only accounts for about 6 percent of the population in Asia and Latin America; however, the proportion of the population aged 65 and over in these countries is expected to double during the next three decades to 12 percent. Aging is occurring at a much slower rate in Africa where wars, famines, and disease continue to take their toll of national populations.

No matter the stage of economic development, national policy-makers must be aware of concern about demographic changes. The growth rate of the population and changes in its age structure require governments to reassess their education, health, and retirement policies. Despite these similarities, population aging affects rich and poor nations differently. The rich nations of the world, especially those with large unfunded social security schemes, face the prospect of increasing numbers of aged and fewer young adults who will be able to support these elders.

Projections in the United States indicate a shortfall of about 2 percent of taxable earnings between the benefits promised to future retirees and the expected tax revenues over the next 75 years. Thus, benefits will have to be reduced or taxes will have to be increased. But the financial problems facing the US Social Security system is substantially less challenging than that confronting other developed nations.

Table 2.8 Population aging by regions of the world: percent of population aged 65 and older

Region	2000	2015	2030
Europe	15.5	18.7	24.3
North America	12.6	14.9	20.3
Oceania	10.2	12.4	16.3
Asia	6.0	7.8	12.0
Latin America/ Caribbean	5.5	7.5	11.6
Near East/ North Africa	4.3	5.3	8.1
Sub-Saharan Africa	2.9	3.2	3.7

Source: US Census Bureau, *International Database*, 2000.
www.census.gov/ipc/www/idbnew.html.

Germany, France, and Italy, for instance, face adjustments of over 5 percent of total income over the next 30 years alone. Rapid increases in required health care costs only exacerbate these cost problems.

In developing countries, the pressures are different. Many developing countries still do not have formal social security systems or these systems cover only a small segment of the population. In other countries, pressures to establish and enhance pre-funded retirement savings schemes may increase. Individual account plans and provident funds such as those in Chile, Singapore, and Australia may become more popular. More than half of men age 60 and over are economically active in developing countries, despite low levels of literacy. In most countries, the proportion of the old who are women is projected to increase, the oldest old will continue to rise as a proportion of the population, and continued low fertility in most of these nations will produce further population aging.

The challenge posed by population aging is that most developing countries must find a way to expand coverage of national retirement systems and increase the level of retirement income at the very time that older populations are increasing rapidly. Thus, the demographic changes are exacerbating the problems of developing adequate national retirement programs. The demographic challenge to the developed countries is how to reform existing social security systems so that they will be affordable and consistent with aged populations. In both cases, careful attention must be paid to the age of eligibility for retirement benefits, the level of retirement benefits, and the treatment of widows.

POPULATION AGING: GOOD NEWS OR BAD?

Longer life spans along with expanding periods of retirement are expected in the twenty-first century. These changes associated with individual aging increase the importance of individuals planning for retirement. Retirement planning requires enhanced financial education, greater savings, and a reassessment of the age of retirement. Increased numbers of older people result in an increase in the old age dependency ratio and place increased financial pressure on retirement and health care systems. These demographic changes raise extremely important questions for individuals and policy-makers. The answers to these questions will determine the nature and the quality of life in the upper ages. Serious discussion at the level of families, communities, and federal policy-makers is needed. Better understanding of the economic and social consequences of societal aging is also necessary. Yet unless we study the economics of old age and the policy questions it poses, we will not be able as a society, to fully understand these consequences and to make better policy decisions.

It would be tragically short-sighted if stereotypes about old age and the traditional family blinded us to the new demographic challenges and real opportunities associated with longer life spans. Many of the dire warnings about the adverse economic effects of population aging could well become self-fulfilling prophecies if nations do not plan for the new demographic realities. At the time most current social policies and cultural norms were put in place during the first half of the twentieth century, life was completely different from what it is today. Not only was life expectancy shorter, but also divorce rates were low, serial marriages were unusual, and the average number of children born to each woman was much higher than what it is today. Influenza, pneumonia, and tuberculosis were the main causes of death. And life expectancy after retirement was relatively short.

The demographic realties of the twenty-first century are very different and require new policies. Hopefully, students reading this book will have a better understanding of future demographic events that are producing individual and population aging. In subsequent chapters, readers are shown how aging will influence national policies and how these policies should be evaluated. "Demography is not destiny," to quote a recent report (NAAS, 1999). Societies and markets can adjust to aging societies. Some institutions will change more slowly than others. The challenge is to be well informed about the economics of population aging so that we better understand the forces at work and can better craft public policy to adapt to these changes.

DISCUSSION QUESTIONS

Comment on the reasonableness of these statements:

1. The primary cause of population aging is a decline in the fertility rate.
2. The optimal age structure of a company's labor force depends on the employment cost of workers at different ages, changes in productivity with age, and the different skills that young and old workers have.
3. Increases in life expectancy at birth are primarily the result of declines in age-specific mortality at ages 65 and older.

4. Governments have been able to alter fertility rates by adopting policies that promote increased births or by policies to lower the birth rates. If you believe this statement is true, name several policies to increase birth rates and several policies that might reduce the number of births.

5. Governments can influence the size and age structure of their populations by changing their immigration policies. Identify some countries that have adopted policies promoting immigration and several countries that have much more restrictive immigration policies.

6. Increasing life expectancy combined with earlier retirement has dramatically increased the number of years the average person spends in retirement. This has been very good for our society.

References

Binstock, R. H., Carstensen, L. L., Carter, D., Estes, C., Foster, D., Friendland, R. B., Goldstein, M., Jackson, J., Lee, R. D., Markus, H., Rando, T., Roden, E., Shoven, J., Smeeding, T. M., and Yeo, G. 2002: *Aging in the 21st Century* (Difficult Dialogues Program, Consensus Report, Institute for Women and Gender). Stanford, CA: Stanford University, 1–18.

Burkhauser, R. V., Daly, M. C., Houtenville, A. J., and Nargis, N. 2002: Self-reported work limitation data: what they can and cannot tell us. *Demography* 39 (3) (August): 541–55.

Crimmins, E., Reynolds, S., and Saito, Y. 1999: Trends in health and ability to work among the older working age population. *Journal of Gerontology* 54 B(I): S31–40.

Cutler, D. M. 2001: The reduction in disability among the elderly. *National Academy of Science* 98 (12) (June 5): 6546–7.

Cutler, D. M. and Meara, E. 2001: *Changes in the Age Distribution of Mortality over the 20th Century.* NBER Working Paper No. 8556 (October). Cambridge, MA: National Bureau of Economic Research. http://papers.nber.org/papers

Himes, C. L. 2001: Elderly Americans. *Population Bulletin* 56 (4). Washington, DC: Population Reference Bureau.

Kinsella, K. and Velkoff, V. 2001: *An Aging World: 2001.* US Census Bureau, Series P-95/01–1. Washington, DC: US Census Bureau.

Lee, R. 1997: Intergenerational relations and the elderly. In Ken Wachter and Caleb Finch (eds.), *Between Zeus and the Salmon: The Biodemography of Longevity,* Washington, DC: National Academy of Sciences Press, 212–33.

Manton, K. G., Corder, L., and Stallard, E. 1997: Chronic disability trends in elderly United States populations: 1982–1994. *Proceedings of the National Academy of Sciences, Medical Sciences* 94: 2593–8.

Minino, A. M. and Smith, B. L. 2001: *National Vital Statistics Reports,* vol. 49, no. 12. Washington, DC: NCHS.

National Academy on an Aging Society 1999: *Demography Is Not Destiny.* Washington, DC: National Academy on an Aging Society.

National Center for Health Statistics 2001: *Health, United States, 2000* (No. 1999–1, January 12, 1999). Washington, DC: Gerontological Society of America.

Smeeding, T. M. 1999: *Social Security Reform: Improving Benefit Adequacy and Economic Security for Women.* Center for Policy Research, Policy Brief No. 16. Syracuse, NY: Syracuse University. http://www-cpr.maxwell.syr.edu/pbriefs/pb16.pdf

United Nations 1997: *The Sex and Age Distribution of the World Populations: The 1996 Revision.* ST/ESA/SER.A/170.UN, NY.

United Nations 2002: Report for Madrid Meeting on World Aging, April. New York: United Nations. http://www.un.org/esa/population/publications/worldageing19502050/

US Census Bureau, International Aging Database 2000: http://www.census.gov/ipc/www/idbnew.html

US Census Bureau 2002: Older Americans month celebrated in May. http://www.census.gov/Press-Release/www/2002/cb02ff07.html (accessed April 30, 2002).

West, L. and Kinsella, K. 1998: *Pension Management and Reform in Asia: An Overview.* NBR Executive Insight. Seattle: National Bureau of Asian Research.

CHAPTER THREE

The Economic Well-Being of Older Americans

LEARNING OBJECTIVES

After completing this chapter, you will be able to:

1 Provide a detailed assessment of the economic well-being of the elderly.
2 Discuss trends in the real and relative economic status of the elderly.
3 Define the concept of poverty and know how it is measured in the United States and in other countries.
4 Describe the importance of assumptions used in the measurement of income and poverty.
5 Discuss how public policies are influenced by poverty and income measures.
6 Assess the significance of including in-kind benefits in determining the economic status of households.
7 Describe the wealth distribution of the population.

CHAPTER OUTLINE

Introduction
The Measurement of Economic Well-Being
Sources and Shares of Income of the Elderly
Income of the Elderly
Poverty among the Elderly
Diversity among the Elderly
The Sensitivity of Income and Poverty Measures to Alternative
  Measurement Assumptions
The Sensitivity of Policy Outcomes to Poverty Measurement Assumptions

INTRODUCTION

The economic well-being of the elderly in America has improved significantly since the 1960s, when over a third of all elderly Americans were poor. The improvement can be seen along a number of dimensions, including absolute money income levels, incomes relative to those of the rest of the population and poverty rates. Similar improvement can be seen with more comprehensive measures of income that include the value of in-kind (or non-cash) benefits, such as Medicare and Medicaid coverage, or housing subsidies.

Despite this generally good news, there exists great diversity among the elderly, and significant pockets of economic distress remain. Even after almost a decade of substantial economic growth at the end of the twentieth century, over 10 percent of older Americans have money incomes below official United States Government poverty thresholds, and many older Americans who are above these thresholds are barely so. Many Americans, especially those who are less educated, who have modest earnings histories or are in poor health, who live alone, who are members of minority groups or who survive into their eighties or nineties, remain at considerable risk of economic deprivation late in life. These elderly tend to depend on public programs, particularly Social Security and Medicare, as the basis for their economic well-being. How the cohorts of baby boomers will fare in their coming retirement years will depend on many factors, including the future state of the economy and capital markets, the timing and nature of labor force withdrawal late in life, and reform initiatives concerning the important social insurance programs that affect elderly populations and their families.

In this chapter, we will discuss and analyze the economic status of older Americans. On what sources of income do the elderly rely? How important is each of them? How has their importance changed over time and how does it differ across the income distribution? How do the incomes of the elderly compare to those of working-age Americans? In making these comparisons, should one consider non-cash or in-kind benefits, which go disproportionately to the elderly, and try to add their value to the cash incomes we usually measure?

Similar questions can be asked about the poverty status of the aged. How are official US poverty thresholds defined? How many elderly are poor, or almost poor? How have elderly poverty rates changed over time, both absolutely and relative to others? How does the probability of being poor in old age vary with race, gender, marital status and other economic and demographic characteristics?

Income is an annual flow, measured over some period of time, often a year. Wealth, in contrast, such as the value of a home or 100 shares of stock, has no time dimension; its units of measurement are simply dollars. What components of wealth are relevant to economic well-being? Most analysts would include the market value of financial assets, real estate and other large capital goods. But what about non-traditional components, such as the value today of the stream of future benefits promised by Social Security or an employer pension? As we will see below, these promises, when viewed as assets, are very important components of the wealth portfolios of many older Americans.

How unequal is the distribution of wealth among the elderly, with and without these non-traditional kinds of wealth? Is it more unequal than the income distribution? How are the wealth accumulations of today's workers, when they reach retirement age, likely to compare to those of their parents, the elderly of today? Are current workers saving enough to continue their current lifestyles during their retirement years ahead?

Finally, as we look ahead into the twenty-first century, should we be optimistic or concerned about the financial well-being of future retirees? How are the income sources that have traditionally supported older Americans likely to fare? About whom should policy-makers be concerned? These are difficult predictions to make, especially in an era where Social Security and Medicare reform are topics of intense political debate.

THE MEASUREMENT OF ECONOMIC WELL-BEING

The well-being of an individual is a very complicated concept. It depends on the person's mental and physical health, living and other social arrangements, personal attitudes, financial resources, and needs. The support infrastructure provided by society is also extremely important. Most of these components of well-being are difficult to quantify and therefore tough to measure. Along this spectrum of difficulty, the easiest dimension may be personal financial resources. There are a number of sophisticated surveys in the United States and elsewhere whose goal is to measure the financial resources available to a representative sample of the population.

The goal is to measure an individual's ability to obtain the goods and services that contribute to his or her economic well-being, and, in some cases, to compare the amount of those resources to the costs of a market basket of necessities. But as we will see, most people live with others and share their personal income and other resources with other family or household members. So while we will focus on the resources available for an individual's consumption, we determine that availability within the income-sharing unit – family or household – in which the person lives. To do so, we must make assumptions about the configuration of the sharing unit, how income is shared within that unit, and the degree to which resources must be increased after adding one more member to maintain the same level of economic well-being for all its members.

The most popular summary measure of purchasing power is annual money income, which adds various components of cash income regularly received by an individual and his or her larger sharing unit. But individuals who live in families or households with the same measured cash income can have very different levels of economic well-being. For instance, households may differ in size, and some adjustment has to be made for the number of people supported by that income. There is a vast literature on the appropriate treatment of family size in measures of economic well-being. Ignoring family size is obviously inappropriate, but utilizing income per capita probably over-adjusts, since it ignores economies of scale – the fact that even if "two can't live as cheaply as one" they can live as well as one on less than twice the income.

Individuals who live in households of the same size, composition, and income can still enjoy different levels of economic well-being. For instance, very different levels of wealth can accompany the same level of income. And not all wealth generates money income and hence will not be captured in an income measure of economic well-being. One family may own a large home, with significant home equity, while another with the same measured income may be paying rent. The owned home can be viewed as generating a stream of imputed rents (which the household "receives" and then "pays" each month or year), but these "transactions" are not traditionally treated or counted as income. But even this measure will under-estimate the real return to housing since the homeowner can at some point sell the house and consume the wealth contained in that asset.

One worker may be eligible for generous employee retirement benefits in a couple of years, while another will be eligible for none. The former worker is obviously better off because of these future benefits, although the benefits do not yet show up in the worker's current income. Finally, one family may be eligible for Medicare or Medicaid coverage while another is not, yet this very important health insurance coverage would not appear as a traditional income source.

Initially we will concentrate on concepts that are typically measured in surveys, and therefore are readily available for analysis. These tend to be annual income flows and stocks of wealth. But we will also discuss some extensions of the traditional measures; in particular, expanded concepts of income that include the value of in-kind benefits (such as Medicare), imputed rent on owner-occupied housing, and wealth concepts that include the present value of future retirement (Social Security and employer pension) benefits.

SOURCES AND SHARES OF INCOME OF THE ELDERLY

SOURCES OF INCOME. Older Americans receive income from a wide variety of sources, including labor earnings, retirement benefits from government and employer pension programs, and the returns from their own accumulated savings, like interest on bonds or savings accounts and dividends from stocks. The most prevalent income source in elderly households is Social Security, or OASDI – the nearly universal old-age, survivors, and disability insurance program. Over 90 percent of American couples in which one or both are aged 65 or over and non-married individuals in this age group receive Social Security benefits, most of which goes to retirees (see table 3.1).[1] About two-thirds of these elderly households receive income from assets (interest, dividends, rents, and royalties), although this is often in small amounts, and therefore this source is less important in the aggregate than its prevalence suggests. About 40 percent receive employer pension

Table 3.1 Income sources of older Americans by age, 2000 (percent of aged units with money income from specified source)

Source	Total	65–69	70–74	75–79	80–84	85+
Social Security	90	86	91	91	94	93
Income from assets	59	60	59	60	62	55
Employer pensions*	41	41	44	43	41	33
Earnings	22	44	26	14	7	4
Veterans' benefits	4	4	4	6	6	3
Public assistance	5	5	5	4	3	6

* Includes income from Railroad Retirement, Government employee pensions, and private pensions and annuities.
Source: SSA (2002a), table 1.1.

benefits, and one in five still have earnings. Other sources are relatively unimportant in aggregate; for example, only about 5 percent report receiving needs-based public assistance, which is primarily Supplemental Security Income.

Table 3.1 also shows how these shares change with the age of the head. The most dramatic change occurs with labor earnings. For households with heads aged 65 through 69, 44 percent have earnings. This drops to only a quarter of those aged 70 to 74, and to 14 percent for those aged 75 through 79. In the oldest category displayed here, those 85 and older, only 4 percent report any earnings during the year – four in a 100 compared to four in ten for those aged 65 to 69 years old. This reflects the retirement process, with workers withdrawing from the labor force as they age.

Other sources change less dramatically with age. Social Security receipt is always high for the elderly, but increases slightly, as some workers have first claimed benefits after age 65. By age 70, when (prior to 2000) people could earn any amount without losing Social Security benefits, the percentage peaks at about 91–94 percent.[2] Pension receipt declines with the age of the recipient, dropping from 44 percent of those aged 70 to 74 years to only one third of those aged 85 or older. This is not because people who have benefits lose them as they age, but rather because recent retirees are more likely to be eligible for pension benefits than are those who retired several decades ago. The prevalence of income from assets declines in the oldest group, which may reflect a cohort effect (like the pension statistics), or the fact that some long-lived Americans consume and then outlive their assets, something that one cannot do with Social Security, which is a lifetime annuity.

SHARES OF INCOME. The receipt of various income sources does not reflect their importance since the magnitude of the income is not considered – a $100 source and a $100,000 source are each counted as a source. Figure 3.1 reflects the share or the proportion of total money income represented by each of the sources discussed for Americans aged 65 and over.[3] If we round off a bit, we see three sources each providing about 20 percent of aggregate income for the elderly (earnings, employer pension income, and income from assets), and one source (the most important one,

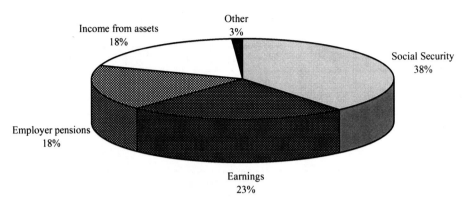

Figure 3.1 Income shares for aged units aged 65 or older, 2000
Source: SSA (2002c), table 7.1.

Social Security) providing 40 percent.[4] Only a small residual (3 percent) comes from all other sources, including means-tested public assistance for the elderly poor.

It is enlightening to observe how the relative importance of these income sources changes with the age and with the income status of the recipient. As seen in figure 3.2, the share of total income from Social Security increases from about 30 percent for those aged 65 to 69 (when many Americans are still working) to well over half for those aged 80 or older. As older Americans leave the labor force, the share of earnings shares drops dramatically with age, from nearly 40 percent for those aged 65 to 69, to only 10 percent for those aged 75 to 79, and 5 percent for those aged 80 or older. The shares from asset income and employer pensions are more stable with age.

Figure 3.3 shows the same type of pie-charts, but with the elderly population disaggregated by income quintile, from the poorest 20 percent (the first quintile) to the richest 20 percent (the fifth quintile). The most significant fact here is that among those in the lowest two quintiles (the poorest 40 percent of older Americans), Social Security provides over 80 percent of all their money income. For the lowest quintile, public assistance (primarily Supplemental Security Income) provides most of the rest, with only 7 percent from all other sources – earnings, pension and income from assets. The poorest elderly simply do not have these sources of income in any significant amount, and subsist almost entirely on government-provided sources.

Among the next 20 percent (the second quintile), asset income and pension income do appear, but together they provide only 12 percent of the total. Even among those with incomes in the middle 20 percent, Social Security provides two dollars out of every three.

The situation is very different at the upper end of the economic scale. Among the 20 percent of the elderly with the highest incomes, earnings are the most important income source (providing over a third of all money income), followed by asset income (a quarter), and Social Security and employer pension benefits (about 20 percent each).

The overwhelming importance of Social Security among low-income elderly can be seen in another way. Among the aged in the lowest two quintiles, about

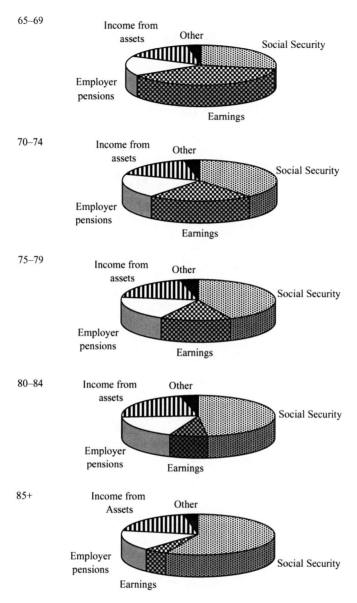

Figure 3.2 Income shares for aged units, by age, 2000 (%)
Source: SSA (2002c), table 7.1.

60 percent of the households receive more than 90 percent of their income from Social Security, and about 85 percent of the households receive more than half of their income from Social Security alone (Social Security Administration, 2002c: table 6.A.2). Even in the fourth quintile, well above the median, nearly half of the households

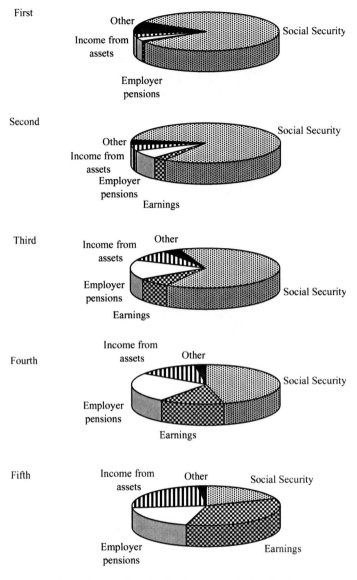

Figure 3.3 Income shares for aged units, by income quintile, 2000
Source: SSA (2002c), table 7.5.

receive more than half of their income from this one source. Social Security is very important to all but the most affluent older Americans.

Those who have earnings or receive pension benefits are rarely found in the lowest quintiles. Among the 20 percent with the lowest incomes, only 4 percent had any earnings at all during the year and only 8 percent received employer pension benefits. Only a quarter had any income from assets. Among the top 20 percent, in sharp contrast, over half (55 percent) had earnings, nearly two-thirds received retirement benefits other than Social Security, and the vast majority (87 percent) reported income from assets (Social Security Administration, 2002c: table 1.6).

The stereotypical "three-legged stool" of income support for the elderly (Social Security, employer pension benefits and income from personal savings) fails to reflect the actual income sources of many older Americans. Two of the three legs (employer pension benefits and income from assets) are usually missing at the lower income levels, while there is a stable, four-legged table (with earnings as the fourth and most important leg) at the upper end of the income distribution.

SOURCES OF INCOME OVER TIME. Sources of income for older Americans have changed during the past four decades. Between 1962 and the late 1970s, the proportion of the elderly units receiving Social Security benefits increased from about 70 to 90 percent, and has remained about 90 percent range ever since (Social Security Administration, 2002b: p. 7). A similar trend is seen for employer pensions. In 1962, only 18 percent of the elderly units received pension benefits. This rose to about 40 percent by the late 1980s, peaked at 45 percent in 1992, and remains near that today. As men retired earlier and earlier during the 1960s and 1970s, the proportion of elderly households with earnings declined from 39 percent in 1962 to only 20 percent in 1986, and has remained around 21 percent since then. The proportion of elderly households receiving asset income peaked at 69 percent in 1990, and has fallen slowly since then, to about 60 percent in 2000. The prevalence of means-tested public assistance has declined dramatically, from 14 percent of all households in 1962 to only half that by the mid-1980s, and even lower today.

SHARES OF INCOME OVER TIME. Social Security grew in importance in the late 1960s and early 1970s because of large increases in Social Security benefits, rising from about 30 percent of aggregate elderly income in 1962 to about 40 percent by the mid-1970s, where it remains today (38 percent in 2000; Social Security Administration, 2002b: pp. 21, 23). The share of total income from pension benefits has also increased, from only 9 percent of the aggregate in 1962 to about 16 percent in the 1970s and 1980s, and nearly 20 percent since the 1990s. The share of elderly income derived from earnings fell through the mid-1980s, from nearly 30 percent in the 1960s to only 16 percent in 1984, as men retired earlier, but has increased recently (to 20 percent by 1996 and 23 percent in 2000), as long-term trends toward earlier and earlier retirement came to a halt, and perhaps even reversed in the late 1990s. "Other" sources (largely public assistance) have almost disappeared from the map, dropping from about 16 percent of aggregate income in 1962 to only 3 percent by the mid-1980s, and the same today.

When one looks at the sources and shares of income among the elderly, over time and today, several conclusions emerge. The first is the overwhelming importance of Social Security benefits for the vast majority of older Americans, especially those at the lower end of the income scale and the oldest of the old. Social Security provides nearly 40 percent of the cash income of those aged 65 and over, over 80 percent for those in the lowest two elderly income quartiles, and nearly 60 percent for those aged 85 and older. The second is the (perhaps surprising) importance of earnings, which provides nearly a quarter of the income of the elderly overall (23 percent in 2000), nearly 40 percent of the income of those aged 65 to 69, and 35 percent for those in the top income quintile of elderly Americans. Earnings and employer pension benefits, as we will see below, are very effective means of keeping older Americans out of poverty. Finally, we note, as we will do again, the tremendous variety and heterogeneity among the elderly. The mean or average, an enticing summary statistic, must always be used with the knowledge of the great variation around it.

With that warning, we turn in more detail to trends in the incomes of older Americans, not by income component, as we have done above, but in total.

INCOME OF THE ELDERLY

MONEY INCOME. In 1999, the median money income for elderly householders (those with a householder aged 65 or older) was approximately $23,000.[5] As seen in figure 3.4, median household income differs dramatically by age, and peaks in the prime working age category (those aged 45 to 54.) Average household income declines and then drops substantially as people move into the traditional retirement ages of 55 to 64, and especially 65 to 74 and above.

Around these averages for any age category, however, is great variation. Figure 3.5 shows the income distribution for households aged 65 to 74 and 75 and older in 1999. There are about 11 million households in the first category and about 10 million in the second. Despite median incomes of over $27,000 and $19,000, respectively, about 13 percent of the households aged 65 to 74 and nearly 19 percent of those aged 75 and older had incomes less than $10,000 in 1999. In that year, the poverty threshold for an aged couple (householder aged 65 or older) was just over $10,000; for an aged individual, just under $8,000. At the other end of the spectrum, 24 percent of the younger group (aged 65 to 74) and 12 percent of the older group (75 and older) had incomes over $50,000.

Within these elderly categories, average incomes can differ dramatically by demographic characteristics. As seen in figure 3.6, the average incomes for black and Hispanic households aged 65 to 74 are only about two-thirds the incomes of analogous white households. For those in the 75 and older category, the ratios are slightly higher, but still only 70 percent.

The US Census Bureau publishes historical tables on median incomes by age category, which documents the dramatic progress over time for the average elderly household. Figure 3.7 compares those aged 65 and over with the overall median for all households in each year, both indexed to 1.0 in 1967. During the 32 years between 1967 and 1999, the overall real (that is, adjusted for inflation) median household income in the United States rose by only 24 percent, less that 1 percent per year. The median elderly household income rose by this much in just six years, from 1967 to 1973, after large increases in Social Security benefits enacted in the late

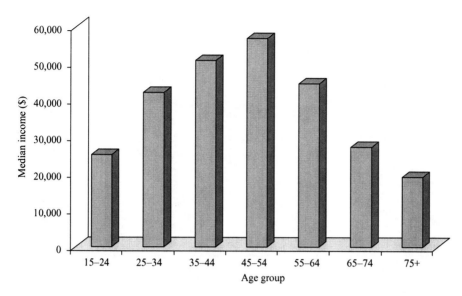

Figure 3.4 Median income, by age of household, 1999
Source: US Census Bureau, 2000a, table 1.

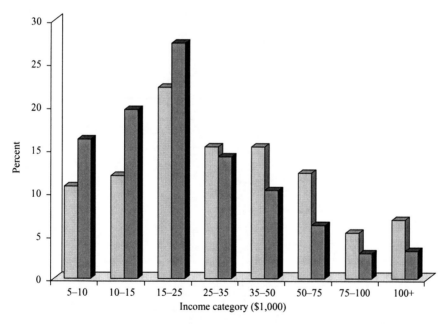

Figure 3.5 Income distribution, households aged 65–74 (left bar) and 75+ (right bar), 1999
Source: US Census Bureau, table 2.

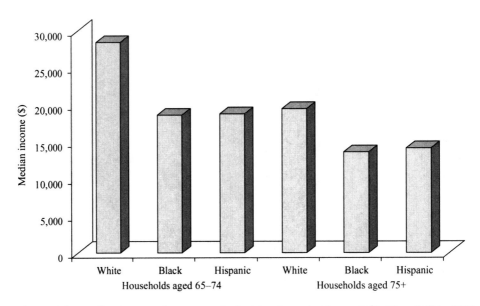

Figure 3.6 Median income, by race and ethnicity, households aged 65–74 and 75+, 1999
Source: US Census Bureau, table 1.

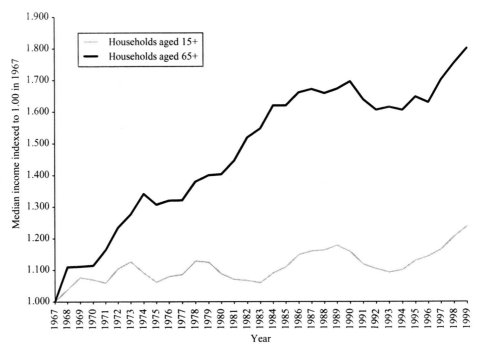

Figure 3.7 Median income, households aged 15+ and 65+, 1967–99
Source: Website (http://www.census.gov/hhes/income/histinc/h10.html).

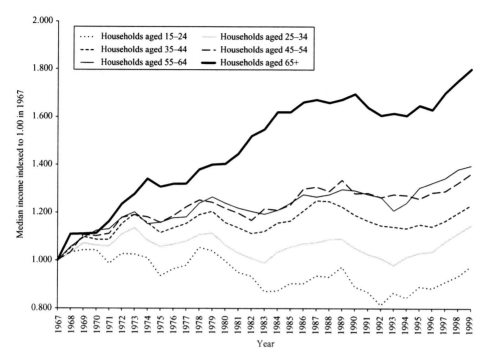

Figure 3.8 Median income, households aged 15–24 through 65+, 1967–99
Source: Website (http://www.census.gov/hhes/income/histinc/h10.html).

1960s and early 1970s. Compared to the original 1967 base, the elderly median rose by 40 percent by 1980, by 70 percent by 1990 and by 80 percent by 1999.

Figure 3.8 disaggregates these time series by age category, and we see that the groups with the two largest percentage increases since 1967 are those that include retirement years – those 65 and older (up 80 percent, as noted above) and those aged 55 to 64, up by half as much, 40 percent. Although those in the prime-working years (45 to 54) are close behind those 10 years older (with an increase of 36 percent), the gains for younger households (aged 25 to 24 and 35 to 44) are much more modest – only 15 and 23 percent. None come close to that of the oldest category.

What is particularly impressive about the 80 percent increase in the median real elderly household income during this third of a century is that it occurred while older men were retiring earlier and earlier, at least for the first half of this period. For example, 50 percent of all men aged 65 (and eligible for full Social Security benefits) were in the labor force in 1970 compared to only 30 percent in 1985, which has crept back to 39 percent by the year 2002. For men aged 62, and just eligible for reduced Social Security benefits, the participation rate fell from 74 to 51 percent between 1970 and 1985, and was slightly higher by 2002 (57 percent.) For men aged 68, the decline was from 38 to 20 percent (in 1985), and back to 30 percent by the year 2002 (Quinn, 2002, updated). Social Security and employer pensions have helped dampen the income declines that accompany departure from the labor force.

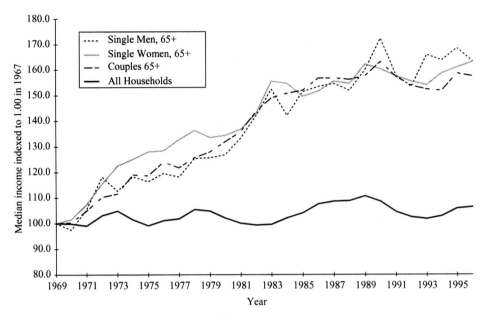

Figure 3.9 Growth in median income, by household type, 1969–96
Source: Website (www.census.gov/hhes/www/mednhhldincome.html).

In a US Census Bureau publication, McNeil (1998) describes the changes in median real income from 1969 to 1996 for all American households and then separately for 12 different household types, including three types of elderly households: (i) married couples with householder aged 65 or over, with no children under 18 in the household; (ii) male one-person households, aged 65 or older; and (iii) female one-person households, aged 65 or older. This is a very useful disaggregation, since the data described above include both couples and single individuals, all aggregated together, and it is possible that these groups might have fared differently.

Of the 12 demographic categories analyzed, the three elderly household types had the three highest percentage increases in median income. While the median income of all households rose by only 6 percent in real terms between 1969 and 1996 the median of the elderly households increased by about 60 percent (see figure 3.9). The overall percentage gains are almost identical for elderly couple and singles. As seen in figure 3.9, most of the increase in the median real income of the elderly occurred by the late 1980s; there has been relatively little change since then.

Incomes of the elderly, on average, have increased significantly in the past several decades, both in absolute terms and adjusted for inflation, and relative to the experiences of the population as a whole. Around these rising averages, however, remain pockets of elderly in severe economic distress – groups that we will analyze and discuss next.

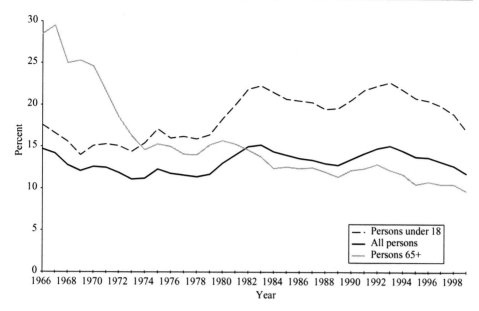

Figure 3.10   Poverty rates by age, 1966–99
Source: US Census Bureau, 2001b.

POVERTY AMONG THE ELDERLY

One of the most noteworthy domestic accomplishments of the past four decades has been the dramatic decrease in poverty among older Americans. This is the mirror image of the increases in average real household incomes noted above. In 1966 and 1967, when the annual time series on poverty rates among separate age categories began, the poverty rate among American elderly (aged 65 and older) was nearly 30 percent. This was twice the rate for the population as a whole and much higher than the rate for children under age 18, which was 17 percent. Estimates from the 1960 Census suggest that even more (35 percent) of American elderly were poor in 1959.

Following large increases in Social Security benefits in the late 1960s and the early 1970s, however, the elderly poverty rate plummeted, falling from about 30 percent in 1967 to less than 15 percent by 1974, and 14 percent in 1977 and 1978 (see figure 3.10). By 1982, the elderly poverty rate was below that for the population as a whole, and it has remained below the overall rate ever since. Since 1980, when the elderly rate increased to about 16 percent, the percentage of older Americans in poverty has slowly declined, moving below 11 percent by 1995 and below 10 percent in 1999. The official 1999 estimate, 9.7 percent, is about two points below the overall rate of 11.8 percent. In contrast to this steady improvement, the trend in poverty rates among children under 18 includes no such good news. The child poverty rate bottomed out at 14 percent in 1969, rose to near or

Box 3.1 *Has the Increase in Social Security Benefits among Older Families Reduced Old-Age Poverty?*

Public policy-makers evaluate the success of social policies in improving the economic well-being of older families using statistics of the type presented in this chapter. Such "evidence-based social policy" provides a rational way to allocate public resources on social problems like poverty. But unlike the natural and behavioral sciences where controlled experiments can be used to test hypotheses (e.g. how safe and effective a given drug is in combating disease, etc.), most public policies questions do not easily lend themselves to such experimental decisions.

In the absence of controlled experiments, social scientists have proposed an array of alternative methods to capture the effect of social policies. Perhaps the most straightforward is the simple thought experiment of comparing "what happened" with what "would have happened" in the absence of the program. The difficulty of using this method of analysis is that while it is possible to know what happened, for instance, to the income of older Americans in the presence of the Social Security program, we will never know for certain what would have happened to them in the absence of Social Security. Hence, it is difficult to answer a policy question like "How much did the increase in Social Security benefits between 1965 and 2000 reduce old-age poverty in the United States?" Nonetheless, policy analysts have tried to do so using a method called comparing the "counterfactual."

For instance, one could use the data discussed in this chapter to look at the household income of older people in 1965 and in 2000 and subtract all Social Security benefits from that household income. This "pre-Social Security" income level could then be compared to the poverty line in 1965 and in 2000. Assuming all else being equal, one could compare the actual poverty rates of older persons in 1965 and in 2000 in the presence of social security with the "counter-factual" poverty rates in the absence of Social Security and assert that this was a reasonable measure of the importance of Social Security on poverty over the period.

But this method of analysis contains a "hidden" assumption that clearly leads to an overstatement of the "true" effect of Social Security on poverty. Subtracting Social Security benefits (which grew dramatically between 1965 and 2000) and assuming that "all else would remain equal" results in the counterfactual income level. While that might be true if the government tomorrow without warning took away all Social Security benefits from older people, it surely would not be true had the system "never existed."

The 2000 data capture the behavioral consequences of a lifetime of the current cohort of older persons who have lived with and counted on the fact that a Social Security system did exist. If it did not exist, they would not have paid

Social Security taxes over their lifetime into the system and their savings and work behavior would have been very different.

As we will discuss in chapters 4 and 5, the Social Security system has had profound effects on the labor force participation rates of Americans. In the absence of our Social Security program, the current older population would have worked longer and saved more over their lifetimes to avoid the very poverty our simple counterfactual showed. While they all would not have been able to avoid poverty at older age, some would have been able to do so. Hence, while it is undoubtedly true that increases in the Social Security system since 1965 have significantly reduced old age poverty, the true effect of the program on poverty is less than this simple "no behavioral change" measure would suggest. To capture the true effect of Social Security on old-age poverty, one must model the behavioral effect of the policy into the counterfactual. This is the more difficult task that economic-based policy analysis tries to do and is what we will discuss in future chapters.

above 20 percent from 1981 through 1996, and has since declined only slightly to 17 percent in 1999.

DIVERSITY AMONG THE ELDERLY

Older Americans are a very diverse demographic group. Although virtually all the traditional measures of economic well-being show significant gains for the elderly over recent decades, these statistics conceal the experiences of specific subgroups of the population. Closer inspection of the income distribution (as noted above) or traditional poverty statistics (below) reveals pockets of economic distress, even after the absolute and relative gains documented above.

Although the elderly are less likely than average to be poor, they are disproportionately represented among the near-poor – those above the poverty threshold, but below 1.25 or 1.50 times the threshold. Figure 3.11 shows the percentage of the total population and the percentage of the elderly population who reside in households with incomes less than 1.00, 1.25, 1.50 and 2.00 times their poverty threshold. While the elderly do have a poverty rate about two percentage points lower than that of the general population, as noted above, they have the same percentage of people with incomes below the 125 percent of the poverty threshold (both about 16 percent) and a higher percentage below the 1.50 (23 percent of the elderly versus 21 percent overall) and 2.00 thresholds (36 versus 30 percent). Over 13 percent of the elderly are near-poor, with incomes between the 1.00 and 1.50 poverty thresholds, compared to only 9 percent of all households.

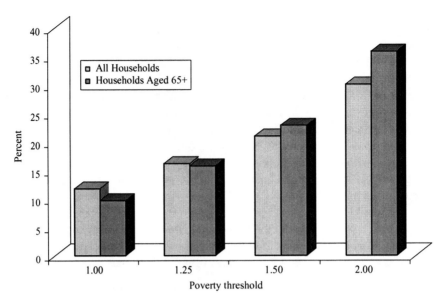

Figure 3.11 Ratio of household income to poverty threshold, all households and households aged 65 and over, 1999
Source: US Census Bureau, 2000b, table 2.

Figure 3.12 illustrates the relationships between gender, age and poverty. Poverty rises with age among the elderly, though more steadily for women than for men. In 2000, the poverty rate was in the 7 to 8 percent range for men aged 65 through 85, and almost 11 percent for men aged 85 and older. Among the older women, the rate rose steadily from 10 percent among the youngest group shown (65–69) to over 15 percent for those 85 and over.

The US Census Bureau estimates that poverty rates among older (65 and older) women are 70 to 80 percent higher than they are for older men (11.8 vs 6.9 percent in 1999; 12.8 vs 7.2 percent in 1998). This occurs for two reasons. The first is that the poverty rate is higher for women than for men in each age group shown in figure 3.13, with the differential expanding with age. The second is a compositional effect. Because women tend to outlive men, a larger percentage of women aged 65 and older than men are in the oldest categories, where poverty rates are highest.

Poverty rates also vary greatly by level of education for older men and women. Of those elderly without a high school diploma, 21 percent were poor in 1992 (15 percent of the men and 26 percent of the women). The poverty rate drops below 10 percent for those with a high school diploma but no college education, to 6 percent for those with some college education but no bachelor's degree, and finally to only 3 percent for older Americans with a bachelor's degree or more. The increase in educational levels over time may be a source of optimism for higher retirement incomes in the future.

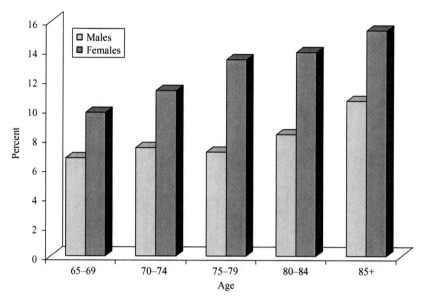

Figure 3.12 Poverty rates by age, men and women aged 65 and above, 2000
Source: SSA (2002c), table 8.2.

Figure 3.13 shows the impact of some other socio-economic characteristics –
race/ethnicity, living arrangements and work status – on the likelihood of being
poor or near-poor. Racial and ethnic differences are significant correlates of poverty
status. Whereas fewer than 8 percent of elderly (non-Hispanic) whites were in
poverty in 1999 (of course, higher for women than for men), over 20 percent of
elderly blacks and Hispanics were poor. About one-third of all elderly blacks
and Hispanics had incomes below 125 percent of the poverty line (not shown in
figure 3.12) and over 40 percent had incomes below 150 percent of the threshold,
compared to only 13 and 19 percent, respectively, for non-Hispanic whites.

Family status is also important. Whereas only about 4 percent of elderly husbands
and wives living in families were poor in 1999, 14 percent of men living alone and 20
percent of all women living alone were poor. About one-third of all elderly men living
alone and 45 percent of such women had incomes below 150 percent of the poverty
line (about $12,000 in 1996) compared to only 12 percent of the married elderly.

When we combine race/ethnicity and living arrangements, some real pockets of
concern appear. For example, in 1999, 44 percent of older black women living alone
were poor, and 70 percent of them had incomes below 150 percent of the poverty line.
For elderly Hispanic women living alone, the analogous figures were even higher – 58
and nearly 80 percent below 100 and 150 percent of the poverty threshold.

Finally, the importance of work experience becomes clear in figure 3.13. Less than
2 percent of the men and women aged 65 or older who worked full-time, year-round
in 1999 were poor. Of the elderly who worked during the year, but did not work

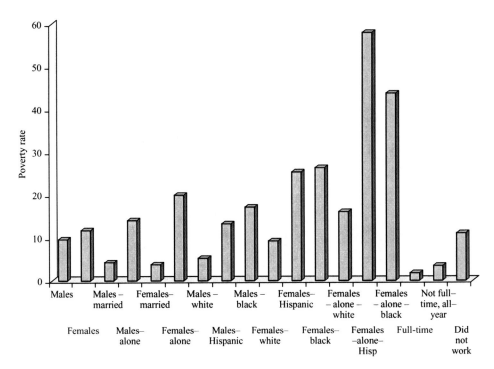

Figure 3.13 Poverty rates by selected demographic characteristics, aged 65 and over, 1999
Source: US Census Bureau, 2000b, tables 2 and 3.

full-time, year-around, only 3 percent (for the men) or 4 percent (for the women) were poor. In contrast, for those elderly who did not work at all during the year, 8 percent of the men and 13 percent of the women fell under the appropriate poverty threshold. How and when people leave the labor force is a very important determinant of their subsequent financial well-being.

When various demographic characteristics are combined, substantial differentials in average income and poverty rates emerge. Only about 3 percent of married (non-Hispanic) white couples aged 65 or older are poor (and far fewer of those in which one or both of the couple are working full-time), compared to about half of all black or Hispanic woman aged 65 or older and living alone. Averages can be deceptive, and as favorable as the post-war experience has been, the data make clear the need to consider the economic well-being of various subgroups of the elderly population, not just the overall averages.

THE SENSITIVITY OF INCOME AND POVERTY MEASURES TO ALTERNATIVE MEASUREMENT ASSUMPTIONS

The previous sections reported official statistics developed by the Social Security Administration and the US Census Bureau to measure the economic well-being and poverty levels of older Americans. But any such measures are sensitive to the assumptions used in their creation. Like the establishment of the official length of a foot, which is said to have been based on the length of the actual foot of a long dead English monarch, there is arbitrariness in official US economic well-being and poverty measures. Hence, it is important to understand both the conceptual and operational judgments that underline our current system for measuring poverty as well as the sensitivity of the levels and trends in measured poverty we observe based on these judgments.

In determining how best to measure poverty and, more broadly, economic well-being, it is important to first ask what the purpose of the measure is. The primary purpose of the poverty measures established by the US Census Bureau is to provide policy-makers with a straightforward and understandable guide for focusing programs on "vulnerable" populations who live below a social mini-mum and for measuring the effectiveness of social programs in reducing that population.

As we will see, the official US poverty measure generally provides reasonable estimates of both. But it is also the case that the methods used to construct the poverty line contain some controversial value judgments that have significant impli-cations for how the level of income necessary to escape poverty has changed over the past 40 years and on the kinds of families that were most likely to be found in poverty over that period.

Based on data from the 1961 Consumer Expenditures Survey, Mollie Orshansky estimated that food purchases equaled about one-third of total expenditures for the median income household in the United States. She then multiplied the cost of a minimum food budget by three for various household types to establish their poverty thresholds (see Ruggles, 1990). These poverty thresholds vary by household size and age. In 1969, the US Bureau of the Budget adopted these thresholds and the equivalence scales (the additional income necessary to keep all members of a family at the same level of economic well-being with the addition of one or more family members) embedded in them for use in all official US measure of poverty. Because "returns to scale" in food purchasing and preparation allowed larger fam-ilies to purchase and prepare a given diet at less than a proportionate increase in cost, the family income necessary to purchase and prepare that food did not rise proportionately with family size. This is reflected in the equivalence scales implicit in our official poverty thresholds to this day.

This set of poverty thresholds by household size has been increased each year to maintain that same level of 1963 purchasing power. Table 3.2 contains official poverty threshold for various size households from 1959–2000. They are based on three principles: an absolute level of poverty based on food consumption in 1961, equivalence scale based on that pattern of food consumption, and the use of the consumer price index since then to increase yearly poverty thresholds. These three principles, which effectively set the income levels necessary for households of var-ious sizes to escape poverty, importantly affect both the level of measured poverty in the United States and its composition to this day.

Table 3.2 Poverty thresholds for nonfarm families of specified size, 1959–2000

Calendar Year	Unrelated individuals	2 Persons	3 Persons	4 Persons	5 Persons	6 Persons
1959	1,467	1,894	2,324	2,973	3,506	3,944
1960	1,490	1,924	2,359	3,022	3,560	4,002
1961	1,506	1,942	2,383	3,054	3,597	4,041
1962	1,519	1,962	2,412	3,089	3,639	4,088
1963	1,539	1,988	2,442	3,128	3,685	4,135
1964	1,558	2,015	2,473	3,169	3,732	4,193
1965	1,582	2,048	2,514	3,223	3,797	4,264
1966	1,628	2,107	2,588	3,317	3,908	4,388
1967	1,675	2,168	2,661	3,410	4,019	4,516
1968	1,748	2,262	2,774	3,553	4,188	4,706
1969	1,840	2,383	2,924	3,743	4,415	4,958
1970	1,954	2,525	3,099	3,968	4,680	5,260
1971	2,040	2,633	3,229	4,137	4,880	5,489
1972	2,109	2,724	3,339	4,275	5,044	5,673
1973	2,247	2,895	3,548	4,540	5,358	6,028
1974	2,495	3,211	3,936	5,038	5,950	6,699
1975	2,724	3,506	4,293	5,500	6,499	7,316
1976	2,884	3,711	4,540	5,815	6,876	7,760
1977	3,075	3,951	4,833	6,191	7,320	8,261
1978	3,311	4,249	5,201	6,662	7,880	8,891
1979	3,689	4,725	5,784	7,412	8,775	9,914
1980	4,190	5,363	6,565	8,414	9,966	11,269
1981	4,620	5,917	7,250	9,287	11,007	12,449
1982	4,901	6,281	7,693	9,862	11,684	13,207
1983	5,061	6,483	7,938	10,178	12,049	13,630
1984	5,278	6,762	8,277	10,609	12,566	14,207
1985	5,469	6,998	8,573	10,989	13,007	14,696
1986	5,572	7,138	8,737	11,203	13,259	14,986
1987	5,778	7,397	9,056	11,611	13,737	15,509
1988	6,022	7,704	9,435	12,092	14,304	16,146
1989	6,310	8,076	9,885	12,674	14,990	16,921
1990	6,652	8,509	10,419	13,359	15,792	17,839
1991	6,932	8,865	10,860	13,924	16,456	18,587
1992	7,143	9,137	11,186	14,335	16,952	19,137
1993	7,363	9,414	11,522	14,763	17,449	19,718
1994	7,547	9,661	11,821	15,141	17,900	20,235
1995	7,763	9,933	12,158	15,569	18,408	20,804
1996	7,995	10,233	12,516	16,036	18,952	21,389
1997	8,183	10,473	12,802	16,400	19,380	21,886
1998	8,316	10,634	13,003	16,660	19,680	22,228

Table 3.2 (*continued*)

Calendar Year	Unrelated individuals	2 Persons	3 Persons	4 Persons	5 Persons	6 Persons
1999	8,501	10,869	13,290	17,029	21,127	22,727
2001	9,039	11,569	14,128	18,104	21,405	24,195

Source: Social Security Administration (2002a), table 3.E1

THE SENSITIVITY OF POLICY OUTCOMES TO POVERTY MEASUREMENT ASSUMPTIONS

ABSOLUTE VERSUS RELATIVE POVERTY THRESHOLDS. The exact poverty thresholds established in 1964 as part of President Lyndon Johnson's "War on Poverty" are as attributable to political and ethical decisions about the part of the lower tail of the income distribution on which public policy should focus as they are to the scientific insight of Orshansky. It is also likely that the simplicity and operational convenience of the poverty measure proposed by Orshansky were as important as the sophistication of its conceptualization of poverty to its later acceptance as the official measure of poverty by the US Bureau of the Budget. Other countries use alternative arbitrary but convenient poverty measures. These other measures also contain assumptions about returns to scale that allow income comparison to be made across different size households. Many of these alternative poverty thresholds are relative in nature; that is, they are some proportion (like 50 percent) of the (household size-adjusted) income of the median person rather than the cost of a specific market basket. As such, they reflect not only the cost of living, but also the standard of living in the society. Of course, choosing 50 percent rather than 45 or 55 percent of the median is as arbitrary as the techniques behind the absolute measure developed by Orshanky. In principle, Orshansky could have chosen some ratio of median household size-adjusted income that would have yielded exactly the same initial poverty thresholds that her measure did. But even if she had, changes in that initial threshold over time would have been dramatically different, since median incomes have risen much faster than the cost of living.

ADJUSTING POVERTY THRESHOLDS BY CHANGES IN PRICES OR REAL GROWTH IN THE ECONOMY. An important policy decision regarding the establishment of an appropriate minimum level of social adequacy in a society is hidden in these two approaches to establishing poverty thresholds. A poverty line automatically tied to median income will increase over time both because of inflation (the price of the same basket of goods increases) and because of real productivity growth in the country (the amount of goods and services available increases). During the past 40 years, median income in the United States has increased dramatically for both reasons. Hence a poverty line that moved with median income would increase in real

terms and the size of the basket of goods and services necessary to reach the politically determined level of social adequacy in a country would increase as the country's median income grew.

In contrast, the official poverty thresholds in the United States have reflected only
the prices of goods and services and not the growth rate in the number of goods
and services available in the country as a whole. Because current poverty thresholds
have been increased only to reflect inflation, they imply that the minimum level of
social adequacy established in 1961 should still be the standard in our richer society
today. If we had increased our poverty threshold to acknowledge both increases in
the cost and the standard of living over the past 40 years, the measured poverty rates
of young and old Americans alike would be substantially higher.

ALTERNATIVE EQUIVALENCE SCALES. Policy-makers and researchers interested in
comparing economic well-being or poverty levels across countries or time must
choose which equivalence scales to employ. To illustrate the sensitivity of the
choice of scale on both the size and composition of poverty across countries, we
draw on the work of Burkhauser et al. (1996).

As discussed above, in order to compare the economic well-being of different
individuals, one must adjust for the fact that household size varies. Empirical measures of poverty assign every person in a household some household size-adjusted
share of the purchasing power of household income.[6] Buhmann et al. (1988) capture the scale elasticity inherent in official poverty thresholds with the following
simple equation:

$$\text{EI} = D/N^e$$

An individual's equalized (or size-adjusted) income (EI) is determined by dividing
total disposable household income (D) by the number of persons in the household
(N) raised to the power (e). Household scale economies are captured by this single parameter. At one extreme, where e equals 1, no economics of scale exists and
a family of two requires twice as much disposable income as a family of one to
reach the same level of equalized income. Operationally, each household member
is assigned the per capita income of the household. At the other extreme, where e
equals 0, economics of scale are perfect so that a household of two or more can
live just as well as a household of one with no increase in their disposable income.
Operationally each person is assigned the income of his or her entire household.
In fact, the true scale economies of household living lie somewhere between these
two extremes.

Table 3.3 shows how much household income thresholds would be increased
with each additional person assuming that a single person household has an
income threshold of 100 in both the United States and Germany using the equivalence scale implicit in their official poverty thresholds. Using the equation above,

Table 3.3 Alternative equivalence scale values for the US and Germany

Number of people in household	Official scales		International experts scale[c]
	U.S.[a]	Germany[b]	
1	100	100	100
2	128	183	141
3	157	244	173
4	201	308	200
5	238	371	224
6	268	435	245
Elasticity scale (e)[d]	0.56	0.81	0.50

[a] Equivalence scale embedded in US Census Bureau poverty threshold.
[b] Equivalence scale embedded in German Public Welfare law (BSHG) since 1991.
[c] Equivalence scale developed by several analysts and used in various studies undertaken on behalf of the Office of Economic Cooperation and Development (Burkhauser et al., 1996, table 1).
[d] Elasticity of scale with respect to household size. Based on $EI = D/N^e$.
Source: Burkhauser et al. (1996)

Burkhauser et al. (1996) established that the implicit scale economics in these two systems are 0.56 and 0.81, respectively, and compare these measures with the .50 scale used in many cross-country comparative studies.

Officially, at least, this implies that the German welfare system believes that returns to scale are much lower as household size increases than is the case either in the United States or in the international expert scale. Operationally, this means that German families of a given size would require more income relative to a single person in their country than would be the case in the United States. For example, a household of two in Germany would require 183 to be equivalent to a single individual with 100, whereas in the United States the same size family would require 128, and using e = 0.5, it would require 141. As the equivalence parameter increases, one will measure a higher proportion of poverty in larger families, and a lower proportion in small ones.

Do these economies of scale assumptions affect social policy? Burkhauser et al. (1996) show that this seemingly innocuous assumption does not matter much in the comparison of overall economic well-being between the two countries. Income inequality and poverty rates are considerable higher in the United States than in Germany regardless of the scale elasticity used. But it matters a great deal in terms of *who* is considered to be poor in the two countries.

Table 3.4, taken from Burkhauser et al. (1996), shows poverty rates in the two countries using the official US equivalence scales, the official German scales, and then those imbedded in the international experts' scale.[7] Overall, poverty rates in

Table 3.4 Measures of the prevalence of poverty for persons within various groups in the US and Germany using different equivalence scale (percentage)

	US			Germany		
	Scales					
Age of head and household type	Official US[a]	Official German[b]	International Experts[c]	Official US[a]	Official German[b]	International Experts[c]
Overall	18.2	17.9	18.2	6.3	5.8	6.4
Aged 65 and Older[d]	21.3	15.5	23.6	9.0	5.6	10.3
Single	41.7	16.6	41.5	15.1	4.0	13.9
Couple	10.3	9.7	11.8	5.5	5.5	8.4
Aged 64 and Younger[d]	17.5	18.2	17.3	5.7	5.9	5.5
All Parents	21.1	23.2	20.5	5.6	7.7	5.0
Single Parent	58.8	59.9	61.5	37.7	30.3	34.1
Two Parents	15.6	17.4	14.3	5.6	7.7	5.1
All Non-Parents	10.9	9.1	11.5	5.8	3.6	6.2

[a] Equivalence scale embedded in US Census Bureau (1989) poverty threshold.

[b] Equivalence scale embedded in German Public Welfare law (BSHG) since 1991.

[c] Equivalence scale developed by several analysts and used in various studies undertaken on behalf of the Office of Economic Cooperation and Development (Burkhauser et al., 1996) and Ruggles (1990).

[d] The age categories, Aged 65 and older and Aged 64 and younger, are all inclusive and hence sum to 100%. Subcategories within these age groups are not all-inclusive and therefore do not sum to age category total.

Source: Burkhauser et al. (1996), table 2, based on the Luxembourg Income Study data from the 1986 US Current Population Survey and the 1984 Germany Socio-Economic Panel.

the United States (the first three columns) are always higher than German poverty rates (the last three columns) regardless of scale, as are the poverty rates of all the subgroups shown. But relative poverty across household types is dramatically affected by the choice of equivalence scales.

For instance, measured poverty among single older persons in the United States in 1985 would be dramatically reduced from 41.7 percent to 16.6 percent by simply adopting German equivalence scales in the United States. Likewise, poverty among older single Germans in 1983 would increase from 4.0 to 15.1 percent by using US equivalence scales in Germany.

Obviously, actual poverty and economic well-being are not so easily transformed, but this example shows the sensitivity of measured poverty to equivalence scales. The reason for the dramatic difference in measured outcomes is that on average younger persons live in larger households than do older persons. The smaller the returns to scale assumed in the equivalence scale (i.e. the larger e is), the higher total household disposable income must be to keep the larger household above the poverty threshold.

As we will discuss later, the same is true with respect to household wealth and its distribution across households of different sizes. Making no adjustments for household size implicitly assumes that household wealth should be measured as if returns to scale in its use are perfect (e = 0; each family member benefits fully from the wealth no matter who consumes it). Such an assumption will overstate the real equalized wealth available to each person in the household and disproportionately overstate, the level of wealth available to larger (and disproportionately younger) households.

Box 3.2 *Measuring Old-age Poverty in a Cross-national Context*

As discussed in the text, official US Census Bureau poverty estimates are based on an absolute measure of poverty that increases each year as average prices increase. Hence it has not changed in real value since the 1960s. In contrast, most poverty estimates outside the United States are based on relative poverty measures that automatically change with changes in the country's median income. Hence over time relative poverty lines will rise faster than our absolute line as long as median income grows in real terms. This means that even if these lines were originally at the same level, measured poverty using the faster growing relative poverty line will define more poverty in a country. Hence while measured poverty rates among older person have fallen dramatically in the past 40 years in the United States, this fall would have been less dramatic if measured with a relative scale.

Table 3.5   Poverty rates of older people using a relative poverty scale [a]

Country	40 percent of median	50 percent of median
Aged 65 and Over		
United States	13.4	22.7
United Kingdom	11.0	23.9
Australia	7.2	28.6
Canada	1.3	6.1
Germany	4.9	8.7
Netherlands	3.2	4.4
Sweden	1.5	6.4
Women Aged 65 and Over		
United States	16.7	27.5
United Kingdom	13.4	34.8
Australia	8.0	34.1
Canada	1.4	8.3
Germany	5.7	10.7
Netherlands	2.9	4.0
Sweden	1.9	9.1
Women Aged 65 and Older Living alone		
United States	26.9	43.1
United Kingdom	23.3	50.1
Australia	12.4	62.1
Canada	2.5	16.2
Germany	9.3	15.9
Netherlands	2.1	3.4
Sweden	3.0	14.7
Women Aged 75 and Older Living alone		
United States	27.7	46.6
United Kingdom	25.2	51.8
Australia	12.3	64.5
Canada	2.4	14.8
Germany	9.9	17.8
Netherlands	1.6	3.1
Sweden	3.1	17.4

[a] Poverty is defined as percentage of population living in households with adjusted disposable income less than 40 or 50percent of median adjusted disposable income for all persons.
Source: Luxembourg Income Study/www.lisproject.org/keyfigures.html.

Luxembourg Income Study (LIS) data are used in table 3.5 to show what elderly poverty rates would look like in the United States if a relative poverty scale were used and how our poverty rates would compare to those of other leading industrialized countries. LIS is a collection of income survey data that has been harmonized exactly for this purpose. LIS contains data for over 25 countries for the period 1975–2000. Poverty estimations are available for all 28 countries at http://www.lisproject.org/keyfigures.html. Poverty rates for seven countries are provided in table 3.5.

Poverty rates are shown for all those aged 65 and over and then for more vulnerable sub-samples: women aged 65 and over, women aged 65 and over who are living alone and women aged 75 and over who are living alone. Poverty rate estimates are presented using poverty lines set at 40 percent of median and 50 percent of median household size adjusted income in each country. The 40 percent standard is above our absolute standard but closer to it than the one-half median standard which would include the "near poor" in the United States (100 to 125 percent poverty range).

Using the 40 percent of median standard, the United States has the highest overall poverty rate by a wide margin. At the 50 percent median standard, poverty rates increase in all countries but less so in the United States which falls to third highest.

Women in general and older women living alone generally do worse than the average older person in all countries. In some nations, for example, Sweden, The Netherlands, Germany, and Canada – older persons do better than others – United States, United Kingdom, Australia. In these last three countries, between 43 and 62 percent of women aged 65 and older living alone, and even higher proportions of the women aged 75 and older living alone, have incomes that are less than 50 percent of the median in their country. In all nations except The Netherlands, poverty rates for the oldest women living alone at the one-half median poverty standard are 15 percent or higher. Thus, single women living alone are far more likely to be in poverty than other older persons in all nations, but this is especially the case in the higher average poverty nations.

INCLUSION OF IN-KIND BENEFITS

There are other measurement issues that can importantly affect both the levels and trends of measured poverty. Measures of economic well-being and poverty are traditionally based on the regular receipt of pre-tax cash income. Tax obligations are not considered, nor are important types of support that are not dispersed to recipients as cash (such as Medicare or Medicaid coverage), nor are assets (like a home) that do not generate a stream of cash income, despite the fact that these support programs and assets can profoundly influence the economic well-being of an individual or a household.

During the past two decades, the US Census Bureau has experimented with alternative income definitions that exclude taxes paid and that include non-cash

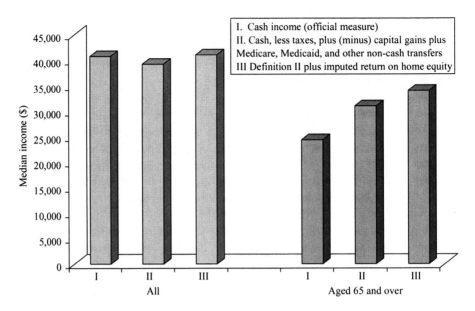

Figure 3.14 Median income under three census income definitions, total population and those aged 65 and over, 1999
Source: US Census Bureau. 2000a, table 13, definitions 1, 14 and 15.

benefits, capital gains and an imputed return on home equity. As we will see, these adjustments disproportionately favor the elderly who tend to be Medicare recipients and home-owners, and who are more likely to have non-taxable income.

Figures 3.14 and 3.15 show median household incomes and the poverty rates for the entire population and for those aged 65 and older using three income definitions:

1 pre-tax cash income only (the traditional measure);
2 cash income after state and federal taxes, plus (or minus) capital gains, plus the value of Medicare, Medicaid and other noncash transfers;
3 the second measure, plus net imputed return on home equity (an imputed rent).

For the population as a whole, all these adjustments together have almost no net impact on median household income – the median declines slightly (about 4 percent) when taxes are subtracted and in-kind benefits added, and then returns to approximately its original value when imputed returns on home equity are included. In sharp contrast, however, the median income of elderly households increases by more than 25 percent when taxes and in-kind benefits are considered, and by over 40 percent when home equity is also included. When the final and broadest Census income measure is used (definition 3, above), the median elderly household income rises from 60 to 83 percent of the overall national median.

Analogous changes occur in the poverty statistics (figure 3.15), which focus on the poorest segments of society, for which Medicaid, housing subsidies, and subsidized

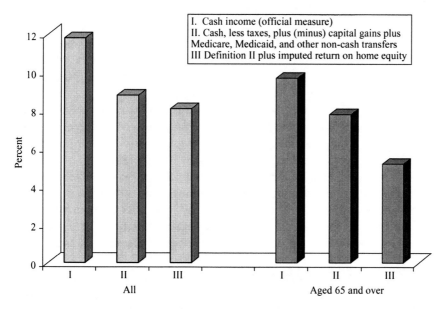

Figure 3.15 Poverty rates under three census income definitions, total population and those aged 65 and over, 1999
Source: US Census Bureau. 2000b, table 5, definitions 1, 14 and 15.

meals are important. When taxes and in-kind benefits are included, and the poverty thresholds kept the same, the national poverty rate declines by about a quarter, from 11.8 to 8.8 percent (in 1999). When home equity is also considered (not an important factor among most of the poverty population), the rate drops a bit more to 8.1 percent – about a 30 percent decline in all.

As with median income, the broader income definitions have a larger impact on the elderly population, whose 1999 poverty rate drops nearly in half (from nearly 10 to 5.2 percent) when taxes, in-kind benefits, and home equity are all included. This decline is much larger than the 30 percent drop for the population as a whole. This confirms the general conclusion that the economic status of the elderly has improved, on average, relative to that of the rest of the population. The inclusion of in-kind benefits makes this even more so.

But these measures have problems of their own. By excluding in-kind transfers, we certainly understate the value of these goods and services to households since their exclusion implicitly assigns a value of zero to their receipt. But to the degree that recipients would not purchase these goods and services at their market price, the use of their market price as a measure of their value to the recipient will overstate their true value.

This is especially true of Medicare and Medicaid. At one time, the actual amounts actually paid by Medicare and Medicaid (e.g. the payment of the individual's hospital and doctor's bills) were used to calculate the value of these benefits to the recipients. This had the odd implication that the sicker a person became, the greater was his economic well-being. For instance, a person lucky enough to receive a heart transplant costing Medicaid $1 million would under such accounting rules be considered a millionaire! A much better estimate of the value of Medicare or Medicaid coverage is not the actual medical expenses paid in a given year, but rather how much that insurance coverage would cost.

The fair market value of this insurance is what is now used to assign a value to those eligible for benefits. But even this improved measure will exaggerate its value to those who, given their incomes, would not have purchased this protection at the fair market price. (See Smeeding, 1992 for a fuller discussion.)

These issues and other have long been discussed in the poverty measurement literature. A panel of experts appointed by the National Academy of Science published recommendations in 1995 (Citro and Michael) and a number of them were utilized in a volume of statistics published by the US Census Bureau in 1999. The recommendations included a broader definition of (disposable) income, excluding payroll and income taxes and job expenses, and including in-kind benefits; a definition of poverty that allows for increases in productivity to effect threshold levels over time; adjustments for geographical differences in the cost-of-living; more sophisticated adjustments for family size; and consideration of out-of-pocket medical expenses.

The Panel recommended that a new definition of family resources be compared to a new definition of a poverty threshold, for families of different compositions in different locales. The new poverty threshold would continue to be based on a basket of consumption goods, but the basket would be expanded from food to represent "a dollar amount for food, clothing, shelter (including utilities), and a small additional amount to allow for other common, everyday needs" (US Census Bureau, 1999: p. 3).

The resources to be compared to these thresholds would include cash income, plus the value of near-money (in-kind benefits) that are available to buy the items in the market basket, minus taxes, work-related expenses (including child-care), child support payments to another household, and household expenditures for medical care or health insurance premiums (ibid.).

Note that these concepts neither include the value of Medicare or Medicaid coverage (on the resource, or income, side), nor the cost of any treatments that these public programs cover (on the expenditure, or threshold, side). Out-of-pocket medical costs, however, are subtracted from income (just like payroll taxes are), since resources spent on medical care or premiums are not available to purchase the necessary items represented by the revised poverty threshold.

Adoption of the National Academy of Science recommendations results in a larger poverty population than the Census estimates, in large part because of the increase in the basic threshold to acknowledge the real growth in the US economy (the increase in the overall standard of living) since 1961. There is a disproportionate increase in measured poverty among the elderly under these revisions, both because of the importance of out-of-pocket medical expenses for this population, even among a population covered by Medicare, and because such a large share of the elderly population was "near-poor" using the official thresholds.

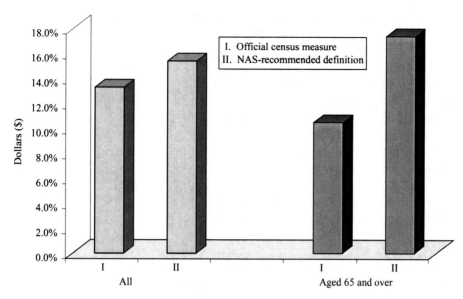

Figure 3.16 Poverty rates under official census and NAS-recommended definitions, total population and those aged 65 and over, 1997
Source: US Census Bureau. 1999, table B2a.

Figure 3.16 illustrates 1997 poverty rates, overall and for the elderly, with and without all the adjustments recommended by the NAS Panel. The adjustments raise the estimated national poverty rate by about two points, and the elderly rate by about seven points. The elderly poverty rate increases from three points below the national average to two points above it.

The revised poverty estimates have not been estimated prior to 1990, so it is not possible to discuss long-range trends under these broader definitions. Between 1990 and 1997, however, the official Census Bureau poverty rate for the elderly declined from 12.2 to 10.5 percent, while the overall rate remained about the same (at about 13.5 percent), showing a small relative improvement for the elderly. With the NAS adjustment, however, the elderly rate stayed the same while the overall rate fell, showing a relative decline in economic status for the elderly during these seven years (ibid.: table B6b).

Nevertheless, we remain convinced of two prior conclusions: that the relative economics status of the elderly has improved significantly over the past four decades, even if not in recent years, and that there remain pockets of economic distress among older Americans, no matter how income and poverty are defined. One source of distress is the high and rising cost of medical care, even for those with government-provided medical insurance. Although progress has been made, there is no cause for complacency.

A POLICY COMPARISON: HOW OLDER PEOPLE FARED DURING
THE GROWTH YEARS OF THE 1980S

Our previous discussion has been based on cross-sectional data that are collected annually by various government agencies to measure the economic well-being of older and younger people at a particular point in time. But these cross-sectional data ignore the fact that the younger people in one year are the older people later. To observe changes in economic well-being over the life course, it is necessary to utilize data that follow the same people over time.

Over the past several decades, data collection has become increasingly sophisticated and there now exist a number of longitudinal data sets that collect socio-economic information on the same individuals over time. These data sets allow researchers to track the economic well-being of individuals as they age.

Table 3.6, taken from Burkhauser et al. (1999), shows that the cross-sectional and longitudinal answers to the question, "How did older people fare over the growth years of the 1980s?" can differ. In the first three columns, data from the Panel Study of Income Dynamics (PSID) are used to analyze how the income (adjusted for household size) of a representative cross-section of Americans in 1983 compares with a similar cross-section in 1989. The sample is then disaggregated to show how older persons and the rest of the population did over the same period. This is exactly the kind of cross-sectional comparisons we have used in the previous discussions in this chapter. These data show how older persons in one year (1983) compare to (different) older persons in another year (1989). The next three columns do something very different; they compare how the same people who were old in the 1983 sample fared in 1983 and then six years later in 1989. The final six columns repeat this exercise using cross-sectional and longitudinal data from the German Socio-Economic Panel.

If the panel data in 1983 capture a random sample of the cross-sectional data in 1983, then columns 1 and 4 should be very similar.[8] The good news for the PSID is that this is almost the case. For the population as a whole, mean and median incomes for 1983 in column 4 are only slightly higher than in column 1. This may be because the attrition of lower-income people from the longitudinal sample between 1983 and 1989, due to death or refusal to respond, is higher than that of higher income people. In addition, there is very little difference in the changes in these average values over the next six years. Both data sets show substantial increases in average real (inflation-adjusted) income as the United States moved from the deep recession of the early 1980s to the business cycle peak of 1989.

Importantly, however, this is not the case for the subsample of older people in 1983 that was followed longitudinally until 1989. While there continue to be small differences in columns 1 and 4 (the 1983 data), there is now a dramatic difference in the changes over time captured in columns 3 and 6. In the cross-section, we observe that the mean and median older person in 1989 had more income than the mean and median older person did in 1983. While the average older person did not enjoy as large an increase in income as the average younger person did

(3–4 percent versus 11–16 percent), we do observe improvements in average elderly household size-adjusted income.

A look at column 6 shows the exact opposite result in the longitudinal data. Those persons who were old in 1983 experienced a significant decline in average income over the six years of substantial economic growth in the 1980s. Which data are telling the truth? Both are, but they are doing so by answering different questions. The panel data is telling us that the real income of those who were 65 or older in 1983 declined over the next six years, by which time they were 71 and older. The reason why, despite this, all older people in 1989 were, on average, better off than all older people in 1983 (which is what the cross-sectional data report) is that the *new* older persons who turned 65 during those six years had incomes high enough to off-set (and more than offset) the real decline in income of those 65 and older in 1983.

Further analysis of the data by Burkhauser et al. shows how this happens. The average (mean) income of persons aged 59 through 64 in 1983, those who would turn 65 during the next six years, was substantially above that of all older persons in 1983 ($23,236 versus $19,623). This was also true in 1989, when these same persons were aged 65 through 70 ($21,228 versus $17,988 for those aged 71 and older). Thus, it is the movement of a richer younger cohort of persons into the older population rather than an increase in the income of those who were already in the 1983 older cohort that explains the cross-sectional results.

WHY DOES THIS MATTER? Statistics are used to help policy-makers resolve problems. Hence, it is critical that we match the appropriate statistics to the appropriate policy question. For instance, in chapter 8, we will discuss the potential consequences of changes in social security rules to bring the system into financial balance over the next several decades. The information in table 3.6 has a substantial bearing on this issue. The growth in the economic well-being of older people in the cross-section was caused by the infusion of a new cohort of older persons who are richer than the earlier cohorts. The average income of these earlier cohorts was actually falling over time. This suggests that if cuts in social security benefits must occur, other things equal, they could be more easily borne by new cohorts of older people (for instance, by raising the normal retirement age for future retirees) than by across-the-board cuts for all older person (for example, by lowering future cost-of-living adjustments.)

Table 3.6 tells another story as well. It suggests that over the growth years in the German economy, the average older German's household income increased from both a cross-sectional and longitudinal perspective. In the cross-section, increases were uniform across the age distribution. Longitudinally, however, the average income of younger Germans grew much faster than that of older Germans. But the fact that the income of older Germans grew at all is noteworthy. As we will see in chapter 7, this was largely due to a German Social Security system that links increases in annual benefits to real increases in wages in the overall economy rather than to increases in prices, as is done in the United States.

Table 3.6 Summary measures of household size-adjusted income and income inequality for persons, by age of individual using cross-sectional and longitudinal data from the United States and Germany

	United States						Germany					
	Cross-sectional[a]			Longitudinal[b]			Cross-sectional[c]			Longitudinal[d]		
			Percent[e]			Percent[f]			Percent[e]			Percent[f]
	1983	1989	Change	1983	1989	Change	1984	1991	Change	1984	1991	Change
Age group	(1)	(2)	(3)	(4)	(5)	(6)	(7)	(8)	(9)	(10)	(11)	(12)
All persons												
Mean	20,509	23,351	13.86	21,254	23,767	11.82	27,763	30,609	10.25	27,460	31,246	13.79
Median	17,518	19,096	9.01	18,271	19,415	6.37	25,154	27,628	9.84	25,284	28,219	13.86
Aged 65 and over												
Mean	18,462	19,231	4.17	19,623	17,988	-8.33	23,634	26,030	10.14	23,386	24,053	2.85
Median	15,089	15,517	2.84	16,701	13,128	-6.93	20,907	22,855	9.32	21,148	21,607	1.22
Aged 64 and younger[g]												
Mean	20,957	24,384	16.35	21,643	24,836	14.75	28,541	31,579	10.64	28,013	32,224	15.03
Median	18,109	20,141	11.22	18,751	20,539	11.61	26,067	28,600	9.86	25,763	29,396	16.20

[a] Post-transfer post-tax household size-adjusted income per individual in 1991 dollars based on cross-sectional data from the *Panel Study of Income Dynamics* (1984, 1990).

[b] Post-transfer post-tax household size-adjusted income per individual in 1991 dollars based on longitudinal data from the *Panel Study of Income Dynamics* (1984, 1990). Sample restricted to individuals observed in both years.

[c] Post-transfer post-tax household size-adjusted income per individual in 1991 deutsche marks based on cross-sectional data from the *German Socio-Economic Panel* (1985, 1992).

[d] Post-transfer post-tax household size-adjusted income per individual in 1991 deutsche marks based on cross-sectional data from the *German Socio-Economic Panel* (1985, 1992). Sample restricted to individuals observed in both years.

[e] This is the ratio of peak-to-trough year values.

[f] For the mean row this is the ratio of peak to trough year values. For the median row, this is the ratio of median change to first year median increase.

[g] In the longitudinal analyses, age is measured in the initial year.

Source: Burkhauser, Crews-Cutts, and Lillard, 1999, table 1; Authors' calculations based on the *Panel Study of Income Dynamics* (1984, 1990) and the *German Socio-Economic Panel* (1985, 1992).

Box 3.3   *Using Longitudinal Data to Compare the Economic Well-Being of Widows Across Countries*

A long-term exit from the labor force is a threat to the household economic well-being of the worker whether caused by unemployment, old age, disability or death. Most modern industrialized countries now have a mixture of private and public institutions to ameliorate the consequences of such exits. Figure 3.17 (see p. 72) shows how the economic well-being of the median widows changed between the year before and the year after the death of her husband in four countries: Canada, Germany, Great Britain and the United States over the 1990s. The widows are disaggregated by the age of their husband at the time of his death. Despite very different mixtures of public and private sources of income in the four countries, the patterns are remarkably similar. Controlling for household size by using an equivalence scale of (0.5) the widows of men aged 62 and above in all four countries have access to household income that ranges from 86 percent to 96 percent of their income when their husbands was alive. Note, however, that these results are quite sensitive to the choice of equivalence scales used. (Why?)

These data come from the Cross-National Equivalent File (CNEF) that contains matched longitudinal data from the British Household Panel Study, Canadian Survey of Labour and Income Dynamics, German Socio-Economic Panel, and United States Panel Study of Income Dynamics. Using CNEF data, researchers can make these kinds of cross-national comparison of employment and economic well-being. For more information on CNEF, visit its web site: http://www.human.cornell.edu/pam/gsoep/equivfil.cfm.

WEALTH AMONG THE ELDERLY

The income and poverty measures discussed above are flow concepts, measuring the flow of economic resources and comparing them to needs over a specific time period, usually a year. In fact, many households have resources other than current income streams (cash or in-kind) on which they can draw to support consumption. Many households have financial assets – accumulated savings and home equity, for example. With the exception of the imputed rent calculation mentioned above and any income flow (like interest or dividends) that financial assets generate, however, these sources are generally ignored in the traditional measures of economic well-being.

Wealth is an alternative measure of financial well-being. It represents the stock of assets that a household owns at a point in time. The units are dollars, not dollars per year. There are difficult measurement issues here too, just as there were above.

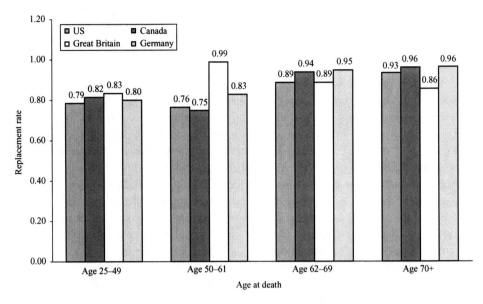

Figure 3.17 Median widows' post-government income replacement rate in the US, Canada, Great Britain, and Germany by husbands' age at death, (e = 0.5)
Source: Final Report to Social Security Administration How Exits from the Labor Force or Death Impact Household Income: A Four Country Comparison of Public and Private Income Support. Burkhauser, Giles, Lillard, and Schwarze, 2002

Many assets are measured directly in dollars, and some of these have fluctuating market values, such as homes, businesses or shares of stock. Other "assets" are harder to measure, such as the right to future retirement benefits from Social Security or from a traditional defined benefit pension plan. One can theoretically calculate the asset equivalent of any future income stream such as anticipated retirement benefits. This is known as its present discounted value – the amount of money today that, if invested at market interest rates, could generate just that future income stream, but these calculations are not normally available in traditional data sets. We will discuss this in greater detail in chapter 7 where we use such calculations to disentangle the insurance and distribution component of Social Security. This issue is of great importance to the elderly, since, it turns out, a significant portion of their (broadly defined) wealth resides in these future retirement benefits. Most of the studies of wealth are based on more traditional and narrow definitions that exclude the value of public and private retirement rights.

The traditional wealth holdings of Americans are more unevenly distributed across households than are their annual incomes. Using data from the Survey of Consumer Finances, Edward Wolff (1998) estimates that the wealthiest 1 percent of all Americans held nearly 40 percent of all household wealth in 1995, and the top 20 percent held 84 percent. Both of these percentages were higher in 1995 than they were in the early 1980s, suggesting that wealth concentration and inequality

Table 3.7 Distribution of total net household wealth by person-based deciles in 1992 and the decile share of 1991 household income and poverty for persons aged 51 through 61

Wealth decile	Mean net household wealth (dollars)	Share of net household wealth (%)	Mean household income (dollars)	Share of household income (%)	Decile poverty rate (%)	Share of total poverty (%)
Bottom	50,270	1.0	16,921	3.2	40	49
2	118,625	2.4	26,024	4.9	19	23
3	181,231	3.7	33,317	6.3	8	9
4	242,450	4.9	40,308	7.6	5	6
5	302,039	6.1	46,063	8.7	2	3
6	372,109	7.6	50,827	9.6	3	3
7	458,460	9.3	55,899	10.6	2	2
8	581,555	11.8	63,277	12.0	1	1
9	781,317	15.9	74,729	14.2	1	1
Top	1,830,966	37.2	120,331	22.8	2	3
All	491,984	100.0	52,774	100.0	8	100
GINI[a]	0.49		0.42			
90–10 Ratio	10.98		8.91			
Theil (0)[b]	0.45		0.35			
Theil (1)[b]	0.47		0.33			

HRS sample weights were used to make the sample representative of men and women aged 51 through 61 in 1992.

[a] All negative values are given a zero value in these calculations.

[b] All negative values are given a value of $1 in these calculations.

Source: Burkhauser and Weathers, 2001, table 3.2; from Health and Retirement Study Wave 1 Final Release.

are not only high but are also increasing. For the narrower concept of financial wealth that excludes home equity, the top 1 and the top 20 percent of all households held even larger proportions of the aggregate in 1995 – 47 and 93 percent, respectively. Both of these percentages have also increased since the early 1980s.

THE WEALTH OF THOSE ON THE VERGE OF RETIREMENT. Burkhauser and Weathers (2001) use data from the longitudinal Health and Retirement Study (HRS) to examine the distribution of wealth among older Americans in the 1990s. Unlike previous studies, they account for difference is household size as discussed above.

Table 3.7 shows the relationship between the distribution of total household wealth (net financial assets as well as assets not normally captured in wealth data – net housing wealth, net Social Security wealth and net previous wealth) and household income. In this table, they do *not* adjust household wealth or income to account for differences in household size. Mean household wealth, broadly defined, was nearly $500,000 for men and women aged 51–61 in 1992. Household wealth was very highly skewed. The top 10 percent of wealth holders, with mean household wealth of over $1.8 million, held over 37 percent of all wealth, while the lowest decile, with

Table 3.8 Effect of changes in equivalence scale on measurement of distribution of total net household wealth by person-based deciles in 1992 for persons aged 51 through 61

Wealth decile	Equivalence scale					
	e = 0		e = 0.5		e = 1.0	
	Mean household wealth (dollars)	Share of household wealth (%)	Mean household wealth (dollars)	Share of household wealth (%)	Mean household wealth (dollars)	Share of household wealth (%)
Bottom	50,270	1.0	34,087	1.1	19,915	0.9
2	118,625	2.4	77,892	2.4	48,845	2.2
3	181,231	3.7	115,628	3.6	73,494	3.3
4	242,450	4.9	155,144	4.8	98,933	4.5
5	302,039	6.1	195,654	6.1	127,397	5.8
6	372,109	7.6	243,018	7.5	160,713	7.3
7	458,460	9.3	301,502	9.3	202,358	9.2
8	581,555	11.8	380,650	11.8	259,947	11.8
9	781,317	15.9	518,343	16.0	362,182	16.4
Top	1,830,966	37.2	1,210,223	37.5	856,065	38.8
All	491,984	100.0	323,251	100.0	221,016	100.0
GINI[a]	0.49		0.49		0.51	
90–10 Ratio	10.98		10.93		12.27	
Theil (0)[b]	0.45		0.49		0.53	
Theil (1)[b]	0.47		0.51		0.53	

HRS sample weights were used to make the sample representative of men and women aged 51 through 61 in 1992.
[a] All negative values are given a zero value in these calculations.
[b] All negative values are given a value of $1 in these calculations.
Source: Burkhauser and Weathers, 2001, table 3.3; from Health and Retirement Study Wave 1 Final Release.

mean wealth of $50,000 per household, owned only 1.0 percent of aggregate wealth. Table 3.7 also shows there is a strong positive correlation between wealth holdings and household income and a strong negative correlation between wealth holdings and the risk of poverty. In addition, it shows that wealth is distributed much more unequally than is income.[9] Table 3.8 shows the impact of various equivalence scales for household size on the wealth statistics of older Americans. While the absolute level of household wealth is greatly affected by assumptions about the returns to scale in household size, there is very little impact on the relative distribution of that wealth. For example, the share of wealth held by the richest decile varies between 37 and 39 percent; that of the lowest decile between 0.9 and 1.1 percent. But table 3.9 shows that the characteristics of those in the bottom of the wealth distribution (i.e., who is there) are just as affected by the choice of equivalence scales, as was the case for the income distribution in table 3.3. When no adjustments are made for household size (e = 0), only 12 percent of those aged 51 to 61

Table 3.9 Effect of changes in equivalence scale on the social characteristics of deciles of net household wealth by person-based deciles in 1992 for persons aged 51 through 61 (in percents)

Wealth decile	Equivalence scale											
	e = 0.0				e = 0.5				e = 1.0			
	Adult couple	Single female	Single male	Total	Adult couple	Single female	Single male	Total	Adult couple	Single female	Single male	Total
Bottom	12	64	24	100	23	58	19	100	37	48	15	100
2	52	32	16	100	58	28	14	100	65	25	10	100
3	71	21	8	100	73	18	9	100	74	17	9	100
4	82	12	6	100	82	13	5	100	80	12	8	100
5	86	9	5	100	86	9	5	100	83	11	6	100
6	85	9	6	100	85	9	6	100	85	10	5	100
7	91	5	4	100	85	8	7	100	85	9	6	100
8	90	6	4	100	85	9	6	100	83	9	8	100
9	92	4	4	100	89	6	5	100	82	11	7	100
Top	93	3	4	100	87	6	7	100	78	11	11	100
All	75	16	9	100	75	16	9	100	75	16	9	100

HRS sample weights were used to make the sample representative of men and women aged 51 through 61 in 1992.
Source: Burkhauser and Weathers, 2001, table 3.4; from Health and Retirement Study Wave 1 Final Release.

in the lowest wealth decile are adult couples. This rises to 23 percent when an e value of 0.5 is used and to 37 percent with an e value of 1.

Finally, table 3.10 shows the relative importance of each component of wealth held by men and women age 51–61 in 1992. Like Wolff (1998), Burkhauser and Weathers (2001) find dramatic inequality in net financial wealth holding. But they also show that net financial wealth makes up only 40 percent of total wealth in this population and that its very skewed distribution (the top decile owns 60 percent of all net financial wealth in this age group) is partially offset by more evenly distributed wealth holdings in home equity, private pensions and especially Social Security (where the wealthiest 10 percent has only 13 percent of total Social Security "wealth.")

WEALTH ACCUMULATIONS OF THE BABY BOOMERS. As we look ahead to future cohorts of elderly Americans, we wonder how their economic well-being in retirement will compare to their current financial status, as workers, and how it will compare to that of their parents – today's elderly. Are today's workers saving enough to maintain their life-styles when they reduce working hours or leave the labor force altogether? Of course, how much saving will be needed depends on many important factors that are subject to considerable uncertainty, including the strength of the economy and assets markets (real estate and financial markets), the structure of important government programs such as Social Security, Medicare and Medicaid, and the timing and nature of their retirement decisions. The latter, in turn, will depend on as well as determine the individuals' health and financial status. Some elderly will have comfortable retirement options while many others will not.

Sabelhaus and Manchester (1995) have studied these questions, and they suggest that many baby boomers are doing as well as or better than their parents were at the same age, both in terms of their current income and the ratio of accumulated wealth to that income. Depending on how the authors adjusted for household size, baby boomers in 1989 had 40 to 80 percent more annual income (adjusted for the cost-of-living), at the median, than their parents did at the same ages, 25 to 44. The percentage gains over time were lowest in the bottom quintile (although even they had higher incomes and higher wealth/income ratios than the earlier generation) and highest at the top, another indication of widening income disparities and reason for concern for those at the bottom end of the socio-economic scale.

Sabelhaus and Manchester temper their generally optimistic story by pointing out that baby boomers aged 25 to 44 in 1989 were still several decades away from retirement and that many unforeseen things would happen during the intervening years. Today's baby-boomers are unlikely to enjoy some at the cohort-specific financial gains that their parents did prior to their retirements. The earlier generations saw dramatic increases in real estate wealth and in Social Security benefits in the late 1960s and early 1970s, as well as the introduction of Medicare. In contrast, members of the baby boom cohort are facing the prospect of Social Security and Medicare benefit cuts or eligibility delays as they approach retirement, and have witnessed significant fluctuations in financial markets – both the boom years of the late 1990s, and the retraction of the early 2000s.

Table 3.10 Distribution of total net household wealth and its components by person-based wealth deciles in 1992 for persons aged 51 through 61 (in 1992 dollars)

Wealth decile	Mean net total wealth	Mean net financial wealth	Mean net housing wealth	Mean net Social Security wealth	Mean net pension wealth
Bottom	34,087	3,808	−5,982	35,142	1,119
Column share	1.1	0.30	−1.33	4.07	0.18
Row share	100	11.17	−17.55	103.09	3.28
2	77,892	6,198	8,769	58,306	4,619
Column share	2.4	0.48	1.95	6.76	0.72
Row share	100	7.96	11.26	74.85	5.93
3	115,628	15,079	18,140	71,875	10,533
Column share	3.6	1.18	4.02	8.33	1.65
Row share	100	13.04	15.69	62.16	9.11
4	155,144	22,834	28,499	83,791	20,021
Column share	4.8	1.78	6.32	9.70	3.13
Row share	100	14.72	18.37	54.01	12.90
5	195,654	34,888	35,820	90,917	34,029
Column share	6.1	2.73	7.95	10.55	5.34
Row share	100	17.83	18.31	46.47	17.39
6	243,018	51,597	44,868	94,952	51,602
Column share	7.5	4.03	9.94	11.00	8.08
Row share	100	21.23	18.46	39.07	21.23
7	301,502	79,608	54,770	99,803	67,321
Column share	9.3	6.21	12.14	11.57	10.55
Row share	100	26.40	18.17	33.10	22.33
8	380,650	109,979	64,768	104,946	100,958
Column share	11.8	8.60	14.38	12.18	15.84
Row share	100	28.89	17.02	27.57	26.52
9	518,343	187,192	76,867	108,921	145,363
Column share	16.0	14.62	17.04	12.62	22.77
Row share	100	36.11	14.83	21.01	28.04
Top	1,210,223	769,235	124,345	114,070	202,574
Column share	37.5	60.08	27.58	13.22	31.75
Row share	100	63.56	10.27	9.43	16.74
All	323,251	128,061	45,092	86,276	63,823
Column share	100	100	100	100	100
Row share	100	39.62	13.95	26.69	19.74
GINI[a]	0.49	0.77	0.57	0.10	0.73
90–10 Ratio	10.93	4058.5	∞	3.46	∞

HRS sample weights were used to make the sample representative of men and women aged 51 through 61 in 1992. Equivalence scale is (e) = 0.5.

Column share is the contribution of a decile to total wealth in percentage terms.

Row share is the contribution of a wealth component to the total wealth of a decile in percentage terms.

[a] All negative values were given a value of 0 in this calculation.

Source: Burkhauser and Weathers, 2001, table 3.7; from Health and Retirement Study Wave 1 Final Release.

A report on the retirement prospects of the baby boomers by the Employee Benefit Research Institute (1994) reached a similar mixed conclusion. After reviewing trends in pension income, savings behavior, and retirement trends, the report predicts that baby boomers, on average, will enjoy a standard of living in retirement that will exceed that of their parents during retirement, but might fall short of their own pre-retirement standards. The report expressed specific concerns about particular subsets of the elderly, such as the less educated, the single, and those without home equity.

More recent studies, employing a variety of methodologies, paint a generally optimistic picture, but, as always, with considerable variation around the mean.[10] Gustman and Steinmeier (1999), for example, with the same sample of Americans aged 51 to 61 (from the Health and Retirement Study) mentioned above, do the thought experiment of converting all of a household's wealth (including the home) into a single annuity (which will last for life), and asking what percentage of a person's final earnings this annuity could provide. For a real annuity (i.e., one that grows with inflation) the answer was about 60 percent, near the bottom edge of the 65 to 85 percent range that financial planners often suggest that retirees need (Uccello, 2001). For a nominal annuity, one that remains constant in dollar but not in real terms, the answer is about 85 percent, but this of course then declines over time.

Moore and Mitchell (2000) asked a very different question with a similar goal: if an individual wanted to maintain his or her consumption levels over time, how much would he or she have to save each year prior to retirement? For someone in the median income family, planning to stop work at age 65, the saving rate was only 7 percent of family earnings – higher than the average saving rate to be sure, but a manageable goal for many American workers. For the same household with an age 62 retirement goal, the saving rate was obviously higher – 16 percent, showing again the importance of the timing of retirement. As with all these studies, however, the variance was large. Moore and Mitchell report that about a third of the households required no additional savings for an age 62 retirement, and slightly more than that needed to save one-fifth or more of their incomes each year to achieve that same goal.

Finally, recent surveys of workers' attitudes and behaviors tell an ambivalent tale. In a 2001 Retirement Confidence Survey, about two-thirds of workers surveyed claimed that they were confident (very or somewhat confident) that they would have enough money "to live comfortably throughout retirement" (Uccello, 2001). Although that may sound encouraging, only half of these workers had actually tried to estimate their retirement needs (and three-quarters of this subset felt confident that could live comfortably in retirement). Three-quarters of the entire sample had begun saving for retirement, yet 60 percent felt that they were behind schedule in planning and saving.

A POPULATION AT RISK?

There is much cause for optimism as we consider the financial well-being of present and future retirees. Life expectancy continues to grow and older Americans are healthier at any given age than were earlier cohorts. The nation as a whole has grown and will continue to grow more prosperous, although the recessionary decline in 2001 and 2002 reminds us of the vagaries of the economy and of asset markets. Real per capita output in the United States doubled between 1960 and 1995, and, at a 2 percent real growth rate would double again by the year 2030, when the last of the baby boomers will have just turned 66. Workers today are earning more than their parents did at the same age, and, so far, are also accumulating more assets relative to their earnings at any given age (Sabelhaus and Manchester, 1995).

As outlined in this chapter, the economic circumstances of older Americans have improved dramatically over the past three decades, absolutely and relative to the rest of the population. Real incomes of the elderly have risen and their poverty rates have declined due in large part to policy initiatives that increased the real value of Social Security benefits. Future retirees will be better educated than today's, and education is correlated with economic success.[11]

Beneath this rosy picture, however, are serious concerns. Although the elderly today are less likely than the average citizen to be poor, they are more likely to be near-poor. Growth in employer pension coverage has stalled since the mid-1970s and an increasing proportion of pension coverage is in defined contribution plans. Although these plans may be superior for mobile workers and may end up providing some retirees with more income than defined benefit plans would, they do shift financial risk from employers to employees, and their eventual impact on the economic well-being of future retirees remains unknown.

The size of some traditionally vulnerable groups is on the rise. The proportion of the elderly who are black is increasing steadily, from about 8 percent today to 10 percent by 2030 and 11 percent by 2050 (US Census Bureau, 1996). Among those aged 65 or older today, about 12 percent are aged 85 or above. This is projected to increase to over 14 percent by 2010, then retreat to about 12 percent in 2020, before rising to nearly one-quarter by the year 2050. Women aged 85 and over, a group particularly prone to poverty, are estimated to rise from about 8 percent of the elderly population today to 10 percent in 2010, then back to about 8 percent in 2020 and 2030, before rising to 14 percent by 2050.

More future retirees are likely to be living alone than was true in earlier generations. More current workers have never been married. Nearly 10 percent of the youngest baby boomers (born between 1956 and 1964) are forecast never to have married by ages 55 to 64, which is twice the rate of their parents. More of those who did marry will become divorced or widowed by the time they reach ages 55 to 64 – 25 to 30 percent compared to 15 to 20 percent of prior cohorts. Finally, childlessness is on the rise. In 1989, 26 percent of couples aged 25 to 34 had no children, compared to only 13 percent of such couples in 1959 (AARP, 1998). These trends will likely increase the percentage of older Americans living alone, from 21 percent of the 1926 to 1935 cohort to 24 percent of those 10 years younger, to 37 percent of the early baby boomers. Income and poverty data suggest that these trends may adversely affect the economic well-being of the elderly in the twenty-first century.

As mentioned above, two factors that aided many of today's retirees may not occur for the baby boomers – dramatic increases in asset prices and increases in real Social Security benefits prior to retirement. In fact, the reverse may occur for persons retiring during the next 30 years. Asset prices may well decline as the large number of future retirees sell the homes and equities they accumulated in anticipation of retirement (Schieber and Shoven, 1997). In addition, there may be benefit decreases or eligibility delays as society decides how to deal with the long-term funding deficits faced by Social Security.

Finally, personal wealth, which can act as a buffer between the income decline that usually accompanies retirement and a decrease in consumption, is inadequate for those persons most at risk of falling into poverty in old age. There is some debate about whether baby boomers on average are saving enough to maintain their current standards of living in retirement, but there is no doubt about the bottom half of the income distribution, especially those who are also in poor health. Their housing equity tends to be modest, and their financial reserves beyond home equity are almost non-existent.

It is important to recognize that people can adjust to changing economic circumstances and policy changes that will adversely affect their well-being. Many Americans will continue to approach traditional retirement ages employed and in good health, with many years of potential retirement ahead of them. If early retirement results in inadequate income over the rest of their expected life span, then the easiest adjustment to anticipated economic distress, for healthy older persons at least, would be to delay their retirement plans. Older Americans may well decide to work longer in the future and use these additional earnings to augment their "retirement" income – to add an important fourth leg to the traditional three-legged retirement stool of personal savings, Social Security and private pension income.

Nonetheless, there will continue to be a portion of the elderly population who will be at serious risk of living the last years of their lives in poverty, especially persons living alone, the most long-lived, the poorly educated, and those without housing equity. Older women, especially minority women, remain a particular concern. Their incomes and assets are much more likely to be inadequate to meet poverty level norms while healthy and much less able to handle the expenses of a catastrophic illness or long-term care when their health fails. For these older Americans especially, those at risk of economic distress late in life, societal decisions about the future structure and funding of Social Security and Medicare will be of the utmost importance.

CONCLUSION

This chapter uses official government statistics on average household income, average wealth, the distribution of income and wealth and poverty to measure both the levels of economic well-being of older Americans and how it has changed over time. On average, older Americans' income and wealth have increased and the share of older Americans in poverty has fallen. But there has also been considerable variation in both the income and wealth outcomes within the older age population.

Equally important, this chapter demonstrates that official policy success indicators (e.g., changes in average income or average wealth, or changes in the poverty rate) are sensitive to the assumptions behind their calculations. Decisions about what is counted as income (e.g. do we include in-kind benefits? do we utilize before or after tax income?) or wealth (do we include housing equity, or the wealth equivalents of future private pensions or Social Security benefits?) will influence the level of the values measured, their distribution across the population, and how they change over time.

Poverty rates are influenced not only by what is counted as income, but also by decisions on the level of income that is considered necessary for a household to be above the poverty line and how those thresholds should change over time. For instance, official US Census Bureau poverty lines have remained at the same real level of income since 1965, even though average real income and the standard of living in the United States have increased substantially since then. Hence, the relative income of those in poverty today is farther below the average American than was the case in 1965.

Choice of equivalence scale will also affect the level of measured income assigned to each person in the economy and, as we have shown, can significantly alter our measure of the relative economic well-being of younger and older persons. It is somewhat disappointing to learn that there is no scientific way to determine precisely the economic well-being of older people, and that all calculations of income, wealth and poverty are imprecise measures that are sensitive to the assumptions made in their calculations. But this is also true of other social policy success measures, such as the inflation rate, the unemployment rate, or the rate of economic growth. Perfection in measurement is impossible, and too high a standard. A better criterion is "Does our policy success measure prove a reasonable indication of the level and trends of the concept we are trying to capture?"

The economic concept of well-being discussed in this chapter is based on a notion of command over resources. In a market-oriented society like ours, this is most clearly measured by a household's control of income and wealth. But as we have discussed, it also includes command over non-income-providing wealth like a home or in-kind transfers. It is also affected by the numbers of persons that must share household resources. We believe that current measures of economic well-being, if used prudently, are useful indices to measure levels and trends in the economic well-being of older Americans.

DISCUSSION QUESTIONS

Comment on the reasonableness of each of these statements:

1. If we used a European-style relative poverty line to determine poverty in the United States, other things equal, measured poverty would be higher in the United States today.

2. Holding the poverty line for a one person household constant, if we used the German equivalence scale rather than the US equivalence scale to determine the poverty lines for other size households, the absolute level of poverty among older people would be higher and their share of the poverty population would increase.

3. The appropriate way to measure in-kind transfers is to assign the market value to the household since that is the price the government paid for them.

4. Why does government provide in-kind transfer to beneficiaries rather than cash?

5. The economic well-being of older people increased over the growth years of the 1980s.

6. The wealth of older people is highly skewed.

7. Older married couples are much more likely to have an adequate level of wealth than are older single persons.

Notes

1   The data generated by the Social Security Administration (SSA) is based on the annual Current Population Survey, a survey of approximately 50,000 households conducted each March by the US Census Bureau. The unit of account in the SSA publications is the aged unit, defined as either a married couple living together with at least one member aged 65 or older, or a nonmarried person aged 65 or older. Many of the SSA publications also contain data for aged units between 55 and 65.

2   Today, anyone over the age of eligibility for full Social Security benefits (soon to be age 66) can earn any amount without losing any Social Security benefits. The much-maligned earning test has been repealed for those over the normal retirement age.

3   Total money income includes the pre-tax value of wages, salaries, and self-employment income, Social Security, public assistance, interest and dividends, unemployment and workman's compensation, retirement benefits and any other source of income that is regularly received. Excluded are capital gains and one-time payments such as insurance settlements. For more detail on the definition of total money income, see Social Security Administration (2002c: p. xii).

4   These data may understate the importance of pensions, since the income derived from the distributions of defined contribution pension proceeds may be listed under "income from assets," even though these assets were initially accumulated through a pension program.

5   The US Census Bureau defines a household as a group of people living together or an individual living alone. The householder is the person who owns or rents the housing unit. If a couple owns the housing unit jointly, the interviewer may list either one as the householder. The "age" of the household is the age of the designated householder. In this chapter, we are primarily interested in households in which the householder is aged 65 or older. For more detail, see US Census Bureau (2000a), Appendix A.

6   They also in general assume that all resources in the household are equally shared.

7   Data are from the 1986 US Current Population Survey and the 1984 German Socio-Economic Panel.

8   The population of people aged 65 and over in 1983 in column 4 is a subsample of column 1's population. It includes only those who answer questions in the PSID in both 1983 and 1989.

9   Note that some individuals even in the highest wealth deciles are considered to be in poverty, using a single year income measure of poverty. This seeming anomaly is caused to some degree by very high business losses and wealth that produces no realized income in that year as well as by measurement error.

10 Uccello (2001) provides a very useful summary of recent research on these issues, including the Gustman and Steinmeier (1999) and Moore and Mitchell (2000) papers mentioned below.

11 Whereas fewer than 15 percent of Americans aged 65 years or older have a bachelor's degree or more, 22 percent of persons aged 55 to 59 and nearly 30 percent of those aged 45 to 49 are college graduates (US Census Bureau, 1997). In 1999, working men aged 65 and over with a bachelor's degree had average earnings over twice as high as that of men with only a high school degree, and over three and a half times higher than someone with less than a 9th grade education. For women aged 65 and over, the analogous figures are similar (US Census Bureau, 2000a, table 9).

References

AARP Public Policy Institute 1998: *Boomers Approaching Midlife: How Secure a Future?* Washington, DC: American Association of Retired Persons.

Buhmann, B., Rainwater, L., Schmaus, G., and Smeeding, T. M. 1988: Equivalence scales, well being, inequality, and poverty: sensitivity estimates across ten countries using the Luxembourg Income Study (LIS) Database. *Review of Income and Wealth* 34 (June): 115–42.

Burkhauser, Richard V., Crews-Cutts, Amy, and Lillard, Dean 1999: How older people in the United States and Germany fared in the growth years of the 1980s: a cross-sectional versus a longitudinal view. *Journal of Gerontology: Social Science* 54B, (5) (September): S279–S290.

Burkhauser, Richard V., Giles, P., Lillard, Dean R., and Schwarze, J. 2002: *Final Report to Social Security Administration: How Exits from the Labor Force or Death Impact Household Income. A Four-Country Comparison of Public and Private Income Support.*

Burkhauser, Richard V., Smeeding, Timothy M., and Merz, Joachim 1996: Relative inequality and poverty in Germany and the United States using alternative equivalency scales. *Review of Income and Wealth* 42 (4) (December): 381–400.

Burkhauser, Richard V. and Weathers, Robert R., II 2001: Access to wealth among older workers and how it is distributed: data from the health and retirement study. In Thomas M. Shapiro and Edward N. Wolfe (eds.), *Assets for the Poor: The Benefits of Spreading Asset Ownership.* New York: Russell Sage Press, 74–131.

Citro, Constance F. and Michael, Robert T. (eds.) 1995: *Measuring Poverty: A New Approach.* Washington, DC: National Academy Press.

Congressional Budget Office 1993: *Baby Boomers in Retirement: An Early Perspective.* Washington, DC: Congress of the United States.

Employee Benefit Research Institute 1994: *Baby Boomers in Retirement: What Are Their Prospects?* (Issue Brief No. 151). Washington, DC: EBRI.

Gustman, Alan L. and Steinmeier, Thomas L. 1999: *Effects of Pensions on Savings: Analysis with Data from the Health and Retirement Study.* (Carnegie-Rochester Conference Series on Public Policy, vol. 50). 271–326.

McNeil, John 1998: *Changes in Median Household Income: 1969 to 1996.* (Current Population Reports, p. 23–196). Washington, DC: US Government Printing Office. http://www.census.gov/hhes/www/mednhhldincome.html

Moore, James F. and Mitchell, Olivia S. 2000: Projected retirement wealth and savings adequacy. In Olivia S. Mitchell, P. Brett Hammond, and Anna M. Rappaport (eds.), *Forecasting Retirement Needs and Retirement Wealth*. Philadelphia: University of Pennsylvania Press, 68–94.

Quinn, Joseph F. 2002: Changing retirement trends and their impact on elderly entitlement programs. In Stuart H. Altman and David I. Shactman (eds.), *Policies for an Aging Society*. Baltimore: Johns Hopkins University Press, 293–315.

Ruggles, Patricia 1990: *Drawing the Line: Alternative Poverty Measures and Their Implications for Public Policy*. Washington, DC: Urban Institute Press.

Sabelhaus, John and Manchester, Joyce 1995: Baby boomers and their parents: how does their economic well-being compare in middle age. *Journal of Human Resources* 30 (4): 791–806.

Schieber, Sylvester and Shoven, John 1997: The consequences of population aging on private pension fund saving and asset markets. In Sylvester Schieber and John Shoven (eds.), *Public Policy Towards Pensions*. Cambridge, MA: MIT Press, 219–46.

Smeeding, T. 1982: Alternative Methods for Valuing Selected In-Kind Transfer Benefits and Measuring their Effect on Poverty. US Bureau of the Census, Technical Paper No. 50. Washington, DC: US Government Printing Office, March.

Smith, James 1997: *The Changing Economic Circumstances of the Elderly: Income, Wealth and Social Security* (Policy Brief No. 8). Syracuse, NY: Syracuse University, Maxwell School.

Social Security Administration 2002a: *Annual Statistical Supplement, 2001*. Washington, DC: US Government Printing Office.

Social Security Administration 2002b: *Income of the Aged Chartbook, 2000* (Office of Policy, Office of Research, Evaluation, and Statistics Publication No. 13–11727, April). Washington, DC: US Government Printing Office.

Social Security Administration 2002c: *Income of the Population 55 or Older, 2000*. (Office of Policy, Office of Research, Evaluation, and Statistics Publication No. 13–11871, February). Washington, DC: US Government Printing Office.

Uccello, Cori E. 2001: *Are Americans Saving Enough for Retirement?* (Issue Brief No. 7, June). Chestnut Hill, MA: Center for Retirement Research at Boston College.

US Census Bureau 1996: *Population Projections of the United States by Age, Sex, Race, and Hispanic Origin: 1995 to 2050* (Current Population Reports, p. 25–1130). Washington, DC: US Government Printing Office.

US Census Bureau 1997: *Educational Attainment in the United States: March 1997* (Current Population Reports, p. 20–493). Washington, DC: US Government Printing Office.

US Census Bureau 1999: *Experimental Poverty Measures: 1990 to 1997* (Current Population Reports, p. 60–205). Washington, DC: US Government Printing Office.

US Census Bureau 2000a: *Money Income in the United States: 1999* (Current Population Reports, p. 60–209). Washington, DC: US Government Printing Office.

US Census Bureau 2000b: *Poverty in the United States: 1999* (Current Population Reports, p. 60–210). Washington, DC: US Government Printing Office.

US Census Bureau 2001a: Historical Income Tables. http://www.census.gov/hhes/income/histinc/inchhdet.html

US Census Bureau 2001b: Historical Poverty Tables. http://www.census.gov/hhes/poverty/histpov/perindex.html

Wolff, Edward N. 1998: Recent trends in the size distribution of household wealth. *Journal of Economic Perspectives* 12 (3): 131–50.

PART TWO

Retirement Planning and Policies

CHAPTER FOUR

Economics of Retirement and Old Age

LEARNING OBJECTIVES

After completing this chapter, you will be able to:

1 Understand the basic economic model of the allocation of resources over a lifetime.
2 Know the meaning of key economic concepts such as opportunity costs, trade-offs, income and substitution effects, present value of future income streams, and compound interest.
3 Analyze how people would save for retirement in the absence of Social Security or employer pensions.
4 Assess the importance of risk and return to retirement savings.
5 Explain the economic reasons for retirement and why retirement rates are higher at particular ages.
6 Describe how public policies alter resource allocation and the timing of retirement.

CHAPTER OUTLINE

Introduction
Basic Economics and Retirement Savings Economics
  Stocks and flows: income and net worth
  Law of compound interest
  Opportunity cost
Economic Models
  Income and substitution effects
  Models and the economics of aging

Life Cycle Model
  Choices made in a life cycle context
  Summary
Role of the Public Sector
  Government as insurer of property rights
  Subsidies to increase savings by individuals
  Social insurance and welfare
  Pay-as-you-go versus self-funded social retirement schemes: the role of population aging
Programs Interactions, Societal Aging, and the Limits of Public Versus Private Responsibility
Discussion Questions
Notes
References

INTRODUCTION

At its heart, this book is about the economics of aging. The purpose of this chapter is to set the stage for later chapters by examining how economists think about the process of aging at both an individual and at a societal level. We begin with a discussion of economics, *per se*, and then move to economic models and their strengths and limitations for analyzing the aging processes. The goal is to provide some of the tools and insights that economists bring to the analysis of individual and population aging. The role of the government in providing financial security is addressed in the final part of the chapter. Later chapters will go into detail on many of the issues introduced here.

BASIC ECONOMICS AND RETIREMENT SAVINGS ECONOMICS

All societies and the individuals in those societies face the same basic economic question of *what* goods and services to produce, *how* to produce them, and *for whom*. All societies make choices in answering these questions by means of a socio-economic system. Most developed economies answer these questions through a market system, one in which the basic decisions are made by individual producers and consumers. These producers and consumers are all striving to achieve their own goals, and in so doing, respond as best they can to the incentives that penalize or reward their activities. In a market system, the primary incentives are expressed in prices that are generated in markets. These prices guide human behavior as households and individuals decide how much of their services to sell in the labor market to producers and how to use the proceeds of this labor (their incomes) to consume and to save and to provide for their old age.

When persons save, they postpone consumption today in return for greater consumption tomorrow. Compensation for this postponement is called interest (or investment) income. Of course, everyone must consume some amount of goods and services from their incomes to survive. The amount consumed today vs tomorrow is also determined both by prices and by individual preferences. These prices include both the dollar amounts spent to consume goods and services today, but also the return to saving which is also a price. Economists call this price the interest rate. Preferences relate to an individual's desire to consume now or wait until later. If the interest rate is high enough or if individuals believe they will need more income later to support future consumption (e.g., in retirement) individuals may postpone current consumption now to have more at a later time.

Stocks and flows: income and net worth

Economics is also about stocks and flows. Flows are amounts received (amounts earned by or transferred to a household or person), and amounts paid for expenditures or for services received over a given period. The earnings of a household plus its return on investments, including pensions, are called its market income (MI). MI is used to pay for consumed goods and services (C) and to either save (S) if consumption is less than income, or to borrow (B), if we consume more than we earn over a given period.

Thus:

$$C + S = MI \quad \text{if } C < MI$$
$$C - B = MI \quad \text{if } C > MI$$

Market income is also used to pay taxes (T) to governments. These taxes may be on income, earnings (such as payroll taxes), property (homes), or on expenditures (sales taxes). Some taxes paid by citizens are returned to them in the form of government transfers (R) that we discuss in a later section. Transfers are payments received as entitlements or in discretionary benefits from other individuals or from governments. For instance, Social Security benefits are transfers, as are food stamps. A household's disposable or "spendable" income (DI) is its market income, net of taxes, after adding back transfers received.

Thus:

$$DI = MI - T + R$$

Each of these items is a flow. Flows are always defined over a period such as a year, month or week.

On the other hand, stocks are defined as an amount at a point in time. Persons hold assets such as the value of savings, investments, homes, other buildings, businesses, vehicles, etc. These assets are defined as a persons (or household's) wealth (W). At any point in time, persons may also have a set of liabilities that are owed to other persons such as home mortgages, car loans, credit card debt, or school loans. These are called debts (D). A person's net worth (NW) is defined as their wealth minus their debts.

$$NW = W - D$$

Stocks change from one period to another. The change in a stock is a flow. If a person is a net saver during a given period, they add to their net worth by either increasing wealth (W) or paying off debts (D).

Thus a person saving for retirement can add to their net worth by saving some of their income. Over time, the process of reducing consumption and adding to savings builds up a stock of wealth that can be used to sustain consumption in retirement. Persons may add to retirement savings through savings plans, pension funds, or other financial vehicles. Persons may also dissave (or reduce net worth), by cashing in pension funds in case of emergencies, or by running down their wealth by consuming more than they are earning.

Law of compound interest

Why is it that financial planners urge young people to save for retirement? How much difference does it make if we start saving for retirement when we are young instead of when we are older? A short foray into financial economics will underscore the power of compound interest and the importance of starting early and then maintaining savings for retirement.

Let's assume you are going to retire at age 65 and want to know the value of saving $1,000 for retirement (until age 65) in any given year. Next, assume there are two types of investments, one yielding a "safe" 5 percent, the other a "risky" 10 percent. Usually, riskier investments have higher interest rates as a reward for those who take these risks (and hence can lose as well as gain), but for now we will abstract from these risks. Suppose you invested $1,000 at age 45 and left it for 20 years? During that period, the initial value (IV) of the investment grows according to the law of compound interest. The future value (FV) will equal $(1 + i)$ where i is the interest rate, compounded over the n years of the investment.

Thus:

$$FV = IV \, (1 + i)^n$$

At the end of one year with an initial investment (IV) of $1000, and an interest rate of 5 percent ($i = .05$), the future value of the asset rises to $1,050 since $50 in interest is added to the initial investment. If $i = .1$, the value rises to $1,100 and $100 of it will be interest.

But the power of compound interest takes hold if the amount left at the end of the first period, the $1,050 (or $1,100) stays invested at the same interest rate over a long number of years. This process is called compounding because not only the does the initial $1000 grow, but also the interest each year is added to savings, and eventually earns interest as well. If a person aged 45 puts aside $1,000 for 20 years at 5 percent, it will be worth $2,653 at age 65. If the interest rate were 10 percent, the amount would $6,727!

Age 45 is about where many people begin to save for retirement. But, instead of starting at age 45, what if one put away $1,000 for retirement at age 25 and left it there for 40 years? Even at a "safe" 5 percent, the $1000 would be worth $7,040 at age 65. If the return were a riskier 10 percent, the $1,000 would grow to $45,259! Thus, beginning to save for retirement at age 25 yields many times larger an amount than waiting to save until reaching age 45. Table 4.1 presents a larger series of returns on an initial investment with constant returns of 5 percent and 10 percent over a number of years. Consistent annual investments, even if small, mount up substantially over time.

RISKY INVESTMENTS AND POSTPONING RETIREMENT. Of course, people would prefer a constant 10 percent return instead of 5 percent. Unfortunately, this is not

Table 4.1 Future value and compound interest for $1,000 invested once and left to grow in an interest-bearing account

Years	Age	FV at i = 0.05	FV at i = 0.10
1	65	$1,050 = 1000 \ (1 + .05)^1$	$1,100 = 1000 \ (1 + .10)^1$
10	55	$1,629 = 1000 \ (1 + .05)^{10}$	$2,594 = 1000 \ (1 + .10)^{10}$
20	45	$2,653 = 1000 \ (1 + .05)^{20}$	$6,727 = 1000 \ (1 + .10)^{20}$
30	35	$4,322 = 1000 \ (1 + .05)^{30}$	$17,449 = 1000 \ (1 + .10)^{30}$
40	25	$7,040 = 1000 \ (1 + .05)^{40}$	$45,259 = 1000 \ (1 + .10)^{40}$

Formula: $FV = IV \ (1 + i)^n$

where:

FV = Future value of investment, assuming money is not withdrawn until age 65.

IV = Initial value of investment made in a given year.

n = Number of years for investment.

i = Interest rate on investment.

Age = age at which you begin to invest for retirement, assuming money is not withdrawn until age 65.

the way that investment works. Few investments can guarantee a constant 10 percent return, especially over a 40-year period. However, over a long period of time, a risky investment, even with ups and downs at any point over the period, usually produces a higher return than a safe, fixed investment. For instance, longer-term certificates of deposit or government bonds may yield the safe 5 percent. Corporate stocks and bonds, on the other hand, are much riskier because they vary with the profitability of the company. They sometimes pay 10 percent, but other times more (e.g., 20 percent per year for the Dow Jones index 1992 to 1999) and sometimes less (e.g., 2 percent in 2000 and −7 percent in 2002). In the past 50 years, however, stocks and bonds have averaged about a 7 percent return. Assuming that the $1,000 is invested for 40 years at 7 percent, this investment will yield $14,974, nearly twice the $7,040 return on the "safe" 5 percent investment. Thus, while it may take a strong stomach to withstand the ups and downs of the stock market over a 40-year period, history has shown that those who do so are likely to be rewarded for taking such risks – not at a peak return, but at a higher return than the low risk investments.

The final basic point to be made is that with investments like these, there is a reward to delaying retirement (or withdrawal of funds). In the example on the final line of table 4.1, the hypothetical individual has saved a single one-time investment of $1,000 for 40 years, depositing the initial amount at age 25, and realizing their investment at age 65 and has $7,040 for his efforts. Now suppose this person decided to work another five years, until age 70, and to leave his retirement savings intact for the five years at the assumed rate of interest? The reward for waiting is an extra $1,945.[1] At a 10 percent interest rate; the difference is $27,631.[2] Thus, postponing retirement by five years may pay handsome dividends to those who hold their accumulated savings.

Of course compound interest works the other way as well. Retiring "early" at age 60 reduces the value of the $1,000 put away at age 25 to $28,102 at the 10 percent interest rate, $17,157 less than if it were left until age 65. Hence, there is a stiff penalty for early withdrawal of funds.

Finally, risky investments at older ages may not always be the best medicine. The 10 percent return over 45 years yields $45,259 at age 65, but if the stock market loses 5 percent per year over the next five years, this $45,259 will fall to only $35,021. Putting the $45,259 at age 65 into a safer 5 percent investment still yields $57,763 at age 70.[3] This is a lesson that many investors on the verge of retirement in 2001 and 2002 have learned the hard way. As most people grow older and retirement is drawing near, switching to a "safe" asset reduces the risks inherent in the stock market. Therefore most savvy investors split their savings by investing larger amounts in "safer" financial vehicles, and putting smaller amounts in "riskier" investments as they draw closer to retirement. This process is called "portfolio diversification."

Opportunity cost

Most of economics is really not about risk and reward in financial markets. Rather it is about behavior, about how people make decisions or "choices" about work, schooling, consumption, etc. While financial behavior is important, there are many other types of behavior that are also of economic importance. One of the most important principles that economists use to describe basic choices is called *opportunity cost*. All actions have cost consequences. We must choose between doing one socio-economic activity (eating, sleeping, working, consuming, saving) vs another. The decision to consume more today means having less saving for tomorrow's consumption, given a fixed level of income. But income, the return for providing labor to employers or from investing in stocks or bonds, can also vary as we have seen above. This is because we can decide, within limits, how much to invest in various types of accounts.

But even more important is the decision of how much to work (vs enjoy leisure). Both the number of hours worked within any one year and the number of total years worked over a lifetime are subject to our discretion. As illustrated above, choosing to stop work (retire) at age 60 vs age 70 may produce more leisure and less work, but it may also have high opportunity costs for investment income, just as choosing risky vs safe investments may have opportunity costs as well. It also means lower income from wages, often at a time when wages are particularly high. Further, the decision to postpone going to work after school to obtain more training usually can yield higher lifetime incomes.

ECONOMIC MODELS

The economic choices people make are governed by prices, preferences, and constraints. Economists describe the process of making these choices by creating *models.* Models are simplifications of reality. They are judged not by their realism, but by their ability to predict or explain reality. Most economic models rely on the role of prices to influence behavior and to help explain the choices that people make as individuals and as societies.

Choices are affected by tastes and preferences, and by constraints. Tastes and preferences are what you would like to do; constraints are limits on these choices. For example, we might prefer to never work, or only to work at a very interesting job that paid a high salary in return for little effort. But ultimately, the best paying jobs require lots of skill, training, and experience, and a great deal of effort as well. Ultimately, the choices we make early in life or even in middle age will determine what opportunities and choices we have later on in life. Constraints may also arise because of factors beyond our control, such as discrimination by race or gender. Before formalizing these choices in a simple economic model of the life-span in the next section, it is important to understand how prices affect choices in an even simpler model.

Income and substitution effects

Every wage, interest rate, or price of consumer goods indicates the economic cost or return for making a particular decision. Every change in price may lead to a change in behavior. Changes in price produce two effects: a *substitution* effect and an *income* effect. The substitution effect is about changes in relative prices. When the price of a consumer good rises, given constant other prices, preferences and income, the consumer will choose to spend less on that good because its price has risen relative to all other goods where prices have remained constant. Thus if bananas are $1.00 a pound this week, you don't buy them. Rather you wait till next week, when you hope they go on sale for, say, 50 cents a pound and at that price become more desirable than other fruit.

The income effect is about the purchasing power of your income. With a fixed income (say, $5,000 per month), higher prices for one good, e.g., clothing, mean that if you consume the same amount of that good, e.g., the same new suit every month, there will be less money for other goods and services. A rise in the price of your favorite designer suit from $500 to $1,000 means that you will have only $4,000, not $4,500 left for other goods and services that month, reducing your ability to buy other goods and services.

Here, the economic model of choice predicts that both the income effect and the substitution effect will lead you to consume fewer of your favorite suits. You may decide to only buy a new suit every other month now, or you may choose a less expensive line of suits. The point is that both effects work in the same direction, reinforcing one another.

If prices of all suits were $250 instead of $500, there would be a completely opposite reaction. Lower prices lead a consumer to buy more goods and services (more suits) and lower prices mean more spending power for a consumer, since after buying the monthly suit at $250, you have an extra $250 left over to spend on other goods and services that month (and you still have your new suit). Falling prices therefore have income and substitution effects that lead you to consume more of these goods and services again because of the reinforcing nature of both types of effects. Economists call the effect of price change in consumer markets "the law of demand," because the law of demand predicts that when prices rise, all else equal, a consumer buys less of a good or service, and when they fall, the consumer buys more. But not all choices are so simple, as one might expect.

Models and the economics of aging

The economics of aging concerns itself with several of these choices, each of which has an opportunity cost, and each of which is governed by substitution and income effects. Here we examine two of the most important of these choices: the decision about how much to work and the decision about whether to save (invest) for old age or to consume. The decision of how many hours to work in a given week is determined by both tastes (preferences for work vs other things) and constraints. For instance, one can work for others for wages and salaries or one can work at home, not for pay but to directly provide goods or services for the family. Alternatively, one can spend hours not working just relaxing or "goofing off." These choices are partially governed by tastes. For instance, you can clean your own home and cook your own dinner, or work enough to be able to afford to pay someone else to clean the house or cook your dinner. Or you might really like sleep and goofing off, even if you have no money to do anything else with your spare time.

These choices are also governed by prices – the monetary return to work (wages) and the cost of purchased services (their money prices and the time costs of household activities) are relevant prices for making the work hours choice. Our choices are also constrained; of course, by the amount of money we have, by commitments we have made to others, (e.g. spouses, children), by the direct enjoyment (or displeasure) we receive from the work we do, and by the preferences and rules of employers who pay us for our work.

Here we simplify the work choice by limiting our model to a single time period, and a single person deciding how many hours to work in a given week. Begin by assuming that a person works 40 hours per week for $30 per hour and thus earns an income of $1,200 per week. Again to simplify, we assume that the employer will allow the worker to make his or her own decision (within some bounds) of how many hours to work per week.[4]

The pay that the worker receives depends on their efforts and on their productivity: the value of the goods and services they produce for their employer. Suppose this worker has just completed some form of advanced training that increases her productivity by a third. The employer now announces that the worker will be paid $40 per hour for her efforts. Thus the return to additional work has now increased by a third. After that change, how many hours will the employee work?

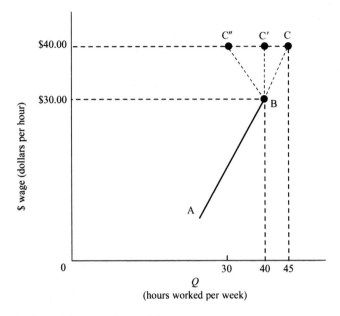

Figure 4.1a   The basic labor supply model

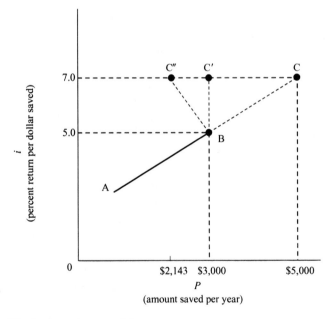

Figure 4.1b   The basic savings model

We first see that that higher wages usually entice workers to increase their hours of labor because of the higher return to work (thus the line A–B in figure 4.1a, below $30 per hour).

The reason for more hours worked at higher wages is that the opportunity cost of *not* working has increased. Every hour that one does not work in the market means one hour less they are paid a given wage. At lower wages, one may choose fewer hours of work in the market and more hours of work at home or more hours of leisure (insuring goods and services, e.g. shopping for new suits!). However, fewer hours worked means less income as well. As wages rise, most persons decide to work more hours (at least up to a point), thus having more money to spend on substitutes for homework (e.g. home cleaning services, and restaurant meals instead of home cooking) but this also means fewer hours for doing things we enjoy more than work!

The decision of how many hours to work, as wages change, also depends on substitution and income effects. But this time they work in opposite directions. Let's go back to the $30 per hour worker who is now offered $40 per hour. Because of the higher return to added market work the person may increase their work hours by moving from B to C, working 5 more hours for an added $200 per week. This is the same substitution effect we talked about before. The worker has selected more hours of work now that the return from those hours has increased. On the other hand, a higher hourly salary means that just working the same 40 hours now brings with it an extra $400 a week (40 hours at $40 per hour vs 40 hours at $30 per hour). If the person works the same 40 hours (B–C'), the worker is already earning more and has more money to spend (or save). This increase in hourly pay therefore has an income effect as well. That is, the extra amount of pay received for each hour already worked means more real income to spend on goods and services (assuming that other prices have not changed). The effect here is that as incomes rise, the employee can expand her range of consumption choices. In order to spend more money effectively, the employee needs and wants more time to enjoy this higher income. However, time is constrained to just so many hours in a week. The dilemma is that working more hours brings higher income, but that income may make the worker want to use some of that income to "buy" more leisure time.

Here the income and substitution effects work in opposite directions, with the substitution effect providing incentives to work more, and the income effect pushing the individual to work less and get more leisure time. In fact, if one were happy with $1,200 per week of income, and valued time not working highly, the same income could now be earned by working only 30 hours a week (at point C ″), giving the worker the initial $1,200 income, but ten more hours a week to enjoy it. Thus the model of hours worked (or labor supplied) does not conclusively predict how an employee might react to a pay increase. Hours worked per week could rise or fall depending on tastes and preferences of the individual. But, it does tell you the trade-offs between more work time, less work time, and the amount of money one has to spend.

The decision to save or consume presents a similar dilemma. Suppose a person has $3,000 per year after paying for necessities (or 5 percent of his annual income of $60,000) and needs to decide whether to spend it or save it for the future. A low risk savings bond carries an interest rate of 5 percent. This means that the person would receive $150 in interest on this savings over the next year (Point B in figure 4.1b). Now suppose the interest rate increases to 7 percent.

With no increase in the risks associated with this investment, the $3,000 per year saved now yields $210 per year interest (B to C'). The substitution effect says that the person ought to increase his savings because the return is higher. For instance, saving an additional $2,000 per year means an extra $140 per year in added income from savings, increasing interest income to $350 per year (at a 7 percent interest rate). This is an extra $140 he would have to consume in goods and services. On the other hand, deciding to save more means consuming less this year. Instead of $57,000 to spend this year, the person would reduce spending to $55,000 if he saved $5,000 instead of $3,000. The cost of increased saving is less consumption in the given year. The substitution effect says that this is not "giving up" consumption, but rather postponing it. At the higher 7 percent interest rate, the extra $2,000 in savings will yield another $140 per year in income next year, and every year thereafter (assuming the $140 is spent each year).[5]

On the other hand, the $3,000 saved would yield an extra $60 per year of income because of the higher 7 percent interest rate. Thus, the person will have an extra $60 per year to spend in the future, with no reduction in current spending. In fact, at a 7 percent interest rate, interest income of $150 requires saving only $2,143, thus providing an extra $857 to spend this year (B to C"). And so, income effects of higher returns on saving may lead the individual to save even less (not more) of his income and to take the $857 and spend it now, rather than later. Again, the model is inconclusive. Faced with a higher return on savings (a higher interest rate), the individual may save more (if the substitution effect dominates) or he may save less (if the income effect dominates). In fact many people feel that during the late 1990s when stock market returns were averaging 20 percent per year, investors spent some of their higher earnings on consumption goods and services and thus, in effect, reduced their savings over what would have occurred if the returns were lower (e.g., moving along the curve "B–C").

Two final comments are in order here. While the simple models of hours worked and savings vs consumption did not yield predictable results, they still were of considerable value because they offer insights into the forces that push or pull an individual to make certain choices. Second, of course, the world is much more complicated than in these simple models. Both the hours worked and the savings/consumption decision can be linked. Higher pay and higher interest rates mean more money to consume or to save. But lower pay (or a layoff and subsequent unemployment) or lower interest rates (or a loss from a risky investment) mean less income and less to consume or save. It is important to put these particular choices into the context of a dynamic longer-term view of individual behavior. We call this the life cycle model because it presents the way that individuals make these same decisions over the course of their lifetime; and this model is particularly relevant for understanding aging issues.

LIFE CYCLE MODEL

The process of aging, from birth until death, can be presented as a model of the economic life cycle. At each stage of the life cycle, an individual makes many important choices: schooling, taking a job, marriage, parenthood, location of residence, job tenure with a given employer, savings and investing (or borrowing and repaying). While most of these choices are made before "old age," they nonetheless have a large and cumulative effect on economic decisions such as retirement (withdrawal from the workforce), living arrangements at older ages, and provisions for long-term care as health status declines. Each person will make these choices, either implicitly or explicitly, as they move through their own life cycle.

Of course, not all of these choices will be unconstrained. Most choices made at earlier ages pose both opportunities and constraints for later choices. And unforeseen events of good luck (e.g., good employment, health, and steady high incomes) or bad luck (e.g., unemployment, disability, and low or erratic incomes) can greatly affect the choices an individual may make. Remember our discussion of compound interest earlier in the chapter.

The simplest model of the life cycle is usually attributed to Albert Ando and Franco Modigliani (1963). In the model, an individual is assumed to begin economic life with no inheritances (money given to them from another generation, e.g., from parents, grandparents) and to end it leaving behind no bequests (e.g., money left to another generation). The individual lives in a world of perfect foresight, borrows when young, earns enough in his working years to both repay these loans and to save for retirement, and saves exactly enough so that when he stops working, he can spend a certain known period of retirement, living off his savings until he dies exactly at the same time that he runs out of money.

This model is depicted in figure 4.2, where one finds a flatter line of total lifetime consumption, compared to income that rises and then falls. During younger ages and at older ages, consumption exceeds income (areas I and III). In the middle period, income exceeds consumption (area II). In the simple model, lifetime consumption equals lifetime income, and thus areas I + III = II.

Even when complications are added, this model can still be very powerful. And, to be more realistic, a number of other factors need to be added to the model. For example, most of us are cared for by our parents when we are young. Thus, much of consumption in period A is financed by parents. Then, we may borrow to pay for additional years of schooling (or that education may also be financed by parents). Most people choose to marry (for at least some period) and to have children. Complicated decisions arise about work and family life since both partners must choose whether to work in the labor market, and how to balance the benefits of marriage and parenthood against the possibility of divorce, chronic illness of self, child or spouse, etc. As we grow older and contemplate retiring from the labor force, we are constrained by imperfect information about how long we will live and how our health will change at older ages. We may well have motives to leave some of our accumulated wealth to our children, either at death through bequests or during our lifetime (*inter vivos* transfers). But even with these complications, the basic life cycle choices and predictions remain the same: consume from the income of others when young (parents or borrowing); attend school (and therefore, beyond age 14 or so, give up some market earnings until, say, age 20–25); work for an

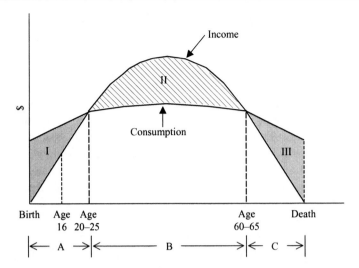

Figure 4.2 Stages of the simple economic life cycle
Major Life Periods:
A. 'Youth': Period when consumption exceeds income (up to age 20–25).
B. 'Working Life': Period where income exceeds consumption (20–25 to 60–65).
C. 'Retirement': Period where consumption exceeds income (60–65 and beyond).

extended period after school and accumulate assets (house, car, savings for retirement). Then, at some point (say, age 60–65) retire from the labor force (often gradually); live in retirement off of savings and then die. Thus the life cycle model, however it may be complicated, still typifies the economic lives and the stages of economic life that almost everyone will experience.

Choices made in a life cycle context

Now let us return to the basic choices made in the original one period model and extend the model to many periods. In so doing, the following individual key choices are made, abstracting for now, from societal trends and from government actions.

SCHOOLING CHOICE. A key choice is to decide how much *human capital* to accumulate when young and then through the rest of the life course. Human capital reflects the skills and knowledge of an individual (Becker, 1964).[6] One can add to human capital by formal education, by job training, and through experience. Most people add to human capital by staying in school beyond the compulsory age and sometimes earning a college or university degree. Some go on further to professional school for law, medicine, or business, for example. Of course, the added years of schooling have both a money cost (tuition) and an opportunity cost (loss of wages while in school). However, for most persons, the investment in more education produces higher levels of skill and abilities (human capital). As these skills are added, the worker becomes more productive and therefore earns more. The higher earnings for college and professional degrees more than compensate for the initial tuition and opportunity cost of schooling, even if the individual has to obtain school loans to make this investment.[7]

SAVING CHOICES: GENERAL. As seen earlier, all individuals can decide to save or consume their market incomes. Borrowing early in life (section A of figure 4.2) means repaying those loans later in life (section B). But then once school loans are paid off, the individual makes additional savings or consumption choices. Most persons have some amount of savings that they have made in case of emergency or unexpected losses. This so-called "precautionary savings" takes place all the time. But once precaution is accounted for, a whole set of new savings choices can be made. Most people save for a down payment on the purchase of a home, and then take out a mortgage to finance the rest of the purchase. Many people who have children save for their education so the children do not have to be indebted early in their work lives (minimizing the area I for their children, in figure 4.2).

SAVING FOR RETIREMENT. The decision to save for retirement competes with other reasons for saving: education (above), new cars, better homes, expensive vacations, etc. And all these reasons for saving compete with the needs for current consumption and instant gratification: meals, wines, expensive suits, swimming pools, etc. One of the major problems with retirement saving is that its benefits are so far away. As we have seen in our exploration of financial economics, compound interest is a mighty tool for accumulated savings. Yet to a 25 year old, a new stereo system, a week in the Bahamas, or a fancier car offer a much more tangible and satisfying return for the $1,000 of retirement savings. Most people, in fact, do not voluntarily choose to make long-term retirement savings decisions at early ages. But many people who would not choose to increase savings by themselves, will subject themselves to "forced" savings via regular deductions from their current salaries (see Box 4.1 on the psychology of retirement saving).

As we shall see later, both employers and government may further help employees to make savings decisions.

RETIREMENT CHOICE. When people approach older age and begin to consider retirement, the fortunate ones will have saved some amount to add to their retirement incomes. These dollars will at least partially offset lost wage income from retirement. In terms of figure 4.2, people presumably look at the amount accumulated in area II (net of borrowing in I which they have repaid) and guess at the amount they will need in period C to maintain consumption at close to their pre-retirement level. The retirement decision is a complex one. Each year of postponed retirement in the simple model yields one more year of earned income, and one more year of compound interest (as we have seen above.) But each additional

Box 4.1   *Why it Takes Psychology to Make People Save*

When it comes to saving for retirement, Americans are not rational. They know they do not put away enough, surveys show. But ask them to save more in their 401(k) plans and they balk. A buck in hand is irresistibly spent. Try a different approach. Ask them to commit now to increasing their savings in the future, make the increase coincide with the next raise, and they cheerfully sign up.

Various quirks embedded in human nature come into play. Saving more in the future seems much less of a sacrifice. When the future arrives, opting out succumbs to inertia. And timing the increase to coincide with a raise, so that one cancels out the other, is much more palatable than a cut in take-home pay. In the human psyche, giving up a raise not yet in hand is easier for people to accept emotionally than a loss, even the illusion of a loss. After all, the money "lost" is still there, in one's savings account.

Standard economics allows for none of these quirks. Over a lifetime, people rationally save an optimal amount, mainstream economics holds. Confronted with the reality that people do not save enough, the mainstream has no solution, except to reiterate that people are rational, so whatever they save must be enough. No wonder behavioral economics is making such a splash, becoming the "in" specialty of young economists from the best graduate schools.

"You have to force savings and take the money away before people have it and can't resist spending it," said Richard H. Thaler, a University of Chicago economist.

Mr Thaler is a pioneer in the development of behavioral economics over the last 25 years, and now he is a leader in finally applying the insights to daily life...

The most promising application so far is retirement savings. At a time when workers must save for their own retirement, they are in danger of inadequate income in old age unless they contribute 10 percent of their pay to 401(k) plans, pension experts say. And that does not count losses in 401(k) money invested in high-technology stocks.

Such hearty contributions are certainly in the interest of the Vanguard Group, which administers 401(k) plans for companies like Philips Electronics North America, a unit of Royal Philips Electronics. Philips also has a stake: under federal law, top executives cannot have retirement savings too out of line with those of ordinary employees.

So Vanguard and Philips turned to Mr. Thaler and to Shlomo Benartzi, at the University of California at Los Angeles. Executives had read a paper they wrote, entitled "Save More Tomorrow," reporting on the results at a Midwestern company where 162 employees, more than half the staff, had agreed in advance to annual increases in their 401(k) contributions, each increase coinciding with a raise. Over three years, the contributions rose to 11.6 percent of income from 3.5 percent.

Most of the 16,000 Philips employees enrolled in 401(k) plans save 6 percent or less. So Philips is experimenting. With Vanguard administering the test and Mr. Thaler and Mr. Benartzi giving advice, the company will ask 2,000 workers next month to commit to annual increases in 401(k) contributions of one, two or three percentage points. The first increase would be in April, when Philips gives annual raises, although this year, in a recession, a raise is not a sure thing, says Lisa Pyne, Philips's benefits director.

Still, she is counting on inertia to keep people from opting out, even the 3 percenters who, absent a raise, might notice the slight decline in take-home pay. "Behavioral economics seems to work," Ms. Pyne said.

Source: Louis Uchitelle. Reprinted with permission of the *New York Times.*

year of work means one less year of being able to visit grandchildren, travel, or enjoy the pleasure of longer life when in good health. There is an entire chapter later in this book about the retirement decision (chapter 5).

LONG-TERM CARE INSURANCE. Of course there is an additional risk that as we age, our health will decline and we will no longer be able to care for ourselves. Being old, frail, and dependent on others for basic care and daily needs is worrisome for most of us. It is possible that we may suddenly die from a heart attack or other "quick" action and not need such care. But, at age 65 there is a 20 percent chance that a woman will need two years (or more) of nursing home care, while a man has a 7 percent chance of such needs (Murtaugh et al., 1995).[8] Since good nursing home care can cost $60,000 or more per year, the need for nursing home care in old age poses a significant financial risk for most people. The private market offers a few alternative ways to account for this risk. Some individuals might be able to self-insure, e.g., by saving an extra $120,000 or more for such an event. Others might find it useful to buy private insurance against such risk. Again price matters, but so does age. As persons become older, the chances of needing long-term care increase, as do the premiums for long-term care insurance policies. While most people are reluctant to purchase long-term care insurance at younger ages (when there is some chance they will not use it and when it is relatively cheap), when they are older and recognize that they might well need such coverage, it becomes very expensive. Again, individuals face a number of trade-offs that affect both their current and future economic well-being. Long-term care insurance is also covered in greater depth in chapter 11.

Summary

In each of the examples given here, private market decisions about human capital, saving for retirement and long-term care insurance are being made by individuals in a dynamic context. Government also plays an active and vital role in most areas in the economics of aging. We now turn to this role, beginning with the economic rationale for government action in aging policy.

ROLE OF THE PUBLIC SECTOR

All modern economies rely to some extent on the public sector to influence economic choice. At the very least, the government plays a role in making private markets work better by guaranteeing people's property rights and by facilitating the exchange of market information. But governments do much more than that in every modern economy.

The traditional reason for public sector involvement in a market economy is market failure. When markets don't work at all, the government substitutes for the market by collecting taxes and providing "public" goods that are available to all without exclusion. National defense is one example of a good that is provided by the public sector because it is impossible or inefficient for the private sector to do so. But how and why does government become involved in the economics of aging? Government intervention is needed to establish property rights guarantees, to subsidize savings, and to provide both social insurance and minimum income protections. Rather than present a complex model of the government's multiple economic roles in the economy, we illustrate their current and potential roles through a number of examples germane to the economics of aging.

Government as insurer of property rights

Self-provision of retirement income is an important goal for individuals. Employers also effectively act as intermediaries for workers as described in Box 4.1. In this area, government's role has been to protect workers' rights to pension promises made by employers. Since 1974, the Employee Retirement Income Security Act (ERISA) has provided workers with insurance that guarantees that promised employer-facilitated occupational pensions will be provided. These are called "occupational" pensions since they are established by both companies and unions – for both public and private sector workers. Government requires these institutions to meet certain standards. Further, ERISA also guards against pension funds running too low to meet obligations and forbids discrimination across various types of workers who are eligible for company pensions. Government also makes separate provision for self-employed workers to set up their own pension funds.

Subsidies to increase savings by individuals

Because greater provision of occupational pensions offers the general public some assurance that they will not have to directly support the elderly as taxpayers, the US government encourages pension contributions by granting tax exclusions for qualified pension plan contributions and by allowing accumulated pension earnings to grow tax-free until they are used as retirement income. Both convey large advantages to employees who invest in pension plans. Without these subsidies, savings would likely be lower.

For instance, as shown earlier in table 4.1, a pension plan, which pays a compound interest rate of 10 percent, turns an initial $1,000 into $45,259 over a 40-year period. Suppose, however, that all contributions to the pension plan were taxed at 30 percent and further, that all earnings from this plan were also taxed at 30 percent. In effect, this reduces the compound interest rate on that $1,000 from 10 percent to 7 percent and the 40-year accumulation falls from $45,259 to $14,974. These tax provisions (income tax deductibility and postponement of income tax on pension earnings until plan realization) make a huge difference for pension accumulation. In 1998 alone, pension plan contributions in the United States allowed citizens to avoid over $53 billion in taxes that would otherwise be collected (US Congress, 2000). This is but one way that governments encourage particular forms of behavior through the tax system. Tax breaks for home mortgages and for employer-sponsored health insurance are two additional ways that tax deductibility encourages particular forms of behavior by changing effective prices through tax subsidies.

In a similar vein, governments encourage human capital accumulation by offering tuition-free tax-financed elementary and secondary schools to every young child and their families. Moreover, government reduces the borrowing costs for attending college by subsidizing college loans, by offering partial tuition grants, and by charging heavily discounted tuition at public universities and colleges. Thus governments also heavily subsidize schooling decisions as well as pension accumulations; they just do it in a different way.

Social insurance and welfare

The costs of insurance in old age can be very high, not only for long-term care insurance (as mentioned earlier), but also for health insurance, *per se*. Moreover, a market economy in general may treat harshly those who cannot compete because of disability, sickness, and unemployment in old age. While private insurance may fill some of these gaps, it does not cover them all. Moreover, even given strong tax incentives, many people do not save adequately for retirement.

One way to overcome inadequate private insurance is to provide public insurance against both seen and unforeseen events. Social insurance is a compulsory risk-sharing scheme whereby workers are forced to contribute tax dollars to a public trust fund and where they become entitled to certain benefits from that fund after having met qualifying requirements. Such programs are called "entitlements." Social insurance also provides protection against risks that the private sector cannot do, bolstering retirement incomes for those with low earnings or gaps in the earnings, for example.

Our "Social Security" system, formally known as the Old Age, Survivors Disability and Health Insurance (OASDHI) system is one such social insurance program. Both employers and employees contribute to the fund (i.e. through FICA taxes), and after contributing a minimal amount for a certain period (e.g. 40 quarters or ten years of employment for retirement), a worker is eligible for various benefits. The largest of these is Old Age Insurance, which offers a level of benefits determined by a formula based on contributions and age of retirement. This system also qualifies workers for Disability Insurance benefits should they become permanently unable to work before age 62. Further, if the insured worker dies, the spouse and younger children are guaranteed some level of income, through the Survivors Insurance benefit. Finally, upon reaching age 65 (or having been on Social Security disability for two years), qualified individuals are entitled to Medicare health insurance benefits. While other parts of this book are devoted to Social Security and Medicare, it is important to know that almost every modern nation has some form of OASDHI system. Further, most have a completely nationalized (government-run) health care system for all persons, regardless of age.

Old age benefits are related to previous contributions, but also reflect other adjustments. The US, like most nations, provides higher benefits to low wage contributors than they would have received had benefits been strictly tied to contributions. Many Western European nations have high "first tier" social retirement benefits that guarantee a non-poor income level to all who are entitled to benefits, and then a second tier benefit that is more closely related to the worker's lifetime contributions to the trust fund. In the US there is not such a distinction within the Social Security program. Instead, the US system relies on a separate means-tested program. In the United States, the Supplemental Security Income (SSI) system guarantees a certain level of benefits to those over age 65 whose earnings; savings and other benefits are less than about $500 per month. In order to qualify for SSI, a person must submit to a thorough income and assets test that proves that they cannot support themselves. Once one qualifies for SSI, they must repeatedly reapply to show they are still needy. SSI also covers the permanently disabled, often limited to those who do not qualify for the Social Security Disability Insurance program. Federal benefit levels in the means-tested SSI program are below the poverty line in the United States and do not provide enough by themselves to be non-poor (although some states supplement the basic SSI levels).

In contrast to health insurance and old age insurance where the OASDHI program meets the needs of most retirees, the United States does not have a contributory social insurance program for long-term care. While workers contributing to private long-term care insurance are provided a tax subsidy, the only other direct government support for long-term care needs comes from the income and means-tested Medicaid program. In effect, those without adequate private long-term care insurance and those without adequate savings for long-term care and nursing home expenses can qualify for Medicaid benefits once they have depleted their assets. And after that, they still must devote most of their incomes to pay for long-term care each year before Medicaid steps in. Many Western nations, notably Canada, Japan, Germany, and Austria, have a contributory social insurance scheme for long-term care. The United States has not developed such a system.

Pay-as-you-go versus self-funded social retirement schemes: the role of population aging

The United States OASDI system and most European social retirement systems are run on what is called a "pay as you go" basis. This means that younger generations of workers pay taxes into trust funds, but those funds are used to support older generations of workers in the same period. In terms of figure 4.2, taxes are paid by workers in life cycle periods A and especially in B, and the elderly in life cycle period C collect these taxes as benefits in the same period. Funds contributed by workers are paid directly to the next generation, with any excess going into a trust fund. Such systems are fundamentally stable and can pay high benefits to older generations as long as populations grow smoothly and other programmatic and demographic features (such as age of receipt of initial benefit and life expectancy in old age) do not dramatically change. However, as we have seen already, most rich nations' social retirement schemes will be coming under pressure as the "baby boom" population ages. The large cohort of persons born between 1946 and 1964 has been dubbed the "baby boom generation." They will reach retirement ages between 2011 and 2029. But even after that, the numbers of people over age 65 will remain high because of longer life expectancies. Moreover, in recent years, people have tended to retire before age 65. Together, these influences put pressure on entitlement schemes funded on a pay-as-you-go basis. To meet the promises of these social retirement systems, either taxes must rise or benefits must be trimmed, or more likely, both actions will be needed in a large number of Western nations, including the United States.

In contrast, many developing nations, notably Australia, Chile and other emerging Asian nations, have begun "self-funded" social retirement systems. Here intergenerational transfers from younger taxpayers to older beneficiaries are far fewer. Instead, when younger workers contribute to their retirement systems, these contributions are invested in public and/or private enterprises and held there until retirement. Benefits are much more directly tied to contributions, and plan contributions do not directly support other generations. For developing nations just starting social retirement schemes, these self-funded systems provide vehicles for forced savings as workers' funds initially grow. Once workers retire, governments must make sure that the return on these investments accrue to the contributors according to plan rules, but since each generation funds only its own retirement, population aging does not have a direct effect on taxes or benefits as with pay-as-you-go systems.

The dilemma faced by richer Western nations such as the United States, but to a much greater degree by Italy, France and Germany, is that converting from a "pay-as-you-go" to a "self-funded" system generates a number of problems. One generation is caught in the transition because taxes to support the older generation must still be paid while at the same time a self-funded system begins. It is particularly awkward to do this at a point in time when the size of the retiring generation is very large. Countries like Chile, where retirement systems were largely nonexistent, have an easier time establishing a funded program because they do not have obligations to those currently in retirement. The United Kingdom is the only modern nation to have at least partially made such a transition and it has faced a number of problems. It may be much easier for governments to limit the growth of pay-as-you-go systems and to add a "second or third" tier of self-funded contributory pensions on top of existing pay-as-you-go systems, than to make a wholesale change over from one system to another (for more on this issue, see chapter 8 and Schieber and Shoven, 1999; Aaron and Reischauer, 1998).

PROGRAM INTERACTIONS, SOCIETAL AGING, AND THE LIMITS OF PUBLIC VERSUS PRIVATE RESPONSIBILITY

Both private pensions and social insurance help support the elderly when they reach retirement age. Part-time work beyond retirement and other non-pension savings also provide income support in old age. Ideally older workers will have many sources of support in old age, including OASI, private pensions, and other savings. However, as noted above, the mix of support varies by both income level and by age. Younger and better-off retirees are liable to have all these types of support. Older women living alone (e.g. those 80 and over) are much more likely to rely on OASI alone. Moreover, some analysts worry that generous provision of public sector support may discourage efforts by individuals to make provisions for their own support.

Another important issue arises from the fact that as the US population ages, it puts enormous pressure on younger taxpayers to support retirees. Some policy changes will be necessary. For example, OASDI taxes would have to rise by about 16 percent to ensure older OASDI benefits under current rules for the next 75 years. And there is tremendous pressure to expand elder health benefits for Medicare to include both prescription drugs and long-term care insurance, neither of which are currently covered by this program. Benefit reductions or greater self-finance of retirement income, health insurance and long-term care could be made to lessen the amount of taxes that need to be paid by future generations of the elderly. But economic growth can soften the impacts of either of these sets of changes. For example, if workers' productivity rises even modestly over time, the share of their incomes devoted to FICA taxes might only need to go up modestly, leaving them with substantially higher incomes than today's workers. Alternatively, if retirees' incomes also rise from private sources, they will be better able to absorb benefit cuts. Thus, much of the debate about Social Security reform in America is about the issue of who will pay for an increasingly older society. What is the proper level of collective (government social insurance and safety net) support vs individual and private sector support for income and insurance in old age? The remaining chapters in this book are designed to shed light on these issues.

DISCUSSION QUESTIONS

Comment on the reasonableness of these statements:

1 A large one-time, lump sum payment is always more valuable than smaller annual payments over many years.
2 A fundamental principle of economic theory is that all actions involve trade-offs. For example, this means that in order to have more income in retirement, a person must consume less during their working years.
3 Social Security is a large proportion of annual income for many older persons. Thus, in the absence of Social Security, these households would be much poorer.
4 Individuals should invest all of their retirement savings in the stock market because the long-run average rate of return on equities is greater than the long-run average return on bonds.
5 Individuals make work and retirement decisions based on the total compensation of employment compared to the value of their leisure time. Knowing this, employers can influence the timing of retirement by choosing certain parameters of their pension plans such as the ages of early and normal retirement.
6 People retire only when they are too old or too sick to continue to work.

Notes

1 Calculate the return reward for the longer period as $1,000 $(1.05)^{45}$ = $8,985 at age 70, $1,945 greater than the $7,040 at age 65.
2 Calculate the extra reward for a larger count with higher interest rate as $1,000 $(1.10)^{45}$ = $72,890, minus the $45,259 realized at age 65, equals $27,361.
3 The student can calculate these figures by taking the $45,259 and using this amount as the IV in the formula in table 4.1. First, see what happens if you lose 5 percent per year for five years $(1 - .05)^5$ and then start with the same $45,259, invested at 5 percent $(1 + .05)^5$ over this time period per year.
4 The "demand" side of the labor market will provide both constraints, e.g. the employees work week is 40 hours, and opportunities, e.g. the choice to work fewer or more hours. But the availability of second jobs, flexible time schedules, etc. means that many workers can effectively decide how many hours per week to work. Here we concentrate on the employee's decision of how many hours to work. In later chapters, we examine the employer's decision of how much labor to demand.

5 Of course, in our earlier discussion, we saw that leaving the money in savings and not spending the $140 per year yields compound interest returns. Apply the formula in table 4.1. How much would this person have in 20 years if they left the additional $2,000 at 7 percent for all 20 years?

6 The notion of treating a human body and mind as a piece of capital – a stock that produces a flow of value – is attributed to Gary Becker (1964; 1993) and to Jacob Mincer (1958). The model has to also been applied to health status as well as productive skills, e.g., Grossman (1972).

7 Several authors have pointed to the fact that the better educated not only earn more, but they make better decisions as consumers, parents, and in terms of their own health. See Haveman and Wolfe (1984; 2001); Wolfe and Zuvekas (1997).

8 Christopher Murtaugh, Peter Kemper, and Brenda Spillman (1995) made these estimates for people who reached age 65 in 1995. Later periods, changing health circumstances and other factors might influence these results. The fraction of women using long-term care in nursing homes is higher than men because most men receive long-term care in old age from their wives. Most women live longer than men in old age (chapter 2) and because younger women marry older men, older women in poor health are more likely to need formal long-term care services than are men.

References

Aaron, Henry J. and Reischauer, Robert D. 1998: *Countdown to Reform: The Great Social Security Debate*. New York: Century Foundation Press.

Ando, Albert and Modigliani, Franco 1963: The life cycle hypothesis of saving. *American Economic Review* 53(1): 55–84.

Becker, Gary 1964: *Human Capital*. Chicago: University of Chicago Press.

Becker, Gary 1993: *Human Capital: A Theoretical and Empirical Analysis, with Special Reference to Education*. Chicago: University of Chicago Press.

Grossman, Michael 1972: *The Demand for Health: A Theoretical and Empirical Investigation*. New York: Columbia University Press, for the National Bureau of Economic Research.

Haveman, Robert H. and Wolfe, Barbara L. 1984: Schooling and well-being: the role of non-market effects. *Journal of Human Resources* 19 (Summer): 378–407.

Haveman, Robert H. and Wolfe, Barbara L. 2001: Accounting for the social and nonmarket effects of education. In I. J. Helliwell (ed.), *The Contribution of Human and Social Capital to Sustained Economic Growth and Well-Being*. Canada: Human Resources Development, and Paris: OECD.

Mincer, Jacob 1958: Investment in human capital and the personal income distribution. *Journal of Political Economy*. 66: 281.

Murtaugh, Christopher M., Kemper, Peter, and Spillman, Brenda C. 1995: Risky business: long-term care insurance underwriting. *Inquiry* 32 (3) (Fall): 271–84.

Schieber, Sylvester J. and Shoven, John B. 1999: *The Real Deal: The History and Future of Social Security*. New Haven, CT: Yale University Press.

US Congress 2000: *2000 Green Book: Background Material and Data on Programs within the Jurisdiciton of the Committee of Ways and Means*. US Congress, House Committee on Ways and Means, Committee Report WMCP: 106–14. Washington, DC: US Government Printing Office.

Wolfe, Barbara L. and Zuvekas, Samuel 1997: Nonmarket outcomes of schooling. *International Journal of Educational Research* 27 (6): 491–502.

CHAPTER FIVE

Work and Retirement

LEARNING OBJECTIVES

After completing this chapter, you will be able to:

1 Present a basic economic model of the retirement decision.
2 Discuss the long-term trend toward early retirement and explain why older men were leaving the labor force at younger ages.
3 Discuss the stability of male labor force participation rates since 1985 and explain why the trend toward early retirement ended.
4 Describe how the pattern of retirement is changing and how more older people are employed in bridge jobs or are part of phased retirement programs.
5 Compare and contrast the patterns of retirement among the developed countries and between the developed and developing countries.
6 Assess the importance of national retirement policies on the proportion of older persons who remain in the labor force.

CHAPTER OUTLINE

Introduction
Determinants of Retirement
Trends in Labor Force Participation among Older Americans
Why the Change in Retirement Patterns?
How do Older Americans Leave the Labor Force?
International Patterns of Retirement
Conclusion
Discussion Questions
Note
References

INTRODUCTION

Most people initially enter the labor force rather early in life, typically between the ages of 16 and 22 in developed countries such as the United States and those in Europe but often much younger in the developing countries. Individuals start their working careers after leaving school, the age of which varies across countries and stages of economic development. For most individuals, income from work will account for most of their lifetime income. Decisions about how long to remain in school, when to enter the labor force, and how many hours to work are among the most important choices individuals make during their lifetimes. During these working years, people must earn enough to finance current consumption while saving sufficient resources to provide for their retirement years. The retirement age will be determined, in part, by when the desired level of wealth is accumulated.

Economists believe that labor supply decisions are based on comparisons of the value of working to the value of other uses of time. The value of working is determined by the compensation paid in exchange for time on the job, as well as other psychic benefits the job may provide. Compensation includes cash earnings and the value of employee benefits. The value of time away from work is a function of the value of time in the home, one's own health along with the health of other family members, and household wealth. The basic economic model of labor supply was discussed in chapter 4 and will now be re-examined to provide a framework to assess how individuals decide to retire. This chapter begins by reviewing the determinants of work and retirement decisions of older persons in the context of this economic model. Labor force participation rates for older persons in the United States over time are then presented and explanations for changes in trends in retirement ages discussed. The chapter concludes with a review of the differences in labor force participation rates of older persons around the world.

DETERMINANTS OF RETIREMENT

The timing of retirement is influenced by, among other things, total compensation from continued employment, personal wealth, family health status, and the availability of other resources in retirement. These factors determine the pay-off of continued employment and thereby affect the value of leisure time (time not working). Individuals consider these factors along with consumption needs in retirement in order to determine the feasibility and desirability of retirement. Economic theory assumes that individuals attempt to maximize their well-being or utility by making choices subject to certain constraints. A simple, one period exposition of this model is:

$$U = f(i,l)$$

Where i = family income that is used to purchase goods and services for consumption, and l = time away from work often referred to as leisure.

Each individual or household attempts to maximize U subject to the constraints that

$$i = wh + rk$$

and

$$l = T - h$$

where w = hourly compensation or the value of working,

h = hours spent working,

r = return on wealth,

k = total household wealth, and

T = total time available, e.g. 24 hours per day.

Individuals will allocate time to working in the labor market as long as the compensation received from working exceeds the value of their time in leisure. If the value of home time (time away from work) exceeds the value that the market places on an individual's time, the person will retire and thus not continue to work. Chapter 4 describes how this model can be extended to a multi-period framework.

Each individual is assumed to be able to assess their total compensation from working and compare it to the value of their time in other pursuits. The value of continuing to work depends on cash compensation or the wage rate, the gain in future Social Security or pension benefits, the value of health insurance coverage, and other benefits of employment. Cash compensation net of taxes represents the direct value of working. Higher hourly compensation provides a greater incentive for individuals to remain at work. Declines in compensation encourage older persons to leave the labor force. Thus, we would expect, other things being equal, individuals with relatively high and growing earnings to remain in the labor force while those with lower and falling earnings to retire.

Company policies concerning the retention of older workers play an important role in determining retirement rates. At one time in the United States, many companies maintained mandatory retirement policies that forced workers to leave the company at specified ages. The 1967 Age Discrimination in Employment Act (ADEA) prohibited discrimination (and therefore mandatory retirement) against workers aged 40 to 65, but companies could legally continue to force workers out at age 65 or later. In 1978, the ADEA was amended to prevent mandatory retirement prior to age 70. Finally, in 1986, the law was again amended to prevent discrimination against workers age 40 and over. As a result, mandatory retirement has been outlawed for the vast majority of American workers, thus eliminating an important impediment to continued employment. In contrast, many other developed countries continue to permit mandatory retirement regulations. For example, mandatory retirement is virtually universal among large employers in Japan.

While mandatory retirement has been virtually eliminated in the United States, other human resource policies continue to have important effects on job opportunities and employment incentives for older workers. Examples include pension plans, retiree health insurance plans, pay raises and promotional opportunities, and corporate culture. Company policies toward hiring and retaining older workers are a function of the national economy and the company's own success. When unemployment rates are low and labor markets tight, companies are more likely to adopt policies encouraging older workers to remain on the job. When unemployment rates are high or when the demand for a company's product is declining, employers may attempt to reduce their labor force through higher rates of retirement among older workers.

Some pension participants are covered by defined benefit plans that promise a specified level of retirement benefits based on years of service and earnings. These plans have a normal retirement age and typically an early retirement age. Prior to the earliest retirement age, an additional year of work generally increases the value of future pension benefits by increasing the number of years of credited service and by raising the average earnings used to calculate benefits. The present value of this increase in benefits is a form of compensation for remaining on the job and it increases the value of working. After the worker has achieved the required age and years of service to be eligible to begin receiving benefits, the pension component of compensation tends to decline with continued employment, and often turns negative, which means that the present value of future benefits declines. This can happen even if future annual benefits increase because of the additional years of employment, if they do not increase enough to compensate for the pension benefits foregone during those additional years of work. These incentives are described in detail in chapter 6 (also see Quadagno and Quinn, 1997).

The decline in the lifetime value of the pension is due to the reduced number of expected years of life expectancy (and therefore pension receipt) as the worker ages. This decline in the total value of pension benefits can be viewed as a reduction in the compensation from continued employment. For example, if a worker earns $50,000 but loses $12,000 in future pension benefits during a year of work, the true compensation is really $38,000, considerably less than the $50,000 plus the likely increase in lifetime benefits earned before the first year of pension eligibility. The reduction in compensation provides workers with an incentive to retire; the larger the decline in true compensation, the stronger the incentive to leave that job.

The retirement incentives of pensions along with special early retirement programs were a major factor in the timing of retirement for many older persons in the 1970s and 1980s. Many companies have offered special early retirement programs that increased pension benefits provided that departure from the firm occurs within a specified time period. These programs were developed by firms to achieve orderly patterns of retirement and to reduce their labor force. The age of pension eligibility is a key factor in the retirement decision. Defined benefit pension plan incentives usually encourage workers to remain with the firm up until the specified retirement age and then provide a strong reason to leave the firm at that time.

Defined contribution pension plans do not have the same type of age-specific retirement incentives. However, both types of pension plans represent accumulated wealth for pension participants and thus provide the potential for income in retirement. As a result of this wealth effect, pension participants typically retire earlier than workers who are not covered by an employer pension plan.

Health insurance is very important to young and old workers. Many Americans receive health insurance as part of their employment compensation packages. The rapid escalation in the cost of health insurance is one of the most significant public policy issues of the 1990s (see the discussion of health insurance in chapters 10 and 11). The value of employer-provided health insurance is an important part of total compensation for older workers, since the cost of individually purchased health insurance can be prohibitively expensive for older persons. Thus, employer-provided health insurance can be an important determinant in the desire to continue at work. Thus, workers with employer-provided health insurance may be reluctant to retire and thus lose this coverage prior to reaching age 65 when they would be eligible for Medicare benefits.

Beginning in the 1960s, many firms, especially larger firms, extended health insurance coverage to retirees. Qualified persons could retire and continue to be covered by the company's health plan. The existence of this benefit substantially reduced the cost of retirement, especially to young retirees not yet eligible for Medicare. As a result, coverage by retiree health insurance provides a strong inducement for older workers to retire. Most of retiree health insurance plans link eligibility for health insurance to eligibility for the company's pension. These eligibility criteria reinforce the effect of the pension eligibility on the timing of retirement. During the past 15 years, the incidence of retiree health programs has been in decline and fewer workers are now covered by these plans (see Employee Benefits Surveys by the Bureau of Labor Statistics for various years). The decline in coverage by retiree health insurance should encourage delayed retirement by older workers.

Greater personal wealth makes retirement more feasible, and should be associated with earlier retirement, other things being equal, as a wealthy individual can more easily finance consumption needs in retirement. In principle, the form of wealth should not matter; however, the prevalence of personal residence as a major component of total wealth may influence retirement decisions. The availability of other financial resources will increase the likelihood of retirement. The most important income source to the majority of older households is Social Security benefits (see chapter 3). Social Security benefits can be received as early as age 62 with full benefits being paid between the ages of 65 and 66 (the age is slowly moving from 65 to 66, and later is legislated to increase further, to age 67, see chapter 7). Parameters of the program can influence the value of remaining on the job. Changes in Social Security from its inception through the 1970s tended to provide increased retirement incentives for older persons. These included more generous benefits and the introduction of an early retirement age. Since the late 1970s, changes have provided greater incentives for older workers to remain on the job.

Americans become eligible for Medicare at age 65. Medicare provides comprehensive health and medical coverage to retired workers and their spouses. Calculating a cash value for Medicare coverage indicates that health insurance represents a significant proportion of the total resources for many households. The existence of Medicare provides the resources for many persons to retire at age 65.

As we will see below, the largest decline in the proportion of older men in the labor force occurs at ages 62 and 65. These are the ages of eligibility for Social

Security and Medicare, which are important factors determining the timing of retirement for many persons. The introduction of Medicare in the late 1960s and the early retirement age for men in 1961 (it was 1956 for women) and the increase in real Social Security benefits in the early 1970s stimulated the decline in participation rates of older men.

The health status of older persons influences their decisions to work in several ways. First, poor health may limit the ability of persons to perform certain tasks. Declines in productivity make firms less willing to hire or retain workers with such limitations. Therefore, job opportunities and wage offers tend to decline with the onset of health problems. Second, poor health makes work more onerous and thus, reduces the desire for work by many older persons. Getting to the workplace and completing a full day on the job become more difficult. Virtually all studies of retirement conclude that personal health is an important factor governing the retirement decisions of older persons. Statistical studies consistently show that adverse health events and poor health in old age reduce the likelihood that an older person will remain in the labor force. Labor force participation among individuals with health impairments is also influenced by the availability of disability benefits (see chapter 9).

The health of one's spouse can also influence work patterns. In this case, there are two conflicting forces. First, the decline in the ability of a spouse to work may reduce family income and increase health care costs. In response, the other partner will tend to increase his or her own work effort to offset the loss in family income. Second, the need to care for a spouse at home may reduce the ability of the healthier person to go to work, lowering expected labor supply. Which of these forces dominates depends on the price of home health care, family income, and the earnings power of the healthy spouse. Older workers make retirement decisions based on expectations for the future, including life expectancy and likely wealth and health status over future years. The importance of these factors has been reduced somewhat by the almost universal coverage of Social Security and Medicare. Chapter 2 provides a review of the changes in life expectancy during the twentieth century and projections of future improvements.

Increases in life expectancy may be a "surprise" to older workers; for example, if during most of their lives they had planned on 15 years of retirement and then, in their final working years or even after retirement, they realize that they can expect to live 20 or more years after retirement. The increase in the difference between the life expectancies of men and women means that the family must plan for a longer period during which the wife survives alone. Planning for widowhood is an important aspect of retirement planning.

Even without increases in life expectancies, the mean lifespan is an average, and many people will survive long past the average. A person who was consuming accumulated assets based on a life expectancy of 15 years will find their ability to maintain their standard of living substantially reduced if they survive for 20 or 30 years. Lifetime annuities help to solve this problem. Social Security, for example, pays benefits, adjusted for inflation, until a person dies. Most defined benefit employer pensions also pay benefits in the form of life annuities, however, defined contribution plans typically provide lump sum distributions. The continuation of Medicare and retiree health insurance until death permit continued access to health services throughout retirement.

The major threat of outliving one's income comes from private assets that may be exhausted prior to death and therefore result in a substantial deterioration in the standard of living. This possibility is increased in the presence of adverse health events that necessitate large private expenditures and limit work opportunities. The probability of substantial health-related expenditures can be reduced through the purchase of private health insurance and is much smaller for those with employer-provided retiree health insurance.

Economists, sociologists, and other social scientists have conducted numerous empirical and theoretical studies of retirement. These studies indicate economic factors such as compensation from working, family wealth, Social Security and employer pension benefits (and the financial incentives imbedded in them), and access to health insurance are strong influences on the retirement decisions. In addition, personal health and the health of other family members play important roles. General labor market conditions are important, as are company and national retirement policies. Changes in these variables over time are significant determinants of the trends in the labor force participation of older persons over time.

TRENDS IN LABOR FORCE PARTICIPATION AMONG OLDER AMERICANS

The two most significant changes in the US labor market during the last half of the twentieth century were the trend toward earlier retirement by older men and the increased levels of female labor force participation at all ages. By most accounts the proportion of older men in the labor force declined throughout much of the twentieth century. In 1950 approximately one of every two men aged 65 and older was in the labor force. The labor force participation rate for men 65 and over had declined to roughly one in six by 1985. With higher lifetime wealth, individuals were choosing to spend more time out of the labor market. This choice was made easier by the increased generosity of Social Security that provided a minimum income in retirement, the establishment of Medicare to provide health insurance to the elderly, and the spread of employer pensions that augmented retirement income for many older Americans.

Table 5.1 illustrates the dramatic changes that have occurred in the labor force participation patterns for older American men during the second half of the twentieth century. It shows the proportion of men at certain specific ages who were in the labor force during various years. A simple definition of the average age of retirement is the age at which half of the population is in the labor force, and half is out. According to this definition, the average retirement age for men dropped from 70 in 1950 to 65 by 1970 and to 62 by 1985 – a remarkable decline of eight years during less than four decades.

Table 5.1 United States labor force participation rates of men by age, 1940 to 2001

Year	Age									
	50	55	60	61	62	63	64	65	66	67
1940[a]		93.8	85.5	83.6	80.0	80.4	77.0	70.0	68.1	60.3
1950[a]		90.6	84.7	82.3	81.2	79.8	76.8	71.7	67.1	59.4
1960[a]		92.8	85.9	81.6	79.8	77.8	71.5	56.8	49.0	42.7
1970	93.4	88.0	81.7	77.8	73.1	62.9	63.1	47.4	39.3	35.9
1975	91.0	86.0	79.0	73.7	68.8	56.6	54.4	41.9	32.6	30.7
1980	92.0	83.5	74.5	71.1	60.7	54.3	53.1	35.3	30.4	28.4
1981	90.7	85.8	73.4	67.9	56.4	54.0	45.9	34.2	29.2	29.3
1982	91.8	88.6	72.5	69.5	53.1	44.4	47.6	32.2	28.9	28.3
1983	90.6	85.5	71.1	67.3	55.4	47.4	41.1	31.7	30.2	26.6
1984	92.1	83.7	71.2	64.6	53.6	49.3	41.9	30.6	26.0	24.8
1985	92.2	84.3	70.8	65.9	50.6	47.5	45.8	32.2	25.8	23.2
1986	90.2	84.9	68.5	66.0	55.5	45.8	37.0	32.1	29.4	23.5
1987	90.3	85.5	70.3	66.0	55.7	46.5	42.5	29.0	31.1	26.0
1988	90.8	82.6	66.4	66.2	53.4	47.5	39.7	32.1	31.0	25.0
1989	91.7	84.2	70.0	65.6	53.2	45.1	40.6	34.2	30.8	26.3
1990	90.9	84.9	71.5	64.2	51.8	47.7	40.2	37.2	27.1	31.2
1991	90.0	84.8	72.5	67.4	49.0	44.4	41.5	29.3	34.4	25.6
1992	92.3	84.1	72.5	65.4	54.0	44.2	38.7	32.2	28.2	26.3
1993	90.3	83.6	71.4	65.8	51.7	46.5	41.0	28.6	29.3	22.0
1994	88.1	82.0	65.2	62.4	46.1	44.2	43.1	32.4	28.8	27.4
1995	88.7	81.8	71.6	62.3	47.9	44.4	41.7	33.6	32.9	26.4
1996	90.6	83.4	70.7	66.7	53.5	46.1	39.0	37.6	33.3	28.2
1997	90.6	83.6	69.4	64.0	54.0	46.8	42.7	28.4	32.0	30.3
1998	90.3	85.0	66.4	66.2	57.2	47.3	38.2	33.0	29.4	25.2
1999	89.8	82.2	71.1	64.5	52.8	47.5	44.8	38.2	28.5	30.5
2000	88.7	78.9	69.3	69.9	53.6	46.3	45.9	38.8	38.0	31.7
2001	87.3	82.7	71.3	65.9	54.1	48.2	42.2	38.7	37.9	30.3

Year	68	69	70	71	72	73	74	75	76	77	78	79	80
1940[a]	58.5	53.3	48.6										
1950[a]	57.7	54.5	49.8		39.3								
1960[a]	42.0	39.0	37.2		28.0								
1970	31.4	29.4	30.5	20.4	20.9	11.9	16.8	12.8	14.0	13.9	9.4	10.6	9.9
1975	31.3	27.9	25.7	24.5	22.5	20.5	14.6	19.7	14.6	13.8	10.2	9.3	8.7
1980	27.2	25.0	24.8	20.2	17.0	14.1	17.4	15.8	14.0	10.8	12.3	8.9	10.6
1981	23.5	25.5	19.2	21.2	17.0	14.6	14.8	14.8	14.3	15.6	6.7	10.4	7.9
1982	25.8	22.3	22.7	15.5	16.1	16.8	14.8	12.5	12.6	11.0	11.3	7.2	6.9
1983	28.7	23.4	18.4	20.1	14.7	15.4	18.6	13.3	8.4	11.0	10.9	9.8	8.3
1984	18.9	23.4	15.4	14.1	17.0	12.0	18.2	15.2	10.3	8.4	14.0	8.9	7.4
1985	20.7	20.7	20.5	18.3	15.1	16.1	9.7	13.0	11.4	7.9	9.6	10.8	7.0
1986	21.7	23.1	17.5	15.2	16.3	16.7	14.6	10.6	7.3	9.6	8.3	8.8	10.4
1987	23.4	21.8	17.8	16.6	13.3	15.8	13.2	10.2	7.4	8.9	10.1	6.4	6.1
1988	20.0	21.6	19.3	15.9	16.6	13.3	13.6	11.7	10.1	6.7	11.2	8.2	8.3
1989	22.7	22.2	21.1	16.9	16.3	13.3	14.0	9.4	9.8	10.9	7.7	9.3	5.6
1990	21.5	20.0	20.3	16.4	17.6	17.3	11.3	10.7	8.9	10.0	11.0	8.5	5.0
1991	25.7	19.6	17.2	18.3	10.3	14.0	13.4	10.5	10.0	8.9	6.2	12.1	6.7
1992	24.4	23.9	18.6	18.5	18.1	14.0	11.8	11.3	9.0	7.5	10.1	6.2	6.6
1993	21.4	19.7	18.3	17.4	14.4	13.8	12.1	10.3	12.7	7.9	7.6	7.9	5.3
1994	22.4	19.8	17.3	14.3	16.9	14.2	11.9	11.5	11.3	9.2	7.3	7.5	10.5
1995	22.4	19.7	20.0	18.1	13.6	15.4	12.9	13.8	9.9	10.4	7.7	12.2	5.2
1996	20.5	21.4	18.9	22.5	19.0	15.7	10.5	11.8	10.0	10.7	8.2	5.7	6.7
1997	25.1	21.6	23.4	22.5	19.0	15.7	10.5	11.8	10.0	10.7	8.2	5.7	6.7
1998	25.8	21.8	21.5	18.5	13.5	12.9	15.2	10.3	10.9	4.8	8.1	7.4	7.5
1999	23.3	19.9	19.3	18.7	18.2	16.0	14.3	11.6	10.5	9.7	5.5	6.5	4.6
2000	25.9	25.7	20.8	20.2	18.3	19.6	15.6	14.0	12.0	9.9	12.7	8.7	9.0
2001	24.4	22.1	24.5	20.2	19.0	16.6	13.8	14.6	11.9	10.3	10.6	8.6	7.7

[a] Based on adjusted US Bureau of the Census labor force participation data. The adjustment is based on the ratio of CPS figures and US Decennial Census figures in 1970.

Source: Bureau of Labor Statistics.

The same dramatic changes in retirement behavior can be seen by observing the age specific labor force participation rates shown in the columns of table 5.1. In 1950, over 70 percent of all 65-year-old men in America were still in the labor force. Their participation rate fell by over 20 percentage points by 1970 and by nearly another 15 points by 1985, when only 32 percent of 65-year-old men remained in the labor force – a decline of nearly 60 percent in 35 years.

About 80 percent of men aged 62 were labor force participants in both 1950 and in 1960, when they were ineligible for early Social Security benefits. In 1961, Congress permitted men to claim benefits at age 62 (as it had for women in 1956), and a steady decline in participation rates followed. By 1975, the age 62 rate was 69 percent, and by 1985 it had dropped to almost 50 percent – a decline of nearly 40 percent in only 25 years.

Even larger percentage declines between 1950 and 1985 occurred for older men – drops of about two-thirds at ages 68, 70, and 72. Declines are also observed below age 62, but they are more modest – about 16 percent at age 60 and 8 percent at 55.

Dora Costa (1998: chapter 2) has shown that this trend toward earlier and earlier retirement can be documented back at least a century – to 1880 in the United States and in several other industrialized nations and argues that this is primarily the result of dramatic increases in national wealth over the past century.

The most recent decades of the retirement trends discussed above are illustrated in figures 5.1 and 5.2 which are taken from Quinn (2002). The figures show the actual labor force participation rates for men aged 60 to 64 and 65 to 69 from 1964 through 1985. A trend line is drawn through these actual participation rates for these years. For men aged 60 to 64, the participation rate fell from 79 to 56 percent between 1964 and 1985 – a drop of almost one-third and an average drop of over one percentage point per year. For men aged 65 to 69, the participation rate declined by almost one-half, from 43 to 24 percent, a drop of almost one percentage point per year.

Since the mid-1980s, male retirement trends have been very different. The actual data through 2002 are also shown in figures 5.1 and 5.2. These figures compare extensions of the prior trend line through the year 2000 (what would have occurred had the prior linear trend continued) with the actual labor force participation rates of these men from the mid-1980s through 2000. Comparing the actual to the projected rates shows that the participation rates are much higher today than the pre-1986 trends would have predicted. The same phenomenon is observed among men at slightly younger and older ages.

As mentioned above, another significant labor market change in the twentieth century was the increasing proportion of women in the labor force, see table 5.2. In 1970, 50 percent of women aged 50 were employed or looking for work. By 1980 59 percent were in the labor force. The labor force participation rate of these women increased to 68 percent in 1990. In 2000, 78 percent of women age 50 were in the labor force. In the first half of the century, relatively few women worked for long periods of time and female participation rates were quite low. Personal retirement was not a separate life phase for most women. Instead, it was the retirement of the husband that marked a family transition in later life. Often, the role of the wife as a homemaker was unchanged with advancing age while retirement from the labor force substantially altered the time allocation of the husband.

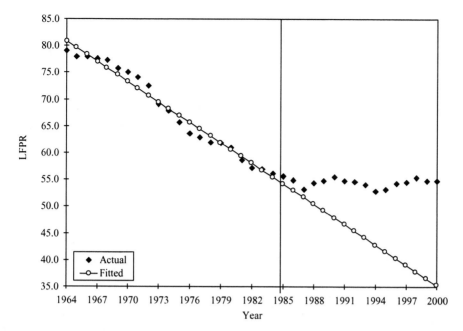

Figure 5.1 Retirement trends, males, aged 60–64
Source: Clark and Quinn, 2002, p. 19.

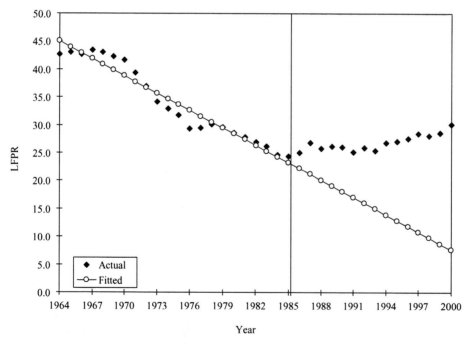

Figure 5.2 Retirement trends, males, aged 65–69
Source: Clark and Quinn, 2002, p. 19.

Table 5.2 United States labor force participation rates of women by age, 1970 to 2001

Year	Age									
	50	55	60	61	62	63	64	65	66	67
1970	49.4	47.7	40.3	32.9	34.0	29.7	23.8	20.2	18.7	14.4
1975	57.4	52.3	42.3	39.9	36.2	27.0	26.4	20.9	14.7	13.0
1980	59.1	52.8	40.4	40.4	31.2	31.5	24.8	19.7	17.8	16.7
1981	60.8	52.9	42.8	38.4	34.4	27.9	25.5	20.3	17.8	17.3
1982	58.7	54.1	41.1	37.6	32.1	27.8	26.3	19.5	16.1	15.2
1983	62.2	54.4	44.7	38.4	33.6	28.1	24.0	17.9	18.3	13.9
1984	64.7	52.5	45.4	38.2	33.2	30.5	22.8	18.8	14.9	14.3
1985	63.3	59.7	41.5	41.5	32.7	28.5	23.4	16.1	14.3	13.9
1986	63.6	56.0	41.7	37.3	33.8	28.7	25.3	19.1	14.6	11.6
1987	66.8	56.7	43.6	37.9	33.2	27.0	27.1	19.4	12.8	16.5
1988	68.0	56.9	44.8	37.6	33.8	27.5	27.7	19.1	16.1	13.6
1989	70.2	59.6	46.0	46.0	36.2	29.6	27.9	22.3	18.7	14.8
1990	68.3	61.0	44.6	41.6	34.2	32.8	26.0	22.3	20.0	16.8
1991	70.7	57.9	44.4	42.3	31.4	28.9	27.1	22.0	19.1	16.5
1992	71.3	60.9	48.6	43.7	33.8	32.0	24.8	19.8	18.9	15.8
1993	72.3	64.3	42.8	46.8	37.0	30.8	28.2	20.8	16.7	16.1
1994	74.7	66.0	47.6	43.9	38.3	33.8	29.3	21.7	18.7	19.2
1995	75.2	62.5	47.2	45.8	38.4	34.0	28.7	22.3	19.2	17.8
1996	75.2	65.2	49.0	47.9	35.1	33.8	32.6	23.0	17.0	18.9
1997	77.5	65.8	49.5	46.0	39.6	34.8	30.7	26.2	19.1	16.5
1998	74.5	67.9	47.3	47.9	42.2	34.7	27.8	26.0	18.9	16.8
1999	77.2	67.8	48.6	40.4	42.4	34.8	30.6	23.4	23.4	21.5
2000	78.0	67.9	48.9	49.5	39.4	36.5	30.8	24.6	24.9	21.2
2001	77.1	67.4	52.5	48.4	41.3	36.6	32.5	25.5	21.2	21.1

	Age												
Year	68	69	70	71	72	73	74	75	76	77	78	79	80
1970	12.5	9.5	9.8	7.6	7.7	6.6	4.6	4.8	3.5	2.3	2.1	3.8	3.8
1975	11.7	11.3	10.0	11.2	7.0	5.4	6.3	4.5	6.7	6.8	2.9	2.9	2.6
1980	12.8	10.2	10.2	10.0	7.4	6.4	6.4	4.6	2.7	3.8	3.3	3.7	0.9
1981	11.8	10.9	8.0	9.5	8.5	7.4	6.5	5.9	5.4	4.6	3.7	3.4	3.0
1982	14.6	9.9	10.5	7.1	8.0	8.1	4.1	5.9	4.0	4.5	3.6	2.0	2.0
1983	13.2	12.9	9.3	7.3	7.5	4.8	7.0	3.0	5.1	3.5	4.6	3.1	2.0
1984	12.1	12.3	11.2	9.8	6.5	5.5	5.4	4.7	2.9	2.0	3.1	3.2	3.1
1985	13.5	11.4	8.3	10.6	8.7	7.7	7.3	4.5	4.5	2.9	1.4	2.5	1.4
1986	12.0	11.4	6.9	5.6	9.0	6.5	7.7	4.5	3.5	4.5	2.1	1.8	1.2
1987	11.4	10.0	6.3	7.6	6.8	6.1	5.7	5.5	4.3	2.6	2.8	3.3	3.7
1988	14.0	10.3	8.2	8.1	7.6	6.3	5.6	5.9	5.3	4.4	2.7	3.7	3.8
1989	13.9	12.2	8.5	9.2	7.4	7.5	7.0	5.5	4.5	5.4	2.4	3.2	2.5
1990	14.4	13.2	14.0	8.1	6.4	5.2	6.4	5.2	4.8	3.6	4.3	2.2	4.1
1991	13.5	11.9	10.8	10.4	7.6	6.2	4.3	5.4	5.7	5.5	3.2	4.1	3.0
1992	14.1	12.2	9.0	10.4	8.3	7.9	6.6	3.8	5.3	3.6	6.0	4.5	2.1
1993	12.1	10.9	12.3	8.8	9.1	6.0	5.7	5.5	3.1	3.5	2.6	2.5	3.5
1994	14.5	11.1	9.8	9.8	8.5	8.3	6.0	5.5	5.7	6.0	1.8	2.4	2.9
1995	14.7	13.0	10.5	8.4	9.9	6.5	5.7	6.6	6.8	5.5	3.4	4.0	1.8
1996	16.4	11.5	10.0	9.9	7.0	8.7	7.1	6.2	6.7	4.8	3.0	5.1	2.8
1997	18.4	16.9	10.5	9.0	10.7	6.3	6.3	6.4	4.9	3.0	4.3	1.7	3.1
1998	15.2	19.1	13.6	10.2	7.0	8.4	7.2	7.4	4.2	4.9	5.7	3.9	4.3
1999	17.8	13.7	14.6	13.0	10.8	6.9	6.7	7.0	5.3	4.8	4.7	5.7	3.7
2000	17.1	17.1	10.0	11.4	11.0	11.1	7.6	7.0	8.6	3.7	4.4	3.7	2.3
2001	17.2	15.1	14.2	10.6	12.4	9.9	10.1	4.6	5.2	5.4	4.6	5.4	1.5

Source: Bureau of Labor Statistics.

Since World War II, more women have entered the labor force, found career jobs, and spent a significant component of their lives working. As a result, the departure from the labor force in late life is now an important process for women as well as men. As their work histories become more like those of men, the same factors influencing retirement become more relevant. Pension and Social Security eligibility, compensation levels, health insurance, and personal wealth have been shown to be important determinants of the timing of retirement of career-oriented women.

As is shown in figures 5.3 and 5.4, the participation patterns of older American women during the two decades discussed above were very different. In fact, there was very little change in the participation rates of women aged 55 to 59 and 60 to 64 (and older, not shown) between the mid-1960s and the mid-1980s, perhaps reflecting the net impact of two offsetting phenomenon – earlier retirement but more women in the labor force. The net changes were on the order of a percentage point per decade, not per year, as with the older men.

The figures extend the pre-1985 trends through 2000, and compare these linear forecast to what actually happened in the work patterns of older women. As with the men, there is a dramatic break from trend; in this case, from a relatively constant participation rate over time to a significant increase in labor force participation after the mid-1980s. As with the men, recent participation rates are much higher than the prior trend would have predicted. The similarity of the break points

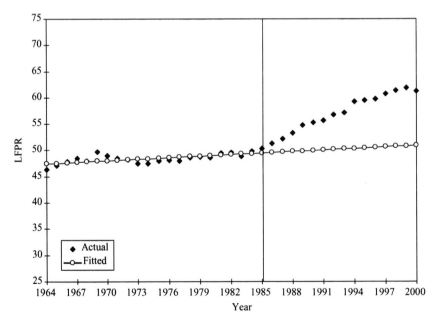

Figure 5.3 Retirement trends, females, aged 55–59
Source: Clark and Quinn, 2002, p. 20.

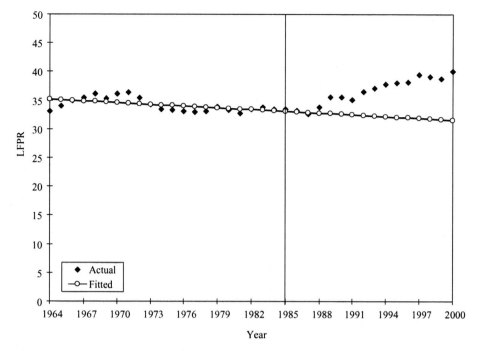

Figure 5.4 Retirement trends, females, aged 60–64
Source: Clark and Quinn, 2002, p. 20.

in the male and female time series is striking and suggests that significant changes have occurred in the US labor market that have altered the timing of retirement among American workers.

WHY THE CHANGE IN RETIREMENT PATTERNS?

What has caused the dramatic breaks from trend in both male and female retirement patterns since the mid-1980s – the ending of the trend toward earlier and earlier retirement among men, and the significant increases in the participation rates of older women? There are two explanations. One emphasizes permanent changes in the retirement environment and argues that we have entered a new era, since these changes are unlikely to be undone. The other argues that it has been a business cycle phenomenon – that the strength of the economy in the late 1980s and 1990s has been key. There is truth in both.

There have been many important societal changes that are consistent with increased work effort late in life. Mandatory retirement was once an important factor in the work lives of many older Americans, covering about half of the workforce, and forcing them out of their jobs at a specific age, usually age 65.

In 1978, the earliest legal age of mandatory retirement was increased from 65 to 70, and then mandatory retirement was eliminated altogether for the vast majority of American workers in 1986. This increased the options of those who had been constrained by the prior policy and who wanted to keep working, and also sent an important message to society that there was no one age appropriate for retirement.

Second, important changes in Social Security have also provided increased incentives for older persons to remain employed. The income that a recipient could earn before losing any Social Security benefits was indexed to wage growth in 1975, and in 1978, higher exempt amounts were introduced for beneficiaries aged 65 through 71. At ages 72 and older, workers could earn any amount and receive full Social Security benefits. In 1983, this earnings test was eliminated for those aged 70 and 71, and in 1990, the benefit loss for each dollar earned over the exempt amount was reduced from 50 to 33 cents for recipients aged 65 to 69. In 2000, Congress eliminated the earnings test altogether for those over the normal retirement age. For those over 62 but younger than the full retirement age, the exempt amounts are increasing dramatically, and by 2002 these younger recipients were able to earn up to $30,000 per year without any loss of benefits (Social Security Administration, 2000: tables 2.A20 and 2.A29).

The liberalization and then elimination of the earning test for persons over the normal retirement age mean that older workers can continue to work and still receive their Social Security benefits. More recently, the gradual increase in the age of normal retirement (from 65 to 66, and later from 66 to 67) is lowering annual Social Security benefits for all retirees, since waiting longer for a given amount is equivalent to receiving less at any given age, thereby encouraging older persons to delay retirement.

Important changes are also underway in the private sector, where there has been an increase in the relative importance of defined contribution employer pension plans, which do not have strong age-specific retirement incentives, at the expense of more traditional defined benefit plans, which do encourage retirement at specific ages.[1] The more recent growth in cash balance plans also means that these participants do not face the early retirement incentives (or, equivalently, work disincentives) that are often imbedded in traditional defined benefit plans.

In addition to these longer-term trends in the structure of employer-sponsored retirement programs, some companies attempted to entice workers to remain on the job at least part time during the late 1990s, with the creation of formal and informal phased retirement programs (Ghent et al., 2002). These programs allow workers to remain on their career jobs while working fewer hours, which some workers find appealing. Still other workers, as we will see below, are moving form career jobs to bridge jobs with new employers in order to withdraw more gradually from the labor force.

The nature of jobs in America is also in transition, with manufacturing on the decline and service employment on the rise. Although there is considerable variation in the nature of jobs within these broad occupational categories, and many service jobs can be grueling, it is probably easier, on average, for older employees to remain working in the new occupational structure. Steuerle et al. (1999, figure 1) estimate that the percentage of American workers in physically demanding jobs has declined from 20 percent in 1950 to 11 percent in 1970, and to 7.5 percent by the mid-1990s.

Finally, older Americans are enjoying longer and healthier lives. The life expectancy of American men at age 65 increased by three years (to almost 16 years) during the second half of the twentieth century, and increased by over four years (to over 19 years) for women. Further increases are projected throughout the next century (US House of Representatives, 1998: table A-2). Crimmins et al. (1999: S31) report significant improvements in the ability to work among men and women in their 60s between 1982 and 1993 – changes large enough that "the percentage unable to work at age 67 in 1993 is lower than the percentage unable to work at age 65 in 1982." Many workers reaching traditional retirement ages can anticipate a healthy decade or two ahead, and, as we will see below, some are deciding that some combination of work and leisure is preferable to all of one or all of the other.

These societal changes describe a retirement environment today that is different from that in the past. Demographic changes and enlightened public policy initiatives have altered the relative attractiveness of work and retirement late in life, in favor of continued work, and, as we have seen, older Americans seem to be responding accordingly.

An alternative hypothesis is that the strong American economy at the end of the twentieth century temporarily delayed the inevitable continuation of the old trends toward earlier and earlier retirement among American men. The unemployment rate declined from nearly 10 percent in the early 1980s to about 5 percent by the end of that decade, and by the year 2000 had fallen to 4 percent – the lowest unemployment rate since the late 1960s (Council of Economic Advisers, 2001: table B-42). Strong labor demand creates employment options for workers of all ages, including older workers. This rapid economic growth may also have changed the attitudes of some employers toward retaining older workers. Instead of encouraging early retirement through pension incentives, buyouts and early retirement windows, some companies tried actively to retain and attract older workers. Low unemployment rates forced companies to reconsider their human resource policies. The shift toward defined contribution and cash balance pension plans is just one manifestation of this change.

Is the current pattern of a more stable male retirement age a permanent change from the prior century's trend or merely a pause in the inevitable long-run decline in the age of retirement? Some argue that the current situation is merely a temporary pause associated with the economic expansion. This view implies that as economic growth slows and unemployment rates rise, companies will once again find ways to encourage older workers to retire and retirement ages will resume their decline. Others point to the more permanent changes in pensions, Social Security and the occupation structure, to the elimination of mandatory retirement, and to improved health among the elderly and increasing life expectancy and argue that these changes will continue to encourage older workers to remain in the labor force beyond normal retirement ages.

HOW DO OLDER AMERICANS LEAVE THE LABOR FORCE?

In the past, the people often thought of retirement as an event, a time when an individual terminated employment on a full-time career job and fully retired, that is stopped working altogether. While still prevalent, this pattern of abrupt labor market withdrawal is not the only or perhaps even the typical way in which most Americans are retiring in the twenty-first century. In fact, some older persons are using phased retirement programs on career jobs while many others are moving from career jobs to new part-time or shorter duration full-time jobs that ease the transition from full-time career work into retirement. The importance of these new paths to retirement is an important change in the retirement process and merits further consideration.

During the 1990s, some companies began exploring ways of modifying their human resource policies to encourage older workers to remain on the job (Watson Wyatt Worldwide, 2001). In some cases, these are selective programs that target particular workers or workers with specific skills that are in high demand. Other firms have adopted general programs that are open to all workers meeting certain age and service requirements. Phased retirement programs can be either formal or informal and can be open to current employees or be used to rehire retired workers. Options for phased retirement include reduced hours per day, fewer days per week or year, extended leaves of absence, job sharing, and rehiring former employees as consultants.

A 1999 survey found that 16 percent of the 586 firms interviewed offered some type of phased retirement program (Watson Wyatt Worldwide, 2001). The incidence of phased retirement varied substantially by industry with 36 percent of educational institutions and 21 percent of public employers offering such a program, compared to only about 10 percent of firms in finance and insurance, manufacturing, utilities, and the trades. Another survey of a similar number of firms found that 23 percent of firms had adopted at least one type of phased retirement program (William Mercer, 2001). This survey reported that among those with phased retirement programs for currently active workers, 47 percent allowed phased retirees to reduce the number of hours they worked. Some 40 to 45 percent of the firms allowed phased retirees to focus on special assignments or do temporary or consulting work. In addition, 59 percent of the responding firms reported that they had policies for the rehiring of former workers. These programs were especially prevalent among government (89 percent) and higher education organizations (88 percent). Most of these programs involved rehiring retirees as part-time or temporary workers or as independent contractors.

Survey evidence on the labor supply side suggests that many current workers want to continue working beyond normal retirement ages. In an AARP survey of 2,000 baby boomers aged 34 to 52, 80 percent said that they expect to keep working at least part-time after age 65, and for a variety of reasons – some because they need the income and some because of the enjoyment it brings (Roper Starch Worldwide, 1998). In a 1998 Employee Benefit Research Institute survey, over 60 percent of workers said that they would work for pay after retirement, again many for financial reasons, and many others to improve their quality of lives (Yakoboski et al., 1998). The stark contrast between these estimates (80 and 60 percent) and the current labor force participation rate of Americans aged 65 to 69 (about 30 percent for men and 20 percent for women) gives one pause about using these survey results as a predictor of the future, but they do suggest that new attitudes toward work late in life are developing in the American workforce.

Analysis indicates that formal phased retirement programs provide workers with new work-retirement options and that many older persons will select this option rather than fully retiring or moving to a bridge job (Allen et al., 2002). In addition to phased retirement, many older persons are opting to remain in the labor force by moving to bridge jobs. These jobs may be full-time or part-time. About 25 percent of the men in the Health and Retirement Survey (HRS) had left their career jobs and were working on a bridge job in 1996 (Quinn, 2002). Another 10 percent of the men in this survey had previously worked on a bridge job but had fully retired by 1996. Thus, approximately one-third of the men in this survey had already selected this type of transition from full-time work to complete retirement, and many others who were still working on a full-time career job undoubtedly would. Women appear even more likely to work on bridge jobs before completely retiring. Of the women in the HRS, about one half of female workers had moved to bridge jobs prior to permanently leaving the labor force.

The precise percentages who retire gradually, using bridge jobs on the way out, depends on technical definition of what is a bridge job, as opposed to another career job. After how many years, for example, does a bridge job become a new career job? But any reasonable definition supports the conclusion that bridge jobs are an important part of the retirement environment in America today, and a substantial minority or perhaps a majority of workers retire in stages. At what stage one is defined as "retired" is arbitrary, and much less important than understanding how older Americans leave their career jobs. It is clear that for many, retirement is not an event; rather, it is a process involving a number of events, the end of which is usually complete labor force withdrawal.

INTERNATIONAL PATTERNS OF RETIREMENT

Economic development produces a series of changes in a country's economic environment that typically result in increases in real income per capita, declines in the rate of population growth and an ensuing aging of the population, changes in the industrial structure of the economy, and the development of national retirement programs. In response to rising income and other socio-economic changes, the proportion of older persons who remain in the labor force tends to decline (Clark et al., 1999). Table 5.3 reports average labor force participation rates in 1990 for workers in each of the three age categories by level of per capita GNP. The income categories are those used by the World Bank to indicate low-, middle-, and high-income countries. Within each income category, labor force participation declines with

Table 5.3   Average labor force participation rates by per capita Gross National Product[a]

Income[b]	N	Men			Women		
		55–59	60–64	65+	55–59	60–64	65+
$0–$610	43	93.0	85.4	66.5	62.5	52.1	33.9
$611–$7,620	63	83.7	66.8	40.5	34.2	25.6	13.9
$7,621 and up	28	78.1	52.1	15.4	40.0	22.1	4.7

[a] Table entries indicate the average LFP rate for all countries within the range for per capita GNP for that row.
[b] The ranges for per capita GNP, in 1990 dollars, come from the World Bank data categories for low, middle, and high income countries.
Source: Clark and Quinn 2002, p. 18.

age. Countries with higher levels of average income have lower rates of labor force participation of older men and women, except for women age 55 to 59. There is a large drop in their labor force participation rate from the low to the middle-income countries, but an increase in their labor force participation rates from the middle- to the high-income countries. This finding appears to reflect the increased labor force participation of women over the past few decades in more developed countries. Research indicates that this has been due to changing social values and the feminist revolution as well as increasing female wage rates, increased educational attainment, enactment of laws banning discrimination on the basis of gender, and declining fertility.

In general, these data support the hypothesis that there is a negative relationship between income and labor force participation. Another interesting observation from table 5.3 is the very large percentage decrease in labor force participation for men and women in high income countries as age increases from the 60 to 64 category to the 65 and older category. There is a 70 percent decline in labor force participation for men (from 52 percent for men aged 60 to 64 to 15 percent for men aged 65 and older) and a 79 percent decline for women (from 22 percent to 5 percent). These are the largest percentage declines across age categories in the table and perhaps reflect the fact that most high-income countries have social security eligibility ages of 65 years old. Thus, this sharp decline in participation rates may be due to the older ages of eligibility for benefits in the high-income sample.

Sorting the individual countries into regions and subregions provides further evidence on the relationship between income and labor force participation. However, variation in the proportion of older workers remaining in the labor force also reflects cultural, ethnic, and religious differences, which the regional sorting may reflect. The regions, as identified by the United Nations, are Asia, Africa, Europe, Latin America and the Caribbean, Oceania, and North America. Table 5.4 contains a listing of labor force participation rates for workers aged 65 and older by geographic region and subregion.

Table 5.4 Labor force participation rates for age 65 and older and per capita income by region

Region[a]	N	Income[b]	Men	Women
Africa	45	$705	64.6	33.8
East	14	419	71.8	44.0
Middle	7	949	67.6	38.5
North	4	1,342	29.2	8.6
South	5	1,524	49.7	17.3
West	15	415	70.8	34.3
Asia	29	$4,994	42.9	14.1
East	4	10,885	32.9	12.1
South central	7	614	57.4	20.4
Southeast	7	2,548	45.2	21.7
West	11	7,196	35.9	5.8
Europe	26	$14,004	11.0	4.7
Eastern/Central	7	2,527	14.9	7.9
North	7	20,369	14.9	5.9
South	5	9,162	10.1	3.4
West	7	22,576	3.8	1.3
Latin America & Caribbean	27	$2,319	44.3	10.9
Caribbean	7	4,326	40.8	14.0
Central America	8	1,405	52.6	10.6
South America	12	1,758	40.7	9.4
North America	2	$21,060	13.5	6.2
Oceania	5	$6,578	36.7	21.2

[a] Countries are grouped by geographical region as specified by the United Nations, except for Eastern/Central Europe.
[b] Table entries for income and LFP rates are averages for all countries in that region.
Source: Clark et al., 1999, p. 418.

Examination of these data supports the finding that regions composed of countries with low average income tend to have higher rates of labor force participation (LFP) among older citizens. A ranking of the regions by income and LFP shows this general pattern, although it is stronger for men than for women. For men, the inverse relationship of income and LFP rates holds, except for Europe, which has lower average incomes than North America, and also slightly lower participation rates among the elderly. For women, Africa has the highest average participation rate and Asia the third highest rate, which corresponds to Africa having the lowest average income and Asia having the third lowest average income. Table 5.4 shows that the corresponding income and labor force participation rankings do not hold for Latin America, Europe, North America, and Oceania.

When comparing subregions, other exceptions to the hypothesis of the inverse relationship between income and elderly labor force participation rates are evident. For example, Northern Africa has lower average income than Southern Africa, but Southern Africa has much higher average participation rates for men and for women. Southeast Asia and Eastern/Central Europe have similar average income levels, but Eastern/Central Europe has participation rates that are about a third of those in Southeast Asia. In fact, the rates for Eastern Europe are much lower than those for many of the subregions that have higher average income levels. These anomalies may reflect religious and cultural differences in the importance of agriculture and oil-based income between countries of Northern and Southern Africa and the vestiges of social welfare systems left over from the days of central planning systems.

CONCLUSION

The decision of when to leave the labor force is one of the most important life cycle choices individuals must make. Economic theory suggests that each person considers their remaining life expectancy and decides how to allocate their resources between current consumption and saving for future consumption and between work and leisure activities. In this chapter we have explored these choices for men and women and for older persons in developed and developing countries. The timing of retirement is influenced by family wealth, earnings potential, and the health status of household members. Government policies such as the age of eligibility for Social Security, the generosity of retirement benefits, and the provision of health care directly affect retirement decisions. Company policies such as mandatory retirement, pension plans, and compensation policies determine the timing of retirement from particular jobs. Economic conditions and the availability of jobs, both full and part-time, are important determinants of the percentage of older persons who remain in the labor force. With the continuation of population aging, retirement policies will become increasingly important.

DISCUSSION QUESTIONS

Comment on the reasonableness of these statements:

1 Throughout most of the twentieth century, men were retiring at earlier and earlier ages. This trend was primarily due to the widespread adoption of mandatory retirement policies by companies interested in pushing older workers off their payrolls.

2 Since 1985, there has been no further decline in the labor force participation rates of older men. This is primarily attributable to the rapid growth of the economy and companies providing more job opportunities to older workers.

3   Gerontologists have long argued that a gradual reduction in hours of work was preferred to the abrupt change from full-time work to complete retirement. Life cycle economic theory also predicts that this would be the preferred pattern of transition from work to retirement. Traditionally this has not been the case, however, recent data suggest that more workers are involved in phased retirement programs and shifting to part-time work prior to completely leaving the labor force. Explain this trend.

4   During periods of recession, companies attempt to reduce the size of their labor force. A preferred method of accomplishing reductions in force is the use of early retirement programs.

5   National Social Security programs influence retirement patterns by changing the incentives to work and retire. These changes have both income and substitution effects. Identify parameters of Social Security that would influence the age at which you expect to retire.

6   Older men in Japan have much higher work rates than older men in Europe. Why?

Note

1   The proportion of employer pension participants whose primary coverage is defined contribution increased from 13 to 42 percent between 1975 and the mid-1990s. Including secondary plans, which are nearly all DC, the proportion of participants with a DC plan more than doubled from 26 to 53 percent over this same time period (Employee Benefit Research Institute, 1997: table 10.2; Olsen and VanDerhei, 1997: table 2).

References

Allen, Steven, Clark, Robert, and Ghent, Linda 2002: Phasing into retirement. Unpublished working paper, Raleigh, NC: North Carolina State University.

Clark, Robert and Quinn, Joseph 2002: Patterns of work and retirement for a new century. *Generations* 26 (11): 17–24.

Clark, Robert, York, Anne, and Anker, Richard 1999: Economic development and labor force participation of older persons. *Population Research and Policy Review* 18(5): 411–32.

Costa, Dora 1998: *The Evolution of Retirement: An American Economic History, 1880–1990.* Chicago: University of Chicago Press.

Council of Economic Advisers 2001: *Economic Report of the President.* Washington, DC: US Government Printing Office.

Crimmins, E., Reynolds, S. and Saito, Y. 1999: Trends in health and ability to work among the older working age population. *Journal of Gerontology* 54 B(I): S31–40.

Employee Benefit Research Institute 1997: *EBRI Data Book on Employee Benefits.* Washington, DC: EBRI.

Ghent, Linda, Allen, Steven, and Clark, Robert 2002: The impact of a new phased retirement option on faculty retirement decisions. *Research on Aging* 23 (6): 671–93.

Olsen, Kelly and VanDerhei, Jack 1997: *Defined Contribution Plan Dominance Grows across Sectors and Employer Sizes, while Mega-defined Benefit Plans Remain Strong.* (Employee

Benefit Research Institute Issue Brief. No. 190). Washington, DC: Employee Benefit Research Institute.

Quadagno, Jill and Quinn, Joseph 1997: Does social security discourage work? In Eric Kingson and James Schulz (eds.), *Social Security in the 21st Century*. New York: Oxford University Press, 127–46.

Quinn, Joseph. 2002. Retirement trends and patterns among older American workers. In Stuart Altman and David Shactman (eds.), *Policies for an Aging Society*. Baltimore: Johns Hopkins University Press, 293–315.

Roper Starch Worldwide. 1998: Boomers look toward retirement. Presentation for the American Association of Retired People, Washington, June, 2.

Social Security Administration 2000: *Annual Statistical Bulletin.* Washington, DC: US Government Printing Office.

Steuerle, Gene, Spiro, Christopher, and Johnson, Richard, W. 1999: Can Americans work longer? In the Urban Institute, *Straight Talk on Social Security and Retirement Policy*, No. 5. Washington DC: The Urban Institute, August.

US House of Representatives, Committee of Ways and Means 1998: *1998 Green Book.* Washington, DC: US Government Printing Office.

Watson Wyatt Worldwide. 2001: *Current Practices in Phased Retirement.* Lake Oswego, OR: People Management Resources.

William M. Mercer Co. 2001: *Capitalizing on an Aging Workforce: Phased Retirement and Other Options.* Chicago: William M. Mercer Co.

Yakoboski, Paul, Ostuw, Pamela, and Hicks, Jennifer 1998: *What is Your Savings Personality? The 1998 Retirement Confidence Survey* (Employee Benefit Research Institute Issue Brief No. 200). Washington, DC: EBRI.

CHAPTER SIX

Retirement Policies and Pension Plans

LEARNING OBJECTIVES

After completing this chapter, you will be able to:

1 Understand the role of pensions in the human resource policies of companies.
2 Understand how pensions alter worker behavior.
3 Discuss the importance of pensions in the total compensation of workers and how this changes with more years of job service.
4 Describe the different types of pension plans and how they have different economic effects.
5 Examine why different types of firms prefer one type of pension plan to another.
6 Examine why different individuals prefer one type of pension plan compared to another.
7 Assess how government regulation affects pension policy.

INTRODUCTION

Employer-provided pensions represent an important component of labor compensation for many workers and a significant cost of production to employers. At the beginning of the twenty-first century, approximately half of the labor force in the United States is covered by a company pension plan. Significant changes have occurred during the past 50 years in pension coverage, the type of pension offered, and the role of pensions in the labor market. The proportion of the labor force participating in a pension plan rose from approximately 25 percent in 1950 to 50 percent in 1974. The growth in participation stalled after the Employee Retirement Income Security Act (ERISA) was enacted in that year. For the past three decades, participation has remained relatively constant at about half of the labor force. The past three decades have also seen a dramatic shift away from the use of traditional defined benefit plans and toward greater utilization of defined contribution plans and more recently, a significant number of large firms have converted their plans to hybrid pension plans including cash balance and pension equity plans.

The primary objectives of compensation and other human resource policies are to attract and retain quality workers and then to have them retire in an orderly manner at appropriate ages. A central component of these human resource policies is the provision of a pension plan. As we learned in chapter 3, company pension plans provide an important part of income in retirement for many older persons and the role of pensions in determining the economic well-being of retirees has expanded during the last half century. In the United States, the federal government has encouraged the establishment of pension plans by providing a preferential tax treatment for qualified plans. In order to attain this tax-qualified status, pension plans must meet certain regulations that seek to insure that companies do not discriminate in favor of high-income workers, provide adequate funding to pay retirement benefits, and meet specific vesting and participation standards.

This chapter reviews the development of employer pension plans in the United States and the growth in pension coverage, discusses the different types of pension plans and how they affect worker behavior, and describes federal regulation of pension plans and how this affects plan administration. Finally, pension plans are examined in relationship to other retirement policies such as mandatory retirement, retiree health insurance, phased retirement plans, and early retirement incentive programs. Thus, the chapter provides an economic framework to evaluate the role of pensions in the labor market including why firms offer pension plans and why workers want to have some of their compensation in the form of a pension.

PENSION ECONOMICS

Economic theory implies that firms are willing to pay workers in accordance with their contribution to the firm, i.e. wages are directly related to the worker's productivity.[1] Compensation can be provided in many forms, with the total cost being the determining factor to the firm. If worker behavior is not affected by the type of compensation, firms can be viewed as neutral sellers of benefits to their employees. In other words, employers are willing to provide whatever combination of cash and benefits workers desire provided that the total cost of employment is not affected. In order to attract certain types of workers, firms may offer particular benefits that these individuals value most highly. This is the fundamental concept behind the theory of compensation wage differentials.[2] However, certain benefits and how they accumulate over time may alter worker behavior and as a result, these benefits can influence labor productivity. If cost savings occur due to this change in behavior, then a dollar of extra benefits would not require a dollar reduction in cash compensation.

The primary reason that workers usually prefer a portion of their total compensation in the form of pension income or other benefits is the favorable tax treatment given to these forms of compensation.[3] Since the 1920s, the federal income tax code has contained provisions that specified that employer contributions to qualified plans and the earnings of these pension trusts were not subject to current taxation but would become taxable income to individuals when the pension income was received. The deferment of income tax liability enables workers to accumulate larger retirement funds through employer-provided pension plans than they could with equivalent dollars paid as current earnings. Pension contributions also are not subject to the payroll taxes for Social Security and Medicare. A numerical example of the value of this preferential tax status of employer-provided pension plans is shown in Box 6.1.

Employers offer pension plans to their employees because they help in the management of human resources including attracting, retaining, and eventually retiring older workers. Some individuals will seek out firms that provide pension plans and alter their careers to remain with these employers, while other workers have a higher preference for current income and will select employers who do not provide deferred compensation. Thus, individuals with low rates of time preference will be more likely to accept pension-covered jobs and then remain with the company until retirement in order to receive the deferred pension payments.[4]

Some pensions impose financial penalties on workers who leave "too early" and thus these firms will have lower turnover rates. Some pension plans have significant retirement incentives at particular ages and thus are able to influence the timing of retirement. These incentive effects can be used by employers to incorporate pension plans into long-term employment contracts. A graphical example of the use of pensions in conjunction with implicit long-term contracts is shown in Box 6.2. These incentives proved to be especially important to companies during periods of downsizing but become liabilities in the tight labor market at the end of the 1990s.[5]

TYPES OF PENSION PLANS

Pension plans have traditionally been divided into two basic types: defined benefit and defined contribution plans. These plan types differ substantially in the manner

Box 6.1 *Tax Advantages of Pension Savings*

The IRS code provides that contributions to a tax-qualified pension plan and the earnings of the pension fund are not subject to current federal income tax. Instead, the pension benefits are taxed when they are received during retirement. This preferential tax advantage provides an incentive for firms to offer a pension plan and for workers to participate in such a plan. The magnitude of this tax effect is shown in the following example.

Consider a worker aged 50 that faces a constant marginal tax rate of 25 percent on all earnings and this tax rate is expected to continue throughout the remainder of the individual's life. The worker is now offered the opportunity to receive an additional $100 in total compensation and the individual has decided that he wants to save all the additional income for retirement. The worker expects to retire at age 65. He can receive the entire $100 in cash or he could have the $100 placed in a defined contribution plan. If the individual selects to receive the $100 in cash, a tax of 25 percent is assessed leaving a net of $75. Assume that these funds are invested at an annual interest rate of 5 percent and held in an account until age 65. Since savings outside of retirement accounts are taxed at the 25 percent rate, the net return on the investment is only 3.75 percent per year $[(5.0 \times (1.00 - 0.25)]$. At age 65 after 15 years of savings, the worker would have $132 in his account.

Alternatively, the worker opts to have his employer deposit the $100 in his individual pension account. No immediate tax is assessed on the contribution and each year the net return on the investment is 5 percent because the earnings of the pension account are not taxed. The pension account grows to $212 at age 65. When the funds are withdrawn from the pension account, the money is taxed at a rate of 25 percent leaving a value of $158. Thus, saving through the pension yields a retirement benefit that is $26 greater than saving outside of a tax-qualified pension plan or a gain of almost 20 percent over the $132 value from savings outside of the pension.

These results can be generalized for savings over the entire lifetime. The value of the preferential tax treatment increases with the individual tax rate and the nominal rate of return on the investment. This implies that more highly compensated workers that are in a higher-income tax bracket receive a greater benefit from this deferment of tax liabilities. The great gain from saving through company pension plans partially explains why workers with higher earnings are more likely to be covered by a pension plan. It can also be shown that the real gain from the tax status of pension plans is the deferral of taxation on the investment return to pension funds and not the deferral of taxes on the initial contribution.

Source: Ippolito (1986).

Box 6.2   *Pensions as a Component of Long-Term Employment Contracts*

Economists have attempted to explain the growth in wages with age and tenure in the context of human capital theory. In general, this theory states that workers with more skills and ability (human capital) receive higher wages and that human capital tends to increase over much of an individual's life, thus generating a rising wage profile with increases in labor market experience (Becker, 1964). Unfortunately, this theory could not explain human resource policies like mandatory retirement and subsidies for early retirement in defined benefit pension plans.

Lazear (1979) developed a theory of implicit long-term contracts in which the firm underpaid the worker early in life (wage less than marginal product) and overpaid them in the latter working years (wage greater than marginal product). In a sense, the underpayment represents a bond posted by the worker that is repaid with interest in subsequent years. Repayment is conditional on the worker remaining with the firm and being a good employee. These contracts help firms attract workers who expect to remain with the firm for many years, thus reducing turnover costs. The contracts also provide incentives for workers not to shirk on the job lest they risk being fired and, therefore, lose the opportunity for the higher wages (figure 6.1). In the repayment phase, the firm has an incentive to lay off workers so as to avoid paying wages in excess of the current contributions to the firm. However, managers recognize that if they renege on the contract they will not be able to use this policy to attract future workers, i.e. their reputation as being unreliable will harm them.

Since firms are overpaying older workers, there needs to be a mechanism to end the contract in an orderly fashion. In the past, mandatory retirement enabled firms to specify the end to such contracts. Even if the worker would

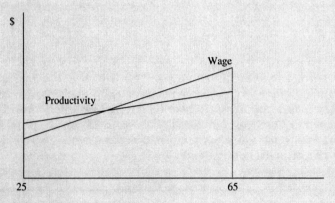

Figure 6.1   Career patterns of wage and productivity

like to remain on the job at the premium wage, they are unable to stay because of mandatory retirement. Another method of accomplishing the same goal is to construct a pension plan that subsidizes early retirement. Such plans enable firms to honor the long-term contract while enticing workers to retire at an appropriate time so that the firm does not have to continue paying wages greater than the marginal product of these workers. Hutchens (1989) provides a straightforward discussion of these issues.

in which benefits are determined, their methods of funding, who bears the investment risk associated with the pension portfolio, the portability of benefits from one company to another, and the regulatory status of the two types of plans.[6] In general, defined benefit plans promise a specified benefit based on years of service, annual earnings, and a generosity parameter chosen by the firm.[7] In defined contribution plans, employers and employees make periodic contributions into individual accounts for each worker and benefits are based on the size of these accounts at retirement. Each type of plan has advantages and disadvantages for workers and for the plan sponsor. Which plan type is best for the firm depends on its human resource needs and objectives. The best type of pension for employees depends on their risk preferences and their expected lifetime work patterns.

Defined benefit plans are usually considered to be good for workers because they provide a specified benefit linked to final annual earnings, coverage is universal among qualified workers, and the employees do not face the investment risk associated with managing a retirement account. Benefits are paid in the form of life annuities with current government regulations requiring that the first option for the pension be a joint and survivor's annuity to protect the financial interests of the spouse of the worker.[8] These annuities provide insurance against retirees outliving their retirement savings. Since the passage of the ERISA in 1974, benefits under defined benefit plans have been insured on a limited basis against the pension fund not being able to pay promised benefits.

The primary disadvantage of defined benefit plans is that workers who change jobs frequently will accumulate considerably lower retirement benefits than those who remain with a single firm. The lower accumulation of benefits is due to formulas that base benefits on earnings in the final years before job termination. These earnings are not indexed so that individuals who leave a pension-covered job relatively early in their careers will have retirement benefits based on average earnings many years in the past. Understanding the nature of benefit accruals is of central importance for pension economics. This lack of portability of benefits creates a significant mobility risk for workers covered by a defined benefit pension plan. Box 6.3 presents a numerical example indicating the lack of portability of pension benefits in defined benefit plans.

The loss in pension benefits that workers face if they change jobs can be an important advantage of defined benefit plans to employers. Imposing such losses on workers who leave is one method that firms can use to reduce their turnover

Box 6.3 *Portability of Pension Benefits*

The pattern of benefit accruals in final pay-defined benefit pension plans
implies that workers who change jobs accumulate smaller retirement benefits
than those who remain with the same employers throughout their careers.
The loss in pension wealth associated with job changes means that retirement
benefits are not portable. Consider the following example. Workers are hired
at age 20 and will retire at age 60. All employers in the economy offer a final
pay defined benefit plan with a benefit formula of

$$B = (0.01) \times (\text{average earnings over the last three years}) \times (\text{years of service}).$$

All workers earn $20,000 the first ten years of employment, $30,000 the next
ten years, $40,000 the third ten years, and $50,000 the last ten years of
employment. Earnings are not affected by job changes.

The impact of job changes on total retirement benefits is easily shown from
this example. A worker who remains with the same firm for 40 years will have
a benefit of $20,000 from this firm (0.01 × $50,000 × 40). Now let the worker
change jobs after 20 years of employment. This person will earn pensions
from both employers. The pension from the first firm will be equal to $6,000
(0.01 × $30,000 × 20) and the pension from the second employer will be
$10,000 (0.01 × $50,000 × 20). Thus, the total pension from the two jobs is
only $16,000. Recall that earnings were not affected by changing jobs and
both firms had identical pensions yet the combined pensions for the job
changer are $4,000 lower than the pension from a single employer based on
40 years of service. The lower combined pension benefit is the result of the
pension from the initial employer being based on final earnings from that job
and not the final earnings of the worker's career. Clark and McDermed (1988)
provided a more detailed discussion of this effect.

Participants in defined contribution plans do not face this loss in pension
wealth with job changes. Their pension is based on contributions into an
individual account that is their property. The funds in the pension account
grow with new contributions and returns on investments. Workers who leave
a firm with this type of pension plan can take the entire value of the pension
with them, thus, there is not a loss in pension wealth with job changes.

rates, i.e. workers who face a loss in their future retirement benefits will be less
likely to leave. Thus, firms that have high costs of hiring and training workers
will be more likely to adopt these types of plans in order to reduce these costs
associated with turnover. Numerous empirical studies confirm that pension-covered
jobs have lower turnover rates than nonpension jobs. In addition, defined benefit plans enable firms to provide substantial incentives for workers to retire at

specified ages such as the normal and early retirement ages. Later in this chapter, we discuss benefit accruals and their incentives on worker behavior.

In the United States, Social Security is a defined benefit program that uses a career-average formula to determine retirement benefits. There are two significant differences between employer-provided defined benefit plans and the national Social Security system. First, the entire labor force is included in the Social Security system. This means that all earnings, whether a worker stays with the same company her entire worklife or whether the worker changes jobs, are used to calculate retirement benefits. Thus, there is no loss in the value of Social Security benefits with job changes, e.g. the benefits are completely portable. Second, earnings are indexed for wage growth so that using a lifetime of earnings does not result in low benefits relative to earnings just before retirement.

One major disadvantage of defined benefit plans to employers is that the cost of federal regulation is more burdensome than that imposed on defined contribution plans. These regulatory costs have proven to be especially high for small firms and research studies indicate that the cost of complying with these regulations is the primary reason why few employers with less than one hundred workers now offer defined benefit plans. Another disadvantage that managers report is that the method of benefit accrual and the value of benefits are more difficult to explain to their employees compared to the value of individual accounts under defined contribution plans. The difficulty in communicating the value of defined benefit plans has led many employers to conclude that their employees do not give them sufficient credit for the costs of defined benefit pensions. Managers often give this as a reason for converting traditional defined benefit plans to pensions with individual accounts that are easier to explain to their workers.

The retirement benefit for participants in defined contribution plans depends on the size of employer and employee contributions throughout the working life and the returns to the investments made with the pension funds. Under these plans, the value of the pension at any point in time is the account balance. If contributions are made at a relatively even rate throughout a worker's career, the value of the account will grow more proportionately than under a defined benefit plan of comparable generosity. Thus, an important advantage of these pension plans is that the benefits are portable and can be transferred with the worker from job to job, i.e. there is no loss in pension benefits with job change. Comparing similar workers covered by the two plan types, workers who move from job to job will accumulate higher retirement benefits if they participate in defined contribution plans.

Potential disadvantages of defined contribution plans for employees are that contributions are often voluntary, workers bear the investment risk of these plans, and the benefits are typically paid in the form of lump sum distributions. Many defined contribution plans require workers to decide if they will make a pension contribution. Employer contributions may be contingent on employee contributions, i.e., if the worker chooses not to contribute to the plan, no employer contributions will be made. Workers who are myopic or have relatively high discount rates may decide not to make pension contributions early in their careers. As a result, they will accumulate relatively low retirement accounts. In defined contribution plans, workers generally must make decisions concerning how to invest their funds. Some participants may invest too conservatively while others may make more risky choices that affect the size of their ultimate retirement accounts. Receipt of retirement monies in a lump sum requires that individuals decide how to manage these funds for the rest of their lives. It creates the possibility that the pension monies will be exhausted before the worker or his or her spouse dies.

Employers find defined contribution plans advantageous because the funding of benefits is more straightforward and the benefit structure is easier to explain to employees. The liability to the plan sponsor is to provide the promised contribution and the firm does not have to worry about future funding nor is it required to purchase insurance against the inability to pay future benefits. The cost of complying with government regulations is lower, enabling the firm to provide higher benefits for the same cost. Employers report that workers find defined contribution plans easier to understand and give the firm more credit for providing these plans compared to a defined benefit plan.

There are also several disadvantages for employers associated with defined contribution plans. Some employees may fail to participate, may begin to make contributions rather late in their careers, or make inappropriate investments and reach retirement ages with inadequate resources to retire. Such workers may then decide to remain with the firm rather than retire at normal ages. It is more difficult for firms to use these plans to influence the quit and retirement behaviors of their employees.

In the past decade, large employers have increasingly converted traditional defined benefit plans into hybrid plans that are referred to as cash balance or pension equity plans.[9] In many regards, the conversion of traditional defined benefit plans into hybrid plans by employers is an attempt to offer workers a pension plan that combines desirable features of both defined benefit and defined contribution plans. Both cash balance and pension equity plans are formally defined benefit plans but they contain many of the features of defined contribution plans that workers seem to prefer. The basic characteristics of defined benefit plans, defined contribution plans, and hybrid plans are shown in table 6.1.

Table 6.1 shows that the contribution and participation features of the hybrid plans closely resemble those found in traditional defined benefit plans. All qualified workers are covered by the plan and the firm typically makes all of the contributions into the pension fund. The firm is responsible for insuring that sufficient monies are in the pension account to pay all promised benefits and the plans are regulated as defined benefit plans. Benefits are specified as an account balance similar to defined contribution plans. Upon leaving the firm, the worker receives the full value of the pension account. The account grows each year from new contributions and from the crediting of a specified return on the existing monies in the account. All benefits are paid as lump sums to departing workers similar to the distributions under a defined contribution plan. In addition, hybrid plans tend to be more age-neutral in their retirement incentives compared to defined benefit plans.

Table 6.1 Features of pensions by plan type

Plan feature	Defined benefit plan	Defined contribution plan	Hybrid plan	Hybrid plan tendency
Employer contributes	Virtually always	Sometimes	Virtually always	DB
Employee contributes	Very rarely	Virtually always	Very rarely	DB
Participation	Automatic	Employee choice	Automatic	DB
Contribution level	Automatic	Employee choice	Automatic	DB
PBGC Insurance	Yes but capped	Not needed	Yes but capped	DB
Early departure penalty	Yes	No	No	DC
Benefits easily portable	No	Yes	Yes	DC
Annual communication	Benefit at end of career	Current balance	Current balance	DC
Retirement incentives	Occur at specific ages	Neutral	Most are neutral	DC
Accrual of benefits	Loaded to career end	Level over career	Level or back loaded	Mixed
Financial market risks	Employer bears	Employee bears	Shared	Mixed
Longevity insurance	Typically yes	Typically no	Not often taken	Mixed

Source: Clark and Schieber (2002).

BENEFIT ACCRUALS

A defined benefit pension plan promises a stream of future income in exchange for the current labor of plan participants while other pension plans specify contributions to an individual account that is invested and grows over time. The present value of the future benefits in retirement under a defined benefit plan is called pension wealth. The change in pension wealth with continued employment is referred to as the benefit accrual.[10] In defined contribution and hybrid plans, pension wealth would simply be the current value of the individual account and the benefit accrual would represent the new contribution into the account along with the return to the investments. Thus, the value of pension wealth and benefit accruals in defined contribution and hybrid plans is rather straightforward – what is the current account balance and how does it change from one year to the next? The evaluation of pension wealth and accruals in defined benefit plans is more complex and it is this complexity that generates many of the incentive effects associated with these plans.

In a typical defined benefit plan with a benefit formula based on final average pay, pension wealth is zero until the individual has been employed long enough to have become vested in the pension, usually five years. Therefore, pension wealth is zero for each year of employment until the worker has completed five years of service. After the fifth year, the worker becomes vested and has a legal claim on benefits based on service to date. At this point, there is a sharp spike in pension wealth from zero to a benefit based on five years of service. Thus, there is a large benefit accrual for this year of employment. Each additional year of service produces further benefit accruals that progressively increase in absolute value and as a percent of annual compensation. This pattern of benefit accrual is often called "backloading" and is the reason that defined benefit plans provide higher benefits to workers who remain with a single company compared to more mobile workers who change jobs throughout their careers.[11]

Defined benefit plans also have additional spikes in benefit accruals when employees reach the age and service requirements for early and normal retirement. Prior to reaching these "magic" dates, benefit accruals are increasing due to additional years of service and increases in average earnings. In addition, if the worker leaves the firm prior to early retirement, future benefits are based on the normal retirement formula, not the early retirement formula. As a result, the worker does not receive any of the early retirement subsidies imbedded in many defined benefit plans.[12] After the worker satisfies the requirements for early or normal retirement, continued employment may continue to increase future benefits; however, the participant must give up a year of benefits in order to remain on the job. Foregoing current benefits results in a sharp decline in benefit accrual and may actually result in negative accruals for some workers – continued employment decreases the present value of pension wealth.

Box 6.4 provides a description of a typical pattern of benefit accruals under a final pay defined benefit plan. The firm can affect the level and rate of change of benefit accruals by selecting specific types of plan provisions. Key parameters of such plans include the age and service requirements for early and normal retirement, the generosity of the plan, and whether there are any limits on the maximum number of years that can be included in the benefit formula. It is these spikes in benefit accruals that provide substantial retirement incentives for workers attaining the early and normal retirement ages. Research studies using company employment records show that the probability of retirement is significantly higher when workers satisfy these retirement requirements.[13]

In contrast, the benefit accruals under a defined contribution plan are more uniform over the working career. Workers and firms make period contributions to the individual's account. The employer's contribution is typically specified as a percent of salary and this does not vary with age or service. Many defined contribution plans are based on voluntary contributions of workers so that accruals may change over time with the employees' decisions; however, the rules governing these contributions tend to be age neutral. Direct contributions from participants are immediately vested while employer contributions are often more quickly vested compared to those in defined benefit plans. The early vesting and the ownership of individual accounts mean that participants in defined contribution plans that change jobs do not suffer the same type of loss in pension wealth as described above for participants in defined benefit plans. In addition, these plans do not have "magic" retirement dates when the pension provides a substantial incentive to retire compared to other ages.[14]

Box 6.4 *Benefit Accruals in Defined Benefit Plans*

The accumulation of pension benefits in final pay defined benefit pension plans produces a pattern of benefit accruals that can alter worker behavior. Examining the change in pension wealth associated with an additional year of work, Kotlikoff and Wise (1985) construct lifetime profiles of benefit accruals using specific plan characteristics. Their analysis shows benefits accruals are zero until the worker becomes vested. The year that the worker becomes vested, the benefit accrual can represent 10 percent or so of annual salary. After this point, benefit accruals drop sharply and represent only a small proportion of salary in the immediate post-vesting period.

The annual benefit accrual as a percent of salary increases continuously until the worker attains the age of early retirement. Depending on length of service, the interest rates, plan generosity, and age of early retirement, accrual rates can become a relatively large percentage of annual salary, in some cases they will be in excess of 20 percent. After reaching the age of early retirement, annual accruals begin to decline and if the worker remains with the firm well past the early retirement age, annual accruals could become negative. The spike at the early retirement age (see figure 6.2) is due to early retirement subsidies imbedded in the pension formula and provides a strong incentive for the worker to retire.

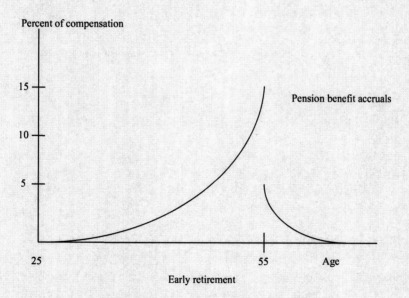

Figure 6.2 Growth in pension benefit with continued employment

PENSIONS AND WORKER BEHAVIOR: EMPIRICAL EVIDENCE

Having demonstrated the economic incentives associated with pension plans, a natural question would be: Do these incentives matter? Or more precisely, how do workers respond to the incentives that pensions provide? For example, do pension participants increase labor productivity, do workers stay longer in pension-covered jobs, and are they more likely to retire at those "magic" retirement dates?

Economic theory predicts that firms will invest more in workers who are likely to remain with them for longer periods of time. Thus, the use of deferred compensation that reduces turnover should lead to increased investment and higher productivity. The risk of losing a pension-covered job also provides an incentive for employees to reduce shirking on the job. Relatively few empirical studies have attempted to estimate productivity effects of pensions. Most of these studies have been conducted by Stuart Dorsey and a series of co-authors. In a review of the literature, Dorsey concluded that the empirical literature supports the view that incentives established by non-portable defined benefit pension plans do enhance productivity and in other research he finds that some of the increased productivity is attributable to increases in on-the-job training.[15]

If participants in pension plans who change jobs suffer a decline in their expected pension wealth, then these workers should have lower turnover rates than employees who are not participating in a pension plan. Considerable evidence supports this conclusion as virtually all empirical studies find that the potential loss of pension wealth discourages mobility.[16] Given the generosity of public pensions, it is not surprising that public employees, especially federal workers, have low quit rates.[17]

Substantial research indicates that participants in pension plans are more likely to retire than those not covered by retirement plans. In addition, participants in defined benefit plans are more likely to retire at specific times such as the early and normal retirement ages. Economic studies using large nationally representative surveys have estimated significant pension effects on the probability of retiring.[18] Similar studies using employment records from individual firms indicate that retirements often occur when workers first reach the age of early or normal retirement.[19] These studies support the predictions from economic theory described above and indicate the importance of pensions as a component of strategic compensation.

DEVELOPMENT OF PENSIONS IN THE UNITED STATES

Throughout the history of western civilization, disability and retirement pensions have been used to reward veterans of military service. Caesars, kings, and other rulers saw the value of providing retirement income to military personnel. Pensions were an inducement to provide needed service and a reward for successful campaigns. This tradition of military pensions quickly became policy in America as the colonies provided pensions to disabled men who were injured defending the colonists and their property. The Continental Congress established pensions for the army and navy during the Revolutionary War and pensions have been part of compensation for military personnel throughout the history of the United States.[20] Interestingly, these nineteenth-century pensions incorporated many of the economic incentives described above in an effort to influence the actions of soldiers and sailors. Box 6.5 describes the differences in funding of the pensions for the army and navy.

Box 6.5 *Funding of Nineteenth-century Military Pensions*

From the earliest days, the American colonies provided pensions to men who were injured defending the colonists and their property. The Continental Congress established separate pensions for the army and the navy during the Revolutionary War. Separate pension plans for the two branches of the military service continued throughout the nineteenth century. The history of these plans indicates that Congress used them to provide income to soldiers injured in battle, to provide performance incentives, to manage the orderly retirement of senior officers, and to respond to political pressures.

During this period, there was an interesting difference in the funding of the pension plans. The army plan was financed from the general revenues of the new country while the navy plan was funded from the sale of prizes seized in navy operations. The funding of the navy pension illustrated an understanding of the potential moral hazard faced by naval personnel to shirk their war responsibilities. In the early 1800s, ships cruised the open seas alone or in small groups and were unable to communicate with the central command. These ships could either engage the enemy at every opportunity and maximize their contributions to the war effort or they could avoid contact with hostile vessels and reduce the threats to themselves. The actual efforts of ships at sea were very hard to judge; however, the outcome of seized cargoes was easier to measure.

To encourage greater effort, Congress established a compensation system for sailors that depended on their performance. The seized cargoes of enemy ships were brought into port and sold. Some of the funds went to current compensation and some of the money was used to fund the navy pension plan. This system of funding and performance pay provided a clear incentive for the ships and their crews to seek out conflict and to bring home the prizes. In contrast, it was much easier to observe and measure the performance of the army. Thus, soldiers were never offered performance-based pay and their pension was funded by the general fund.

Of course, the use of prizes created an irregular source of monies for the navy pension plan. During wars, there were ample opportunities for prizes while during periods of peace new revenues were much smaller. The history of the management of the navy pension fund provides a unique opportunity to observe how in the nineteenth century the US government managed a pension account, responded to changes in labor market conditions, linked the pension to mandatory retirement, and invested the public monies in private equities. This story is told by Clark et al. (2003).

Public pensions for civilian workers came much later. Beginning in the mid-nineteenth century, many of the largest cities began providing disability and retirement benefits to employees in their police and fire departments along with teachers. Massachusetts established the first retirement plans for general state employees in 1911. After many years of considering pension legislation, the Congress established the federal civil service pension in 1920. Thus, by the 1920s, pension coverage was widespread in the public sector with all federal employees participating in a plan and an increasing share of state and local employees included in some type of pension plan. Virtually all of these public pensions were defined benefit plans that determined retirement benefits as a function of years of service and average pay. Most of these plans were used in conjunction with mandatory retirement policies and most required the worker to remain with the government until the specified retirement age. Thus, public employees were forced to leave their jobs at a specified age but were provided with a public pension in order to smooth their transition from work to retirement.[21]

Private employers were slower to introduce pension plans into their compensation packages. The first formal pension plan in the private sector was created by the American Express Corporation in 1875. At the beginning of the twentieth century, only a few companies were providing retirement plans for their employees. Reports indicate that there were only 12 private pensions in the United States in 1900 but by 1916 this number had increased to 117 and by the mid-1920s, there were about 200 plans in existence. These early pension plans were generally noncontributory, defined benefit plans that paid relatively low benefits and could be terminated at the discretion of the employer.[22]

By 1929, just under 4 million workers were covered by a pension representing 14 percent of the nonagricultural, privately employed labor force. Most of the pension participants were employed by railroads, public utilities, and manufacturing firms. Most of the pension-covered jobs were with large firms with more than 1,000 employees.[23] The growth of pension coverage slowed during the 1930s in conjunction with the adverse economic conditions as fewer new plans were established and many existing plans were terminated.[24] As a result of the ebb and flow of plan adoption, the proportion of the labor force covered by a pension was about the same in 1940 as it had been in 1929. In the post-World War II years, pension coverage expanded rapidly as employment in companies with existing pension plans expanded, new plans were adopted, and unions became more interested in negotiating pensions as part of labor contracts.[25] The continued growth in pension coverage raised the proportion of the private labor force that was participating in a pension to just over 40 percent in 1960 and further to approximately 50 percent by the mid-1970s.

The pension coverage rate has remained relatively stable over the past 25 years so that at the beginning of the twenty-first century about half of the labor force continues to be employed in jobs that include a pension plan.[26] A variety of explanations has been presented to explain the stagnation in pension coverage including revisions in the tax code lowering marginal tax rates, employment growth in sectors that have traditionally not offered pensions, slow or no growth in employment in large manufacturing firms, and higher administrative costs of offering tax-qualified pensions.

Coverage rates differ substantially by individual characteristics. In general, men are more likely to be in pension-covered jobs than women, although the coverage rate for women has been increasing while the proportion of men who are participating in a pension has been decreasing. Public employees are much more likely to have a pension than private employees. Full-time employees have much higher pension coverage rates than part-time employees and workers employed by large firms are more likely to have a pension than those that work for small firms. Pension coverage rates increase with annual earnings and with employee age.[27]

CHANGING UNIVERSE OF PENSION PLANS

During the past three decades, the proportion of the labor force covered by a pension has remained relatively stable; however, there have been significant changes in the composition of pensions. Historically, most employers with a retirement plan offered defined benefit pension plans. Since the passage of ERISA in 1974, there has been a pronounced movement away from the use of defined benefit plans and toward a greater reliance on defined contribution plans. For example, the proportion of the private labor force covered by a defined benefit plan declined from 38 percent in 1980 to 23 percent in 1995 (see table 6.2). This resulted in a decline in the proportion of pension participants with primary coverage in a defined benefit plan dropping from 83 percent to 50 percent. This transition has occurred primarily among small employers. The number of defined benefit plans with fewer than 1,000 workers dropped from 92,000 in 1980 to 38,000 in 1998.[28] However, some large employers have also terminated their defined benefit plans in order to establish defined contribution plans. Sixteen of the members of the Fortune list of the largest 100 publicly traded corporations in the United States now offer a defined contribution plan as their primary pension plan.

This rapid change in the use of defined contribution and defined benefit pension plans is the result of a series of regulatory, economic, and demographic changes. Changes in federal pension regulations beginning with ERISA but continuing over the next two decades increased the cost of offering a pension plan. These higher regulatory costs fell more heavily on defined benefit plans, thus increasing the relative cost of offering a defined benefit plan compared to offering a defined contribution plan. The increase in administrative costs associated with these regulatory changes increased the per participant cost for small plans more than the cost for large plans.[29] This higher burden on smaller plans is the primary reason for the collapse in the use of defined benefit plans among small employers. In addition, a change in tax policy in the 1980s allowed employee contributions to tax-qualified pension plans to be tax-deductible. This paved the way for the development of 401(k) plans that are now the fastest growing type of pensions. In recent years,

Table 6.2 Percent of private labor force covered by
a pension

Year	Percent LF covered by pension	Percent LF covered by DB pension
1980	46	36
1981	46	37
1982	45	36
1983	46	35
1984	46	34
1985	46	33
1986	46	32
1987	46	31
1988	45	30
1989	45	29
1990	45	28
1991	45	27
1992	46	26
1993	46	26
1994	45	24
1995	46	23

Source: Pension Benefit Guaranty Corporation, 1999.

employment growth has been greater among firms that have traditionally offered defined contribution plans and slower among firms with defined benefit plans. These changes have lowered the proportion of pension participants with defined benefit coverage. Finally, changes in the composition of the labor force and greater awareness that most workers do not spend their entire careers with the same firm may have altered worker preferences for the two types of plans.[30]

During the past decade, another significant change in the structure of pension plans has been occurring; the conversion of traditional defined benefit plans to hybrid plans such as cash balance and pension equity plans.[31] The recent movement toward hybrid plans is occurring primarily among larger employers including some of the most recognizable corporations in America.[32] The conversion of retirement plans to hybrid plans is the result of employers seeking to eliminate early retirement subsidies in their pension plans, a desire to have a more certain assessment of pension costs, the belief that employees better understand and appreciate retirement plans with individual accounts, and in some instances, the conversion process is made in conjunction with a restructuring of compensation that reduces pension costs.[33]

The trend toward pension plans with individual accounts is expected to continue in the twenty-first century as more firms offer defined contribution and hybrid plans and fewer rely on traditional defined benefit plans. In general, this will mean that most workers will have the opportunity to accumulate greater retirement benefits because of the portability features of these plans. Defined contribution and hybrid plans typically provide benefits more evenly between short-service and long-tenured employees compared to final pay, defined benefit plans. Thus, the transition to these plans creates winners as well as losers.[34] Increased utilization of defined contribution plans also means that individual workers must assume more responsibility for managing their own retirement accounts since these plans often require voluntary contributions and self-management of investment decisions. Box 6.6 describes a study examining how contribution and participation rates vary with age, annual earnings, and gender.

Box 6.6   *Retirement Savings in 401(k) Plans*

In the past 15 years, 401(k) plans have emerged as the fastest-growing type of pension plan. Over one quarter of pension participants now have 401(k) plans as their primary pension plan and millions more have supplemental coverage in such a plan. Virtually all 401(k) plans require workers to decide whether they want to make any contribution to the plan, how much they want to contribute, and how the funds will be invested. The voluntary nature of these plans and increased investment risk associated with the plans creates advantages and disadvantages for workers. Policy-makers are concerned about workers who start contributing too late in life or who contribute too little each year to accumulate needed retirement funds. Concern is also expressed that low wage workers will be less likely to contribute to these voluntary plans and that some individuals will select investments that yield only modest returns.

Statistical evidence provided by Clark et al. (2000) shows that participation rates in 401(k) plans increase with annual earnings and age. The proportion of employees with incomes in excess of $50,000 who make an annual contribution is somewhat higher than the participation rate for workers with lower earnings. Also the participation rate for those over age 30 is greater than that for employees in their twenties. Limited evidence indicates that participation rates can be increased with higher employer matching contributions and better communication concerning the value of the pension. The proportion of salary contributed to the pension each year also rises with age and earnings up until the point where maximum contribution limits restrict further employee contributions.

Choice of investment funds can make a significant difference in the ultimate level of the pension account at retirement. In general, the proportion of pension assets in 401(k) plans invested in equities declines with age as workers seek to reduce the volatility of their account balances as they approach retirement. The proportion of investments held in equities increases with annual earnings. Despite claims to the contrary, this study found no significant difference between the investment behavior of men and women in their 401(k) accounts.

GOVERNMENT REGULATION OF PRIVATE PENSIONS

Federal regulation of private employer pensions has primarily focused on the treatment of contributions to pension funds and the earnings of those funds, funding and insurance requirements to make pensions safer investments for workers, and regulation that attempt to prevent discrimination across workers based on age and level of earnings. The United States, like all modern industrialized countries, has a sophisticated Social Security system to protect workers' economic well-being as they move out of the labor force and into retirement. But unlike most other countries, social policy in the United States has also consistently encouraged the formation of a voluntary system of private employer pensions to insure workers against the economic consequences of the labor market that exists at older ages. As discussed above, this private pension system predates Social Security.

Federal income tax policy has been the primary policy instrument for encouraging the growth of private employer pensions. It is in the interest of society for government to encourage private savings since increased investment will lead to greater economic growth. Furthermore, some analysts argue that taxing the returns from savings and investment is "double taxation" because federal income tax was already paid when the money was first earned. Therefore this money is taxed both when it is initially earned and when it generates additional income from savings and investments. No such double taxation is placed on the use of that money for consumption. Hence this double taxation will encourage current consumption at the expense of savings and investments. Reduced private saving will lead to greater reliance on social security for income at older ages. Conversely, other analysts argue that higher-income families are the ones most likely to save and invest either on their own or through company pension plans. The ability to pay (vertical equity) is an appropriate criterion for tax policy. Thus, higher-income families should pay more taxes, not less. It is further argued that income from all sources should be taxed equally (horizontal equity).

Within the context of these broad policy objectives, the federal government has adopted tax policies that favor workers saving through company pension plans. To receive this tax-qualified status, pension plans must comply with a wide variety of rules and regulations. We now examine these tax policies and pension regulations in detail. Federal tax policy encourages companies to provide pension plans as part of their compensation by affording plans that meet certain requirements such as a preferential tax status. In general, the objectives of the requirements are to ensure that plan participants ultimately receive the promised benefits and that pension coverage is offered to all workers, not simply the highly compensated. The requirements for tax-qualified status have changed over time and become increasingly complex requiring plan sponsors to incur increased administrative costs.[35] As described above, many firms have decided the tax advantage does not offset the regulatory costs of offering such a plan.

Beginning with the establishment of the federal income tax, employer-provided pensions have been subject to certain regulations if they were to merit preferential tax treatment. The initial tax law of 1913 specified that reasonable pension payments would not be taxable to participants until benefits were paid; however, the earnings of the pension fund were taxable to the plan sponsor, the covered employees, or the pension itself. The 1921 Revenue Act exempted the income of the pension fund from current taxation.

Initially, pension funds could be started and then terminated without penalty so that a plan sponsor could set up a plan in good times and receive the tax advantage and then terminate the plan in adverse circumstances. This created an opportunity for tax arbitrage. The 1938 Revenue Act required that funds in retirement plans be used for the exclusive benefit of employees covered under the plans until all obligations were met. The 1942 Revenue Act introduced first guidelines aimed at preventing the adoption of plans only for shareholders, officers, and highly compensated workers. Thus, if a firm wanted to establish a tax-qualified pension plan, this plan must not discriminate against low-wage employees. The primary purpose of this nondiscrimination standard was to prevent the benefits supported by the tax treatment from flowing solely to high-income employees.[36]

Beginning with the passage of ERISA in 1974, the federal government established a wide-ranging set of requirements for a plan to achieve tax-qualified status. These include: vesting, participation, funding, and insurance standards. Vesting occurs when a worker has a legal claim on a future retirement benefit. Prior to ERISA, many firms required a worker to remain with the firm for many years to earn a pension benefit and the worker might also have to remain with the firm up until the specified retirement age. ERISA established a maximum vesting standard of ten years. This was subsequently reduced to five years. Thus, a participant in a defined benefit plan who remains with the firm for five years will earn a retirement benefit based on the benefit formula in effect at the time of termination and his average earnings at that time. When the worker leaves the firm, the benefit is frozen at that level. Defined contribution plans face the same vesting standards; however, many plans vest employer contributions sooner than five years and employee contributions are always immediately vested. Federal regulations have also established maximum requirements for participation in the pension plan including all employees who work more than 1,000 hours per year, have been with company for at least one year, and are at least age 21.

ERISA also introduced limits on benefits in tax-qualified plans. The maximum benefit that could be funded in a defined benefit plan was set at $75,000 and the maximum contribution in a defined contribution plan was $25,000. These limits were initially indexed to the Consumer Price Index. Subsequent legislation has periodically changed these limits. Over time these limits have become binding on an increasing number of pension participants. Had the indexation remained in place, the maximum fundable defined benefit would had been $227,230 in 1999. Instead, after various legislated changes, the fundable limit was $130,000. Similarly, the maximum contribution limit would have been $75,743 if the 1974 standard with indexation had remained in effect. Instead, the actual 1999 maximum contribution was set at $30,000.

Regulations have also been enacted to limit the degree of integration of pension benefits with Social Security. Since Social Security benefits provide a greater replacement ratio for low-wage workers, pension benefit and contribution formulas have been allowed to provide somewhat greater benefits to high-wage employees. Integration of pension benefits with Social Security has been a very controversial issue because the integrated plans tend to reduce the pension benefits of low-paid workers relative to those provided to highly compensated workers. Over time, the maximum amount of integration permitted by tax-qualified plans has been reduced in an effort to limit this reduction in benefits to lower paid employees.

ERISA established the Pension Benefit Guaranty Corporation (PBGC) to institute a system of insurance that would enable workers to know that they would receive a retirement benefit even if their employer went bankrupt. The PBGC is chaired by the Secretary of Labor with the Secretary of Treasury and the Secretary of Commerce also serving as board members. All sponsors of defined benefit pensions must purchase insurance from the PBGC. This insurance guarantees the payment of all basic benefits up to a limit even if the plan has insufficient assets to make all promised payments. When a plan terminates with insufficient assets, the plan is brought under the PBGC's control and the PBGC assumes the administration of the plan. Thus, the mandating of pension insurance increases the likelihood that pension participants will receive the benefits that they have been promised. To reduce exposure to risk of default, federal regulations have also established funding standards for defined benefit pension plans.[37] The accounting profession has also established reporting and funding standards for deferred compensation plans.

OTHER RETIREMENT POLICIES

In addition to pension plans, firms often use other benefit and human resource policies to achieve the desired level of retirements. These policies include mandatory retirement, special early retirement programs, phased retirement programs, and retiree health insurance. In most cases, these policies are developed in conjunction with pension plans in an effort to provide incentives for workers to retire at the desired ages. The history, legal status, and effects of these programs are described below.

Mandatory retirement

Mandatory retirement allows firms to specify a definite end to a working career so that all workers know that at a certain age they must leave the job. Such policies enable the firm to plan for an orderly transition of its labor force, eliminate older workers whose productivity and performance may be declining, and thereby open up new jobs for younger workers. Knowing that there is a fixed termination point to employment allows companies to adopt policies such as the long-term contracts and compensation policies described above. Historically, mandatory retirement policies have been closely linked with employer-provided pension plans so that workers forced to retire would receive retirement income from the pension.

In the nineteenth century, mandatory retirement policies were introduced by public employers to terminate older workers from the payrolls. Older workers were perceived to be less productive than their younger colleagues. The US military established mandatory policies for officers at the onset of the Civil War in an effort to improve the fighting ability of the troops. Retired officers became eligible for pensions and could be recalled if needed. Compulsory retirement also spread through civilian public employment as pensions were introduced at the state, local, and federal levels.[38] In the private sector, mandatory retirement became more prevalent in the twentieth century primarily among large employers who provided their employees a pension plan.

The use of mandatory retirement became the subject of federal regulation beginning in 1967 with the passage of the Age Discrimination in Employment Act (ADEA) that precluded discrimination on the basis of age for workers between 40 and 65. Initially, ADEA allowed firms to continue imposing mandatory retirement at age 65 or older. In 1978, ADEA was amended to protect workers aged 40 to 70, thus precluding mandatory retirement prior to age 70. And finally in 1986, ADEA was further amended to prevent discrimination against all workers over the age of 40. This action effectively eliminated the use of mandatory retirement in the United States except in certain public safety occupations. Mandatory retirement is widely used in many countries around the world and in most countries, the age of compulsory retirement is the same as the normal retirement age for national or company-based pension benefits.[39]

When mandatory retirement was part of company human resource policies in the United States, many people believed that it was a significant factor causing older workers to leave the labor force. Economic studies of retirement proved that this was not the case. First, less than half of the labor force was covered by mandatory retirement provisions and, second, many employees working for firms with such policies retired long before the age of mandatory retirement. Thus, in the aggregate, mandatory retirement had only a limited effect on the labor force participation rate of older persons.[40] This does not mean that the compulsory retirement did not limit the employment options for many workers. The ending of mandatory retirement gave workers a new employment right which many have chosen to exercise and remain in their career jobs.

Special early retirement programs

During periods of slow economic growth, many companies have established early retirement programs that provide temporary incentives for workers to retire. These early retirement programs are often called window plans. Such plans generally provide additional pension benefits for workers who retire within a specified time period, i.e. the retirement window opens and then closes. Early retirement plans can take many forms but they are frequently linked to existing defined benefit pension plans. If the worker retires under the window plan, the pension benefit is often calculated by adding additional years of service or by treating the worker as if they are several years older. Thus, the annual pension benefit will be higher than it otherwise would have been provided the worker leaves the firm during the enrollment period. Window plans were frequently introduced and then reintroduced by large corporations in the 1980s and early 1990s as firms attempted to downsize their workforces to face the new realities of global competition.[41]

Employees respond to early retirement plans by retiring earlier than they had planned. As a result, a firm is able to reduce the number of employees without having to resort to formal layoffs. This reduces the cost of active workers, however, pension expenditures are increased. The higher pension expenditures may not be considered a problem if the plan is overfunded. Early retirement plans are less effective if the objective is to address age structure or skill mismatches in the labor force since higher pension costs are coupled with additional costs of hiring new employees. To be effective in enticing additional retirements, early retirement plans must be generous enough to make retirement more attractive to older employees than continuing on the job.

One problem often associated with early retirement plans is that highly productive workers which the company would like to retain are the first to accept the incentive payments while lower quality workers often remain on the job. This pattern of acceptance occurs because high quality workers are likely to have other employment opportunities and thus, they can take the incentive payment and move to another firm, perhaps even a competitor of the career employer. In contrast, low quality workers will not have such opportunities and must decide whether complete retirement is more desirable than remaining on the job.

Interestingly, companies were much less likely to offer early retirement programs at the beginning of the twenty-first century. Rapid economic growth and a slowly growing labor force pushed unemployment rates to record lows. In response, companies were no longer attempting to entice older workers to retire. Instead, many companies attempted to eliminate the early retirement incentives in their pension plans.

Phased retirement programs

Recently, some employers have begun to offer a new type of retirement plan, a phased retirement program, to workers who meet certain age and service requirements. Generally, phased retirement programs offer workers the opportunity to reduce their hours of work in exchange for a reduction in salary. For example, a plan could provide half-time pay for half-time work. Such a plan would allow employees to select from three possible choices: full-time pay for full-time work, half-time pay for half-time work, or complete retirement with a pension. Employers seeking to encourage employees to enter phased retirement might offer to subsidize partial retirees by paying 60 percent of the full-time salary for half-time work.

Gerontologists, policy-makers, and social scientists have long argued that a smoother transition from full-time employment to complete retirement would be more desirable than an abrupt shift from full-time work to full-time retirement. While workers have always been free to leave a career job and find part-time work with another employer, reducing hours on one's career job has often been difficult if not impossible for many workers. Phased retirement programs offer such a new option to employees.

Phased retirement on a career job has been limited for several reasons.[42] First, participants in final pay defined benefit plans would suffer losses in future benefits if their years in phased retirement were to be included in the benefit calculation. Thus, employees would tend to prefer to retire from their career jobs, begin their pensions from that employer, and find new part-time work. Second, this problem could be eliminated if the workers could retire from the career employers, begin their pensions, and then be rehired by the same firm. Currently, ERISA does not allow in-service distributions or payment of pension benefits – thus, employees cannot elect to retire, start a pension, and then work part-time for the same company. Public sector employers are not subject to ERISA and many public, educational institutions have initiated phased retirement programs.[43]

Phased retirement programs offer several advantages to workers and firms. Part-time work may be desirable to many older employees. These may be employees who otherwise would have left the firm but are now willing to remain on the job part-time or they may be employees who would have stayed on the job full-time but prefer part-time work. Determining the response to phased retirement programs is critical to understanding how to evaluate the success of such plans. Little research is currently available concerning the impact of phased retirement plans.[44]

Retiree health insurance

Another important benefit program that significantly affects the retirement decision is retiree health insurance. Many employers provide health insurance to their employees. This is an important and valuable employee benefit. Individuals considering retirement must consider how they will purchase health insurance after they leave their company and are no longer able to participate in the firm's health insurance plan. If they were to purchase individual medical insurance policies in the private market, the cost could be $3,000 to $5,000 per year. Retirees will become eligible for Medicare coverage when they reach age 65 and this would substantially reduce the cost of obtaining a specified level of health coverage. Thus, the problem of obtaining adequate health insurance after retirement primarily affects early retirees aged 50 to 64.[45]

Beginning in the 1960s after the establishment of Medicare, many large corporations instituted retiree health plans that permitted retirees to remain in the company health insurance plan, generally under the same conditions as active workers. The value of this benefit increases the probability of retirement for workers who qualify for retiree health insurance compared to those workers who do not have such coverage.[46] Thus, firms seeking to encourage early retirement will be more likely to offer this benefit. Retiree health insurance plans are typically offered by firms that also provide pension plans. The joint provision of these two types of retirement plans further facilitates the transition from work to retirement.[47]

The incidence of retiree health plans has declined substantially over the past decade even among large employers. The decline in coverage has been due to rising health care costs and the aging of the workforce so that the costs of retiree health care increased as a part of total compensation. In addition, cutbacks in coverage by Medicare tended to raise employer costs since these plans are secondary payers of health costs for retirees over the age of 65.[48] Changes in accounting rules requiring firms to explicitly recognize the accrued costs of these programs also led many firms to terminate these plans.

DISCUSSION QUESTIONS

Comment on the reasonableness of these statements:

1 Pension plans are important human resource policies that help companies attract, retain, motivate, and ultimately retire workers.
2 Over the past 30 years, an increasing proportion of pension participants are covered by defined contribution plans. Explain the reasons for this trend.
3 The conversion of traditional defined benefit plans to cash balance plans adversely affects the retirement income of all workers.
4 Participants in defined benefit plans have less portable benefits than those in defined contribution plans.
5 Participants in defined contribution plans bear the investment risk associated with pension funds while participants in defined benefit plans do not.
6 Coverage by a retiree health insurance plan is an important factor in the early retirement decision. If this statement is true, why are these plans becoming less common?

Notes

1 Modern labor economics is based on the theory of marginal productivity. The theory states that in competitive labor markets, the equilibrium wage paid to workers is equal to the increase in revenues attributable to hiring one additional worker (marginal product of the last worker times the product price). This is the profit-maximizing level of employment.

2   The theory of compensating wage differentials states that total labor costs determine how many workers firms will employ. Labor market conditions determine the equilibrium level of total labor costs. Wages are adjusted downward as the company allocates more dollars to pension contributions or any other employee benefits. In essence, workers buy the benefits from the firm in the form of lower wages.

3   Workers also prefer to purchase some benefits from their employer because the company can buy the benefit for all of its workers at a lower price than the individual could buy the same benefit. Health insurance provides an example of this type of cost savings from group coverage.

4   Ippolito (1997) describes this sorting mechanism in considerable detail. Also see Salop and Salop (1976) for a theory of sorting in the labor market.

5   Many large employers eliminated the early retirement incentives in their pension plans in the past ten years by converting traditional defined benefit plans to hybrid plans (Clark and Schieber, 2002).

6   McGill et al. (1996) is the best reference for readers interested in understanding the differences in these two plan types.

7   Some plans have benefit formulas that specify benefits as a dollar amount per year of service. These formulas are most commonly found in plans that are part of collectively bargained contracts.

8   This requirement was instituted in 1984 as part of the Retirement Equity Act.

9   These plan conversions often result in some older, more senior workers having lower retirement benefits than they expected, even though most workers covered by these plans will ultimately have greater retirement benefits. This result is due to greater portability of benefits in the hybrid plans so that workers who leave the firm prior to the early retirement age accrue greater benefits (Clark and Schieber, 2002).

10 Ippolito (1985) introduced the distinction between the benefits that workers are legally entitled to based on the formal pension contract and earnings to date and benefits that they could expect to receive if they remained with the firm until early retirement based on projected earnings at retirement. The difference between this expected benefit (the stay pension) and the legal benefit (the leave pension) is the loss associated with early departure from the firm. The loss in pension wealth with job changes increases with age and job tenure until the worker qualifies for early retirement. As noted earlier, the larger this loss, the less likely workers are to leave the firm.

11 The nature of this backloading is clearly described in a series of papers by Kotlikoff and Wise (1985; 1989).

12 The key element in the early retirement subsidy is that employees can retire at an earlier age than that specified as the normal retirement age and that benefits are not actuarially reduced. In other words, the present value of pension wealth is greater under the early retirement formula compared to the normal retirement formula.

13 See, for example, Kotlikoff and Wise (1985; 1989) and Lumsdaine et al. (1997).

14 In contrast to spikes in benefit accruals after early and normal retirement ages in defined benefit plans, the value of the individual accounts in defined contribution plans continue to increase more smoothly. When a participant in a defined contribution plan remains on the job, her individual account continues to increase in value due to new contributions and the return on prior investments. A year of benefits is not lost, instead, future annual benefits will be higher because the worker will be converting the lump sum amount into an annuity at a later age and hence have fewer years of expected life remaining.

15 For a more detailed discussion of the relationship between pensions and productivity, see Dorsey (1995), Dorsey et al. (1998), and Dorsey and Macpherson (1997).

16 The interested reader should examine the results presented in Allen et al. (1993), Evan and Macpherson (1996), Ippolito (1991), and Lazear and Moore (1988).

17 See Ippolito (1987) for estimates of the impact of the Civil Service pension on the quit rates of federal employees.

18 Important retirement studies and summaries of the literature include Fields and Mitchell (1984), Anderson et al. (1999), Kotlikoff and Wise (1989), and Quinn et al. (1990).

19 Studies of retirement in individual firms are provided by Burkhauser (1979), Kotlikoff and Wise (1985, 1989), and Lumsdaine et al. (1997).

20 Clark et al. (2003, forthcoming) present a history of the development and management of public pensions in the United States from colonial times through 1920.

21 The development of public pensions in the United States occurs at the same time that public employment is changing from a patronage system to one based on merit. It is unlikely that employees would be willing to have a significant component of their income contingent on remaining on the job until retirement if there were a high probability of being fired after every election. Thus, pensions became a part of compensation in the public sector when public employment became a more stable career path.

22 Interesting accounts of the development of private pensions in the United States can be found in Latimer (1932) and Conyngton (1926). Also see Costa (1998).

23 Epstein (1928) describes this early development of private pensions and how it affected the income of aged Americans. He noted that because of high turnover rates and long vesting periods, relatively few of those employed by firms offering a pension ever received a pension benefit.

24 Corson and McConnell (1956) report that between 1929 and 1932, 45 pension plans covering approximately 100,000 employees were terminated in the manufacturing sector.

25 For an assessment of the development of pensions during this period, see Munnell (1982).

26 Current data on pension coverage can be found on websites of the Bureau of Labor Statistics (www.bls.gov), the Employee Benefit Research Institute (www.ebri.org), and the Pension Benefit Guaranty Corporation (www.pbgc.gov).

27 Coverage rate data can be found in a variety of surveys including the Current Population Survey, Survey of Consumer Expenditures, and the Employee Benefit Surveys.

28 These data can be found in Pension Benefit Guaranty Corporation (1999).

29 The best study of trends in administrative costs for pension plans is Hustead (1998).

30 Economic studies examining the change from defined benefit to defined contribution plans include Clark and McDermed (1990), Gustman and Steinmeier (1992), Ippolito (1995), and Papke (1999).

31 A cash balance plan defines a worker's individual pension account based on annual employer contributions plus a credited interest rate on the existing account balance. A pension equity plan defines the benefit as a percentage of final average earnings for each year of service under the plan. Both of these hybrid plans specify the benefit in terms of the account balance payable at termination rather than as an annuity in the traditional manner of a defined benefit plan.

32 Analysis of the conversion of traditional defined benefit plans to hybrid plans is provided in a series of papers by Clark and Schieber (2002, 2003 forthcoming).

33 Clark and Schieber (2003 forthcoming) examine the reasons for plan conversions along with their impact on workers of different characteristics.

34 See Clark and Schieber (2003 forthcoming) for discussion of the distribution of winners and losers from such transitions.

35 Federal regulations and how they affect pension participants and plan sponsors are described in McGill et al. (1996).

36 Such tax treatment reduces federal tax revenues relative to treating pension contributions as normal income. Today, this concept is referred to as a tax expenditure. Pension tax expenditures at the end of the twentieth century were one of the largest such items in the federal budget. See Clark and Wolper (1997).

37 In an odd turn of events, the federal government instituted full funding standards in the 1980s, thus limiting the amount of money a plan sponsor could contribute to the pension plan. These regulations were adopted during a period of large government deficits with the objective of limiting losses in current tax revenues due to pension contributions. These standards helped to increase tax revenues but also put the funding of some pension plans in jeopardy.

38 Clark et al. (2003 forthcoming) describe the emergence of public sector pensions and the use of mandatory retirement.

39 Clark (1991) provides a detailed assessment of the incidence of mandatory retirement in Japan and how companies link compulsory retirement with pension plans and other aspects of the compensation system.

40 For estimates of the impact of mandatory retirement on the labor supply of older persons, see Burkhauser and Quinn (1983), Barker and Clark (1980), and Halperin (1978).

41 Early retirement programs have also been introduced by many educational institutions in the face of adverse budgetary conditions. Switkes (2000) provides an overview of the effectiveness of a series of window plans offered by the University of California.

42 Watson Wyatt Worldwide (1999) reports that 16 percent of the nearly 600 employers they surveyed have some form of phased retirement arrangements. Phased retirement programs were most prevalent among educational institutions with 36 percent of these employers offering such programs.

43 An example of a phased retirement program is the plan introduced by the University of North Carolina system. This plan provides for half-time pay for half-time work for tenured faculty who give up tenure in exchange for entering the program.

44 Ghent et al. (2001) estimate that phased retirement plans have increased the number of total retirements (complete and phased) because most of the phased retirees would have remained on the job full-time rather than retiring if the program had not been in place.

45 Many retirees aged 65 and over purchase additional insurance to cover health care cost not included in Medicare. These gaps in coverage mean that even these older retirees who are participating in Medicare will be interested in additional health insurance.

46 Limited statistical evidence supports the conclusion that workers covered by retiree health insurance are more likely to retire than comparable workers without such coverage, see Currie and Madrian (1998).

47 Clark et al. (1994) show the close relationship between retiree health plans and pension plans.

48 For retirees over the age of 65, Medicare is the primary payer of medical bills and company-provided insurance is a secondary payer. Thus, declines in Medicare reimbursements would lead to an increase in company payments. For active workers over the age of 65,

company policies are the primary payers of medical bills while Medicare is the secondary payer.

References

Allen, Steven, Clark, Robert, and McDermed, Ann 1993: Pension bonding and lifetime jobs. *Journal of Human Resources* 28 (3): 463–81.

Anderson, Patricia, Gustman, Alan, and Steinmeier, Thomas 1999: Trends in male labor force participation and retirement. *Journal of Labor Economics* 17 (4): 757–83.

Barker, David and Clark, Robert 1980: Mandatory retirement and labor force participation of respondents in the retirement history study. *Social Security Bulletin* 43 (11): 20–9.

Becker, Gary 1964: *Human Capital*. New York: Columbia University Press.

Burkhauser, Richard 1979: The pension acceptance decision of older workers, *Journal of Human Resources* 14 (Winter): 63.

Burkhauser, Richard and Quinn, Joseph 1983: Is mandatory retirement overrated? *Journal of Human Resources* 18 (3): 337–58.

Clark, Robert 1991: *Retirement Systems in Japan*. Homewood, IL: Dow Jones-Irwin.

Clark, Robert and McDermed, Ann 1988: Pension wealth and job changes: the effects of vesting, portability, and lump-sum distributions. *The Gerontologist* 28: 524–32.

Clark, Robert and McDermed, Ann 1990: *The Choice of Pension Plans in a Changing Regulatory Environment*. Washington, DC: American Enterprise Institute.

Clark, Robert and Schieber, Sylvester 2002: Taking the subsidy out of early retirement: the story behind the conversion to hybrid pensions. In Olivia Mitchell, Zvi Bodie, Brett Hammond, and Steve Zeldes (eds.), *Innovations in Managing the Financial Risks of Retirement*. Philadelphia: University of Pennsylvania Press, 149–74.

Clark, Robert and Schieber, Sylvester 2003, forthcoming: An empirical analysis of the transition to hybrid pension plans in the United States. In William Gale, John Shoven, and Mark Warshawsky (eds.), *Public Policies and Private Pensions*. Washington, DC: Brookings Institution.

Clark, Robert and Wolper, Elisa 1997: Pension tax expenditures: magnitude, distribution, and economic effects. In Sylvester Schieber and John Shoven (eds.), *Public Policy towards Pensions*. New York: Twentieth Century Fund, 41–84.

Clark, Robert, Craig, Lee, and Wilson, Jack 2003, forthcoming: *History of Public Sector Pensions in the United States*. Philadelphia: University of Pennsylvania Press.

Clark, Robert, Ghent, Linda, and Headen, Alvin 1994: Retiree health insurance and pension coverage. *Journal of Gerontology* 49: S53–62.

Clark, Robert, Goodfellow, Gordon, Schieber, Sylvester, and Warwick, Drew 2000: Making the most of 401(k) plans: Who's choosing what and why? In Olivia Mitchell, Brett Hammond, and Anna Rappaport (eds.), *Forecasting Retirement Needs and Retirement Wealth*. Philadelphia: University of Pennsylvania Press, 95–138.

Clark, Robert, Haley, John, and Schieber, Sylvester 2001: Adopting hybrid pension plans: Financial and communication issues. *Benefits Quarterly* 17 (1): 8.

Conyngton, Mary 1926: Industrial pension for old age and disability. *Monthly Labor Review* 22: 21–56.

Corson, J. J. and McConnell, J. W. 1956: *Economic Needs of Older People*. New York: The Twentieth Century Fund.

Costa, Dora 1998: *The Evolution of Retirement: An American History, 1880–1990*. Chicago: University of Chicago Press.

Currie, Janet and Madrian, Brigitte 1998: Health, health insurance, and the labor market. In David Card and Orley Ashenfelter (eds.), *Handbook of Labor Economics*. Amsterdam: Elsevier Science.

Dorsey, Stuart 1995: Pension portability and labor market efficiency. *Industrial and Labor Relations Review* 48 (2): 276–92.

Dorsey, Stuart, Cornwell, Christopher, and Macpherson, David 1998: *Pensions and Productivity*. Kalamazoo, MI: Upjohn Institute for Employment Research.

Dorsey, Stuart and Macpherson, David 1997: Pensions and training. *Industrial Relations* 36 (1): 81–96.

Epstein, Abraham 1928: *The Challenge of the Aged*. New York: Vanguard Press.

Evan, William and Macpherson, David 1996: Employer size and labor turnover: the role of pensions. *Industrial and Labor Relations Review* 49 (4): 707–28.

Fields, Gary and Mitchell, Olivia 1984: *Retirement, Pensions, and Social Security*. Cambridge, MA: MIT Press.

Ghent, Linda, Allen, Steven, and Clark, Robert 2001: The impact of a new phased retirement option on faculty retirement decisions. *Research on Aging* 23 (6): 671–93.

Gustman, Alan and Steinmeier, Thomas 1992: The stampede toward defined contribution pension plans: fact or fiction? *Industrial Relations* 31 (2): 361–9.

Halperin, Janice 1978: Raising the mandatory retirement age: its effect on the employment of older workers. *New England Economic Review* May/June: 23–35.

Hustead, Edward 1998: Trends in retirement income plan administrative expenses. In Olivia Mitchell (ed.), *Living with Defined Contribution Pensions*. Philadelphia: University of Pennsylvania Press, 166–77.

Hutchens, Robert M. 1989: Seniority, wages and productivity: a turbulent decade. *Journal of Economic Perspectives* 3 (4): 49–64.

Ippolito, Richard 1985: The labor contract and true economic pension liabilities. *American Economic Review* 75 (5): 1031–43.

Ippolito, Richard 1986: *Pensions, Economics, and Public Policy*. Homewood, IL: Dow Jones-Irwin.

Ippolito, Richard 1987: Why federal workers don't quit. *Journal of Human Resources* 22: 281–99.

Ippolito, Richard 1991: Encouraging long-term tenure: wage tilt or pensions? *Industrial and Labor Relations Review* 44 (3): 520–35.

Ippolito, Richard 1995: Towards explaining the growth of defined contribution plans. *Industrial Relations* 34 (1): 1–20.

Ippolito, Richard 1997: *Pension Plans and Employee Performance*. Chicago: University of Chicago Press.

Kotlikoff, Laurence and Wise, David 1985: Labor compensation and the structure of private pension plans: evidence for contractual vs. spot labor markets. In David Wise (ed.), *Pensions, Labor, and Individual Choice*. Chicago: University of Chicago Press, 55–85.

Kotlikoff, Laurence and Wise, David 1989: *The Wage Carrot and the Pension Stick*. Kalamazoo, MI: Upjohn Institute for Employment Research.

Latimer, Murray Webb 1932: *Industrial Pension Systems in the United States and Canada*. New York: Industrial Relations Counselors.

Lazear, Edward 1979: Why is there mandatory retirement? *Journal of Political Economy* 87 (6): 1261–84.

Lazear, Edward and Moore, Robert 1988: Pensions and turnover. In Zvi Bodie, John Shoven, and David Wise (eds.), *Pensions in the U.S. Economy*. Chicago: University of Chicago Press, 163–88.

Lumsdaine, Robin, Stock, James, and Wise, David 1997: Retirement incentives. In Michael Hurd and Naohiro Yashiro (eds.), *The Economic Effects of Aging in the United States and Japan*. Chicago: University of Chicago Press, 261–93.

McGill, Dan, Brown, Kyle, Haley, John, and Schieber, Sylvester 1996: *Fundamentals of Private Pensions*. Philadelphia: University of Pennsylvania Press.

Munnell, Alicia 1982: *The Economics of Private Pensions*. Washington, DC: Brookings Institution.

Papke, Leslie 1999: Are 401(k) plans replacing other employer-provided pensions? *Journal of Human Resources* 34 (2): 311–25.

Pension Benefit Guaranty Corporation 1999: *Pension Insurance Data Book: 1998*. Washington, DC: PBGC.

Quinn, Joseph, Burkhauser, Richard, and Myers, Daniel 1990: *Passing the Torch: The Influence of Economic Incentives on Work and Retirement*. Kalamazoo, MI: Upjohn Institute for Employment Research.

Salop, Joanne and Salop, Steven 1976: Self selection and turnover in the labor market. *Quarterly Journal of Economics* 90: 619–27.

Switkes, Ellen 2000: The University of California Voluntary Early Retirement Incentive Programs. In Robert Clark and Brett Hammond (eds.), *To Retire or Not? Retirement Policy and Practice in Higher Education*. Philadelphia: University of Pennsylvania Press.

Watson Wyatt Worldwide 1999: *Phased Retirement: Reshaping the End of Work*. Bethesda, MD: Watson Wyatt Worldwide.

PART THREE

Social Security Programs and Reforms

CHAPTER SEVEN

Social Security Benefits and Program Objectives: An Individual Perspective

LEARNING OBJECTIVES

After completing this chapter, you will be able to:

1 Calculate your Social Security benefit.
2 State the policy objectives of Social Security and relate them to principles of insurance and income redistribution.
3 Disentangle the insurance and redistributive components of Social Security by comparing the expected implied rate of return to your payroll taxes with an actuarially fair one and relate this to the concept of getting your money's worth.
4 Use this method to evaluate the redistributive components of Social Security across different types of households (e.g. single persons, one-earner married couples, two-earner married couples, etc.) using concepts of horizontal and vertical equity. Show how single person households receive dramatically different retirement benefits from married couples and how the treatment of married couples depends on whether both members work or not.
5 Discuss the growth of social welfare spending over the past four decades.
6 Debate the merits of the current tax and benefit structure of Social Security and how changes in this structure would impact on different kinds of households.

CHAPTER OUTLINE

Introduction
How Old-Age, Survivors, and Disability Insurance Works
  Social Security taxes
  Insured status
  Benefit computation
  Indexation and benefit calculation
  Retirement age
  Spouse benefits
  Survivor benefits
What are the Policy Objectives of the OASDI Tax and Benefit Structure?
Trends in Social Welfare Spending in the United States
Disentangling the Insurance and Redistributive Components of Social Security
  Balancing the insurance and redistributive goals of OASI
  Who gets what from OASI
Evaluating Social Security Policies
  Money's worth issues
  The disparate treatment of single individuals and married couples
  Does this method of calculating benefits make sense?
  The treatment of women more generally
  Earnings sharing
  Thinking through the consequences of policy changes
Conclusion
Discussion Questions
Notes
References

INTRODUCTION

The Old-Age, Survivors, and Disability Insurance (OASDI) program or "Social Security" is the largest single government program in the United States and similar retirement programs represent a considerable portion of national governmental expenditures in most developed countries. In 2001, the US Social Security system paid cash benefits of approximately $432 billion to 46 million people. OASDI had revenues of $602 billion from the Social Security payroll taxes paid by 153 million employees and self-employed workers. Today, the average retired American family receives more income from Social Security than from any other source of income and the average American worker pays more in Social Security taxes than in federal income taxes (this comparison assigns both the employer and employee Social Security payroll tax payments to the individual). Thus, for most Americans, Social Security is a program that they will be significantly involved with over their entire lifetime from their first job until their death.

Given its importance to their lives, it is surprising that relatively few Americans understand how Social Security actually works, its primary policy objectives, and whether it has been or will be a "good deal" financially for them or for the country. The central focus of this chapter is to describe how Social Security benefits are calculated and how they vary across family types and cohorts. The analysis examines the insurance and redistribution goals of Social Security and provides the reader with a method of disentangling the implications of these two important and sometimes contradictory goals. Using the method developed in this chapter, the reader can evaluate the successes and failures of OASDI in achieving its broader social goals and whether the program is likely to be a good deal from an individual's money's worth perspective. Proposed reforms to Social Security are then examined using this method of analysis.

HOW OLD-AGE, SURVIVORS, AND DISABILITY INSURANCE WORKS

The most up-to-date and complete source of information on the operations of OASDI and its major characteristics is *The Annual Statistical Supplement to the Social Security Bulletin* (http://www.ssa.gov/statistics/Supplement/2001/supp01.pdf). This reference contains a detailed history of all Social Security programs, including a systematic discussion of changes in their complex tax and benefits structures. In addition, it contains detailed information on the populations currently paying Social Security taxes and those receiving Social Security benefits. Anyone interested in learning more about Social Security as a program should consult this government publication.

The aim of this section is to provide a general description of how the major components of the OASDI programs operate. The discussion is based primarily on information provided in the *Annual Statistical Supplement*. The analysis does not attempt to provide the reader with a detailed description of every Social Security program tax and benefit rule. Instead, the description of the programs is intended to provide enough information so the reader can understand the basics of how benefits are calculated and using this information examine the difficult policy trade-offs that are behind these rules. The information and method of analysis presented below will enable each person to determine how the parameters of the system affect different types of households and the value of their participation in Social Security.

In this chapter, we focus on the relationship between Social Security taxes and benefits from the individual's perspective. The discussion focuses on the so-called "money's worth" issues as well as redistributive features in current Social Security rules. In chapter 8, we will discuss broader Social Security budgetary issues including policies relating to how Social Security programs are financed and the proposals that are currently being made to address the long-term financing problems facing Social Security. Finally, the disability components of Social Security are examined in chapter 9.

Social Security taxes

A worker contributes to Social Security either through the payroll tax (Federal Insurance Contribution Act or FICA) or the self-employment tax (Self-Employed Contribution Act or SECA). For workers, employers match the contributions of their employees while self-employed persons pay the combined tax but receive a special federal income tax offset, which effectively reduces their total contribution. Maximum annual earnings subject to these taxes were $84,900 in 2002. Social Security taxes were paid by 96 percent of American workers. Workers who remain outside of the Social Security system include some long-term federal workers, railroad workers, some state employees, some low-earning domestic or farm workers, and the self-employed who have very low earnings.

The maximum amount of earnings subject to the payroll tax is increased automatically each year by the rate of growth of the national average annual earnings. In 2002, the payroll tax for both employees and employers was 6.2 percent for OASDI (5.3 percent for OASI and 0.9 percent for DI). FICA taxes are also paid to fund the Medicare program. In 2002, the payroll tax for both employers and employees was 1.45 percent. Since 1994, this payroll tax for Medicare has been paid on all wages and self-employed earnings without limit. The Medicare program is examined in more detail in chapters 10 and 11.

Insured status

To be eligible for Old-Age or Disability Insurance benefits a worker must earn a minimum number of credits based on covered work. These credits are called quarters of coverage. In 2002, an individual was credited with a quarter of coverage for each $870 in covered earnings. A worker can earn up to a maximum of four quarters per year. Thus, earnings of $3,480 yielded four quarters of coverage in 2002. The earnings required for a quarter of credited coverage increases each year based on changes in the national average annual earnings. An individual must be aged 62 and have 40 quarters of coverage to be eligible for Old-Age Insurance benefits. For workers who become disabled or die before age 62, the number of quarters of coverage needed for benefits depends on their age at the time of disability or death.

Benefit computation

The Primary Insurance Amount (PIA) is the monthly benefit amount paid to workers who initially accept OAI benefits at the normal retirement age or who receive disability benefits at any age. The PIA is also the base figure from which monthly benefit amounts are paid to the worker's family members or survivors. The PIA is derived from the worker's annual taxable earnings, averaged over their covered work life. Determination of an individual's PIA calculation involves three steps:

1 *Indexing of past earnings.* The worker's annual taxable earnings after 1950 are indexed to reflect the real value of those earnings in monetary units relative to the year just before first eligibility for retirement, disability, or death benefits (the second year before a worker reaches age 62, becomes disabled or dies). For someone dying in 2000, earnings in 1973 of $10,000 would be adjusted for average earnings growth between 1973 and 1998 by multiplying $10,000 by $28,861.44 (average labor earnings in 1998) and dividing by $7,580.16 (average labor earnings in 1973). That is, adjusting for real growth in average earnings, a worker with earnings of $10,000 in 1973 would have been credited with indexed earnings of $38,075 for that year.

2 *Determine AIME.* The Average Indexed Monthly Earnings (AIME) is an approximation of workers average real earnings over their work lives. The AIME is measured in a dollar amount that reflects real earnings just before retirement age, disability, or death. The period used to calculate AIME equals the number of full calendar years elapsing between age 21 and the year of first eligibility. For those who first become eligible for retirement benefits at age 62 the number of relevant years is 40. The lowest five years of indexed earnings are ignored in calculating the AIME. Thus, an individual's AIME is derived by first adding the highest 35 years of indexed earnings (out of the 40 possible years) and then dividing this total by 420 (35 years times 12 months). Workers disabled before age 47 can exclude between zero and four years.

3 *Computing the PIA.* A three-step benefit formula is used to compute the PIA from the AIME. The formula is weighted to provide a higher PIA-to-AIME ratio to those with lower earnings. The ratio of PIA to AIME is often referred to as the replacement ratio. The progressive benefit formula results in the replacement ratio

declining as AIME rises. For workers who reached age 62, became disabled, or died in 2001, the formula provides a PIA equal to the sum of:

90 percent of the first $561 of AIME, plus
32 percent of the next $2,820 of AIME, plus
15 percent of AIME over $3,381

Beginning with the first year of eligibility, the PIA is increased annually in January by cost-of-living adjustments (COLA). The COLA is based on the rate of increase in the Consumer Price Index (CPI) for the previous year.

The dollar amounts in the PIA formula produce three AIME brackets called bend points. The bend points are increased each year in proportion to increases in the average annual earnings level. Importantly, the benefit formula used to determine the PIA of a worker depends on their year of eligibility (reaching age 62, becoming disabled or dying), not the year they first receive benefits. For those who retire at age 65 in 2002, the PIA would be calculated using the eligibility rules that prevailed in 1999. Their actual PIA at retirement would be increased using the appropriate COLA increases for the years between 1999 and 2002. During most years, prices rise more slowly than do average national annual earnings and as a result, the indexation after age 62 tends to be lower than the indexation before age 62.

Indexation and benefit calculation

Since 1972, most aspects of Social Security have been indexed to either the growth in average earnings or changes in the CPI. The primary objectives of the indexation have been to keep initial retirement benefits increasing at the same rate as real wages, to keep benefits in retirement rising at the same rate as consumer prices, and to keep the tax revenues rising with the growth of earnings. The first objective is accomplished through the indexing of past earnings and the indexing of the bend points. As a result of these policies, a person in 2020 should have approximately the same replacement ratio from Social Security as a person who was in the same position in the earning distribution in 2000. For example, persons with earnings always at the taxable maximum should have approximately the same replacement ratio whether they are retiring in 2000, 2010, or 2020. The second objective is achieved by indexing retirement benefits to changes in the CPI. This indexation of benefits results in retirees receiving the same real Social Security benefit throughout their retirement years. The final objective is achieved by indexing the maximum taxable earnings to the growth of average earnings in the economy. Thus, as earnings rise, so do tax revenues.

These benefits provisions result in a very complex calculation to determine the benefits that a person will actually receive. Readers can use the information in Box 7.1 to calculate sample retirement benefits for workers retiring at different years with alternative earnings records.

Box 7.1 *How to Figure Your AIME and PIA*

AIME calculation

1 In column C of table 7.1, enter your earnings for each year after 1950. If your earnings for any year were more than the Maximum Taxable Amount, use the maximum only
2 Multiply the earnings for all years by the Index Factors in Column D. The index factors make past earnings comparable to the level of earnings today. Enter the results of your multiplication in column E, Indexed Earnings.
3 If you were born after January 1, 1929, use the best 35 years of earnings (after indexing) to figure your AIME. If you have fewer than 35 years of earnings, use zero for each of the remaining years.
4 In table 7.1, put check marks in column F by the years of highest indexed earnings shown in column E. Continue until you have checked 35 years.
5 Add up all the indexed earnings in column E for the years you have checked in column F.
6 Divide the total earnings shown in step 5 by 420 (35 years × 12 months) to get your AIME (drop cents).

Table 7.1 Worksheet for figuring your indexed earnings only if born after 1938

A	B	C	D	E	F	G
Calendar year	Maximum taxable amount $	Enter your taxable earnings	Index factor	(C*D) Indexed earnings	High years	Earnings required for a credit $
1951	3,600		10.88535			50
1952	3,600		10.24775			50
1953	3,600		9.70550			50
1954	3,600		9.65568			50
1955	4,200		9.22926			50
1956	4,200		8.62592			50
1957	4,200		8.36688			50
1958	4,200		8.29382			50
1959	4,800		7.90234			50
1960	4,800		7.60393			50
1961	4,800		7.45574			50
1962	4,800		7.10021			50
1963	4,800		6.93026			50
1964	4,800		6.65815			50
1965	4,800		6.54039			50
1966	6,600		6.17003			50
1967	6,600		5.84448			50
1968	7,800		5.46862			50

Table 7.1   (*continued*)

A	B	C	D	E	F	G
	Maximum	Enter your		(C*D)		Earnings
Calendar	taxable	taxable	Index	Indexed		required for
year	amount $	earnings	factor	earnings	High years	a credit $
1969	7,800		5.16985			50
1970	7,800		4.92542			50
1971	7,800		4.68977			50
1972	9,000		4.27119			50
1973	10,800		4.01968			50
1974	13,200		3.79414			50
1975	14,100		3.53031			50
1976	15,300		3.30243			50
1977	16,500		3.11570			50
1978	17,700		2.88649			250
1979	22,900		2.65429			260
1980	25,900		2.43497			290
1981	29,700		2.21227			310
1982	32,400		2.09684			340
1983	35,700		1.99943			370
1984	37,800		1.88842			390
1985	39,600		1.81125			410
1986	42,000		1.75904			440
1987	43,800		1.65359			460
1988	45,000		1.57597			470
1989	48,000		1.51595			500
1990	51,300		1.44901			520
1991	53,400		1.39696			540
1992	55,500		1.32851			570
1993	57,600		1.31718			590
1994	60,600		1.28275			620
1995	61,200		1.23331			630
1996	62,700		1.17581			640
1997	65,400		1.11098			670
1998	68,400		1.05573			700
1999	72,600		1.00000			740
2000	76,200		1.00000			780
2001	80,400		1.00000			830

Index factors change each year based on US average wage.
Source: William Mercer, 2002.

Now to figure your PIA

7   For those taking retirement benefits at age 62 this is straightforward. Use
the PIA rules in place in the year you reach age 62. For instance, someone

aged 62 in 2001 must use:

> 90 percent of the first $561 of AIME
> 32 percent of next $2,820 of AIME
> 15 percent of AIME is excess of $3,381.

8   For those who retire at age 65, one would begin with this same procedure, estimating PIA using rules in place when you were age 62; but you increase this value by the increases in prices between age 62 and 65.

Source: Adapted from information in William Mercer, 2002.

Table 7.2   Increasing normal retirement age for OASI retirement benefits

Year of birth	Normal retirement age
1937 and before	65 years
1938	65 years 2 months
1939	65 years 4 months
1940	65 years 6 months
1941	65 years 8 months
1942	65 years 10 months
1943–54	66 years
1955	66 years 2 months
1956	66 years 4 months
1957	66 years 6 months
1958	66 years 8 months
1959	66 years 10 months
1960 and later	67 years

Source: The Annual Statistical Supplement to the Social Security Bulletin (2002).

Retirement age

The earliest age of eligibility for OAI is 62. The full or normal retirement age is the earliest age at which an unreduced PIA is paid. Historically, the normal retirement age for Social Security has been 65. However, Social Security reforms adopted in 1983 specified that the normal retirement age for full benefits would begin to rise for persons who were born in 1938 or later. The normal retirement age is gradually being increased and will reach age 67 for persons who become age 62 in 2022. Table 7.2 shows the gradual increase in the retirement age that is set by current law.

The earliest a person can start retirement benefits is age 62. The early retirement age is not increased under current law and will remain at age 62. Persons who accept retirement benefits before the full retirement age will have their PIA reduced by 5/9 of 1 percent for the first 36 months and 5/12 of 1 percent for the next 24 months.

Prior to 2000, a worker retiring at age 62 would receive annual payment of 0.08 PIA:

$$\text{Age 62 Benefit} = [\text{PIA} - (36)\ (5/9\ \text{percent})\ \text{PIA}] = 0.8\ \text{PIA}.$$

As the normal retirement age is increased, the age 62 benefit will be reduced further. In 2022, a worker retiring at age 62, would only receive a monthly payment of 0.7 PIA:

$$\begin{aligned}\text{Age 62 Benefit} = [\text{PIA} &- (36)\ (5/9\ \text{percent})\ \text{PIA} \\ &- (24)\ (5/12\ \text{percent})\ \text{PIA}] = 0.7\ \text{PIA}.\end{aligned}$$

A worker who postpones receiving retirement benefits beyond the normal retirement age will receive a higher monthly benefit. This delayed retirement credit has been changed many times to provide older persons with a greater economic incentive to postpone receiving Social Security benefits. When the normal retirement age reaches 67, workers will be given an 8 percent increase in their PIA for each year they delay receiving Social Security benefits until age 70. Thus, a worker who starts retirement benefits at age 70 will receive a payment of 1.24 PIA:

$$\text{Age 70 Benefit} = [\text{PIA} + (3)(0.08)\ \text{PIA}] = 1.24\ \text{PIA}.$$

Spouse benefits

A spouse receives 50 percent of the worker's PIA (regardless of the worker's actual benefit amount), if the spouse has attained full retirement age. Benefits are payable to unmarried, divorced spouses of retirement age who were married at least ten years to the worker. However, in all cases, spouses must effectively choose to receive the larger of either their spouse benefit or their own worker benefit. Technically, spouses always receive benefits based on their own earnings record and then if their own retired worker benefit is less than one half of their spouses PIA, they are awarded the difference as a reduced spouse benefit. Thus, their total benefit is equal to one half the PIA of their spouse. This is, of course, the same benefit they would have received if they had never worked.

Survivor benefits

Widows and widowers of fully insured workers are eligible for unreduced PIA benefits at full retirement age. Surviving divorced spouses can also receive PIA benefits if they were married to the worker for at least ten years and had not remarried before age 60.

WHAT ARE THE POLICY OBJECTIVES OF THE OASDI TAX AND BENEFIT STRUCTURE?

The relationship between Social Security taxes paid and Social Security benefits received is both complex and contradictory. The reason is that OASDI has elements of both a private insurance system and a government program that taxes one group

---

Box 7.2 *Social Welfare Expenditures*

Social welfare expenditures represent a large and growing component of the federal budget. Table 7.3 shows that total social welfare expenditures have grown as a share of gross domestic product (the value of all final goods and service produced in a year in the United States) over the last half of the twentieth century. In the period between 1965 and 1975, the share of GDP used for federal social welfare expenditures grew from 11.0 to 18.2 percent. Growth since then has been more modest. In 1995, 20.9 percent of GDP was used for social welfare expenditures. Future growth in these programs will be driven by the aging of the population and whether the programs are modified in the face of rising costs.

Source: Annual Statistical Supplements (2002: table 3.A.1, p. 134).

---

in order to provide income to another group. In a private insurance system, each person must pay a premium that equals the expected value of the benefits provided by the insurance company. This actuarial principle defines all types of private insurance schemes including life, health, and retirement. Government programs can use this actuarial principle for certain programs, however, the insurance principle can be commingled with a desire to provide certain groups with additional benefits they do not personally finance.

Table 7.3 shows that total social welfare program expenditures by the federal government exceeded $1.5 trillion in 1995. About one-half ($705 billion) of these expenditures was spent on social insurance programs. OASDI and Medicare ($496 billion) made up the largest share of these expenditures followed by Public Employee Retirement ($128 billion), Worker Compensation ($43 billion), and Unemployment Insurance ($26 billion). All of these programs share a common characteristic. The payments made to beneficiaries are based on specific payments made to the program either directly by them or by their employees. This link between payments and benefits is in contrast to other social welfare expenditures such as public aid ($254 billion), health plans ($85 billion), veterans programs ($39 billion), education ($366 billion), housing ($29 billion), and all others ($27 billion). These programs have no direct relationship between individual taxes paid for the programs and individual benefits received.

Social insurance programs have a component of private insurance that distinguishes them from more general transfer programs that have no such *quid pro quo*. A person's eligibility for welfare payments or other forms of public aid (Public Assistance, Supplemental Security Income (SSI), food stamps, etc.) is not dependent on his or her past contributions to these programs. Rather, these pure welfare programs are based on need or some combination of need and other personal characteristics (age 65 for SSI, having dependent children for welfare, etc.).

Table 7.3 Gross Domestic Product and social welfare expenditures under public programs, fiscal years 1965–1995[1]

Item	1965	1970	1975	1980	1985	1990[2]	1992[2]	1993[2]	1994[2]	1995
					Amount (in millions)					
Gross Domestic Product	$701,000	$1,023,100	$1,590,800	$2,718,900	$4,108,000	$5,682,900	$6,149,300	$6,476,600	$6,837,100	$7,186,900
Total Social Welfare expenditures[3]	77,084	145,979	288,967	492,213	731,840	1,048,951	1,266,504	1,366,743	1,435,714	1,505,136
Social Insurance	28,123	54,691	123,013	369,595	513,822	618,938	659,210	683,210	683,779	705,483
Public Aid	6,283	16,488	41,447	72,703	98,362	146,811	207,953	221,000	238,025	253,530
Health and Medical Programs	6,155	10,300	16,535	26,762	38,643	61,684	70,143	74,706	80,130	85,507
Veteran's Programs	6,031	9,078	17,019	21,466	27,042	30,916	35,642	36,378	37,895	39,072
Education	28,108	50,846	80,834	121,050	172,048	258,332	292,145	331,997	344,091	365,625
Housing	318	701	3,172	6,879	12,598	19,468	20,151	20,782	27,032	29,361
Other Social Welfare	2,066	4,145	6,947	13,599	13,552	17,918	21,532	22,670	24,762	26,558
All heath and medical care[4]	9,302	24,801	51,022	99,145	170,665	274,472	353,174	381,710	408,780	435,075
					As percent of Gross Domestic Product					
Gross Domestic Product	100.0	100.0	100.0	100.0	100.0	100.0	100.0	100.0	100.0	100.0
Total Social Welfare expenditures	11.0	14.3	18.2	18.1	17.8	18.5	20.6	21.1	21.0	20.9
Social Insurance	4.0	5.3	7.7	8.5	9.0	9.0	10.1	10.2	10.0	9.8
Public Aid	.9	1.6	2.6	2.7	2.4	2.6	3.4	3.4	3.5	3.5
Health and Medical Programs	.9	1.0	1.0	1.0	.9	1.1	1.1	1.2	1.2	1.2
Veteran's Programs	.9	.9	1.1	.8	.7	.5	.6	.6	.6	.5
Education	4.0	5.0	5.1	4.5	4.2	4.5	4.8	5.1	5.1	5.1
Housing	(5)	.1	.2	.3	.3	.3	.3	.3	.4	.4
Other Social Welfare	.3	.4	.4	.5	.3	.3	.4	.4	.4	.4
All health and medical care	1.3	2.4	3.2	3.6	4.2	4.8	5.7	5.9	6.0	6.1

[1] Through 1976, fiscal year ended June 30 for federal government, most states, and some localities. Beginning in 1977, federal fiscal year ended September 30.
[2] Revised data
[3] Represents program and administrative expenditures from federal state and local public revenues and trusts funds under public law. Includes worker's compensation and temporary disability insurance payments made through private carriers and self-insurers. Includes capital outlay and some expenditures abroad.
[4] Combines "health and medical program" with medical services provided in connection with social insurances, public aid, veterans', and "other social welfare" categories.
[5] Less than 0.05 percent.

Source: Annual Statistical Supplement 2001 (2002) Table 3.A.1 p. 134, based on Gross Domestic Product data from Department of Commerce, Survey of Current Business. GDP figures revised in 1996 to reflect changes in the source data. Social welfare expenditures data taken or estimated from Federal Budgets, Consensus of Governments, and reports of administering agencies.

Social insurance programs are often described as programs that provide benefits to individuals based on an earned right. In this respect, social insurance programs are similar to private insurance because eligibility for benefits and the amount of the benefit are dependent to some degree on past tax payments. However, the exact relationship between payments and benefits for social insurance is typically quite different from that found in private insurance, i.e. benefits may be more or less than the amount that could be purchased by their tax payments.

Premiums for private insurance against various forms of risk are closely related to the average risk of the event occurring for members in the relevant risk pool. Every reader should be able to relate their premiums for life insurance, car insurance, or health insurance to the specific risk of certain events occurring. Individuals who live in wood houses must pay higher premiums for their fire insurance, other things being equal, than persons who live in brick homes. Older persons must pay higher premiums for life insurance while teenagers pay more for car insurance. In private insurance, there is a very close relationship between the expected cost of the event the person is insuring against and the premium the person must pay the insurance provider to accept responsibility for payment if the event should occur. Moreover, the premium is freely contracted between individual buyers and the company selling private insurance. Thus, the market place will ultimately determine the price of most forms of privately purchased insurance.

In addition to providing individual insurance against the risk of certain outcomes such as death, disability or old age, social insurance has another policy goal. OASDI is intended to redistribute income from higher-income families to lower-income families within a given age group or cohort of persons born at the same time. This redistributive goal is one that OASDI shares with other welfare programs. The tension between the insurance goal of paying the fair market price for benefits and the redistribution goal of providing enhanced benefits to certain groups has resulted in contradictory tax and benefit structures.

TRENDS IN SOCIAL WELFARE SPENDING IN THE UNITED STATES

From a political perspective, social insurance programs and especially, Old-Age Survivors, Disability, and Health Insurance (OASDHI) have had more consistent political support than other social welfare programs over the past half century. Table 7.4 (column 1) shows the total amount of social welfare expenditures (excluding education) from 1950 through 1995 in nominal dollars (unadjusted for inflation). Column 2 shows these social welfare expenditures (excluding education) as a share of Gross Domestic Product (GDP). GDP is of the value of all final goods and services produced in the United States during a particular year. The share of GDP going to those receiving social welfare expenditures has risen from 4.9 percent in 1950 to 15.8 percent in 1995. OASDHI expenditures have also been continuously increasing (column 3) rising from 0.3 percent of GDP in 1950 to 6.9 percent

Table 7.4 Social indicators

Years	Social welfare expenditures[a] (billion)	Social welfare expenditures	Social security expenditures	Non-social security expenditures	Overall poverty rate	Poverty rates for those aged 65 and over
		Share of Gross Domestic Products				
1950	14.1	4.9	0.3	4.7	39.8	59.0
1960	34.3	6.8	2.2	4.6	22.4	35.2
1968	72.9	8.8	3.5	5.3	12.8	25.0
1972	129.9	11.8	4.4	7.4	11.9	18.6
1976	239.6	14.7	5.6	9.2	11.8	15.0
1980	369.1	13.8	5.7	8.1	13.0	15.7
1984	517.5	14.0	6.5	7.5	14.4	12.4
1988	667.4	13.9	6.2	7.6	13.0	12.0
1992	972.1	15.8	6.8	9.0	14.5	12.9
1995	1140.0	15.8	6.9	8.9	13.8	10.5

[a] Social welfare expenditures include all social insurance, public aid, health and medical, veteran (except education) housing, and other social welfare programs. Social Security here is defined as Old-Age, Survivors, Disability, and Health Insurance programs. These figures are based on data from social welfare expenditures under public programs published in Table 3.A.1 p. 134 of the *Annual Statistical Supplement to the Social Security Bulletin*, 2000, and analogous table, in earlier years.

Source. Columns 2 through 5: *Annual Statistical Supplements to the Social Security Bulletin*, 2002, Table 3.A.1, p. 134.

Columns 6 and 7: 1950: Smolesky, Danziger and Gottschalk (1988), 2002, Table 3;

1960–90: US Census Bureau (2002), Tables 2 and 3.

of GDP in 1995. This increase is attributable to the maturing of the OASI program and the introduction of DI and HI to the system. The path for all other social welfare expenditures has been more erratic. Non-OASDHI expenditures (column 4) grew modestly as a percent of GDP between 1950 and 1968 and then nearly doubled through 1976. But following this 1976 peak, expenditures for these programs as a percent of GDP fell to a low of 7.5 percent in 1984 before slowly rising again to around 9.0 percent in the 1990s.

Table 7.5 illustrates changes in social welfare spending across presidential administrations. Social welfare expenditures are influenced by decisions made by all three branches of government. However, this single table shows that growth in OASDHI as a share of GDP has been positive across all presidential administrations from Eisenhower through Clinton. In contrast, non-Social Security welfare expenditures as a percent of GDP grew dramatically during the Nixon and Ford Administrations and fell modestly during the Carter and Reagan Administrations.

Tables 7.4 and 7.5 also show how overall poverty rates and the poverty rates of those aged 65 and over have changed since 1950. The tremendous increase in social welfare expenditures between 1950 and 1976 is correlated with dramatic reductions in overall poverty (from 39.8 percent to 11.8 percent) and old-age poverty (from 59.0 percent to 15.0 percent). The decline in non-Social Security expenditures since 1976 is correlated with an increase in poverty since then, while the continuing increases in Social Security expenditure are correlated with a further decline in poverty at older ages. Since 1984, the poverty rate of those aged 65 and over has fallen below that of younger people. A more detailed discussion of trends in poverty was provided in chapter 3.

Substantial increases in GDP between 1995 and 2000 lowered the poverty rates of all age groups but older persons continue to have significantly lower poverty rates than younger persons. It is likely that the major shift in social welfare expenditures toward OASDHI is primarily responsible for both the absolute decline in the poverty rate at older ages as well as the relative decline in old-age poverty that has occurred since 1950.

DISENTANGLING THE INSURANCE AND REDISTRIBUTIVE COMPONENTS OF SOCIAL SECURITY

The most common method of measuring poverty or income inequality and the impact of government programs on the poverty rate is based on a single-year perspective. Within this time frame, Social Security appears to have a profound intergenerational effect. In any given year, young workers pay taxes and retirees receive benefits. This mechanism gives the appearance of significant redistribution of income from the young to the elderly. From this single-year perspective, the effect of Social Security on intra-generational transfers (redistribution within a given age cohort) is also quite large. Since Social Security is the major source of income for older persons in middle- and low-income families, the data appear to indicate significant redistribution to persons in the lower half of the income distribution.

Table 7.5 Percentage changes in social welfare spending and poverty rates across presidential administrations

| Administration | Percentage change in social welfare share[a] | | Percentage change in social security welfare share[b] | Percentage change in non-social security share[c] | Percentage change in overall poverty[d] | Percentage change in elderly poverty[e] |
| | Gross Domestic Product | | | | | |
	Per year					
Eisenhower, 1950–1960f	39	3.9	—	–2	–44	–39
Kennedy-Johnson, 1960–1968	29	3.6	59	15	–43	–31
Nixon-Ford, 1968–1976	67	8.4	60	74	–8	–40
Carter, 1976–1980	–6	–1.5	2	–12	10	5
Reagan, 1980–1988	1	0.3	9	–6	0	–24
Bush, 1988–1992	14	3.5	10	18	12	8
Reagan/Bush, 1980–1992	14	1.2	19	11	12	–18
Clinton, 1992–1995	0	0	1	–1	–5	–19

[a] Percentage changes from table 7.3, column 3.
[b] Percentage changes from table 7.3, column 4.
[c] Percentage changes from table 7.3, column 5.
[d] Percentage changes from table 7.3, column 6.
[e] Percentage changes from table 7.3, column 7.
[f] The Eisenhower Administration began in 1952, but our data are for 1950 and 1960.
Source. See Table 7.3.

Such single-period measures provide a good first approximation of the ultimate redistributive consequences of pure welfare programs because general revenues are used to fund programs like Supplemental Security Income or Food Stamps. This is the case because those taxes directly redistribute income from taxpayers to beneficiaries without taxpayers receiving a promise of future benefits. But single-year indicators are much poorer measures of the influence of social insurance programs like OASDI on poverty rates or income distribution. Using a single period measure of income redistribution to estimate the influence of OASDI will grossly distort the true redistributive properties of Social Security by confusing redistribution across people with redistribution across a given individual's life.

It is more appropriate to recognize the temporal nature of Social Security (the relationship between taxes paid at younger ages and benefits received at older ages) and measure its effect on the well-being of individuals over their entire lifetime. This lifetime perspective separates Social Security benefits received in old age into two components. The first is a simple return on past taxes paid into the system. This can be thought of as the government taking a dollar out of your pocket when you are young and then returning the dollar back to you with interest when you are older. If benefits in old age exceed the lifetime tax payments plus compounded returns, the additional money received by one individual must come from somebody else's taxes. This excess of present value of benefits over the lifetime taxes paid represents the true positive transfers Social Security provide in old age. From a lifetime perspective, only that part of the Social Security tax paid by workers at younger ages which is not reimbursed to the same individual (or that individual's family or estate) at older ages represents a true redistribution of income away from younger workers.

Balancing the insurance and redistributive goals of OASI

In 1935, during the midst of the Great Depression, Congress passed the Social Security Act, which created a pension program for retired workers known as Old-Age Insurance (OAI). Supporters of the Act were motivated not only by the poor financial status of the elderly, but also, and perhaps chiefly, by the unemployment rate that prevailed among younger men in their prime working years. Because it offered pensions to workers aged 65 and older on the condition that they withdraw completely from the labor force, OAI was viewed as a way of increasing the number of jobs available for younger workers (Altmeyer, 1968).

The primary objective of OAI was to replace earnings that ceased when older workers retired. Benefits were to be related to total wage earnings of workers, over their entire lifetime (up to maximum of three thousand dollars per year), and were to be financed with wage-related contributions paid by employees and their employers. However, even this original program was intended to redistribute income to some degree to those at the low end of the income scale through the use of a progressive benefit structure.

The initial legislation provided that retirement benefits would be paid to qualified workers beginning in 1942. It soon became clear that Social Security would provide only minimal benefits to workers who were already close to retirement in 1935. These relatively low benefits were due to the fact that older workers would have only a few years of work life remaining to accumulate credits toward retirement benefits. Even in the long term, after workers had paid into the system over an entire lifetime, benefits would still be very small for many workers with a history of low earnings.

In recognition of this deficiency, the 1939 Amendments to the Social Security Act dramatically increased the benefits going to the first generation of recipients and mandated that a greater share of benefits would go to low-income workers. To provide greater benefits to first generation retirees, the original funding principles of Social Security were largely abandoned. This meant there was a shift from the expected full funding principles similar to those of a private annuity insurance plan to a pay-as-you-go funding system. In the new system, the contributions of current workers were not invested in the general economy for distribution to them in later years. Rather, current contributions were used to pay benefits to current retirees and only a small reserve fund was created. This allowed the first several generations of recipients to receive benefits far in excess of those attributable to their contributions and those of their employers. To provide increased benefits to low-wage workers, the benefit formula was made more progressive and benefits were extended to a worker's spouse and children.

The current system retains the mix of insurance and redistributive principles that emerged from the 1939 Amendments. As described above, there is a link between benefits and contributions. Monthly benefits are paid as a matter of earned right and are related to earnings on which Social Security taxes are paid. The amount of the monthly benefit is determined by first computing workers' AIME from their Social Security earnings records. But there is also a significant redistribution component. The PIA calculation disproportionately replaces average earnings for lower earners. Replacement rates are even higher in the presence of a spouse since the spouse receives 0.5 PIA.

Who gets what from OASI

Steuerle and Bakija (1994) used a lifetime perspective of redistribution within and across individuals to simulate the true transfer provided by OASI over its history to different simulated groups of beneficiaries. Table 7.6, developed by Steuerle and Bakija (1994), shows the total value of OASI benefits received and taxes (and foregone interest) paid for various hypothetical workers using the actual tax and benefit rules in the system. The type of workers considered in this analysis are: single males, single females, married couples where only one spouse works, and married couples where both spouses work. In each of these four groups, the workers are either low, average, or high wage workers over their lifetimes. To show how

Table 7.6 Lifetime OASI benefits, taxes, and transfers (in thousands of constant 1993 dollars)

Year cohort turns 65		Single male			Single female			One-earner couple			Two-earner couple		
		Low Wage	Avg. Wage	High Wage	Low Wage	Avg. Wage	High Wage	Low Wage	Avg. Wage	High Wage	Low Wage	Avg. Wage	High Wage
1960	Benefits	30.1	45.5	50.6	45.7	69.0	76.7	66.3	98.9	111.0	76.8	102.0	122.1
	Taxes	4.0	9.0	13.8	4.3	9.6	14.6	4.0	9.0	13.8	8.4	13.3	23.4
	Net Transfer	26.1	36.5	36.8	41.4	59.4	62.1	62.3	89.9	97.2	68.4	88.7	98.7
1980	Benefits	54.3	90.2	114.6	80.8	134.3	170.5	129.3	209.9	264.3	146.9	208.4	273.2
	Taxes	22.9	51.0	71.9	24.2	53.9	76.1	22.9	51.0	71.9	47.2	75.2	125.7
	Net Transfer	31.4	39.3	42.7	56.6	80.5	94.4	106.4	158.9	192.4	99.7	133.3	147.5
1995	Benefits	58.0	95.7	133.6	80.6	132.9	185.5	134.9	223.4	305.4	155.2	226.6	312.6
	Taxes	45.4	100.8	170.7	47.2	104.8	179.0	45.4	100.8	170.7	92.5	148.0	275.5
	Net Transfer	12.6	−5.1	−37.1	33.4	28.1	6.5	89.5	122.5	134.7	62.6	78.6	37.1
2010	Benefits	69.0	115.2	175.9	93.6	156.1	238.4	154.6	258.8	388.6	178.9	261.7	394.2
	Taxes	68.2	151.5	310.8	70.4	156.5	322.4	68.2	151.5	310.8	138.6	221.9	467.3
	Net Transfer	0.9	−36.3	−135.0	23.2	−0.4	−84.1	86.5	107.3	77.7	40.3	39.8	−73.1
2030	Benefits	84.0	139.6	220.3	113.7	189.0	298.1	187.4	312.8	493.0	215.9	316.5	498.1
	Taxes	88.1	195.9	468.8	91.3	202.8	485.4	88.1	195.8	468.8	179.4	287.1	671.6
	Net Transfer	−4.1	−56.2	−248.5	22.5	−13.8	−187.3	99.3	117.0	24.2	36.5	29.4	−173.5

All amounts are discounted to present value at age 65 using a 2 percent real interest rate. Adjusts for chance of death in all years after age 21. Includes actuarial value of all OASI workers, spousal, and survivors benefits payable over a lifetime, includes both employer and employee portions of OASI payroll tax. Couples are assumed to be the same age and to have two children born when parents are age 25 and 30. Assumes retirement at the OASI Normal Retirement age. Projections are based on the intermediate assumptions from the 1993 OASI Bard of Trustees report. AOSI tax rate is assumed to set at 10.65 percent after 1992.
Source: Steuerle and Bakija (1994).

the pattern of net Social Security transfers has changed over the history of the program, the workers considered turn age 65 at various years between 1960 and 2030. Of course, Steuerle and Bakija did not know how the future would turn out, so all tax and benefit projections are made based on rules as of 1993.

Using the concept of intertemporal redistribution, an actuarially fair system in this table, would yield net transfers of zero for all groups. Such a system would redistribute income across individuals' lifetimes, thus "insuring" income at older ages that was more consistent with their level of income at younger ages but would provide no real transfers across people. Such a program based solely on private insurance principles would not have satisfied the intent of Congress to both provide immediate transfers to a first generation of older Americans and permanently redistribute money within a given age cohort from high to low earners.

Given the redistrubutive goals Congress intended OASI to satisfy, it is not surprising that those who first received OASI benefits at age 65 in 1960, that is, those in the cohort of people who were age 44 in 1939 when the 1939 Amendment to the Social Security Act transformed OASI into a major redistributional program, received substantial positive transfers over their lifetimes. All hypothetical workers, high and low labor earners; men and women; married and single, are estimated to receive more in lifetime OASI benefits than they and their employers paid in OASI taxes plus interest over their lifetimes.[1]

It is important to understand why net transfers vary so much across the various subgroups in Table 7.6:

1 *High vs. low earners.* Holding gender and marital status constant, it is clear that the progressive PIA formula provides a much greater rate of return to low-earning workers than to average and high earners within a given age cohort. In the early years of the program, the rate of return was higher for low earners, the actual size of their net transfer was lower because they contributed much less into the program over their lifetime (see row 1, table 7.6). In 1960, low earning males received over 7.5 times as much in benefits as they and their employers paid in taxes (30.1 ÷ 4.0 = 7.52) while highly paid workers received 3.67 (50.6 ÷ 13.8 = 3.67) times as much. However, the absolute dollar amount of the transfer was much less for the low earners compared to the high earners ($26,100 for the low wage men and $36,800 for the men with high lifetime earnings).

2 *Men vs. women.* Single females do better than single males because the system is gender-neutral with respect to its benefit rules. Private insurance annuities that pay yearly benefits of a given amount would be forced to charge women as a class more for this old age insurance than men as a class because historically women have lived longer than men. Thus, women have a higher probability of experiencing the risk of reaching old age than do men and hence of receiving a retirement benefit. Therefore, women can expect to receive greater lifetime benefits than men, holding all other factors constant. As a result, gender-neutral annuities will not be actuarially fair. Rather they provide the average woman a net transfer at the expense of the average man. For the same reason, differential

death rates, gender-neutral life insurance will not be actuarially fair. Such life insurance policies will provide the beneficiaries of the average man a net transfer at the expense of the average woman, since the average man is more likely to die at a given age than is the average woman.

It is important to note that what is fair from an actuarial point of view may not be considered fair from a social point of view. In the 1980s, the United States Supreme Court in a series of rulings (Los Angeles vs. Manhart, 1978; Arizona vs. Norris, 1983, etc.) required all private retirement plans to be gender-neutral, based on their interpretation of Title VII of the Civil Rights Act of 1964.[2]

3   *Single vs. married worker.* A one-earner couple with exactly the same earning history as a single worker receives greater net transfers than does a single worker. This occurs because the couple receives a worker and a spouse benefit equal to 150 percent of the PIA received by the single worker alone. The extra benefit is received even though the couple paid the same tax rate as a single worker. The net transfer to a one-earner couple is more than 150 percent that of a single male because the spouse will receive a survivor benefit equal to the worker's PIA once the worker dies while no survivor benefits are paid to the estate of a single worker. Because single males are expected to live fewer years than single females, the difference in net transfers between one-earner couples and single men is much greater than it is between one-earner couples and single females. The average two-earner couple also receives greater net transfers than the average single male or single female for the same reasons.

4   *Past generations vs. future generations.* The large across-generational transfers available to the first generation of Social Security beneficiaries made possible by the switch in 1939 to a pay-as-you-go funding system permitted all early beneficiaries to receive benefits far in excess of an actuarially fair system based on their contributions alone. By 1980, a new cohort of beneficiaries who were only age 24 in 1939 entered the old-age retirement rolls. Remarkably their net transfers were even larger than those of previous generations of beneficiaries. This was made possible by substantial increases in OASI benefits made in the 1970s. Between 1972 and 1980, real Social Security benefits increased by over 50 percent (see Anderson et al., 1986). This was caused by sharp increases in the PIA formula and by errors in the way past wages and future benefit increases were indexed that were never fully corrected for this particular cohort of beneficiaries.

By 1995, the tax increases necessary to pay for these increased benefits as well as the correction of the double indexing problem had been worked into the system as had the future reduction in benefits (via extension of the age of full retirement to 67). This dramatically reduced net transfers for future generations.[3] After 1995, the within cohort transfers necessary to redistribute benefits from high earners to low earners, from men to women and from single persons to married persons (especially to one-earner couples) are finally being felt. Even if current tax and benefit levels are maintained, (and that is unlikely, given the long-run financial problem with OASI discussed in chapter 8), the expected future net transfers will be negative for many high earners, most single workers, and some two-earner couples by 2030. Net transfers will be smaller for all workers because the across-cohort transfers that offset negative within cohort transfers dictated by the redistributive aspects of OASI benefit determination rules are no longer available.

EVALUATING SOCIAL SECURITY POLICIES

The previous section provides an important yardstick for measuring how Social Security affects economic well-being across a lifetime for different types of people. The critical insight behind this thought experiment is that Social Security is a multi-period social insurance program that combines private insurance and income distributional goals. The appropriate mix of insurance and redistribution that should be incorporated into OASDI ultimately is the value judgment that will always be at the heart of Social Security policy debates. Reasonable arguments can be made that either the insurance or redistributive components of OASI should be changed or that the overall size of the OASI program should grow or shrink.

What is less debatable is how the size of the insurance and redistributional components of OASI should be measured. To fully understand how OASI impacts the economic well-being of people, a lifetime perspective is necessary. To disentangle the redistributive from the insurance components of Social Security, the appropriate comparison, the policy counterfactual, is between an annuity provided by private insurance and the current government program. The lifetime net transfer provided by OASI is then the difference between benefits provided by the current system and what would have been provided by a private system. Given this objective information, policy-makers can then make normative determinations as to whether this transfer is in the appropriate direction and of the appropriate size.

Money's worth issues

Much of the current discussion about Social Security reform centers on whether OASI provides people with their money's worth. In its simplest form, one can think of this as a question about how the net transfers in the current system compare with those from a private actuarially fair system. As we have seen, intergenerational transfers have offset the within-cohort redistributive components of OASI through much of the first 50 years of the program. Thus, there were net positive transfers to all members of those early retiring cohorts and as a result, each Social Security participant received benefits in excess of his or her tax payments plus interest. Thus, each person received more than his or her money's worth from Social Security.

The continuation of large intergenerational transfers is no longer politically possible. The increases to currently retiring cohorts necessary to yield returns similar to those of previous generations of retirees are technically possible to achieve but only by dramatically increasing the taxes levied on each subsequent generation. Furthermore, paying off the liabilities related to these even larger future benefit promises would be even more difficult to achieve by their children (see chapter 8). Thus, what may really be at the heart of this money's worth discussion is the same controversy that surrounds other welfare programs, that is, what types of households are truly deserving of net positive transfers, how large should they be, and who should pay for them. As shown in tables 7.4 and 7.5, public attitudes and subsequent public policies to the degree they are reflected in non-Social Security social welfare spending have changed substantially in this regard over the last half century.

What is clear with respect to the money's worth discussion is that it is inappropriate to simply compare the implied rate of return on OASI taxes to that of the return on private market investments as a measure of OASI success. The redistributive components of OASI intentionally provide a lower return for men, higher earners, single workers and two-earner couples than the one they would receive in a purely private insurance system. More appropriate questions that should be asked in a money's worth context are whether and to what degree are transfers from these groups to women, low earners, and one-earner couples socially appropriate on traditional redistribution grounds. It is to these questions that we now turn. The next chapter poses other questions that should be examined within the money's worth context. Could alternative funding mechanisms (investment in the stock market, individualized accounts, etc.) increase the overall return to a given cohort?

The disparate treatment of single individuals and married couples

As table 7.6 showed, the net positive transfer to married couples is larger than is the transfer to single individuals. This cannot be justified on insurance grounds. Clearly from a strict money's worth perspective OASI is a better deal for married couples than for single individuals. Hence, this difference must be justified on redistributional grounds. In so doing, we turn to two basic economic principles used to judge the fairness of such transfers: horizontal equity and vertical equity.

Horizontal equity argues that with respect to government tax and benefits, equals should be treated equally. This concept implies that those who have the same amount of income should be taxed at the same rate or should receive the same benefits. Vertical equity argues that ability to pay or level of need is a fair method of determining the size of taxes assessed or benefits received. Hence, those with higher income should pay more in taxes and receive less in benefits than those with lower income. How much higher taxes or lower benefits should be, is a more difficult issue with regard to the vertical equity concept.

Table 7.7 shows the OASI benefits payable to a single person, a one-earner couple, and a two-earner couple. In the case of the single person and the one-earner couple, the earnings record of the worker is assumed to equal the taxable maximum for the OASI program in each of the 35 years used to calculate the worker's

Table 7.7 Benefits payable to single persons and couples in 2001 with identical total earnings through 2000[a]

| Family status[a,b] | Social Security benefits | | | |
	Average lifetime earnings	Retirement and spouse	Survivor	Survivor benefit/couple benefit
Single Person	$66,324	$18,440	–	–
One Earner Couple				
Husband	$66,324	$18,440		
Wife	–	$ 9,220		2/3
Total	$66,324	$27,660	$18,440	
Two Earner Couple				
Husband	$33,162	$13,655		
Wife	$33,162	$13,655		1/2
Total	$66,324	$27,310	$13,655	

[a] This example assumes that the single person as well as both the husband and wife are age 65 in 2001 when they retire.

[b] This example is a one-earner couple, where the husband has earned the taxable maximum over his career, and a two-earner couple who have each earned one-half the taxable maximum. Earnings are assumed to begin at age 22, and retirement occurs at the beginning of the year. The single person has the same earning history as the husband in the one-earner couple.

Source: Based on information from table 2.A.27 p. 119 and table 2.A.28 pp. 120–121 Social Security Administration (2002).

AIME in 2001 when the worker retires at age 65. In the case of the two-earner couple, both spouses are assumed to earn exactly one-half the taxable maximum over those same 35 years. The husband and wife are aged 65 in all cases. In 2001, a worker aged 65 who earned the taxable maximum over all his or her working years would have had an annualized AIME of $66,324.

These household types are chosen because all three families considered in the example have identical annual earnings throughout their work lives. Therefore, each family would have paid exactly the same amount of taxes into the OASI system. On strict insurance grounds, they should receive exactly the same lifetime benefit. But as can be seen in table 7.7, these equal tax payments yielded dramatically different yearly benefits for the three families. While everyone is alive, the single worker receives $18,440 per year based on his or her PIA. The one-earner couple receives $27,660 which is a sum of the worker's PIA and the spouse's 0.5 of the worker's PIA. Each of the workers in the two-earner couple receives $13,655 for a total of $27,310.

The reason a worker who earns $33,162 receives more than one-half of the PIA of a worker who earns $66,324 is that the PIA formula is tilted towards lower-income workers. (This is especially true in this case since each of the earners in the two-earner couple have AIMEs that fall within the first two PIA brackets, while almost one-half of the AIME of the earner in the one-earner couple is in the third PIA bracket.) The reason why the two-earner couple receives less in total bene-fits than the one-earner couple is that each can only claim their own PIA or a spouse's benefit based on their partner's PIA. But the spouse benefit based on the earnings stream of either worker in the two-career couple is only $6,828. Hence, the two-earner couple, despite paying the same in total OASI taxes, receives more than the single worker but less than the one-earner couple.

The disparity in benefits across the three families following the death of the worker (or spouse) is even greater. When the single worker dies, his or her estate receives nothing based on the worker's PIA. In contrast, the survivor benefit for the one-earner couple is $18,440 (the worker PIA). This is effectively a joint-and-two-thirds annuity. That is, the survivor receives two-thirds of the total amount provided to the couple when both were alive. In contrast, the death of one mem-ber of the two-earner couple results in an effective survivors' benefit of $13,655 based on the higher PIA paid to the two workers while both were alive. (Note in this special case, both spouses have the same PIA.) This effectively results in a joint-and-one-half annuity.

Not only does this result in a much lower level of benefits compared to the survivor benefit of the one-earner couple but it also yields a much lower level of benefits for the survivor relative to benefits when both members of the two-earner family were alive. Surely Social Security policy did not intend that the drop in benefits to a survivor should be a function of the relative share of a couple's labor earnings earned by the husband and the wife over their lifetime. Yet, this is how current OASI rules operate.

Does this method of calculating benefits make sense?

One can argue on redistributional grounds that a married couple that earns the same amount and pays the same amount of taxes as single worker should receive more in benefits. The reason is that a married couple has two persons to support in retirement whereas the single person has only one person to support. This ver-tical equity argument is consistent with the logic behind our official measures of poverty in the United States that establishes higher poverty thresholds for a two-person family than for a one-person family. (See chapter 3 for a discussion of these measurement issues.)

It is likely that in 1939, this was the logic behind the creation of the spouse bene-fit. It also explains the creation of the survivor's benefit at no actuarial cost to the married couple. (A private annuity requires a higher premium or a lower yearly benefit for covering the higher risk of paying two people benefits until they both die.) Under Social Security, married persons neither pay more for OASI coverage nor do they receive less per year than do single persons. While neither the spouse nor the survivor benefit is justified on insurance grounds, they can be justified on vertical equity grounds within a social insurance system.

More difficult to justify is the difference between benefits for one- and two-earner couples who pay the same amount of taxes into the system. A former chief actuary of Social Security has tried justifying this policy. His argument is presented in Box 7.3. In this memo, which is more formally discussed in Myers (1982), it is argued that:

> the two-earner couple has *lower* net earnings when account is taken of various elements such as the non-earner spouse of the one-earner couple devoting her/his time at home providing incomes-saving things (for example lower cost of food) that the two-earner couple do not have time to do . . .Thus, in this case the one-earner family is really a *higher* income family than the two-earner one, and the higher Social Security benefits are proper as a recognition thereof. (emphasis added)

This statement can be examined using the methods we have developed to capture insurance and redistribution components of OASI. It is correct to argue that the one-earner couple actually is better off than the two-earner couple with the same

---

Box 7.3 *Memorandum*

TO: Richard V. Burkhauser
FROM: Robert J. Myers
DATE: September 17, 1992
SUBJECT: Relative Benefits of Single-Earner and Two-Earner Couples

At the meeting of the Women and Retirement Study Group of the House Select Committee on Aging on 9/11, you mentioned that the Social Security retirement benefits of a one-earner couple with the same total earnings as those of a two-earner couple are higher than the benefits of the latter couple.

   This is factually correct, but in my view the analysis is improper, because the two couples do not have the same net earnings, on the average. The two-earner couple has lower net earnings when account is taken of various elements, such as the non-earner spouse of the one-earner couple devoting her/his time at home producing income-savings things (e.g. lower cost for food) that the two-earner couple does not have time to do, and such as the one-earner family having lower costs for transportation to work, meals at work, clothes for work, and (where children are present) child care. Thus, in this case the one-earner family is really a higher income family than the two-earner one, and the higher Social Security benefits are proper as a recognition thereof (and also of the economic efforts of the non-earners) Comments? Rebuttal?

Source: Personal correspondence from Robert Myers to Richard Burkhauser.

earnings, if the one-earner couple manages to earn that money in less time. Under such circumstances, the extra non-market work time available to the one-earner couple makes them economically better off. But on redistributional grounds (vertical equity) most people would agree that this suggests that the one-earner couple should receive less rather than more in OASI benefits at older ages than the two-earner couple, given the fact that the one-earner couple pay the same amount of OASI taxes as the two-earner couple at younger ages. The memo confuses the insurance and redistributional aspects of OASI. On insurance grounds those who pay more into the system should receive more in benefits. But in this case, the one-earner couple did not pay OASI taxes on their additional non-market activities; so one cannot argue that on insurance grounds they should receive benefits for such uncovered work activities. This discussion shows the power of clear thinking in disentangling the two often-contradictory goals of OASI.

It is unlikely that Social Security policy-makers in 1939 consciously considered the implication of treating one-and two-earner couples differently. Rather, in 1939, when two-earner couples were rare, it is more likely that on redistributional grounds they provided spouse and survivor benefits to "traditional" male heads of households without considering the implication this would have in our twenty-first-century society in which both members of a typical married couple are likely to have large periods of market work during their married life.

The treatment of women more generally

OASI was developed in an era when few married women worked outside the household, few marriages ended in divorce, and few children were born outside marriage. Therefore, it is not surprising, as we saw in table 7.6, that OASI provides the greatest protection to married couples. While some changes in program rules since 1939 have made men and women who do not belong to this most favored family type somewhat better off relative to traditional families, the OASI protection provided non-traditional families continues to be less than that provided more traditional lifelong one-earner families.

Earlier we discussed the disproportional net transfers to one-earner couples relative to two-earner couples, but more general issues can be raised with respect to the reasonableness of the current method of providing additional benefits to married couples via the spouse benefit.

1   A spouse benefit is equal to 0.5 of the worker's PIA. But why is this an appropriate amount? Based on current equivalence scales used to set the poverty line for two- and one-person families, a spouse benefit of 0.25 is more appropriate (see chapter 3).

2   Alternatively a spouse benefit might be considered on insurance grounds as a payment for non-market work or for the raising of children. But if so, why not require married couples to pay OASI taxes on this work? Alternatively if on

redistributional grounds this is a social payment to unpaid labor, why is the non-market work of the spouse of a higher earner worth more than that of a lower earner? Why are benefits paid regardless of whether or not the spouse actually raised children?

While OASI treats one-earner couples more generously than two-earner couples, the risk of lost benefits following divorce is much greater for a woman (who is usually the non-wage-earning spouse) in one-earner families. A spouse's benefit is only paid to a divorced spouse if he or she has been married ten years. Hence, a non-market working spouse is not vested in an OASI pension until she or he has been married ten years. Furthermore, even after ten years, at divorce the worker receives the PIA. The spouse only receives 0.5 PIA. This 67–33 percent split is less than the 50–50 percent split of other assets earned during a marriage in community property states. Thus, while long lasting one-earner marriages yield higher benefits for the families of non-market working women, such women experience greater losses than do market working wives if they divorce.

Earnings sharing

A major alternative to the current treatment of Social Security tax and benefits that would dramatically change the treatment of men and women within the Social Security system is the concept of earnings sharing. Currently the property rights to OASI benefits are based directly on an individual's earnings record. A spouse who does not work in the market receives benefits through his/her working spouse's earnings record. An alternative method of assigning property rights is to divide total Social Security earnings of a married couple in a year (or month) equally between the two. These equally divided earnings would then be used to calculate individual AIMEs. This treatment of family income would make OASI more consistent with current Federal Income Tax policy where a married couple files a joint-return and taxes are paid by the couple on the combined income of the couple regardless of who earns the money.

This simple but powerful idea (changing the property right from the individual earner in a family to an equally shared family concept) would do much to end the inconsistent treatment of one- and two-earner couples in the OASI system. For instance, returning to table 7.7, the distribution of family earnings between the husband and wife would no longer lead to different benefits either when both partners are alive or for the survivor. Both members of the couple would have their own separate and equally proportioned earnings record. These records would be based on their highest 35 years of earnings and would look exactly like the two-earner couple records in table 7.7. Regardless of how actual wages were earned by the husband and wife, each would have an AIME of $33,162 since each partner's AIME would be based on one-half of the total couple's earnings for each year they were married.

Note that while a one-earner couple would no longer be more favorably treated than a two-earner couple, they would not lose one-third of their former benefits, despite giving up the spouse benefit. The disproportionate PIA return on lower AIMEs would offset much of this loss. However, unless changed, simple earnings sharing would lead to a joint and one-half annuity. This distribution of funds across the family's life cycle could easily be changed to a joint and two-thirds annuity by, for instance, changing the method of calculating survivor benefits to equal two-thirds of the couple's summed PIAs.

In addition, earnings sharing would insure that each member of a divorced couple would receive one-half of the earnings record of the couple while married and will do so immediately but not after ten years. Finally, because of the progressive PIA relationship to AIME, married couples would continue to do better than a single person with the same earning history.

Earnings sharing was widely discussed in the 1970s and 1980s (see Burkhauser and Holden, 1982) but was never enacted. In part, this was the result of the administrative complexity of keeping Social Security records on married couples, rather than on individuals. But a more likely reason earnings sharing never gained sufficient political support was that in a budget neutral world, gains by some would have to be paid for by losses to others. In a period when Social Security was rewarding all beneficiaries more than the expected value of their contributions, it was difficult to get the political process focused on even the most obvious oddities of its redistributional components if it meant that any one group would lose. But as the disproportionate gains to one-earner couples in the next 50 years become more obvious, especially when compared to the negative returns of some two-earner couples and most single persons, perhaps earning sharing will be revisited.

The method of disentangling the insurance and redistribution components of OASI described in this chapter makes it obvious that the implementation of earnings sharing will result in some men and women losing benefits while other men and women will gain. But the progressive PIA structure will cushion the loss of the spouse benefit for one-earner couples. In addition, even modest increases in the market work of the previously non-market working spouse in a one-earner couple will further offset the loss of the spouse benefit.

A far less radical policy change proposed by Burkhauser and Smeeding (1994) would offset some of the problems in the current treatment of one- and two-earner couples. They propose that the OASI lifetime benefit payout be shifted from a joint and two-thirds to a joint and three-quarters annuity for all couples but that the survivor benefit be based on the sum of the PIA of both members of the couple. The information in table 7.7 shows that this would increase the survivor's benefit from $18,440 to $20,745 for the one-earner couple but would increase the survivor's benefit from $13,655 to $20,483 for the two-earner couple. This would equalize the survivors' benefit to three-quarters of the benefit paid while both the husband and wife were alive for all survivors and do so using a modified earnings sharing concept. This policy would make the redistributive component of OASI for one- and two-earner couples more horizontally equitable.

Furthermore, a survivor's benefit that was 75 percent of the couple's benefit would be closer to the 80 percent of the couple's combined benefit necessary to keep the survivor at the same standard of living after the other spouse's death, according to official poverty scale measures discussed in chapter 3. To make this larger survivor's benefit cost-neutral, one could slightly reduce the bend points for establishing PIAs for all workers. This would have the effect of shifting Social Security benefits from couples (both one- and two-earners) while married to the survivor of both types of couples. Thus, Social Security benefits would be shifted from a period of the life cycle when both members of the couple are alive and their poverty rates are low to a later period when only the survivor remains and poverty rates are much higher. Note, this proposed change is not primarily redistributive in nature, but mostly an adjustment in the timing of insurance from the time when both spouses are alive to the time when only the survivor remains. It does, however, result in income being redistributed from single persons to married persons.

Thinking through the consequences of policy changes

The current tax and benefit rules for OASI were largely set in 1939 although major revision with respect to indexing of benefits and the size of the PIA were implemented in the 1970s and 1980s. Seemingly small changes in these rules can have significant effects on the insurance and redistributional components of OASI. Using the analytical tools described in this chapter, it is possible to approximate who gets what from any proposed change.

One way of doing so is to think about how cost-neutral proposals for OASI changes would affect different groups in the short and long run. It is useful to recognize in such thought experiments that any increase in benefits must be paid for either by fewer benefits to others or by increases in taxes. For instance, let's return to our discussion of the treatment of singles, one-earner couples, and two-earner couples and think through the consequences of ending the spouse benefit.

We have already discussed the problems associated with this method of redistributing income to larger families. Ending the spouse benefit would make OASI more actuarially fair. Who would be hurt and who would be helped by such a change? Single persons clearly gain because they are not eligible to receive a spouse benefit, so any reduction in this benefit will in the long-run result in a tax saving to them. One-earner couples are clearly hurt since they are the primary beneficiaries of this benefit, and any tax savings will be less than their loss in benefits. Two-earner couples are likely to gain overall by the change but not every two-earner couple will gain. For couples whose lower earner has a PIA which is equal to or greater than 0.5 of the higher earner's PIA, the spouse benefit is completely irrelevant, but a spouse whose PIA is less than .5 of their spouse's PIA, the spouse benefit does provide additional revenues. On the whole, the tax savings gained by ending the spouse benefit is likely to offset the loss of spouse benefits for most two-earner couples.

Because OASI is a pay-as-you-go system, any change in benefits will immediately be felt in tax savings. However, in the real world it is unlikely that current benefits would be taken away from current recipients or excess taxes returned to the taxpayers. Changing the rules of the game after people have retired is neither fair nor good social policy. Changing the rules for younger people who have time to adjust to the new rules is both fairer and is a better policy. This is especially true because the longer people have to adjust to a policy change before it is enacted; the better able they are to offset its negative consequences to them.

This is a critical point that makes all of our discussion of the redistribution consequences of policies an approximation of the actual consequences of policy change. Most first-order estimates of how a policy change will affect people assume no behavioral change. That is, it is implicitly assumed that people will behave in exactly the same way whether or not the policy exists. It most cases, this assumption can be shown to be false. (See our discussion of the labor supply effects of Social Security rates in chapter 5.) Policy-makers should recognize and plan for behavioral responses to policy changes.

CONCLUSION

This chapter provides a comprehensive overview of the calculation of individual retirement benefits under Social Security by describing the benefit formula and illustrating how different family types receive different levels of benefits. A central part of the chapter is devoted to developing a method of disentangling the insurance and redistributional aspects of OASI. By recognizing the intertemporal period aspect of social insurance programs like OASI one can more coherently evaluate the consequences of any Social Security tax and benefit rule change. Using the methods described in the chapter, the reader can evaluate winners and losers of various types of policy changes. Students are encouraged to consider how they would be affected by some of the policy changes discussed in this chapter. Do you expect to be a winner or loser if the benefit structure is changed? Can you now explain why?

Let us now compare the Social Security systems in other countries (Box 7.4).

DISCUSSION QUESTIONS

Comment on the reasonableness of each of these statements:

1   Social Security's rate of return is inferior to a private insurance system. Therefore, it is an inferior system.
2   Social Security is a fair system for all.
3   In 2000, for every dollar of Social Security taxes paid by Hispanics, Hispanics received $0.95 in Social Security benefits, while for every dollar of Social Security taxes whites paid, whites received $1.02. This is evidence that Social Security disproportionately favors whites.

Box 7.4   *International Comparison: Germany and Japan*

All modern industrialized countries and many developing countries have Social Security systems. Most have the same pay-as-you-go structure and have had to make the same insurance/redistribution trade-offs that have been discussed in this chapter. We briefly examine the Social Security systems of two developed countries and describe their benefit formulas and tax policies.

The Federal Republic of Germany has one of the oldest old-age retirement programs. Like the United States, benefits in Germany are based on the individual earnings record of each worker. The goal of the system is to keep workers at approximately these same levels in the income distributions after retirement as before. Unlike the United States, the German system does not use either a PIA mechanism or the spouse benefit to explicitly redistribute benefits from low to high earners or from one- to two-person households. Nonetheless, the system is not a "pure" insurance system and does contain transfer to "non-contributors."

The German system redistributes income from workers who explicitly contribute to the system to those who do not make annual contributions through the use of "earnings credits." These credits are given to individuals who perform appropriate social tasks such as child rearing, attending school, etc. These credits are then used together with actual earnings on which taxes are paid to calculate benefits. In addition, a survivor benefit is provided to widows that is not available to the estates of single persons. After retirement, benefits are adjusted by a wage index rather than the price index used in the United States.

The Japanese Social Security system is composed of two plans. Virtually, all persons are covered by the National Pension (NP). Self-employed persons and their spouses, unemployed persons, and students are required to make monthly payments of a specified amount of yen each month to earn a month of credited service. At retirement, the pension is determined by multiplying a specific amount of yen times the number of months of coverage. All employees are covered by the Employees' Pension Insurance system (EPI). Workers and their employers pay 17.3 percent of covered earnings (shared equally) as a payroll tax. Annual payments yield years of coverage. At retirement, workers receive a benefit that is equal to 0.7125 times their annual salary times the number of years of coverage. The payroll tax also supports the worker and his or her spouse's participation in the National Pension. Thus, the retired worker would receive an EPI benefit and an NP benefit while the spouse would receive an NP benefit.

A retired worker with a spouse would receive a combined benefit of 50 to 60 percent of average earnings. If the worker dies, the surviving spouse continues to receive their own NP benefit plus the earnings-related EPI survivor's benefit that is 75 percent of the retired worker benefit. Thus, the surviving spouse would receive a total benefit that is approximately 60 percent of the benefit the couple was receiving while both persons were alive. For self-employed persons, the surviving spouse continues to receive only their own NP benefit. Thus benefits decline by approximately 50 percent. No benefits are provided to the estates of single individuals upon their death.

4　On average, African-Americans have shorter life spans than whites. This is evidence that Social Security disproportionately favors whites.

5　Two-earner couples who contribute the same amount into the system over their lifetime as one-earner couples or single people have no reason to complain that they receive less than one-earner couples since both receive more than single people.

6　Consider three groups of Social Security participants – single persons, one-earner couples and two-earner couples. Discuss the distributional consequences on each of these groups of the implementation of the following Social Security system changes (assume Social Security taxes will be raised or lowered to assure sufficient funding):

(a) Ending the spouse benefit.

(b) Ending the survivor benefit.

(c) Instituting a pure individualized account system where each person's taxes are placed in their own personalized account for them to invest as they see fit.

(d) Instituting an actuarially fair system.

(e) Granting gay couples the same legal rights to Social Security benefits as married couples.

Notes

1　Burkhauser and Warlick (1981) first used this methodology on various cohorts of people found in the 1973 Social Security Exact Match File. They showed that all early cohorts of Social Security beneficiaries received benefits in excess of their contribution plus interests but that the returns were projected to fall over time.

2　However, the McCarren–Ferguson Act specifically exempts the private insurance industry from Title VII. For a more detailed discussion of gender issues in pension plan, see Burkhauser (1996).

3　The Greenspan Commission of 1983 set the ground rules for the last great change in the Social Security rules.

References

Altmeyer, Arthur, J. 1968: *The Formative Years of Social Security: A Chronicle of Social Security Legislation and Administration, 1934–1954.* Madison, WI: University of Wisconsin Press.

Anderson, Kathryn H., Burkhauser, Richard V., and Quinn, Joseph F. 1986: Do retirement dreams come true: the effect of unanticipated events on retirement plans. *Industrial and Labor Relations Review* 39 (4) (July): 518–26.

The Annual Statistical Supplement to the Social Security Bulletin (2002) (http://www.ssa.gov/ statistics/supplement/2001/supp01.pdf) Table 3.A.1, p. 134.

Arizona Governing Committee vs. Norris, No. 82–85 slip op. at 1, July 6, US 1983.

Burkhauser, Richard V. 1996: Touching the third rail: time to return the retirement age for early Social Security benefits to 65. *The Gerontologist* 36 (6) (December): 726–7.

Burkhauser, Richard V. and Holden, Karen C. (eds.) 1982: *A Challenge to Social Security: The Changing Roles of Women and Men in American Society.* New York: Academic Press.

Burkhauser, Richard V. and Smeeding, Timothy M. 1994: *Social Security Reform: A Budget Neutral Approach to Reducing Older Women's Disproportionate Risk of Poverty* (Policy Brief). Syracuse, NY: Syracuse University.

Burkhauser, Richard V. and Warlick, Jennifer L. 1981: Disentangling the annuity and redistributive aspects of Social Security in the United States. *Review of Income and Wealth* 27 (December): 401–21.

Los Angeles vs. Manhart, 435 US 702. 1978.

Myers, Robert, J. 1982: Incremental change in Social Security needed to result in equal and fair treatment of men and women. In Richard V. Burkhauser and Karen C. Holden (eds.), *A Challenge to Social Security: The Changing Roles of Women and Men in American Society.* New York: Academic Press: 235–45.

Smolensky, Eugene, Danziger, Sheldon, and Gottschalk, Peter 1988: The declining significance of age in the U.S.: trends in well-being of children and the elderly since 1939. In John M. Palmer, Timothy M. Smeeding, and Barbara Boyle Terrey (eds.), *The Vulnerable.* Washington, DC: Urban Institute Press, 29–53.

Social Security Administration 1975–2002: *Annual Statistical Supplements to the Social Security Bulletin 1975–2002.* Washington, DC: US Government Printing Office.

Steuerle, C. Eugene and Bakija, Jon M. 1994: *Retooling Social Security for the 21st Century.* Washington, DC: Urban Institute Press.

US Census Bureau 2002: Current Population Survey, Annual Demographic Supplement, Poverty and Health Statistics Branch, HHES. (http://www.census.gov/hhes/poverty/histpov/ perindex.html)

William Mercer, Inc, 2002: 2002 Guide to Social Security and Medicare. Louisville. KY: William M. Mercer, Inc.

CHAPTER EIGHT

Social Security Financing and Reform Issues

LEARNING OBJECTIVES

After completing this chapter, you will be able to:

1 Discuss the long-run financial status of Social Security including the growth and depletion of the Trust Fund, the 75-year deficit, and the ultimate tax rate needed to finance the current system.
2 Describe reform proposals presented by various commissions, advisory boards, and other policy-makers.
3 Consider the merits of restructuring Social Security to include individual accounts as a component of the national retirement program.
4 Debate the merits of keeping the current structure but changing benefit calculations in the treatment of low-income workers, women, widows, and spousal benefits.

INTRODUCTION

In chapter 7, we analyzed Social Security from an individual's perspective. In this chapter, we focus on how the old age, survivors and disability components of Social Security are financed and on the long-run financial problems that the program faces, which must be resolved during the next several decades. We will examine various types of reform proposals and discuss a set of criteria that can be used to evaluate them.

FULLY FUNDED VS. PAY-AS-YOU-GO SYSTEMS

Federal legislation requires that private annuity systems must be "fully funded" or if not, be attempting to address their shortage of assets compared to existing liabilities.[1] This requirement is intended to assure that all promises to pay benefits in the future are backed by assets held today. In other words, were future revenues to disappear, the funds currently held in trust would be sufficient to pay all benefits already earned. To insure these promises are kept, the firm must have assets on hand equal to the present value of all its future liabilities.

The 1939 Amendments to the Social Security Act transformed OASI from a fully funded system in which future payments were to be drawn primary from assets generated by prior contributions of individual workers over their working lives.[2] Instead, as discussed in chapter 7, the 1939 Amendments allowed current OASI contributions to be used to pay several generations of OASI beneficiaries lifetime benefits far in excess of what their contributions would have entitled them to in a fully-funded, actuarially fair private annuity system. As table 7.6 in chapter 7 demonstrated, substantial increases in benefits legislated during the 1960s and 1970s allowed even those who had paid into the OASI over their entire working lives to receive greater than actuarially fair benefits. For most current and prior beneficiaries, Social Security has provided and continues to provide more income during their retirement years than their contributions, and those of their employers, would have generated in other similarly safe investments.

However, these decisions to turn Social Security into a "pay-as-you-go" system, in which current receipts were used to "overpay" earlier generations, created a system in which each generation of retirees is now dependent on the next generation of workers to provide the resources for their retirement benefits. In principal, this is a fully functional system because, unlike a private firm, the government has the power to levy the taxes necessary to insure payments to current and future retirees, as it has done in the past. However, as we will see, additional Social Security taxes would be needed to pay currently promised benefits in the future. The projected increases in taxes to sustain the current benefit structure have prompted proposals for other ways of balancing the future cost of Social Security benefits.

To understand the roots of Social Security's long-run financial difficulties, it is useful to more fully discuss how the books are balanced in a pay-as-you-go system.[3]

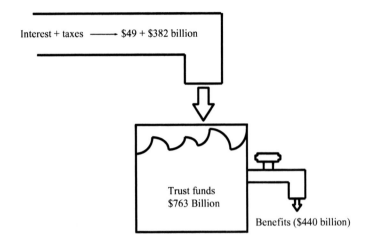

Interest + taxes ⟶ $49 + $382 billion

Trust funds
$763 Billion

Benefits ($440 billion)

Figure 8.1 A Pay-As-You-Go system
Source: Based on Board of Trustee Annual Report 2002 values.

Figure 8.1 shows a water barrel with a faucet at the top and a spigot at the bottom. Social Security revenues (taxes collected and interest paid on current Trust Funds assets) can be viewed as water flowing into the barrel. Benefits can be seen as water leaving the barrel.[4] The Trust Fund is represented by the quantity of water in the barrel at any time. The water entering or leaving the barrel is a flow, denoted in dollars during some time period, like a year. The amount of water in the barrel is a stock of assets, denoted in dollars. When Social Security revenues exceed expenditures in a year, total Trust Funds assets increase, i.e., the water rises. When the reverse is true, the barrel begins to drain. If expenditures exceed revenues for long enough, the barrel will eventually empty as past accumulated surpluses are used to supplement current revenues in order to meet current obligations. Were the Trust Funds to disappear, and if current benefits promised exceeded the tax revenues being generated, Social Security would technically be insolvent and thus, unable to meet its promised obligations in full. Note that this would not imply that Social Security would disappear. Revenues would continue to flow into system but they would be insufficient to pay the promised benefits. Thus, if no additional money were made available to Social Security, benefits would have to be less than what the retirees were promised in that year.

This concept of insolvency, which occurs only when current benefit claims cannot be paid in full, is a far different concept of insolvency from that applied to the private insurance industry. From a private actuarial point of view, insolvency would occur as soon as the assets in the barrel plus anticipated revenues were judged to be insufficient to meet current payments as well as all future promised payments. At that point, the insurance company or retirement plan would have to respond to this shortfall by increasing revenues to the system to maintain a projected balance between revenues and a Trust Fund and expected liabilities. Nonetheless, to understand the financial problems of the current system it is still useful to continue with the single period barrel analogy.

The inflow of revenues and the outflow of benefits are influenced by several demographic factors that were discussed in chapter 2. More formally, Equation 8.1 shows that:

$$
\begin{aligned}
(\text{Trust Funds}) \times &\left(\begin{array}{c} \text{Return on} \\ \text{Trust Funds} \end{array}\right) + \left(\begin{array}{c} \text{Working Age} \\ \text{Population} \end{array}\right) \times \left(\frac{\text{Employed}}{\text{Working Age Population}}\right) \\
&\times \left(\begin{array}{c} \text{Average} \\ \text{Covered Earnings} \end{array}\right) \times \left(\begin{array}{c} \text{Tax} \\ \text{Rate} \end{array}\right) \\
&= \left(\begin{array}{c} \text{Retired} \\ \text{Age Population} \end{array}\right) \times \frac{\text{Beneficiaries}}{\text{Retired Age Population}} \times \left(\begin{array}{c} \text{Average} \\ \text{Benefits} \end{array}\right)
\end{aligned}
$$

$$(8.1)$$

Total revenues flowing into the system depend on two sources. The first, and smaller, is the return earned on Trust Fund assets. The earnings from the investment of funds depends on the size of the Trust Fund and how the funds are invested. Current law requires that all Trust Fund assets be invested in US government bonds, which pay interest to the Social Security system. The second, and the far more important source of revenue, is the OASI taxes paid by the current working age population and their employers. The amount of these revenues depends on the number of workers, the proportion of them who are in OASI-covered employment (which is the vast majority), their average annual covered earnings, and the tax rate paid by them and their employers. Multiplying these factors together and adding them to revenue from the Trust Fund will yield total OASI revenues.[5]

Expenditures are equal to the size of the retirement age population, the percentage of that population that receives OASI benefits, and the average size of that benefit. Multiplying these factors yields total OASI expenditures for the year.

Annual revenues increase over time as the size of the Trust Fund grows, as the return on the Trust Fund assets increase, as the size of the working-age population grows, as the share of the working age population employed in Social Security covered work increases, and as their average covered earnings increase. Yearly expenditures increase as the size of the retirement age population grows, as the share of that population receiving benefits increases and as average benefit increase.

In the early years of the system, growth in the size of the working age population covered by Social Security taxes allowed substantial increases in benefits to be made to a much smaller beneficiary population with no immediate increases in taxes. There were many contributing workers for each retiree. But over the next century, the reverse will occur. The ratio of covered workers per OASDI beneficiary, about 3.4 in 2001, is projected to drop to 3.1 by 2010, and to 2.1 by 2030, when the baby boom cohorts are nearly fully retired. This will require either increases in revenues via Trust Fund earnings or increased tax revenues to maintain the same level of benefits for the growing beneficiary population. As we will see, business cycle effects (e.g., the high growth years of the 1990s) can slow the need for tax increases, if they generate higher taxable wage earnings. This is one reason why the projected year in which the Trust Fund would be depleted was pushed back from 2029 in the 1997 Social Security Trustees Report to 2041 in the 2002 Report. These "year of depletion" projections will continue to change with changing assumptions about the future. What will not change are the long-term demographic forces that are currently adding large surpluses to the Social Security Trust Fund and which will generate even greater projected declines in the Trust Fund as the baby boomers begin to retire.

SOCIAL SECURITY FINANCES

In 2001, Social Security paid out $388 billion in old-age and survivors (OASI) benefits to 39 million retired workers and their dependents and survivors.[6] Total expenditures, including administrative expenses and payments to the Railroad Retirement Fund were $394 billion. During that same year, OASI received over $540 billion in revenues (primarily Social Security taxes on current earnings (85 percent), but also interest from Trust Fund reserves (13 percent) and some income tax receipts on benefits currently paid to high income retirees (2 percent)), generating a net surplus for the year of over $146 billion. This surplus was added to prior surpluses in the OASI Trust Fund. At the end of 2002, OASI Trust Fund assets totaled a record $1.07 trillion.

During the same year, the Social Security Disability program (DI), with nearly 7 million beneficiaries, generated a surplus of $20 billion, with revenues of $87 billion and expenditures of $68 billion. This surplus increased the Disability Trust Fund to $161 billion. Together, the OASI and DI Trust Funds totaled about $1.4 trillion at the beginning of 2003, which is about 2.9 times the total benefit payments estimated for 2003. These Trust Funds are projected to increase to nearly $3.7 trillion by the beginning of 2016, about 4.7 times estimated expenditures during 2016.[7] While these forecasts may sound reassuring from a single period accounting perspective, they mask serious long-run financial problems in the years farther ahead.

The Trustees of Social Security produce an Annual Report each year which documents the current finances of the system and also projects for 75 years (about a lifetime) the annual revenues and expenditures expected, based on current rules.[8] Financial problems emerge in the second half of this time period. Although current revenues substantially exceed current revenues (the barrel is filling), and will continue to do so for two more decades (see below), the flow will be reversed beginning around 2025. Projected expenditures begin to exceed projected revenues as the baby boom cohorts reach traditional retirement age. Ultimately, the Trust Funds – the amount of water accumulating now and in the near future in our barrel – will not be sufficient to offset anticipated shortfalls. This means that there is a long-run unfunded Social Security liability. Adjustments must be made in the system to rectify this underfunding.

When will the Trust Funds run out?

According to the intermediate projections in the 2003 Trustees report, Social Security tax revenues will exceed expenditures until 2018.[9] All OASDI revenues (payroll taxes, income tax receipts and returns on the Trust Fund assets) will exceed expenditures until 2028.[10] Thereafter, given the retirements of the baby boomers, expenditures outpace revenues, and the Trust Funds will be drawn down and eventually exhausted in order to cover the annual shortfalls. According to 2002 estimates, the combined Old-Age, Survivors and Disability Trust Funds would last until about 2042 if we did nothing in the interim. Thereafter revenues would be sufficient to cover only about two-thirds of promised obligations.[11] Note that even in this unfortunate eventuality, Social Security would not disappear and benefit checks stop, since considerable annual revenues would still be forthcoming.

How large is the deficit?

Looking over the entire 75-year projection period, the estimated shortfall in revenues is 1.92 percent of Social Security coverage wage earnings.[12] In other words, an increase of 1 percentage point in the OASDI payroll tax rate paid by both employers and employees (from 6.20 to 7.20 percent for each) would be more than sufficient to eliminate the current 75-year deficit if implemented immediately. This would increase the Social Security tax rate by 16 percent (7.2/6.2 = 1.16). Alternatively, a similar percentage decrease in benefits for all current and future OASDI recipients would balance the system over the next 75 years.

Although a 16 percent increase in Social Security taxes or a 16 percent decrease in benefits would represent a substantial change, it would be a change of a magnitude that has been legislated before.[13] From this perspective, the problem over the next 75 years is a serious but manageable one. However, the longer we wait to implement the tax increases or benefit reductions, the larger the eventual increase in payroll taxes or the decline in benefits must be, since the demographic forces affecting equation 8.1 continue to grow. It should also be noted that benefit reductions for current beneficiaries are highly unlikely. Excluding current beneficiaries and perhaps those on the verge of retirement implies that even large cuts must be imposed on future generations of retirees to close the revenue gap.

While the demographic forces we describe are real, we have seen that the projected date that the Trust Funds will be depleted is subject to substantial variation. As they peer into the future, the Social Security actuaries must make predictions on such variable and fluctuating factors as birth and death rates, marriage and divorce rates, immigration trends, real wage gains, disability incidence, and retirement patterns. Even modest changes in these economic and demographic assumptions can have major consequences when extrapolated out over 75 years. We have already seen that changes in the forecasts of these factors during a six year period have postponed the year of Trust Fund depletion by more than a decade.

Recognizing this, the Social Security Trustees provide two other sets of projections into the future: low-cost and high cost. In the more optimistic (for Social Security finances) low-cost scenario, with lower predicted increases in wage and price levels, a lower average unemployment rate, higher fertility rates and immigration flows, and a lower life expectancy (and this is the optimistic view!), the Trust Funds are never depleted. The ratio of the Trust Funds to annual outlays rises from the current 2.9 to 6.1 in 2019, and remains around 5.0 through 2080. In the high cost-scenario, however, with more pessimistic assumptions about the factor mentioned above, the combined OASDI Trust Fund ratio peaks at 3.6 on 2012, and the Funds are depleted in 2031, more than a decade earlier than in the intermediate scenario.

Some analysts say that the intermediate projections are overly pessimistic, and that they *overestimate* the magnitude of the problems ahead. These critics anticipate greater economic growth than the intermediate assumptions allow, and also argue that the official measure of inflation, the consumer price index, overstates increases in the cost-of-living. In fact, a Presidential Commission charged to study this issue estimated that the CPI overstates true inflation by slightly over 1 percentage point per year.[14] If the inflation numbers used in the Social Security estimates were adjusted down by that amount, about two-thirds of the 75-year deficit would disappear, leaving us with a much more manageable problem. (This would, of course, mean lower nominal benefits for future beneficiaries, but ones more in keeping with the true inflation rate.)

On the other hand, other critics argue that these forecasts *underestimate* the gravity of the situation. They point out that the large annual deficits at the end of the 75-year window equal nearly 7 percent of covered payroll in 2080 under the intermediate estimates. Thus, delaying reform rapidly worsens the long-range forecasting as current surplus years are replaced by years of large deficits as the projection period is extended another year.[15] In other words, even if we did alter taxes or benefits in such a way as to eliminate the current 75-year average deficit, the deficit would reappear the next year, as a new high distant deficit year is added to the calculation. The true long-run deficit, going beyond Social Security's accounting window, is therefore much larger than the 75-year estimates.[16]

In addition, these forecasts do not include the significant Medicare (the H in OASDHI) funding problems (see chapter 10), which are much more imminent, more intractable, and which will soon exceed the OASDI deficits. Although the problems (and potential solutions) facing the Old-Age, Survivors, and Disability programs are very different from those of Medicare, critics argue that it is a mistake to discuss one without the other. What might look like a manageable solution when OASDI is viewed alone (for example, an increase in the combined payroll tax of less than 2 percentage points) might look considerably less so when added to what must be done to rectify Medicare's finances.

A pay-as-you-go system offers tremendous flexibility in the short run (which can and did in fact stretch over many decades) to provide benefits to early recipients far in excess of their contributions into the system. As a society, we chose to do this, and it enabled the within-cohort redistributional transfers from high lifetime earners to low lifetime earners to be more than offset for even the highest-earning contributors in past retirement cohorts. As we saw in chapter 7, Steuerle and Bakija (1994) estimated the net dollar transfer to typical Social Security beneficiaries in various cohorts, defined by family type and gender (single males, single females, and, one- and two-earner couples) at three different wage levels (low, average, and high).[17] Nearly all are net gainers relative to an actuarially fair system; that is, the present value of their benefits exceeds the present value of their and their employers' contributions, had the latter been conservatively invested at a 2 percent real rate of return. Although the net transfer as a percentage of lifetime income tends to be the highest for the low earners, because of the progressive redistributive nature of the program, the absolute dollar amount of the transfer was generally highest for the high earners reaching age 65. All the cohorts were net winners, which is partially responsible for the historic popularity of the Social Security system.

Because of the demographic changes described in chapter 2 – the change in the age structure from a triangular to a rectangular shape, caused both by the number of baby boomers and by increases in life expectancy – the net transfers to recipients are now declining, and for many high earners and some middle-income earners, they have already turned negative (i.e., the expected return on the contributions is less than a 2 percent real return, which is what is assumed for alternative "investments.") These participants can anticipate being net contributors to the system over their lifetimes, which is what is intended in an explicitly redistributional system. In the past, the redistributive nature of the program has been masked by the even larger net transfers from workers to retirees of all income levels. Maintaining universal support for Social Security under the current and future circumstances, in a program with clear net winners and net losers, is more difficult to achieve. As discussed in the context of figure 8.1, demographic forces require policy-makers to raise revenues or reduce or (equivalently) delay benefits to guarantee the long-run financial stability of our Social Security system.

PROPOSED SOLUTIONS TO THE LONG-TERM FINANCING OF OASI

Despite the complexity of much of the discussion about Social Security finances and the myriad proposals for reform, the types of options are surprisingly simple. Because long-run expenditures exceed long-run revenues, either future Social Security revenues must be increased or future benefits decreased (or equivalently, delayed). All reform proposals suggest some combination of these solutions. The proposals differ dramatically on the relative magnitude of revenue increases and benefit decreases and how they are achieved. In addition, the incidence or burden of higher taxes or lower benefits varies greatly across reform proposals. In reviewing reform proposals it is important to distinguish between changes made to eliminate the financial problem and changes made to address other perceived inequities in the current system.

As we will see below, some of the discussion related to Social Security reform has focused on increasing revenues from the first part of the revenue equation – the return on the rapidly growing Trust Fund revenues. In theory, this could occur by allowing the investment of Trust Fund assets in higher yielding instruments, such as corporate equities. Investment in nongovernmental equities and debt is the least revolutionary "privatization" proposal for increasing revenue. This would entail investing Trust Fund assets, while they are available, in private capital markets. Over most long-run periods, such investments have had a higher rate of return than government bonds, in which under current law all Trust Fund assets must currently be invested.

Implementation of this would have no direct effect on the insurance or redistributional components in the current system; rather, if history is an accurate guide, there would just be more money for Social Security to meet its obligations. However, the proposal has the potential of putting what will grow into a many trillion dollar portfolio into the hands of a politically appointed and perhaps politically influenced investment board. This board would be empowered to make investment decisions that could significantly affect the US economy and other economies in which they might or might not choose to invest. Proponents of this approach usually suggest that Social Security would not pick and choose individual assets, but rather purchase a broad passive portfolio of stocks. Opponents question the ability of Congress to remain distant, and fear that agendas other than maximizing Trust Fund returns (given a reasonable level of risk) would become intertwined with these important investment decisions. For example, investment policies might reflect national policies to ostracize certain nations, invest in certain regions of the United States to foster economic development, or avoid certain investments such as tobacco stocks.

A second and much more revolutionary type of privatization proposal would allow some part of the taxes paid by individuals, or additional taxes over and above the current levy, to be placed in individuals' own private accounts. These funds would be owned by and invested by individuals, with varying degrees of discretion. Proponents assume that the individuals' investments would provide more retirement income than the same funds would generate under Social Security benefit rules, especially after the tax increases or benefit decreases needed to rectify the current long-run actuarial imbalance described above.

This would be a revolutionary program design change along several dimensions. First, it would shift at least part of OASDI from a *defined benefit* pension program – one that guarantees a benefit related to past earnings – to a *defined contribution* pension—one that gives the worker greater flexibility in the types of asset held, but which no longer provides a guaranteed benefit in retirement. Such a retirement system would require decisions by workers concerning the choice of assets in their funds, and, in some plans, the amount contributed. Eventual retirement income would then depend on the amount invested and on the future returns on the assets chosen. While defined contribution plans are now common in the private sector and performed well during the growth years of the 1990s, their inclusion in Social Security would lead to much greater variation in retirement income than occurs under the current system, both across individuals and over time, along with the prospect of higher average yields.[18] The historic increase in the stock market in the 1990s followed by the substantial drop in 2001 and 2002 is evidence of the volatility of these market investments.

Second, implementation of substantial privatization would alter the mix of social insurance and income redistribution, both of which are important in the current system. Currently, we have a mandatory system in which the ratio of expected benefits to lifetime contribution declines as lifetime earnings increase. Furthermore, Social Security assumes a certain amount of myopia on the part of participants, acknowledging that everyone does not always make the best decisions for their own lifetime well-being, especially regarding consumption now versus the future. Under privatization, other things equal, there is less redistribution (since none exists in a private defined contribution retirement account), but more individual discretion and potentially a larger pool of retirement income overall.

As we will see below, many privatization proponents do recognize the importance of the redistribution components of the current system, and propose a "two-pillar" system with that in mind. The first pillar tends to provide a defined benefit, which could look like a pared-down version of the current system, with progressive benefits based on one's earnings history, or even a flat rate demogrant, with the same dollar amount for all eligible workers. A second pillar is the privatized component, with individuals allowed some freedom in their choice of assets, based on the level of financial risk they are willing to face.

Our discussion of Social Security reform proposals will focus on the major alternatives that have been proposed to assure long-term financial stability to the US Social Security system and to maintain both its insurance and redistributive goals. In that context, the introduction of private accounts is considered to be a revolutionary change since it would fundamentally change the structure of the current system by introducing a defined contribution component.

Some international comparisons

The adoption of individual accounts would be a revolutionary structural change for the United States, however, many other countries have already established Social Security systems that are partially or completely based on individual accounts. Fox and Palmer (2001) provide a useful taxonomy of Social Security structures throughout the world and show that our defined benefit, mixed insurance and redistributive, partially funded system is only one of many alternatives that could meet both the insurance and redistributive goals of society. More importantly, they show that over the 1990s there has been a substantial movement in other countries away from traditional single-pillar defined benefit partially funded systems toward more mixed systems that include a private account.

Fox and Palmer place Social Security programs into three broad categories:

1   First-pillar plans are large, mandatory, public or quasi-public systems with both intra- and inter-generational redistribution as well as insurance aspects. They can be either defined benefits plans or what they call "notional defined contribution" plans. Similar to defined benefit plans, notional defined contribution plans are financed by taxes on labor earnings. Returns on these contributions are indexed to some measure of economic growth. For example, in Sweden, returns are linked to changes in nominal per capita wages while in Italy, contributions are credited with returns based on the growth of the gross domestic product. The annuity from these "accumulated" contributions is based on current average gender neutral life-expectancy at the age of retirement.[19] These plans can be fully or partially funded, or completely unfunded.

2   Second-pillar plans are fully funded, defined contribution systems in which benefits depend on the assets in individuals' accounts. But these accounts can be centralized and government managed or managed by the individuals. They also include as a separate category "provident funds," which are also individual account plans but all participants are credited with a common return to their account balance.

3   Finally, some countries have adopted Social Security systems that contain both of these pillars although the proportion of benefits achieved from the two pillars varies substantially across countries.

Table 8.1 shows that in 1994, with the exception of Australia, Switzerland and the United Kingdom (all of whom had blended systems), the Social Security systems of all of the OECD countries (including the United States) had only a first-pillar defined benefit component. The same was true of most of the rest of the world. The vast majority of other countries had traditional "provident funds" that are basically pure fully funded private market-based insurance plans. Only Chile had an individual accounts system.

Five years later, another OECD country, Sweden, had adopted a blended system as had four Latin American countries, three Central and Eastern European countries, and two Far Eastern countries. In addition, three more Latin American countries joined the ranks of Chile with only individualized accounts. Several other countries had shifted to notional defined contribution systems. As discussed above, while similar to traditional defined benefit systems, these plans shift some of the "risk" of future demographic change to future retirees by automatically adjusting future yearly benefits to future changes in life expectancy.

The motivation for introducing individualized accounts varied across countries. Fox and Palmer argue that the primary objective of this movement was in the long run to reduce promised benefits of their pay-as-you-go systems that had been inflated by population aging. But the proponents of this change also believed that shifting the management of the funds into the market would result in higher returns, greater transparency (a clearer delineation of the insurance and redistributive components of the system), and greater individual choice.

What also seems clear is that the changes that occurred in the majority of these countries in the 1990s were not as great as those in Chile, which moved from an unfunded defined benefit plan to a fully funded individualized plan. Most countries that moved towards individualized accounts did so while reforming aspects of their defined benefit plan, not abandoning it. This suggests that while the introduction of a second pillar might be revolutionary with respect to structure, it need not be so with respect to the fundamental commitment of a Social Security program to preserve both its insurance and redistributive goals within a long-term financially secure system. This suggests that it is important to focus on what the ultimate consequences of any proposed change in Social Security policy would be on the insurance and distribution goals, rather than to simply focus on the structure changes proposed to achieve them.

SOME SPECIFIC REFORM PROPOSALS

Many specific proposals have been forwarded in the name of Social Security reform, and we now review some prototype plans for modifying Social Security to address the long-run financing problems. These proposals range from modest tweaking of the parameters of the current system to a bail-out of Social Security by using general funds, and to a total restructuring of the system. Any of these approaches could be used to solve the long-term (75-year, or beyond) financial shortcomings of the current system. The question is which is best for the workers and retirees of the future and what types of modification are consistent with the overall objectives of this retirement program.

President Clinton appointed the 1994–96 Social Security Advisory Council and gave it the task of developing a plan to recommend changes in Social Security that would restore its financial balance. The Council failed to reach a consensus on a strategy to address the financial imbalance of the current system. Instead, three reform proposals were presented by different factions within the Council. A fourth was proposed by the Clinton/Gore administration itself. Since the Council issued its report, several others have been made and the proponents of the three Council recommendations have amended their proposals in response to criticisms. In 2001, President George W. Bush appointed another commission to propose changes in Social Security consistent with his views. Together, these five reform proposals provide a good selection of options from across the political and philosophical spectra for reforming Social Security.

Before the Social Security Administration became a separate administrative unit, Social Security Advisory Councils were typically appointed every four years by the Secretary of Health and Human Services. These councils were asked to address some aspect of Social Security and make specific recommendations for change. The focus of the 1994–96 Council was the long-range finances of OASDI. The members generally agreed on the magnitude and timing of the deficit, but they disagreed vociferously on the best response. Rather than present a single consensus position, as prior Councils usually did, the members outlined three very different approaches, all of which dealt with the 75-year deficit.[20] Two maintained the current basic

Table 8.1 National pension system architecture, 1994 and 1999

Year	First-pillar only		Second-pillar only		
	DB	NDC	Provident fund	Individual accounts	Blend
1994	OECD (rest) Latin America Central and Eastern Europe and Former Soviet Union (FSU) (most) Middle East and North Africa, Africa (most) Cambodia, China, Rep. of Korea, Laos PDR, Philippines, Vietnam, Malaysia (public), Indonesia (public)		Gambia, Kenya, Tanzania, Uganda, Zambia Asian Islands, Papua New Guinea, Singapore, Malaysia, Indonesia	Chile	Australia, Switzerland, United Kingdom

India (public)		Brunei, Thailand, India, Nepal, Sri Lanka		
Sri Lanka (public)				
1999 OECD (rest)	Italy			Australia, Switzerland, United Kingdom
Latin America (rest)			Bolivia, Chile, El Salvador, Mexico	Argentina, Colombia, Peru, Uruguay
Central and Eastern Europe and FSU (rest)	Kyrgyz Rep.	Kazakhstan		Croatia, Hungary, Latvia, Poland
Africa (most)	Gambia, Kenya, Tanzania, Uganda, Zambia			
Cambodia, Korea, Laos, Philippines, Vietnam	China, Mongolia	Asian Islands, Papua, New Guinea, Singapore		
Indonesia (public)		Indonesia, Malaysia		
Malaysia (public)				Hong Kong (PRC), Thailand
Sri Lanka (public)		Nepal, Sri Lanka	India	

Source: Fox and Palmer (2001), table 3.1, p. 93.

structure of Social Security; two proposed blended two-pillar systems containing a mandatory individual retirement account (privatization) for all workers, and all three proposed utilizing private capital markets for the first time.

First, the most traditional approach was represented by the *Maintenance of Benefits* plan, which would simply raise the revenues needed to finance the benefits that have been promised under current rules. It proposed no major new benefit cuts, but rather generated new revenues in a number of ways; for example, by the additional federal income taxation of most Social Security benefits (all but the employee's initial contributions would be taxable income when the benefits are paid), by mandating the inclusion of all new state and local employees in the Social Security system, and by proposing a 1.6 percentage point increase in the total employer–employee payroll tax, but not for about 50 years. Small benefit reductions would follow from increasing the number of years used to calculate AIME from 35 to 38.

These changes were not sufficient to eliminate the 75-year funding gap. Thus, to address the remaining shortfall the proponents of this plan proposed to study the investment of some of the Social Security Trust Funds in the private equities markets in order to increase the return on these rapidly accumulating assets. With the exception of this last component, this is the traditional approach, to raise revenues to meet the obligations under current law. Even with the investment of Trust Fund assets in private equities, this plan did not address the on-going budget shortfall after the 75-year projection period. During the past few years, the authors of this plan have presented additional ways of increasing revenues and making marginal changes in the benefit structure in order to more fully eliminate the funding shortfall. In a real sense, this plan and others like it propose to eliminate the financial shortfall through minor reductions in benefits accompanied by whatever tax increases are necessary to generate the required income to pay promised benefits while maintaining the basic structure of the current Social Security system.

Second, an alternative to the traditional approach was the *Individual Accounts* plan. Compared to the Maintenance of Benefits plan, it proposes smaller revenue increases (for example, there is no future increase in the payroll tax rate needed) and larger benefit decreases (mostly for future middle- and upper-income recipients) to close the funding gap. This plan would also increase the normal retirement age to 67 more quickly than is currently legislated, after which it would be indexed to changes in longevity, which is estimated to add about one month to the normal retirement age every two years.[21] This part of the Individual Accounts plan can be summarized as reducing promised benefits sufficiently to eliminate the financial shortfall while holding taxes constant. The basic benefit structure of Social Security is maintained but benefits are substantially reduced.

To compensate for the lower benefits that would accrue under the proposed benefit formula, this plan recommended an immediate *additional* mandatory payroll contribution of 1.6 percent of covered payroll that would go into an Individual Account. These accounts would be administered by the Social Security Administration, over which the contributor would have some limited discretion (e.g., choice among a small number of mutual funds.) This is a new concept for Social

Security – a real account owned by the contributor, with a balance reflecting that individual's investment choices. At or after age 62, the individual could tap the assets in this account, but only by purchasing a monthly annuity provided by the Government. In this sense, even the new component resembles the current system, since beneficiaries could not access these funds in a lump sum, and one could not out-live the annuity. As discussed in table 8.1, two-pillar systems of this type have been adopted by several other countries. In fact, Sweden added just such a mandatory two-percentage point individualized account to their defined benefit first pillar in the 1990s.

Third, the more revolutionary proposal to come out of the Advisory Council was the *Personal Security Account* plan. Although this plan included some of the features of the other two proposals (e.g., the additional federal income taxation of Social Security benefits, the inclusion of new state and local employees, and the acceleration of the normal retirement age and then its indexation to longevity), it also envisioned more fundamental change in the structure of Social Security. The plan proposed to continue survivors and dependants programs (which utilize about 2.4 of the 12.4 percent combined payroll tax) and divide the remaining ten percentage points in half to create an explicit two-pillar system. The first pillar would provide a flat-rate benefit for all those fully insured, independent of one's earnings history.[22]

The other five points would be used to create a mandatory retirement account. In contrast to the Individual Accounts plan, these funds would be controlled entirely by the individual, like the Keogh or Individual Retirement Accounts that already exist, outside of Social Security but within some broad regulatory structure. Note that the funds here (the 5 percent) are being *carved out* of the existing Social Security tax, rather than being added to it. Like the more modest Individual Accounts plan, this would create a (large, in this case) defined contribution component whose eventual value would depend on the choice and performance of the individual investments. At or after age 62, the proceeds could be taken out in a lump-sum (unlike in the Individual Account plan) or used to purchase an annuity.

Because of the diversion of 5 percentage points from Social Security's already inadequate future revenue stream, additional funds would be required to finance future Social Security obligations, even with the decline in the defined benefit payments proposed. The Personal Security Account plan envisioned transitional borrowing by Social Security from the federal government. This loan would be repaid with the proceeds of an additional payroll tax of about 1.5 percent of covered earnings over about 70 years. This two pillar plan would have had important effects on the way benefits were distributed. It is less clear how much it would have actually affected the balance of insurance and redistributive components of the current system.

This plan explicitly acknowledges the long-run unfunded liabilities of Social Security. When matured after 75 years, this would be a fully funded plan and there would be no outstanding liabilities. Revisions of this plan have eliminated the transitional tax and replaced it with permanent mandatory contributions to individual accounts. The revised plans leave more money for the payment of the flat benefit. This plan solves the long-run funding problem by dramatically altering the structure of Social Security to rely to a substantial degree on individual accounts.

Fourth, the *Clinton Administration plan* added a fourth alternative by proposing something not seriously considered since the early days of Social Security – the allocation of general revenues (a proportion of the future surpluses forecast during the Clinton Administration) to finance Social Security expenditures.[23] Some of these funds could be invested for Social Security in the private equities markets, and the rest would be used to retire existing government debt (i.e., to purchase back government bonds from the public.) Although many analysts would consider this good for the economy, lowering interest rates and thereby encouraging investment, these bond purchases would have no direct impact on Social Security finances.

The core of the Clinton/Gore plan was to give government securities to the Social Security administration, in addition to those purchased with past and future Trust Fund surpluses. These bonds would be redeemed in the future when Social Security revenues no longer fully support expenditures. Were this done, Social Security finances would certainly look better, because they would own these new assets that they did not have before. To some, this appears to be simply an accounting gimmick, since nothing is being pre-paid with the bond transfers (in contrast to the equities purchases.) The strategy delays dealing with the deficits until they arise, at which time Social Security begins to redeem its expanded stock of government bonds. At that point, the government would have to raise taxes, lower other expenditures, or refinance the debt by selling equivalent amounts to the public.

On the other hand, these future Social Security obligations *are* government liabilities, unless the benefit rules are changed. As described earlier in this chapter, they would appear on a corporate balance sheet, but they do not appear in federal government finances, which focuses on year-by-year cash flows, not future obligations. The issuing of this debt would make *explicit* an obligation that is currently implicit and therefore largely invisible. One might just as well argue that the accounting gimmick is *not* to recognize these future obligations explicitly, as this plan would do. Note that when the bonds are redeemed, the funds, if generated by taxes, would come from general tax revenues, not from the Social Security payroll tax. Personal and corporate income taxes are more progressive forms of taxation than is the payroll tax on which Social Security currently depends.

The essence of this plan is to retain the current benefit structure and eliminate the shortfall in revenues through the use of higher taxes. However, in this case, the additional revenues would come from general revenues and not the payroll tax that has been the primary source of revenues to Social Security. Many countries already use general revenues to partially support their Social Security systems. As noted above, partial reliance on income taxes has different distributional effects compared to complete reliance on the payroll tax.

Finally, more recently, in the *Bush Administration plan*, President George W. Bush created an advisory Commission to improve the fiscal sustainability of Social Security, while adhering to six principles.[24] The President required that reforms could not change the benefits of current or near-retirees, could not raise Social Security payroll taxes and could not directly invest Social Security funds in the stock market. In addition, they had to preserve the disability and survivors' components of Social Security, dedicate all of the Social Security surpluses to Social Security only, and had to include voluntary, individually controlled personal retirement accounts.

Although the Commission proposed three plans, the philosophy of the group is well represented by their second plan, which would establish voluntary personal accounts without any additional taxes from employers or employees.[25] This plan, which is more fully described in Cogan and Mitchell (2003), tackled the long-run funding problem in two ways. The first and most important was to reduce the payroll tax shortfall between long-term Social Security revenues and expenditures (averaging about 2 percent of covered payroll over the next 75 years) by shifting the calculation of an individual's average indexed monthly earnings (AIME) from a wage-based to a price-based index. In other words, past earnings would be inflated to present dollars using an index of *price* changes rather that the higher index of *wage* changes, as is currently done. This change would eliminate Social Security long-term liability of payroll and create a *surplus* of about 0.20 percent of payroll over the 75-year evaluation period. The change would not begin until 2009 so that inflation-adjusted benefits received by future retirees would still be slightly higher than those received by workers who retired in 2001, the last year of their evaluation.

This proposed change satisfies President Bush's requirement that no current or near-retirees lose benefits. However, it does so, only in the sense that real benefits to new beneficiaries will not decline. In fact, this change would profoundly reduce social security liabilities by holding real Social Security benefits near their current levels (other things being equal) as real wages grow over time. Future beneficiaries will receive much lower real benefits than those promised under current law and its wage-based AIME. Hence, the replacement rates for all future beneficiaries will decline.

The Commission also proposed to use the additional funds made available from this general reduction in future promised benefits (0.20 percent of payroll) to increase the benefits of vulnerable groups, such as low-wage workers and widows of deceased low-wage workers. The proposal would provide a guaranteed minimum benefit of 120 percent of the poverty threshold for long-term (at least 30 years) contributors to the first-pillar system. The result of these two changes is a significantly smaller first-pillar system than the one currently promised, but one that is more redistributive.

It is interesting to note that this part of the reform package (the price indexing of past wages) is the key to reducing the long-term financial problems of the system, yet it has received far less scrutiny than the Commission's other major proposal – the individualized accounts.

The Commission opted to add a second pillar to the smaller but more progressive defined benefit first pillar discussed above. This second pillar would consist of pure insurance-based individualized accounts. Both pillars would be fully funded. Workers would be allowed, but not required, to allocate up to 4 percentage points of their payroll taxes (to a maximum of $1,000, later indexed by the rate of average wage growth) to a personal account.

In exchange for their reduced contributions to the Social Security system, their future traditional Social Security benefits would be actuarially decreased by the amount of the allocation to the personal account, compounded at a real interest rate (that is, over the rate of inflation) of 2 percent.[26] In other words, participants would be trading off a decline in their traditional benefits for the proceeds of a new individual retirement account, financed by a part of their current contributions. If the retirement account grows at more than 2 percent above the rate of inflation, the recipient will be better off with the account than without.[27] Although the proposal forecasts a positive cash flow for Social Security at the end of the 75-year accounting period and forever more (in contrast to the forecasts of the current system), it requires transfers from general revenues during the period 2025 through 2054.[28]

This Commission's proposal offers another method of reducing future benefits compared to those specified in current law while holding the tax rate constant. It then offers individuals the opportunity to establish individual accounts without higher contributions but at the expense of a lower traditional Social Security benefit.

These five plans illustrate the range of options that are being considered to eliminate the long-term gap in Social Security revenues. Equation 8.1 clearly shows that given the demographic changes that are expected to occur, benefits must be reduced or taxes raised. In general, the Maintain Benefits Plan and the Clinton/Gore Plan argue for retaining the current benefit structure as well as the level of currently promised benefits. The financing gap is closed by higher taxes. The Maintain Benefit plan would use higher payroll taxes while the Clinton/Gore plan uses monies from the general fund. The Individual Accounts plan and the recommendation of the Bush Commission attempt to solve the funding problem by maintaining the basic structure of Social Security but substantially reducing future benefits while holding the payroll tax rate constant. The Individual Accounts plan has a mandatory additional contribution that would go into an individual account while the Bush Commission plan would allow voluntary individual accounts that would further reduce the benefits for future retirees. The policy choices are starkly revealed by these plans: maintain benefits and increase taxes or cut benefits and maintain the tax rate.

The Personal Security Accounts and to a certain extent the Individual Accounts plan and the Bush Commission plan also propose a fundamental change in Social Security through the introduction of individual accounts. As our discussion throughout this chapter has shown, changes in the benefit structure, allowing investment of the Trust Fund assets in private equities, or the introduction of individual accounts can be considered separately from the need to resolve the funding gap or in conjunction with financial reforms.

All these proposals are feasible. The unfunded liabilities over the next 75 years are moderate enough, relative to covered payroll, that tax increases, benefit decreases or some combination of both could eliminate this problem for 75 years without major structural changes. Despite some serious transition problems, the more revolutionary privatization reform plans could also work, and move us, in principle, toward a fully funded system that would solve the problem forever. What is true of all the plans is that the longer we wait to implement them, the greater the increases in taxes or reductions in benefits must be to solve the financial problems that lie ahead.

CRITERIA FOR SOCIAL SECURITY REFORM

The Social Security system is a complex institution that plays many roles simultaneously (Quinn, 1999). Certain aspects resemble a *savings* program, like a bank account or a pension, because it reallocates income over time, collecting contributions during working years and then distributing benefits during retirement. But Social Security also has *insurance* components, since it replaces some of the earnings lost following the disability or death of a covered worker, tempering the decline in the family's economic well-being. Finally, the Social Security system is a very important *income redistribution* program. Its progressive benefit structure transfers income from participants with high lifetime earnings to those with low earnings histories. Of all the federal transfer programs, it is the only one that explicitly bases the transfer on a *lifetime* measure of economic status – average earnings over most of an individual's working life.[29]

These multiple roles create multiple goals for Social Security, and therefore multiple evaluation criteria. The insurance and income redistribution roles suggest that *income adequacy* should be a primary concern. Are the benefits sufficient for recipients to maintain some minimum standard of living in old age? The savings component, on the other hand, suggests that we also consider *individual equity*. What is the relationship between what a worker (and employer) contributes to the system and what that individual can expect to receive in the future? Is Social Security a good investment?

The magnitude of the Social Security system suggests that it might also have macroeconomic effects. If it affects the labor supply or savings behavior of individuals, or the actions of firms or the government, it may influence the rate of *economic growth* of the economy. Since future retirees will not be consuming Social Security checks or Trust Fund reserves, but rather the goods and services actually being produced during their retirement years, the productive capacity of the economy in the future will be a primary determinant of the economic well-being of future workers and retirees alike.[30]

Other important considerations include the administrative costs of proposed reforms, their impact on public confidence in the program, and the complexity and ease of transition of reform. One must also consider the complicated effects of reform on other sources of retirement income – employer pension benefits, asset income and earnings. Finally, it is important to consider the impact of changing a program as long-lived and important as Social Security on social cohesiveness.

Income adequacy

The Social Security system grew out of the nation's experiences during the Great Depression, when unemployment, poverty, and income insecurity were widespread.[31] The Social Security program was developed with both insurance and redistributional components. A primary goal was to assist in the provision of income security in retirement without the stigma of a public assistance or welfare system. One had to contribute to the program in order to receive benefits, and the benefits were therefore viewed as an earned right rather than as public charity.

Without Social Security benefits, many more older Americans would (and did) enter their retirement years without adequate income. Some of these at-risk citizens have lived in or near poverty all their lives, with irregular work histories and without pension coverage. Because of their low earnings, many have been unable to save on their own. Others have been myopic, and have either refused to consider the savings needed to support consumption in retirement or miscalculating what would be required. Others may have had bad luck in the choice of a profession or a geographic locale, or been hampered by limited personal endowments. Social insurance is designed to dampen the economic implications of such unfortunate circumstances.

Although Social Security was not designed to be a sole source of support for older Americans, income adequacy remains the primary and most important criterion by which to judge the success of the program. Income adequacy can be measured in at least two ways – relative to one's prior income (for example, what proportion of pre-retirement earnings does Social Security replace?) or relative to some absolute measure of need, like a poverty threshold. One of the program's greatest accomplishments was the dramatic reduction in elderly poverty, from about 30 percent of those aged 65 and over (and twice the national average) in 1967, to half that rate only seven years later, following large increases in real Social Security benefits beginning in the late 1960s and early 1970s. This decline in elderly poverty occurred during a time when Americans were retiring earlier and earlier, making the dramatic increases in economic well-being all the more remarkable. Since 1982, the elderly poverty rate has been below that of the rest of the population, and Social Security is an important reason for this.

Neither a replacement rate nor a poverty index is a perfect measure of income adequacy. A replacement rate is static in nature. It compares retirement income in the first year of retirement to earnings the year before, and ignores changes thereafter. Depending on whether or not income sources are indexed to inflation, a given initial replacement rate could be associated with very different levels of economic well-being later on.

The American poverty thresholds are an absolute measure, based on the cost of a particular basket of consumption goods. Although the cost of the basket is adjusted for price changes, the market basket itself is not adjusted for the changes in the overall standard-of-living that occur over time as real incomes in society rise. In other words, the American concept of poverty adjusts for the cost-of-living but not for the standard-of-living. Nonetheless, both the replacement rate and the poverty rate are useful summary statistics. The latter has the advantage of focusing attention on those at the lower end of the income distribution, those most dependent on Social Security benefits in retirement.

A closely related issue is that of risk – who will bear the risk if economic forecasts turn out to be inaccurate, as they undoubtedly will? What if the equities markets or the economy do not perform as they have (on average) in the past? In a defined benefit plan, the risk falls primarily on whoever promised the benefit, e.g., the government, for Social Security, or the firm sponsoring an employer pension plan. In a defined contribution plan, in contrast, the financial risk falls on the individual.

Individual equity

Whereas income adequacy is one goal for evaluating a Social Security program, individual equity is another. This criterion focuses on the relationship between an individual's total contributions to the system (the payroll tax paid by the employee and employer) and the total benefits that that same individual (and related beneficiaries) is likely to receive in return. From the start, Social Security has emphasized that it was not simply a redistributive welfare program but one in which benefits were related to contributions.

Historically, criticism of Social Security on individual equity has not been an important part of the Social Security debate. One reason, as discussed above, is that before the system matured, all could expect to receive more in retirement benefit than what their (and their employers') contributions would have produced had the funds been invested in similarly safe investments. Favorable demographics – the triangular age distribution and the high ratio of Social Security contributors to beneficiaries – coupled with significant real wage growth permitted generous benefits to retirees without undue burden on workers and employers.[32] Because of the progressive nature and the gender neutrality of the benefit structure, the "rate of return" varied with income level (it is higher the lower one's average lifetime earnings) and gender (since women live longer than men) (see chapter 7). [33] But Social Security was a great deal – a great investment, in today's parlance – for all types of current and prior retirees, and therefore individual equity was not a bone of contention.

But this will not be the case for current cohorts of contributors. Because of the aging of the population and the subsequent decline in the ratio of Social Security contributors to recipients, rates of return from Social Security are falling, and for most high-wage workers, will drop below what alternative uses of the funds might generate. Too many younger workers, therefore, participation in the Social Security system no longer looks like a good "investment." Despite the fact that Social Security was not designed as a pure investment, it is not surprising, given the size of today's payroll tax contributions, that "money's worth" calculations are now part of the reform debate and that they have engendered some adverse reactions to the traditionally popular Social Security system.[34]

The comparison here is between expected lifetime Social Security contributions and expected benefits, and the goal is a closer relation between the two. According to this individual equity criterion, as the system fails to yield a normal return based on individual contribution, the system becomes less of an actuarially fair insurance system and the payroll tax is seen as just another tax to be avoided.

Economic growth

Social Security expenditures are the largest single item in the federal budget. In 2001, Social Security outlays, excluding Medicare, totaled $439 billion, nearly a quarter of all federal government expenditures, and over 4 percent of gross domestic product. Changes in a program of this magnitude can have macroeconomic effects and may influence the state of the economy.

As mentioned above, economic growth is key to the Social Security reform debate because the consumption of future retirees will come from the goods and services being produced at that time. Social Security benefits and other retirement income sources will provide a claim on future output. Much of the discussion about Social Security reform focuses on the distribution of future output – the share that retirees will or should have. As important as the share of the pie, however, is the size of pie being shared.

There are two primary ways in which the Social Security program can affect economic growth, through its influence on individual work decisions and through its impact on aggregate national saving.

1 *Individual work decisions.* The Social Security system can affect labor supply decisions both during the work life and, more importantly, during typical retirement ages. To the extent that participation in the system increases the lifetime wealth of participants, as it has for current and previous cohorts of retirees, it should increase the consumption of all normal goods, including leisure. Much of this increased leisure has been taken late in life, in the form of earlier retirement (see chapter 5). Research suggests that increases in Social Security wealth may be responsible for about one-third of the post-war decline in elderly labor force participation rates.[35]

   But Social Security taxes and benefits also affect the net wage rate earned by current workers. To the extent that employees view their mandatory OASDI contribution as a tax, it lowers the marginal wage rate for those earning below the maximum taxable earnings.[36] This could have a distortionary effect on labor supply, although evidence suggests that it is a small one, at least for primary workers (Council of Economic Advisors, 1997: 115). Once one is eligible for Social Security benefits, however, the incentives get more complicated. Between ages 62 and 65, earnings over the exempt amount have two offsetting effects.

They decrease current benefits because of the earnings test (and benefits are reduced to zero, if earnings are high enough), but they also increase the future benefits. Depending on one's life expectancy and other factors, the net result could be an increase or a decrease in expected total Social Security benefits. One's true compensation during the year of work includes both the paycheck and the change (the increase or decrease) in lifetime Social Security benefits. If the total amount of expected lifetime Social Security benefits declines with additional work, then Social Security acts as a tax, equivalent to a pay cut. To the extent that additional work provides both a paycheck and an increase in lifetime benefits, Social Security acts as a subsidy, and increases true compensation. Considerable research has shown that workers do respond to these incentives, and that they are more likely to leave a job and often the labor force as well, the stronger the retirement incentives (the implicit pay cuts) they face.[37]

Reform proposals that either tighten the relationship between contributions and benefits or make the benefit calculation rules at retirement more age-neutral will reduce the labor market distortions of the system.

2 *Individual consumption-saving decisions.* Social Security rules can also influence the allocation of income between consumption and saving. Many analysts believe that Americans save too little to maintain consumption levels after retirement. Americans save less than they used to, and less than the citizens of many other industrialized countries.[38]

Economic theory and common sense suggest that the provision of retirement income through public (Social Security) or private (employer pensions) mechanisms should affect the amount of saving that individuals will do on their own for retirement. The higher the Social Security or employer pension benefits promised or the level of private saving mandated (for example, through a mandatory individual retirement account plan, as seen in several Social Security reform proposals), other things being equal, the less one has to save through other means to maintain a given standard of living. But other things may not be equal. Retirement decisions are affected by the generosity of Social Security benefits, which creates an offsetting effect. An increase in benefits and therefore an earlier planned labor market exit could induce an *increase* in private saving to finance the additional years of retirement (Council of Economic Advisors, 1997: 109).

The theoretical effect of the Social Security system on private saving is ambiguous, as are the findings in the empirical literature.[39] This same ambiguity is found in the related literature on the impact of government savings incentives, such as favorable IRA and 401(k) tax provisions, on net private savings. Some authors find considerable net new saving, while others, sometimes analyzing the same data, find that the saving in these vehicles is just a re-allocation of saving that would have occurred in other forms.[40] In a recent Congressional Budget Office study, the majority of the cross-sectional empirical articles surveyed found that increases in Social Security wealth do have a negative impact on private savings.[41]

Regardless of the difficulty of calculating the exact effect, the impact of proposed Social Security reforms on the private saving decisions is an important evaluation criterion, because this will influence the amount of asset income that individuals can rely on in retirement, the amount of capital accumulation in the nation (see below) and therefore the future productive capacity of the economy at large.

Aggregate national saving

Private saving by individuals is only one part of aggregate saving. Another key component is federal government saving, through the Social Security program directly and through the rest of the federal budget.[42] The Social Security system is currently running large surpluses. In 2001, an OASDI surplus of over $140 billion was added to Trust Fund reserves. This lowered the official federal government deficit by the same amount. Assets in the OASDI Trust Funds are projected to increase to $7.2 trillion by 2027, and then fall, according to the intermediate forecasts of the Social Security Trustees (Board of Trustees Annual Report, 2002).

Social Security reform could change government saving in two ways. First, modifications could directly affect the revenue or expenditure stream of Social Security and, second, changes could indirectly affect other government decisions. For example, reform proposals that reduce Social Security surpluses (e.g., by diverting some of the revenue stream into mandatory individual savings accounts) would increase the measured government deficit. How would the federal government respond to the increased deficit? Would Congress attempt to maintain the current budget path by reducing spending or raising other taxes to replace the diverted revenue stream? If so, this would represent an increase in aggregate savings. Or would Congress slow the time path to budget balance, by maintaining current expenditure and taxation plans and borrowing the diverted funds from the market (from the individuals themselves) rather than from the Social Security Trust Funds? In the latter case, the measured increase in private saving (the new savings accounts) would be offset by the increase in government dissaving, and national saving would remain unchanged.[43]

Forecasts of this type are extremely difficult, because they require predictions of future Congressional behavior. Nonetheless, they should be included in the discussion, because the behavioral decisions made could have significant effects on aggregate national saving and therefore on future economic growth.

CONCLUSION

Using the criteria discussed above, one can discuss the types of policy options proposed to close the long-run financial gap between anticipated Social Security revenues and expenditures.

First, *benefit decreases versus revenue increases.* Closing the fiscal imbalance with additional revenues rather than benefit decreases would increase the size of the

Social Security program by further shifting funds from workers to retirees. Increasing Social Security revenues would increase (or least not decrease) the level of the Social Security safety net (income adequacy), but at the cost of higher taxes and less consumption at younger ages. While this would improve single period measures of poverty at older ages and reduce income fluctuations due to old age, death, or disability and strengthen the financial integrity of the system, a larger program (especially if funded by larger payroll taxes) would further increase the risk of reduced work and savings, hampering economic growth.

Closing the fiscal imbalance with benefit decreases rather than additional revenues would decrease the size of the program by reducing the funds that are shifted from workers to retirees. But current workers would eventually receive these lower benefits. Lower Social Security benefits would reduce the social security safety net at older ages but would also lower taxes (or at least not increase them) and allow more consumption at younger ages. This could worsen single period measures of poverty at older ages and increase income fluctuations due to old age, death, or disability. But a smaller program would reduce the risk of reduced work and savings.

As discussed above and in chapter 5, OASI benefits and the incentives they include can induce older workers to leave the labor force earlier than they otherwise would. A smaller program that provides lower benefits, especially if combined with an increase in the early age of retirement, is likely to reduce this effect. In addition, payroll taxes may discourage work at younger ages, a labor market distortion that is more likely to decline if the OASI system is reduced in size via benefit cuts rather than increased in size via payroll tax increases.

Second, *alternative types of benefit decreases.* Benefit decreases can come in various forms, from across-the-board declines to decreases that fall disproportionately on high-income retirees. Or they can come from delaying the early or normal retirement age of future beneficiaries, reducing future cost-of-living adjustments, increasing the taxability of benefits, or means-testing the benefits of current and future retirees.

The least harmful benefit decreases from an equity viewpoint would be ones that fell on those most able to adjust to them, either because they have both more time to adjust (i.e., are not on the threshold of retirement) and/or had more financial resources to draw upon (i.e., the wealthy). That suggests that most benefit reductions should be targeted on future rather than on current or near-beneficiaries. Not only is the current working age population younger, with more time to adjust to future benefit declines, but they will have longer life expectancies, be healthier, and be better able to continue to work at older ages than past generations. Hence, retirement income lost via increasing the early and normal retirement ages can be made up by increased work before retirement by future aged cohorts. Reducing the benefits of current retirees is much less likely to be made up by increased work.

Future benefits could be lowered more gradually via adjustments in the calculation of average indexed monthly earnings (as the Bush Commission suggests) or through adjustments to price increases in the cost-of-living adjustment formula (as the Boskin Commission findings would suggest). Such changes would also disproportionately fall on younger cohorts, since in the long run this would provide lower replacement rates. But altering the inflation adjustment would also impact current retirees who would see declines, relative to the current rules, in their future benefits. Because Social Security plays such a large part in the income of older persons in the bottom half of the income distribution, even these gradual changes in benefits could have significant effects on their economic well being.

Third, *alternative types of revenue increases.* Revenue increases can also come in many forms, from a simple increase in the payroll tax rate to raising the earnings limit on which payroll taxes are paid, or simply by adding general revenues into the Social Security Trust Fund. Raising the payroll tax rate is the most direct and traditional means of increasing revenues. Unlike raising the earnings maximum, it would have no direct impact on the size of future benefits. In contrast, some of the increase in revenues caused by raising the earnings maximum would lead to increases in average indexed monthly earnings, and hence future benefits. Because of this partial benefit offset, this would not be as effective a means of increasing net revenues into the system.

Moving to general revenue financing would be a major break from the traditional link between payroll taxes and benefits based on those earnings. However, general revenues are a much more effective method of taxation for pure welfare programs that have no *quid pro quo.* In the event that Social Security moved to a more explicit two-pillar system where the first pillar was the same for all and the second pillar was a privatized system, using general revenues to fund the first-pillar benefits might make sense.

Finally, *the timing of reform.* A pay-as-you-go system has the disadvantage of not forcing change via "insolvency" until the Trust Funds run out, at which time the changes necessary to correct the long term financing problems would be enormous. If we wait for decades to legislate changes in future revenues or expenditures, it will require enormous tax increases or benefit reductions to close the gap. Much less onerous measures could bring Social Security into long-run financial stability if we act promptly. Prompt action also permits some time lag between the legislation and implementation, permitting those affected time to adjust their work and savings behavior to the new environment. For example, if we decide to offset the increased expenditures caused by greater longevity by raising the early (age 62) and normal (already legislated to increase from 65 to 67) retirement ages, it is important to announce such changes well in advance of their actual implementation so that changes in retirement plans need not be made abruptly. The long lead time between now and the potential insolvency of Social Security permits society to debate the options, as we already are, and choose the reform package that best balances the complex goals of the Social Security system.

DISCUSSION QUESTIONS

Comment on the reasonableness of each of these statements:

1   The OASI Trust Fund will not be fully depleted for about four decades. Therefore there is no need to worry about the Social Security system going bankrupt until then.

2   The introduction of individualized accounts into Social Security would disproportionately help high-wage earners at the expense of low-wage earners.

3   No system can achieve both the insurance and redistributive goals of our current Social Security system and contain individualized accounts.

4   Program reforms that maintain benefits and raise taxes are to be preferred to those that cut benefits and keep taxes the same since the former provide greater protection to older persons.

5   Two-pillar Social Security systems that clearly separate the income adequacy (redistributive) and individual equity (insurance) goals of Social Security are preferred to single-pillar systems which combines these two goals.

6   A smaller but more progressive (redistributive) Social Security system is preferred to a larger but less progressive (redistributive) system.

Notes

1   The Employee Retirement Income Security Act passed in 1974 specifies funding rules for defined benefit pension plans sponsored by employers. Essentially, companies are required to fund all newly accrued liabilities and to contribute additional funds to reduce any unfunded existing liabilities. See McGill et al. (1996).

2   There are many outstanding books on the early history of Social Security. Two of the best are Arthur Altmeyer (1968) and Martha Derthick (1979).

3   Each Social Security program – OASI, DI and HI – has its own Trust Fund. The OASI and DI funds are often combined in the analysis of future funding. HI (Medicare) is not considered in this chapter.

4   Since 1983, in addition to Social Security Taxes on employers and employees, each year the Treasury Department transfers to the OASDI Trust Funds an amount equal to income tax receipts attributable to inclusion of Social Security benefits in taxable income.

5   Since 1983 Federal Income taxes paid on the Social Security benefits are also put into the Trust Fund.

6   These statistics are taken from *The 2002 Annual Report of the Board of Trustees of the Federal Old-Age and Survivors Insurance and Disability Insurance Trust Funds*, issued on March 26, 2002. See table II.B1. The Report is available at http://www.ssa.gov/OACT/TR/TR02/tr02.pdf.

7   *The 2002 Annual Report*, table VI.E9.

8   A very useful overview of Social Security forecast issues can be found in an article by Stephen C. Goss, "Measuring Solvency in the Social Security System," in *Prospects for Social Security Reform*, edited by Olivia S. Mitchell, Robert J. Myers and Howard Young (Philadelphia: University of Pennsylvania Press, 1999, pp. 16–36).

9   *The 2002 Annual Report*, p. 3.

10 *Ibid.*, p. 14.

11 *Ibid.*, pp. 14–15.

12 Ibid., p. 2. The estimated size of this long-term deficit has been declining in recent years, from 2.23 percent of covered payroll in the 1997 Trustees' report to 1.86% in the 2001 report and 1.87 percent in the 2002 Report (see *The 2002 Annual Report*, table VI.B1.) Over the same six years, the estimated date of the combined OASI and DI Trust Fund exhaustion, assuming no changes in the programs, has moved out by 12 years, from 2029 to 2041.

13 The 1983 Amendments to the Social Security Act legislated an increase in the Normal Retirement Age from 65 to 67, which is currently underway. This is the equivalent of an across-the-board benefit cut on the order of 16 percent.

14 The report of the Advisory Commission to Study the Consumer Price Index (often referred to as the Boskin Commission) can be seen at http://www.ssa.gov/history/reports/boskinrpt.html.

15 *The 2002 Annual Report*, table IV.B1.

16 More fundamentally, critics of the current system argue that a 75-year window distorts the budget scoring of fully funded alternatives to the current system by over counting declines in benefits during the first 25 years of a reform and ignoring savings that occur thereafter. For instance, Cogan and Mitchell (2003) show that using an infinite time horizon dramatically improves the budget scoring of the Bush Commission Plan since revenues past the 75-year point are substantially greater than projected expenditures over an infinite time horizon.

17 "Retooling Social Security for the 21st Century," *Social Security Bulletin* 60 (2), 1997, pp. 37–60.

18 Since the early 1990s, there have been more participants in defined contribution plans than in the traditional defined benefit plans. The number in the latter have been about the same (about 40 million) since the late 1970s, while the number of defined contribution participants has increased dramatically (from 16 million in 1978 to nearly 55 million in 1998), and is still rising. This growth reflects the popularity of 401(k)-type plans. See Chart 2–2 in the Council of Economic Advisors, *Economic Report of the President, 2002*, available at: http://w3.access.gpo.gov/usbudget/fy2003/pdf/2002_erp.pdf

19 By waiting until the person reaches retirement age to fix the life expectancy component of the annuity, increases in the average life expectancy of succeeding cohorts of retired workers are systematically accounted for. See Fox and Palmer (2001) for a fuller discussion.

20 Much of the discussion in this section is based on the analysis in Quinn (1999). The three reform proposals are described in detail in the *Report of the 1994–1996 Advisory Council on Social Security*, vol. 1: *Findings and Recommendations*, January 1997, pp. 25–33, which is available at http://www.ssa.gov/history/reports/adcouncil/ report/toc.htm. The plans are also discussed and analyzed in chapter 3 of the Council of Economic Advisors, *Economic Report of the President*, February 1997 (http://w3. access.gpo.gov/usbudget/fy1998/pdf/erp.pdf)

21 Legislation passed in 1983 is currently increasing the normal retirement age from 65 to 66 over a six-year period (by 2 months per year), and then, after a 12-year hiatus, from 66 to 67, over another six-year period. The Individual Accounts plan (and the Personal Security Account plan below) would eliminate the 12-year hiatus, and raise the age from 65 to 67 in one 12-year period. An increase in the normal retirement

age (waiting longer for a given benefit amount) is equivalent to an across-the-board benefit decrease (getting less at any given age.)

22   The amount proposed was $410 per month (in 1996 dollars), about two-thirds of the poverty level for an elderly person living alone, and about 60% of the average retiree benefit in 1996. The flat-rate tier I benefit would be wage-indexed until the worker was eligible to retire, and price-indexed thereafter.

23   Currently general revenues are included in the Trust Fund only under the narrow condition that revenue from Federal Income Tax payments made on Social Security benefits paid to higher income families are now credited to the Trust Fund.

24   The Report of the President's Commission, entitled *Strengthening Social Security and Creating Personal Wealth for All Americans*, was issued on December 21, 2001, and is available at http://www.ssa.gov/commission/Final_report.pdf.

25   The Council of Economic Advisors, *Economic Report of the President, 2002*, pp. 79–84, describes the advantages of personal accounts, from the Administration's perspective.

26   See the President's Commission's *Strengthening Social Security* (2001: p. 99), for a discussion of the offset procedure.

27   The Commission assumes a pre-retirement portfolio that is 50 percent equities and 50 percent bonds (30 percent corporate bonds and 20 percent government bonds.) They project future rates of return of 6.5 percent for equities, 3.5 percent for corporate bonds and 3.0 percent for government bonds. With an estimate of administrative costs (0.3 percent of account balances), the Commission estimates that the net real rate of return on the mixed portfolio would be 4.6 percent. Since this is considerably greater than the 2 percent real rate used to calculate the decline in traditional benefits that participants would suffer for any funds allocated to the personal account, all participants are forecast to be better off under the new system than under a reformed current system, with future benefits decreased enough to make Social Security fiscally sound (see the President's Commission *Report*, 2001: pp. 97–8).

28   The general revenues are required to make up for what is estimated to be 0.7 percentage point deficit in payroll tax. The Commission argues that this shortfall would be completely offset by future surpluses that are outside the 75-year window.

29   Chapter 2 of the *Economic Report of the President, 2002* (cited above) contains a section on the rationale for Social Security which discusses many of these same issues.

30   These criteria – income adequacy, individual equity and economic growth – can be seen in the evaluation criteria developed the Technical Panel on Trends and Issues in Retirement Savings, which reported to President Clinton's 1994–96 Advisory Council on Social Security. The Technical Panel Report can be found at: http://www.ssa.gov/history/reports/adcouncil/tirs1.txt.

31   See Council of Economic Advisors, *Economic Report of the President* (2002: pp. 74–9).

32   In 1960, the maximum annual OASDI contribution of the employee and employer combined was only $288, about $1,700 in 2002 dollars. In 1970, the maximum was $655, about $3,000 in 2001 dollars. In 2002, the maximum combined OASDI contribution was over $10,500, excluding the Medicare contribution, more than a six-fold increase in real terms since 1960.

33   The House Committee on Ways and Means (1993: pp. 1301–5) has also calculated net transfers and the ratio of benefits to taxes for men and women at three earnings levels

retiring in 1980, 1992 and 2000. Finally, Burtless and Bosworth (1997: figure 2) have estimated internal rates of return on OASDI contributions, for low, average and high-wage workers, by birth cohort. All these estimates tell the same story – low-wage workers have a higher rage of return than high-wage workers, and early cohorts (those born in the 1920s and 1930s) have a higher rate of return than subsequent cohorts will.

34   Dean Leimer provides an excellent nontechnical discussion of frequently used money's worth measures, the assumptions behind them, and their uses and limitations, in "A Guide to Social Security Money's Worth Issues" (*Social Security Bulletin* 58 (2) 1995: 3–20). Another useful reference on these issues is "Social Security Money's Worth," by Olivia Mitchell, John Geanakoplos and Stephen Zeldes in *Prospects for Social Security Reform*, edited by Olivia S. Mitchell, Robert J. Myers and Howard Young (Philadelphia, PA: University of Pennsylvania Press, 1999, pp. 79–151).

35   See Hausman and Wise (1985) and Ippolito (1990). Hurd and Boskin (1984) attributed nearly all of the decline in the labor force participation rates of older Americans to the generosity of Social Security. Moffit (1984) is skeptical of the claims, and points out that aggregate Social Security wealth rose significantly in the 1950s (because of increases in coverage; more categories of workers were included in the system, and they enjoyed large windfall increases in wealth) without any dramatic declines in labor force participation rates.

36   In fact, the payroll tax is not a pure tax for most workers, since the earnings associated with the payroll tax increase future Social Security benefits. As discussed above, for most current and past retirees, Social Security has in fact been a substantial wage *subsidy*, not a tax, since each dollar of contribution has generated several dollars of eventual benefit. For many workers today, however, this will not be the case. And even those for whom the "tax" is really a subsidy may not view it that way at the time that the payroll contribution is being deducted from their paychecks.

37   For more discussion of these issues and this literature, see Quinn et al. (1990), Quadagno and Quinn (1997) and the Social Security Advisory Council Technical Panel (1997: 13–20).

38   Gramlich (1997: table 9.1) estimates that private saving, calculated from the National Income and Product Accounts, has dropped by about one third, as a percentage of gross national product, since the 1960s. Aggregate national saving has dropped more dramatically, from 8.6 percent (during 1962–65) to only 2.0 percent (during 1991–94) of GNP, primarily because of the large increases in federal government deficits.

      At the individual level, Poterba et al. (1996) estimate that the median level of personal financial assets (excluding housing and estimated Social Security and pension rights) of households with heads aged 55 to 64 was only $8,300 in 1991.

      Trends and issues in national saving are discussed by the Technical Panel (1997: 41–8).

39   The Council of Economic Advisors' report (1997: 108–10) contains a concise discussion of the effects of Social Security on saving, distinguishing among three different time periods, the start-up phase, the current mature system, and the future.

40   This debate is nicely summarized by the titles of two reviews of the literature, "How Retirement Saving Programs Increase Saving" and "The Illusory Effects of Saving Incentives on Saving." See Poterb, et al. (1996) and Engen et al. (1996) for these opposing views, both in the same issue of the *Journal of Economic Perspectives*.

41   CBO reference; mentioned in Council of Economic Advisors, *Economic Report of the President*, (2002: 79).

42   Ibid., pp. 73–4.

43 This assumes that individuals do not offset some of the mandated savings themselves. Bosworth (1996: 104–5) and Burtless and Bosworth (1997: 8) argue that it is difficult to use Social Security accumulations to augment national savings, because, in practice, the surpluses are integrated into the federal budget and treated like any other revenue source. This same argument suggests, however, that reducing Social Security surpluses, as the Personal Security Account plan proposes, might lead to Congressional actions to offset this loss in revenues, and therefore an increase in national saving.

References

Advisory Commission to Study the Consumer Price Index (often referred to as the Boskin Commission): http://www.ssa.gov/history/reports/boskinrpt.html

Altmeyer, Arthur 1968: *The Formative Years of Social Security*. Madison, WI: University of Wisconsin Press.

Board of Trustees Annual Report 2002: *The 2002 Annual Report of the Board of Trustees of the Federal Old-Age and Survivors Insurance and Disability Insurance Trust Funds* (March 26). http://www.ssa.gov/OACT/TR/TR02/tr02.pdf

Bosworth, Barry P. 1996: Fund accumulation: how much? How managed? in Peter A. Diamond, David C. Lindeman and Howard Young (eds), *Social Security: What Role for the Future?* Washington, DC: National Academy of Social Insurance: 89–115.

Burtless, Gary and Bosworth, Barry 1997: *Privatizing Social Security: The Troubling Trade-Offs*. Brookings Policy Brief No. 14. Washington, DC: The Brookings Institution, March. CBO.

Cogan, John F. and Mitchell, Olivia S. 2003: The role of economic policy in social security reform: perspectives from the President's Commission. *Journal of Economic Perspectives*, 17 (2): 149–72.

Committee on Ways and Means, US House of Representatives 1993: *1993 Green Book*. Washington, DC: US Government Printing Office.

Council of Economic Advisors 1997: *Economic Report of the President*, February 1997 http://w3.access.gpo.gov/usbudget/fy1998/pdf/erp.pdf

Council of Economic Advisors 2002: *Economic Report of the President*, http://w3.access.gpo.gov/usbudget/fy2003/pdf/2002_erp.pdf

Derthick, Martha 1979: *Policymaking for Social Security*. Washington, DC: Brookings Institution.

Engen, Eric M., Gale, William G. and Scholz, John Karl 1996: The illusory effects of saving incentives on saving, *Journal of Economic Perspectives* 10 (4): 113–38.

Fox, Louise and Palmer, Edward 2001: New approaches to multipillar pension systems: What in the world is going on? In Robert Holzmann and Joseph C. Stiglitz (eds.), *New Ideas about Old Age Security: Toward Sustainable Pension Systems in the Twenty-First Century*. Washington, DC: World Bank.

Goss, Stephen C. 1999: Measuring solvency in the social security system. In Olivia S. Mitchell, Robert J. Myers, and Howard Young (eds.), *Prospects for Social Security Reform*. Philadelphia: University of Pennsylvania Press, 16–36.

Gramlich, Edward M. 1997: How does Social Security affect the economy? In Eric R. Kingson and James H. Schulz (eds), *Social Security in the 21st Century* New York: Oxford University Press: 147–55.

Hausman, Jerry A. and Wise. David A. 1985: Social Security, health status, and retirement. In David Wise (ed), *Pensions, Labor, and Individual Choice*. Chicago: The University of Chicago Press: 159–91.

Hurd, Michael D and Boskin, Michael J. 1984: The effect of Social Security on retirement in the early 1970s, *Quarterly Journal of Economics* 99 (4): 767–90.

Ippolito, Richard A. 1990: Toward explaining early retirement after 1970, *Industrial and Labor Relations Review* 43 (5): 556–69.

Leimer, Dean 1995: A guide to social security money's worth issues. *Social Security Bulletin* 58 (2): 3–20.

McGill, Dan, Brown, Kyle, Hayley, John, and Schieber, Sylvester 1996: *Fundamentals of Private Pensions*. Philadelphia: University of Philadelphia Press.

Mitchell, Olivia, Geanakoplos, John and Zeldes, Stephen 1999: Social security money's worth. In Olivia S. Mitchell, Robert J. Myers and Howard Young (eds.), *Prospects for Social Security Reform*. Philadelphia: University of Pennsylvania Press: 79–151.

Mitchell, Olivia S., Myers, Robert J. and Young, Howard 1999: *Prospects for Social Security Reform*. Philadelphia, PA: University of Pennsylvania Press.

Moffitt, Robert A. 1984: Trends in Social Security wealth by cohort. In Marilyn Moon (ed.), *Economic Transfers in the United States*. Chicago: The University of Chicago Press: 327–47.

Poterba, James M, Venti, Steven F. and Wise, David A. 1996: How retirement saving programs increase saving, *Journal of Economic Perspectives* 10 (4): 91–112.

President's Commission 2001: *Strengthening Social Security and Creating Personal Wealth for All Americans* (December 21). http://www.ssa.gov/commission/Final_report.pdf

Quadagno, Jill and Quinn Joseph F. 1997: Does Social Security discourage work? In Eric R. Kingson and James H. Schulz (eds), *Social Security in the 21st Century*. New York: Oxford University Press: 127–46.

Quinn, Joseph 1999: Criteria for Evaluating Social Security Reform. In Olivia Mitchell, Robert J. Myers and Howard Young (eds.), *Prospects for Social Security Reform*. Philadelphia: University of Philadelphia Press: 37–59.

Quinn, Joseph 2002: Social Security Reform: Options for the future. *Journal of Applied Gerontology* 2(2): 257–72.

Quinn, Joseph, Burkhauser, Richard, and Myers, Daniel 1990: *Passing the Torch: The Influence of Economic Incentives on Work and Retirement*. Kalamazoo, MI: Upjohn Institute for Employment Research.

Social Security Advisory Council Technical Panel 1997: *Report of the 1994–1996 Advisory Council on Social Security*, vol. 1: *Findings and Recommendations* (January). 25–33. http://www.ssa.gov/history/reports/adcouncil/report/toc.htm

Steuerle, Eugene and Bakija, Jon 1994: Retooling social security for the 21st century. *Social Security Bulletin* 60 (2): 37–60.

CHAPTER NINE

*Disability Policy**

LEARNING OBJECTIVES

After completing this chapter, you will be able to:

1 Describe the Social Security Disability Insurance program including eligibility conditions, work restrictions, and the benefit formula.
2 Discuss the Supplemental Security Income program and how it relates to Social Security Disability Insurance.
3 Examine why disability insurance should be part of national retirement policies.
4 Explain the link between the generosity of disability benefits and labor force participation rates.

CHAPTER OUTLINE

* This chapter is adapted from Bound and Burkhauser (1999), Burkhauser and Daly (2002), and Daly and Burkhauser (2003).

INTRODUCTION

In chapter 7, we showed how OASI ameliorates the risks associated with the transition from work to retirement at older ages. In this chapter, we examine how the risks associated with the onset of a work-limiting health condition that occurs at younger ages are ameliorated via both Social Security Disability Insurance (SSDI) and Supplemental Security Income (SSI). It is important to have a chapter on disability policy in a book on aging for a number of reasons. Social welfare policy has traditionally used age as the boundary between those who are "old" and hence, "not expected to work" and those who are "young" and hence, are expected to work. But while age is certainly correlated with one's ability to work, it is not a perfect correlation. Hence, all mature social insurance systems also provide income protection for those who are unable to work because of a disability that occurs before Social Security retirement age.

More fundamentally, "aging" does not begin at any prescribed age. Hence, it is important to focus on two programs that have provided significant benefits to those who for the most part are permanently exiting from the labor force. Furthermore, as discussed in chapter 7, the "normal" retirement age for OASI benefits is currently being pushed back. In doing so, it is important to understand how other programs like SSDI and SSI will be affected. Finally, and more broadly, it is important to see how OASI, SSDI, and SSI fit into the larger US social welfare system that attempts to ameliorate the economic consequences of long-term exits from the labor market for workers and their families at all ages.

The prevalence of work-related health impairments increases with age and accelerates for those aged 50 and over. Hence, SSDI and SSI are natural extensions of the insurance provided older workers to those who are unable to work but are not yet eligible for OASI.[1] SSDI is a social insurance program targeted on regularly employed workers who have qualified by working an appropriate period of time. Their disability must completely prevent them from working. SSI is a means-tested welfare program, providing a minimum cash benefit to those meeting the same medical standards as SSDI but lacking the time in covered employment to qualify for SSDI benefits.

Historically, disability policy in the United States has been based on these two income transfer programs. Rehabilitation and employment protection programs have played a much less important role. However, in the 1990s, cultural pressures to incorporate and accommodate diversity led to anti-discrimination laws such as the Americans with Disabilities Act (ADA) of 1990. These laws emerged as major tools to integrate people with disabilities into the work force. Title I of the ADA requires employers to make reasonable accommodations to workers with disabilities unless this would cause undue hardship on the operation of business. On July 26, 1992, all employers of 25 or more workers were subject to its rules. Two years later, anti-discrimination standards were extended to all employers of 15 or more workers. Workers who believe they have been discriminated against based on their disability have the right to sue their employer. (For a more complete discussion of the ADA and its provisions, see West, 1996.)

The passage of the ADA was intended to give US disability policy a new, more employment-oriented focus. The hope was that the removal of disability-related barriers to employment would allow and encourage many individuals with disabilities to continue in the labor market until normal retirement age. However, post-ADA research on the employment and benefit receipt of those with disabilities suggests the greatest impact of federal government policy on people with permanent disabilities continues to be felt through the income transfer programs, rather than through employment protections.[2]

This chapter provides a context in which to understand and evaluate the goals and effectiveness of US disability policy and how it fits into the broader US social welfare system. It begins by reviewing the major components of SSDI and SSI and how they have changed over time. It then shows how programs' rules themselves may effect the decision to apply for SSDI and SSI benefits. Trends in employment and disability benefit receipt among those with disabilities are considered, paying particular attention to the past 15 years. The difficult equity and efficiency trade-offs inherent in the targeting of benefits to the heterogeneous population with disabilities and the challenges they cause in forming new policies effecting older workers are discussed at the end of the chapter.

HOW SOCIAL SECURITY DISABILITY INSURANCE (SSDI) WORKS

In many ways, the rules for SSDI and SSI mirror the rules for OASI discussed in chapter 7. But in a critical way SSDI and SSI are fundamentally more difficult to administer than OASI. It is much more difficult to determine "disability" than "old age." Most of the controversy over SSDI and SSI policy is centered on this issue of eligibility.

The age at which a person is "old enough" to be eligible for normal OASI benefits is arbitrary and is currently increasing from age 65 to age 67. But the value of using an age criteria to establish OASI eligibility is that it is straightforward to verify. Establishing an operational definition of disability is a much more complex and difficult task. The result is a set of eligibility rules far more complicated to administer in a consistent way over time and location.

Social Security Disability Insurance (SSDI) is part of the Old-Age, Survivor, and Disability Insurance (OASDI) program. SSDI was first included in the 1956 Social Security Amendments, and benefits for the dependants of disabled workers were added in the 1958 Amendments. Eligibility for most types of OASDI benefits including SSDI requires that the worker be "fully insured." To be fully insured, a worker must earn a certain number of credits based on work in "covered" employment or self-employment. These credits are measured in terms of quarters of coverage.

For workers who become disabled or die before age 62, the quarters of coverage needed for fully insured status depends on their age at the time of onset of disability or death. A minimum of six quarters of coverage is required. Thus, SSDI coverage is targeted on workers with a recent history of covered employment or self-employment. Younger workers can become eligible but they must work at least modestly over a three-year period to receive minimum benefits. Unpaid work in the home is not credited toward eligibility.[3]

Disability is defined as "the inability to engage in substantial gainful activity (SGA), by reasons of medically determinable physical or mental impairment that is expected to result in death or last at least 12 months." Applicants must be unable to do any work that exists in the national economy for which they are qualified by virtue of age, education, and work experience.

A five-step procedure is used for initial disability determination as outlined in figure 9.1. First, the state disability examiner checks to see if the applicant is making more than the SGA amount – $780 per month in 2002. Second, the examiner determines if the applicant has a severe impairment that is expected to last 12 months or result in death. In 2000, 20 percent of applicants for SSDI were denied benefits on these grounds. Third, the examiner looks to see if the impairment meets or exceeds medical listings. If the applicant passes these three stages, he/she is eligible. In 2000, 19 percent of applicants were given benefits at this step.

The fourth step offers those who do not meet the medical listings a chance for eligibility based on residual functional capacity. If they are found to be able to perform past relevant work they are denied (20 percent were denied at this step). If not, in the fifth step, the examiner determines if the impairment prevents the applicant from doing any other work in the economy. Here vocational factors are considered. An age, education, and work skills grid is used for this purpose (16 percent were accepted and 22 percent denied at this step). In 2000, 38 percent of initial applicants were accepted onto the SSDI rolls.

In short, a medical definition based primarily on medical listing but with some effort to define them in terms of function is used. But for those who do not meet this test, age, education, and skill level are considered in relationship to any possible job in the economy, not past employment.

By law, SGA is related to "any work that exists in the national economy for which they are qualified by virtue of age, education, and work experiences." No distinctions are made based on employment status or public–private sector employment, but blue-collar vs white-collar distinctions are effectively considered in the sense that past job skills are taken into consideration. That is, blue-collar workers are not expected to be able to find a white-collar job, which might be less physically demanding. Labor market conditions are not formally taken into account in assessing disability. However, Stapleton et al. (1998) show that SSDI applications and awards appear sensitive to business cycles. That is, other things equal, both applications and awards rise during recessions and fall during periods of economic growth.

Benefit levels for SSDI are determined in a manner similar to that of OASI. A Primary Insurance Amount (PIA), a monthly benefit amount, is payable to the worker upon retirement (OASI) or entitlement to disability benefits (SSDI). The PIA is derived from the worker's annual FICA taxable earnings, averaged over a time period that encompasses most of the worker's adult years.

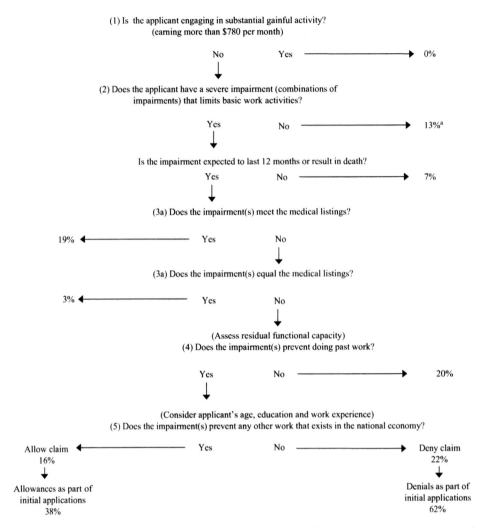

Figure 9.1 SSA initial disability determinations: sequential decision making process and outcomes of decisions on initial SSDI applications, 2000

[a] This response includes 5 percent of claims that were denied because the applicant failed to cooperate in obtaining evidence needed for the claim. The other 8 percent were denied for "impairment not severe."

Source: Daly and Burkhauser (2003) using SSA Office of Disability data, SSA-831 Disability Decision file.

The PIA computation is a progressive function of a worker's AIME (average indexed monthly earnings) amount. The length of the computation period used is based on the number of full calendar years elapsing after age 27 and up to the year of first eligibility. Then up to five dropout years (the lowest earnings years) are subtracted from the calculation. For workers who become disabled before age 47, the number of dropout years is lower. The minimum length of the computation is two years. Hence, younger disability recipients are permitted to use fewer years to determine their AIME to make up for the fact that their wages are low relative to what older workers receive.

Spouses of both SSDI and OASI beneficiaries are first eligible for monthly benefits at age 62. If they wait until age 65, they receive 50 percent of the worker's PIA. If they claim benefits between 62 and 65, they receive an actuarially reduced amount.[4]

SSDI requires a five-month waiting period before permanent benefits are paid. Medicare benefits begin after an additional two-year waiting period. All SSDI beneficiaries are subject to Continuing Disability Reviews (CDRs), although the reviews have been performed only sporadically over time. Legislation in the early 1980s changed the criteria for the reviews, requiring SSA to demonstrate not only that a person is capable of SGA but that he or she has experienced a medical improvement since the initial evaluation. The number of people who exit SSDI due to medical recovery is extremely small.

While SSDI is a federal program, disability determination for the program is done by the individual states. State disability officers use the five-step procedure described above. These officers are generally not medical doctors. The evidence they use in their determination can be provided by private physicians treating the applicants or by medical doctors contracted by state administrators to perform the examinations. The state examiners work in teams. Applicants who are denied benefits can ask for a reconsideration of the denial of benefits. The application for admission into the program is then reviewed by a second team of state examiners. If they are rejected after reconsideration, individuals may appeal to an administrative law judge. It is at this stage that applicants will for the first time come face-to-face with a person who has responsibility for determining their eligibility. Individuals denied at this stage may appeal the decision to the Social Security Appeals Council and then to the District Courts.

There is wide variation in the acceptance rate of SSDI applicants across states and over time. Between 1974 and 1993 mean disability allowance rate states varied from highs of 48 percent in Delaware, New Jersey and Rhode Island to lows of 28 percent in Louisiana and 30 percent in West Virginia (see Burkhauser, Butler, and Weathers, 2002). These variations are unlikely to be caused exclusively by differences in underlying medical conditions and vocational characteristics.

SSDI beneficiaries are permitted to work and receive benefits. However, after a trial work period, earnings above SGA can trigger a CDR. This review ordinarily finds work recovery and results in the loss of *all* benefits. In 2002, SGA was $780 per month. Earnings below $780 per month but above $300 per month can be used as evidence along with other factors. Earnings below $300 per month are not considered.

There are "trial work" options that permit temporary suspension of SGA. The principal SSDI work incentive is the Trial Work Period (TWP). All SSDI beneficiaries are entitled to a nine-month TWP in which full benefits continue regardless of the amount of earnings. Each month that the beneficiary earns above $300 is counted as a trial work month. When the beneficiary has accumulated nine such months (not necessarily sequentially) within a rolling 60-month period, the TWP is completed. If after TWP, the beneficiary earns above SGA, benefits continue for a three-month period and then stop. The beneficiary is then in the extended period of eligibility (EPE) during which benefits are paid for any month in which earnings are below SGA. This effectively gives a beneficiary a three-year "grace period" to test his/her ability to sustain employment.

Former EPE persons may reapply for benefits without being subject to the five-month waiting period for SSDI benefits or the 24-month waiting period for Medicare as long as they reapply within five years of leaving the rolls.

In addition to the general incentives, the costs of certain impairment-related work expenses as well as employer subsidies are deducted from earnings – personal assistants, etc. – when determining initial eligibility as well as when evaluating a post-entitlement work attempt.

A BRIEF HISTORY OF SSDI POLICY

SSDI experienced rapid increases in its rolls in the 1970s that led to a series of reforms in the late 1970s and early 1980s aimed at reducing this growth. A substantial part of SSDI growth in the 1970s was the result of increases in replacement rates (both intentionally via increases in the PIA formula and unintentionally via an unintentional double indexing of benefits for inflation), less restrictive medical standards, increased use of vocation criteria (step 4 in figure 9.1), and eliminating systematic administrative review of initial eligibility decisions (fewer CDRs).

The 1980 Amendment to the Social Security Act reduced replacement rates, increased work incentives, and tightened administrative control. Examples of work incentives include increasing the period of time that benefits and medical coverage could continue over the trial work period and allowing easier return if a job is lost. Tightening administration controls included much greater use of CDRs. Primarily through the vigorous use of CDRs, the disability rolls fell substantially between 1981

Box 9.1 *How Working-Age Men with Disabilities Fared in the 1990s*

In chapter 3, we showed how Current Population Survey data could be used to estimate the economic well being of older Americans. Stapleton and Burkhauser (2003) use these same methods to look at the economic well being of working age (aged 25–61) men and women and how it changed over the business cycle of the 1990s. In table 9.1, updated by Burkhauser and Stapleton (2003) we see that the economic well-being of both those with and without disabilities fell (as measured either by mean or median household-size adjusted real income) between the peak year 1989 and the trough year 1992 of the 1990s' business cycle. But over the next eight years of economic growth, the economic well being of all four groups increased. However, over the entire business cycle from peak year 1989 to peak year 2000, the economic well-being of those without disabilities rose more rapidly, and the mean household-size adjusted income of men with disabilities actually fell over this period.

Table 9.1 Mean and median household-size-adjusted real income of civilians aged 25–61, by gender and disability status[a]

	Year			Percentage change[c]		
Population[b]	1989	1992	2000	1989–1992	1992–2000	1989–2000
Mean household income						
Men without disabilities	35,863	33,968	39,401	−5.4	14.8	9.4
Men with disabilities	21,178	19,774	20,572	−6.9	4.0	−2.9
Women without disabilities	32,430	31,247	36,774	−3.7	16.2	12.6
Women with disabilities	19,629	18,401	20,762	−6.5	12.1	5.6
Median household income						
Men without disabilities	31,899	30,253	34,146	−5.3	12.1	6.8
Men with disabilities	16,905	15,741	16,063	−7.1	2.0	−5.1
Women without disabilities	28,921	27,933	32,042	−3.5	13.7	10.2
Women with disabilities	14,939	13,589	15,633	−9.5	14.0	4.5

[a] Those less than age 25 or more than age 61 or in the Armed Forces are excluded. Persons are considered to have a disability if they report having a health problem or disability that prevents them from working or limits the kind or amount of work they can do. All dollar amounts are in 2000 dollars. Because top coding rules have varied over the history of the CPS, we consistently top code all income at the lowest common income percentile in all years across the CPS data from 1976–2001. Burkhauser, Daly and Houtenville (2001) handled this problem by excluding the top and bottom 1 percent of the distribution.

[b] Disability status is for the year following the income year. In 1994, there were several changes in the CPS. It moved fully to computer-assisted survey interviews. Sample weights based on the 1980 Census were replaced with sample weights based on the 1990 Census. The Monthly Basic Survey was revised, and three new disability questions were added. It is possible that these changes affected the measurement of the population with disabilities either through changes in the sample weights or in the way respondents answered disability questions.

[c] When calculating percentage change, we use the average of the two years as the base.

Source: Stapleton and Burkhauser (2003). Revised and updated calculations of Burkhauser, Daly and Houtenville (2001) using March Current Population Survey, 1990–2001.

and 1983 despite the most serious recession since the 1930s. This led to a major political outcry and a policy reversal in 1984.

The 1984 Amendment to the Social Security Act required the federal government to issue new standards for mental impairments that focused on an individual's functioning in a work environment. The law also required that the combined effect of multiple impairments be considered in cases where no single impairment met the medical listings. Most importantly, SSA was now required to provide proof of medical improvement before benefits could be terminated via a CDR.

Economic growth over the remainder of the decade prevented substantial increases in the rolls but a recession in the early 1990s led to a rapid rise in the rolls and increases in the acceptance of applications which reached 1970s' levels. The most rapid increases came among those classified as having mental disorders. Those with this condition substantially increased as a share of all new beneficiaries. Between 1972 and 1982 their share increased from 9.9 percent to 10.6 percent. In contrast, between 1982 and 1992, the share of those new beneficiaries reporting a mental disorder skyrocketed from 10.6 percent to 25.7 percent. Eight years of continuous economic growth between 1992 and 2000 considerably reduced the increases in the SSDI rolls, although the share of younger workers (who disproportionately report mental disorders) coming onto the rolls continues to increase.

Benefit levels continue to increase automatically based on an inflation index (COLA) for those on the rolls and due to increases in real lifetime wages (AIME) for those coming into the rolls. Because the average age for new beneficiaries is dropping, benefit duration is likely to grow.

The disability rights community and some sections of the medical community are urging a shift from a medical listing model in which medical conditions are the primary standard on which to determine eligibility to a more function-based standard. This was the motivation for the change in the medical listing for mental disorders in the early 1980s. The growth in the population with mental disorders on the rolls since then has raised concerns that moving to a more function-based criterion would lower eligibility standards. While there are several ongoing studies of function-based standards, none have, as yet, been implemented. In fact, the 1996 Amendment to the Social Security Act moved the medical listing in the opposite direction. In response to concerns over the increase in the number of people coming onto the disability rolls based on mental disorders, some functional listings (e.g. maladaptive behavior disorder) were eliminated. But most of these changes focused on the SSI disability children's program.

The OASDI-related FICA tax rate has increased from 10.16 percent in 1980 (5.08 for both employer and employee) with a taxable maximum of $25,900 to a tax rate of 12.40 percent (6.20 percent for employer and employee) in 2002 with a taxable maximum of $84,900. Social Security taxes are now a larger burden on the majority of taxpayers than the federal income tax. The share of this tax going to the OASI and the SSDI Trust Funds has varied over the period to balance revenues in each fund. SSDI-based FICA tax rates have varied from 1.0 to 1.88 over the period. As discussed in chapter 8, concerns about the long-run viability of both the OASI and

SSDI programs have raised issues about the long-term tax burden the system will impose on future generations. To date, little of a structural nature has been done to provide longer-term financial stability to OASDI.

A major new piece of legislation – the Ticket to Work and Work Incentive Improvement Act of 1999 (TWWIIA) – is attempting to increase the movement of SSDI beneficiaries into the labor market. Final regulations for its implementation were issued December 28, 2001. TWWIIA establishes a voucher system by which SSDI and SSI recipients are given a ticket that allows them to contract with public and/or private providers of rehabilitation services. The bulk of the payments for these services are rendered once the individual leaves the rolls and returns to work. In essence, this moves the risk of a failed investment in an individual from SSA to the public or private providers. The goals of the ticket are three-fold: (1) to get SSA out of the quality assurance business with regard to rehabilitation and employment services; (2) to make providers accountable for the success or failure of their clients; and (3) to give disability beneficiaries the power to shop around and find the services that best matches their needs. (See Berkowitz and Burkhauser, 1996, and Bound and Burkhauser, 1999, for histories of SSDI policies.)

HOW SUPPLEMENTAL SECURITY INCOME (SSI) WORKS

The Supplemental Security Income (SSI) program is a nationwide federal assistance cash transfer program for aged, blind, and disabled individuals with low incomes. SSI was enacted in 1972 and began paying benefits in 1974, replacing a patchwork of state-run entitlement programs created under the Social Security Act of 1935 and its Amendments in 1950. The establishment of SSI was the culmination of a four-year debate over a more overarching welfare reform proposal – the Family Assistance Plan (FAP) – intended to extend the federal social safety net to *all* low-income households. While Congress eventually rejected the universality of FAP, it passed SSI, a categorical welfare program based on the same negative income tax principle of FAP but targeted on a subset of low-income individuals not expected to work – aged (65 or older), blind, and disabled adults and blind and disabled children.

FAP departed from existing welfare policy in three important ways: (1) it was universal rather then categorical, with low income and assets as the only eligibility criteria; (2) it was run through the federal tax system rather than administered by state and local governments; and (3) it had a low benefit reduction rate (that is, how fast the benefits would decline as incomes rose), in keeping with the notion that low tax rates provide desired work incentives. SSI was categorical but tried to retain the other two features of FAP. It targets blind and disabled adults and children (as well as the aged) who have income and assets below a prescribed minimum.

SSI uses the same definition of disability (SGA) and the same five-step process to determine eligibility based on the ability to work (the SGA as defined above for SSDI). Unlike SSDI that is a social insurance program, SSI is a pure welfare program and hence requires no work-based *quid pro quo*. That is, previous work history and tax contributions are not an eligibility requirement. Instead, the program is both income- and asset-tested. To be eligible for SSI, an individual's countable income must be less than the federal benefits rate (FBR) – $780 per month ($9,360 per year) in 2002 – and countable resources must be less than $2,000. For couples, the amounts are 150 percent of the individual limits. Not all income is countable. Exclusions include a $20 monthly income disregard on all forms of income with the exception of means-tested income and an additional $65 per month disregard for any labor earnings. After these disregards, for every $1 in labor earnings a worker loses $0.50 in SSI benefits.

In calculating SSI benefits, in-kind assistance from government programs like Food Stamps and public housing do not reduce an individual's overall SSI benefit, but SSI benefits are counted as income and hence reduce Food Stamp benefits. The same is true for other means-tested transfer programs. This can lead to very high disincentives for working since individuals are subject to what are effectively very high tax rates on work. All other benefits from government programs (such as Social Security Disability Insurance) reduce SSI benefits dollar for dollar. Countable resources include resources other than the home a person lives in, their car (depending on use or value), and a limited amount of life insurance and burial funds.

In general, SSI beneficiaries with no countable income receive a federal cash payment of $544 per month in 2002 ($817 for a jointly eligible couple). The federal benefit increased each January by the cost-of-living index used to adjust all Social Security (OASDI) benefits. Some states supplement this minimum. Benefits vary by state and by whether a person is living independently or in an institution. Excluding state supplements, SSI payments represent about 75 percent of the official US Census Bureau poverty threshold for an eligible individual, and about 90 percent of the threshold for an eligible couple; these percentages have remained relatively constant over time. In most states, SSI recipients automatically become eligible for Medicaid and Food Stamps without a separate application. Since 1986, SSI benefits and eligibility for Medicaid have been continued for those who earn about the SGA ($780 per month in 2002); this is known as 1619(b) status. Adult SSI recipients with disabilities also are eligible for federally funded, state-administered vocational rehabilitation and for the new Ticket to Work and Work Incentive Improvement Act (TWWIIA) program.

There are no universal social assistance programs in the United States. The closest we came to passing such a program was FAP. Since the 1996 welfare reforms, the United States no longer has any categorical income programs that offer open-ended cash transfers except for SSI. For instance, Aid for Dependent Children was renamed Temporary Assistance to Needy Families (TANF) with five-year term limits. In addition, SSI in most cases offers higher cash benefits than TANF. Furthermore, because the federal government pays the bulk of SSI benefits (100 percent in some states), while the individual states pay for TANF, states have a financial incentive to move individuals from state-financed welfare programs to federally funded SSI. Over the history of SSI, changes in its eligibility standard have driven most changes in the SSI benefit population.

Note, however, that to receive SSI benefits, low-income persons must pass the disability eligibility criteria. No partial SSI disability benefits are available. SGA is intended to exclude from eligibility all but the totally disabled. However, since 1986, permanent work above SGA is possible for those in SSI and SGA is no longer binding (nor are CDRs regularly conducted). This in effect allows SSI recipients to permanently work and receive benefits once they get on the program. But as discussed above, those who work have their SSI benefits substantially reduced. This means test is enforced on a monthly basis.

Further, loss of other benefits (e.g. Food Stamps, housing subsidies, the Earned Income Tax Credit, etc.) can also discourage work efforts. Economists refer to these benefit reductions as effective marginal taxes. That is, the tax rate reflects how much a one dollar increase in earnings reduces other benefits. In this case, the effective marginal tax on work can be above 80 percent. Only a small percentage of SSI beneficiaries work and even fewer leave the SSI rolls for work reasons. Section 1619(b) also allows individuals whose SSI cash benefits are phased out due to labor earnings to retain eligibility for Medicaid until they earn income around the full value of all lost transfer benefits. About 1.3 percent of SSI-disabled adults continue to receive Medicaid benefits despite reaching an income level sufficient to end SSI cash benefits.

A BRIEF HISTORY OF SSI POLICY

The SSI program has grown substantially since benefits were first paid in 1974. However, its growth has varied over time both overall and within the three populations targeted for benefits (see figure 9.2). Originally considered a program for the elderly, SSI is now dominated by adults and children with disabilities. In 1974, the majority of the SSI caseload was aged 65 or over. The number of aged beneficiaries peaked at 2.5 million in 1975, gradually dropped to around 2 million in 1982 and has remained at about that level. The decline in the elderly population on SSI between 1975 and 1982 is largely due to the significant increases in OASI benefits over the period. The modest increases in OASI since then have been sufficient to prevent increases in the older population on SSI.

In contrast, the number of blind and disabled adults (aged 18–64) on SSI has more than doubled since 1974, with the most rapid growth after 1982. In December 2001, 3.8 million adults aged 18–64 received SSI benefits, about 2.1 million more than in 1982. As is true for SSDI, growth in the blind and disabled adult SSI rolls after 1982 is primarily related to changes in eligibility criteria. In 1984, there were important changes both in the medical listing for mental disorders and in the criteria for CDR removals. Thereafter, yearly program growth in SSI exceeded that of SSDI in every year including the rapid growth years of the early 1990s. As was the case with SSDI, there has been a significant increase in the share of new

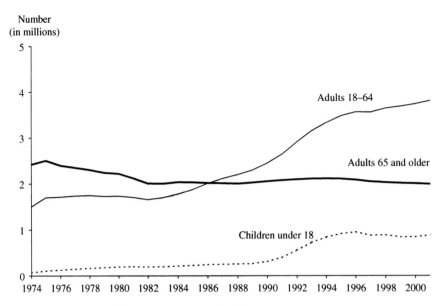

Figure 9.2   SSI caseloads by age group, 1974–2001
Source: Annual Statistical Supplement, SSA various years.

beneficiaries with mental disorders since the early 1980s. It was not until the welfare reforms of 1996 that SSI disability growth finally returned to pre-1984 levels.

The number of blind and disabled SSI recipients who are under age 18 has also
grown substantially in recent years. Between 1974 and 1989, the child caseload
increased modestly to about 185,000. However, following the Zebley decision in
1990, the number of blind and disabled children rose, rapidly reaching 955,000 by
1996. The Zebley decision greatly broadened eligibility for children by requiring
SSA to use an equivalent vocational criterion (step 4 of figure 9.1) in SSI-children
determination. Prior to this Supreme Court decision, children, unlike adults, were
denied benefits if they did not meet or exceed the medical listing (step 3 of figure 9.1).
The rapid growth of the SSI disabled adults and children caseload in the early 1990s
caused Congress to once again modify the eligibility standards in 1996 and to move
them closer to pre-Zebley days. Since then, the SSI disability benefits have grown
more slowly.

The SSI caseload is on average much younger, as a result of the rapid growth in
the adult and child disabled caseload. In 1974, 60 percent of SSI beneficiaries were
aged 65 and over. In 2002, only 30 percent were elderly. The policy changes that have
had the most important effect on program size are related to eligibility standards.
Unlike several European countries, the United States has no universal guaranteed
income floor. There is a clear tension between those who would like to keep SSI a
narrow categorical program from those people unable to do any work because of
a disability or old age and those who would like SSI to meet the need for a universal cash transfer program targeted on all low-income households (FAP). Reforms

in AFDC that led to the creation of term limits in the new TANF program will further heighten the urgency of this latter group to expand the SSI target population, since SSI is now the only long-term cash transfer program in the United States.

The passage of TWWIIA offers some hope that more SSI recipients will volunteer for vocational and work-related training and that more beneficiaries will enter the labor force and reduce their need for SSI benefits. But it is less likely that TWWIIA will impact on SSI recipients than on SSDI recipients. First, SSDI recipients, on average, have had much more work experience and have non-disability-related characteristics that would suggest more success in job placement. Hence, TWWIIA service providers are more likely to take a chance on the SSDI population than on the SSI population because their payments are almost exclusively based on placing recipients in jobs and getting them completely off the SSDI or SSI rolls. Second, the financial rewards for placing SSDI beneficiaries in jobs are greater than for placing SSI beneficiaries, since TWWIIA payments are based on Trust Fund savings and SSDI beneficiaries receive higher benefits than SSI beneficiaries.

A far more difficult issue is the relationship between SSI and other transfer programs targeted at low-income people. The 1996 welfare reforms dramatically reduced benefits for AFDC recipients by limiting lifetime access to TANF benefits to five years. A strong economy since 1996 together with these reforms dramatically reduced TANF rolls. Some of this reduction was simply a transfer from the TANF to the SSI rolls but most has been the result of welfare mothers finding jobs. But it is impossible to predict what will happen if recovery from the 2001 recession stalls or when the business cycle next turns down. The recession of 2001 reduced the demand for low skilled labor in the United States, and resulted in increased pressure on all targeted welfare programs. Undoubtedly, some of this pressure will be felt by the SSI program and we know that acceptance rates have risen despite increases in applications during previous economic downturns. Unless TANF rules are relaxed or unemployment insurance is extended, SSI is likely to be seen as the main source of income for long-term displaced, low-income workers with significant disabilities.

PROGRAM PARTICIPATION AND WORK INCENTIVES OF SSI AND SSDI

Supplemental Security Income

The economics of program participation and labor supply for individuals potentially eligible for SSI mirrors the analyses of these issues in other social assistance programs such as AFDC and TANF. In these models individuals make choices that depend on the income gained from the program and the costs of participating, including the time and money costs associated with applying for and maintaining eligibility for benefits.

To see how this works in the case of SSI, consider the conventional labor-leisure model shown in figure 9.3. It compares the budget constraint of an SSI program with a 50 percent marginal tax rate, (t = 0.5) and one with a marginal tax rate of 100 percent (t = 1.0). Segment ACDE of the figure represents the budget constraint of those not categorically eligible for SSI. The line has a slope equal to the hourly wage rate. Segment ABCDE applies to those same individuals if they are categorically eligible and they face a marginal tax rate of 100 percent. Benefits are taxed one dollar for each dollar earned and phased out at the break-even level (point C). That is, even though they are categorically eligible for benefits, their labor earnings offset all SSI benefits at hours levels greater than point C. Segment ABDE applies to those same people but now they face a marginal tax rate of 50 percent. Benefits are taxed at a rate of 50 cents per dollar earned and the break-even hours point is D. Under this model, categorical eligibility for SSI benefits unambiguously reduces work effort relative to not being categorically eligible. There is an income effect associated with the guarantee (AB), and a substitution effect associated with the marginal tax rate (BC or BD). The income and substitution effects work in the same direction, and hours of work among participants fall. Only those whose optimal hours worked prior to program eligibility were beyond the break-even hours point may not be affected and even then it will depend on the shape of their indifference curve (i.e. some would be willing to accept less income by substantially reducing work and living on program benefits).

The next question to ask is what happens if the marginal tax rate is reduced. Here the answer is unclear; the net effect of a reduction in t, from 100 percent (BC) to 50 percent (BD), is ambiguous. The arrows in the figure 9.3 show the various responses that could occur following a reduction in the marginal tax rate (represented by a shift from segment BC to BD). For individuals initially receiving SSI benefits and not working (i.e. initially at point B), a reduction in the tax rate may encourage participants to work more, represented by arrow 1. At the same time, a reduction in t expands the range of individuals eligible for benefits, and brings some portion of those categorically eligible but not previously receiving SSI onto the rolls. As these individuals move onto SSI their work effort is reduced, as shown by arrow 2. Arrow 3 shows that some categorically eligible individuals who continue to earn too much under the lower tax rate may be motivated to reduce their hours of work enough to become eligible for benefits, thereby combining work and SSI benefits. Finally, it also is possible that a reduction in t will increase payments by enough to induce previously eligible persons on earnings grounds but not on categorical grounds (segment AC) to risk entry onto the rolls.

Taking each of these possibilities into account, the net effect of a lower marginal tax rate on work effort is ambiguous. The only thing that is clear is that lower marginal tax rates increase caseloads. A lower tax rate makes more categorically eligible individuals eligible for the program on income grounds and, given positive take-up rates, unambiguously boosts the number of individuals on the rolls. Moreover, by lowering the costs associated with staying on the rolls, lower marginal tax rates reduce exit rates from the program, thereby increasing caseloads. Finally, lower marginal tax rates may induce those on the margin of categorical eligibility on health grounds to apply for benefits since the gains to program acceptance have

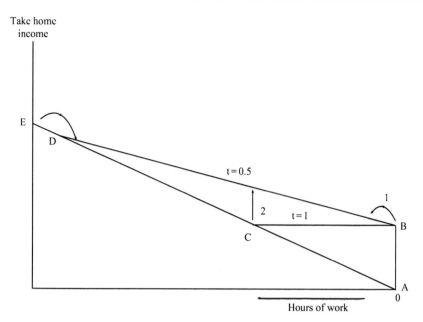

Figure 9.3 SSI budget constraints with differential marginal tax rates (BC: Marginal Tax Rate = 100%, BD: Marginal Tax Rate = 50%)
Source: Burkhauser and Daly (2002).

increased. (Note figure 9.3 is a simplified version of current SSI rules. It ignores the small monthly disregards on all income and labor earnings. How would the inclusion of this disregard in figure 9.3 change the figure? How would it influence employment and program participation?)

Unlike SSI benefits for the elderly, where categorical age eligibility is easily demonstrated and benefit receipt is automatic if one meets the means test, categorical eligibility for SSI benefits is more difficult to demonstrate. Thus, eligibility for benefits is not certain and models of SSI application must take this risk of non-acceptance into consideration. In general, those considering applying for SSI will value disability benefits with a probability of less than one. Holding the underlying health condition constant, the probability of acceptance onto the rolls will depend on the disability screening process. Conditional on the same impairment, tighter eligibility criteria are likely to increase the probability of denial and reduce the expected value of applying. In contrast, looser criteria increase the probability of acceptance and increase the expected value of applying. In either case, individuals facing uncertainty surrounding acceptance, informational hurdles, or stigma associated with benefit receipt, may be induced to participate by the increase in benefits associated with the lower marginal tax rate.

If those categorically eligible for benefits on health grounds are completely unable to perform any substantial gainful activity under any circumstances, then there is no need to lower the marginal tax rate on SSI, since those on the program are neither expected or able to work. However, to the extent that work is both possible and expected for people with disabilities who meet the other eligibility criteria, policy discussions with respect to trade-offs between tax rates, guarantees, and break-even points become much closer to those taking place for other income maintenance programs.

The same model also incorporates stigma and other fixed program costs. As in other income maintenance programs, the presence of stigma and other program costs associated with applying for benefits explains why some categorically eligible individuals are observed on segment ACD. As fixed program costs and stigma decline, participation among this group will rise. What the model in figure 9.3 does not show are potential program interaction effects. The actual budget constraint facing those categorically eligible for SSI benefits is more complex, with more nonlinearities due to the accumulation of taxes from multiple programs. In like manner, multiple program eligibility will cause complications for those interested in the behavioral effects of other transfer programs. Burkhauser and Smeeding (1981) and Powers and Neumark (2001) show the incentives to accept actuarially reduced Social Security benefits (OASI) at younger retirement ages are increased for those who would be eligible for both SSI and OASI at age 65, since OASI benefits after a small disregard are taxed on a dollar for dollar basis by SSI.

Social Security Disability Insurance

While SSDI is a social insurance program rather than a social assistance program, the same kind of analysis can be used to show how changes in its tax rate on benefits can influence program participation and work. In figure 9.4 line segment ABCDE represents the budget constraint of a person who is eligible for a monthly SSDI benefit (PIA) of BA and can work up to (d) hours without loss of benefits. At (d) hours, monthly labor earnings reach the SGA level ($780 per month in 2002) and trigger a review (CDR) of program eligibility. (Note that the hours of work that one can work before reaching $780 depends on one's hourly wage rate.) The result is a benefit "cliff" at $780 (a marginal tax rate of infinity) that will result in the loss of all benefits if one more dollar is earned from work. (This is a highly simplified version of the incentive structure of SSDI. As discussed above, an SSDI beneficiary would in fact have a trial work period that would allow him or her to continue to receive benefits for at least 12 months. But after this time period all benefits are lost.) This is a very powerful signal to beneficiaries that additional work will be severely penalized. Using the same logic as discussed above, you should be able to trace out the potential implications on the employment of those currently on the SSDI program of a relaxation of this tax rate as well as its implications for entry onto the SSDI rolls and overall program costs.

The Ticket to Work and Work Incentives Improvement Act of 1999 (TWWIIA) included a requirement that the Social Security Administration conduct a demonstration project to evaluate the cost and other effects of an SSDI benefit offset (tax)

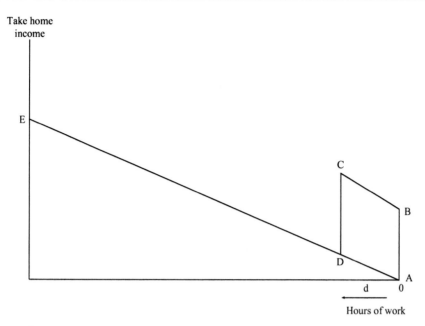

Figure 9.4 SSDI budget constraints with differential marginal tax rates (BC: Marginal Tax Rate = 100%, BD: Marginal Tax Rate = 50%)
Source: Burkhauser and Daly (2002).

of 50 percent to replace the benefit cliff in the current program. At the time this book went to press, the design for this demonstration had not been finalized. One issue in particular had not been resolved – what should be the level of the disregard before the tax went into effect?

If left at $780 per month, this would mean that the break-even point would be at a very high income level for those with high PIAs and might dramatically increase program participation and hence program costs. Lowering the disregard would lower the break-even point and hence the incentive for higher wage earners to enter the program. However lowering the disregard below the current $780 per month level would potentially make some current beneficiaries who work worse off. (Convince yourself that this could be the case using figure 9.4. Show that it could also make them better off. Why?)

It was argued that it would be unethical to run a demonstration using current beneficiaries to test the behavioral implications of a lower disregard. In order for a demonstration to capture the effect of a change in a program, it must compare a "treatment" group (the group that experiences the change in policy) with a "control" group (the group that continues under the old policy). But these two groups have to be the same in all other ways in order to isolate the impact of the treatment on behavior. (This is a much more sophisticated method of measuring the impact of a policy than the "counterfactual" method discussed in chapter 3. Demonstrations are actually able to show behavior in the presence and in the absence of a new policy. This is an example of social science using the methods of the physical sciences to empirically test the effectiveness of a policy.) Thus current beneficiaries would have to be "randomly" assigned into the two groups and the assignment would have to be mandatory.

The ethical issue is, should current beneficiaries be assigned into a group that could lead to their receiving less income than they received prior to assignment? This is the type of ethical issue that is often considered by the human subjects committees at research universities.

While this issue may make it unethical to test this policy in this way, it is nonetheless the case that most changes in government policies help some groups and hurt others. Hopefully the net effect of such policy changes is a net gain for society as a whole. But, it is a rare policy change that makes no one worse off. (See Ticket to Work and Work Incentives Advisory Panel, 2002, for a fuller discussion of the issues surrounding the appropriate design for a demonstration of a 50 percent tax rate for SSDI.)

Balancing efficiency and equity concerns

Our discussion above has focused on the behavioral effects of the SSI and SSDI programs. This focus on the efficiency costs of induced behavioral change ignores the social benefits of SSI and SSDI and may lead some to conclude that socially optimal SSI and SSDI programs would have no behavioral impact on benefit applications or work. This conclusion is inappropriate for two reasons. First, even if actual disability status were perfectly observable, society would probably still want to target some level of benefits on disadvantaged low-income workers and their families even if it resulted in some efficiency losses. Hence the more important question is not whether there are program-related behavioral changes but whether they are small relative to the social gains from redistributing income to less advantaged persons. Analyses of the welfare implications of the SSI and SSDI programs should focus on this second and more important question.

Second, in a world where the socially appropriate eligibility standards for SSI and SSDI are difficult to assess, some individuals will be denied benefits who are less capable of work than is socially acceptable. In such a world, more lenient eligibility criteria will involve a trade-off between the reduction of type II errors on the one hand and the additional costs of type I errors on the other. The issue is: in the presence of uncertainty, do the social benefits outweigh the efficiency costs arising from increasing the probability of guaranteeing an income floor to those below some minimum level of work capacity at the cost of also providing these funds to some who are more capable of work? In both cases, it is appropriate to assign some value to SSI and SSDI as mechanisms for providing social protection against the economic consequences of aging and disability for disadvantaged workers. To do otherwise would be to hold too narrow a view from a social policy perspective. See Bound et al. (2001) for a fuller discussion of these issues.

TRENDS IN EMPLOYMENT RATES AND BENEFIT CASELOADS FOR PEOPLE WITH DISABILITIES

In 2000, about 7.7 million individuals, 5.3 percent of the working-age population, received federal disability payments. Within this group, 50 percent received only SSDI, 37 percent received only SSI, and 13 percent received benefits from both programs. Expenditures on the two programs totaled about $76 billion in 2000 – $56 billion on SSDI and $20 billion for SSI.

As figure 9.5, taken from Burkhauser and Daly (2002), shows, employment rates for those with disabilities as well as SSDI and SSI caseloads have varied greatly over the past two decades, fluctuating with the economy, changes in benefit eligibility criteria, and the implementation of other public policies intended to support people with disabilities. The figure shows employment rates of working-age men and women with self-reported disabilities (using Current Population Survey data) and the number of individuals receiving disability benefits (based on data from the

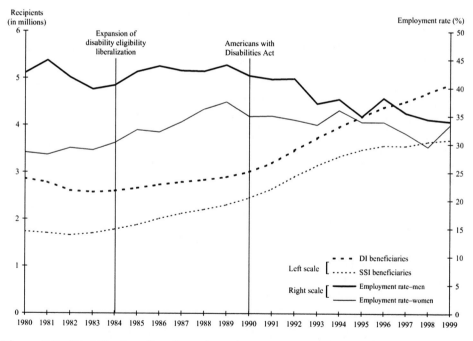

Figure 9.5 Disability benefit rolls and employment rates among working-age men and women with disabilities
Source: Burkhauser and Daly (2002).

Box 9.2   *The Increasing Dependence of Working-Age People with Disabilities on DI and SSI*

The decline in the employment of working age people with disabilities and the increase in their prevalence on DI and SSI captured in figure 9.5 is reinforced by a comparison of their mean labor earnings and income from DI and SSI shown below. (Note this includes those with zero labor earnings and DI or SSI income.) Table 9.2 from Stapleton and Burkhauser (2003) shows that the labor earnings of men with and without disabilities fell from peak year 1989 to trough year 1992 but then rose over the growth years of 1990s for men without disabilities but fell even more for men with disabilities despite the growing economy. On net, the real labor earnings of men with disabilities grew by 9.1 percent over the 1990s' business cycle while the labor earnings of men with disabilities fell by 34.6 percent. The story is not quite so bad for women with disabilities. While they did not do as well as women without disabilities over the same period, their labor earnings did increase.

In contrast, the mean DI and SSI benefit for men and women with disabilities increased dramatically in the 1990s. This offset to a larger extent the decline in the labor earnings of men with disabilities and explains why their household income was not more substantially affected by their decline in employment.

Table 9.2   Mean real income from own labor earnings and own Social security Disability insurance (DI) and Supplemental Security Income (SSI) for civilians aged 25–61, by gender and disability status[a]

Income source/population[b]	Year			Percentage change[c]		
	1989	1992	2000	1989–1992	1992–2000	1989–2000
Own labor earnings						
Men without disabilities	33,820	31,434	37,046	−7.3	16.4	9.1
Men with disabilities	8,058	6,793	5,680	−17.0	−17.8	−34.6
Women without disabilities	16,065	16,632	20,240	3.5	19.6	23.0
Women with disabilities	4,250	4,092	4,880	−3.8	17.6	13.8
Own DI/SSI						
Men without disabilities	50	71	76	33.5	7.0	40.3
Men with disabilities	3,013	3,356	4,237	10.8	23.2	33.8
Women without disabilities	164	150	149	−8.7	−1.1	−9.8
Women with disabilities	2,004	2,380	3,292	17.2	32.1	48.6

See notes for table 9.1.
Source: Stapleton and Burkhauser (2003). Revised and updated calculations of Burkhauser, Daly, and Houtenville (2001) using March Current Population Survey, 1990–2001.

Social Security Administration) for the period 1980–99.[5] Also indicated in the figure are a few key events: when disability screening was liberalized in 1984 and the passage of the ADA in 1990.

The trends in figure 9.5 highlight the major concerns of disability policy-makers over the past two decades. First, the number of disability beneficiaries has increased continuously since the eligibility expansion and liberalization in 1984, with especially strong growth during the 1990s (application and acceptance rates in the 1990s rivaled those experienced during the expansion period of the late 1970s). Second, while employment rates for those with self-reported work limitations rose through the economic expansion of the late 1980s, they have fallen almost continuously since, even during the strong expansion of the 1990s.

Different analysts have reached different conclusions about these patterns. Kaye (2003) for example, argues that rising benefit rolls and declining employment rates among those with disabilities in the 1990s were caused by dramatic increases in the severity of impairments. Hence, for Kaye, the recent trends are health-based and not a reflection of changes in public policy. Other researchers have taken a more social environment-oriented view. For example, DeLeire (2000) and Acemoglu and Angrist (2003) attribute the downturn in employment among those with disabilities in the 1990s to the passage of the ADA. Bound and Waidman (2002) argue that changes in benefit eligibility and generosity made it easier and more profitable for workers to leave the labor force and take benefits.

Autor and Duggan (2002) suggest that a combination of disability benefits that replaced a greater share of labor earnings and declining job opportunities for low-skilled workers induced an increasing share of workers to choose benefits over employment. While the issue is by no means settled, it is likely that changes in the social environment, rather than changes in health, are driving the rise in benefit rolls and the decline in employment among those with disabilities. Which one of the many changing social variables deserves the most credit is a matter for future research, but in all likelihood the true cause is a combination of factors, rather than a single policy action or identifiable event. (See Stapleton and Burkhauser, 2003, for a fuller evaluation of this literature.)

While researchers debate the reasons for the declining employment and rising benefit rates of men and women with disabilities during the 1990s, policy-makers are debating whether these outcomes are signs of success or failure of US disability policy. For some advocates of those with disabilities, the increasing disability benefit rolls reflect an appropriate increase in support for a group of workers with limited labor market opportunities. For others, the increased rolls reflect the shortcomings of a transfer-focused policy that has failed to provide the necessary supports (e.g., universal health insurance, rehabilitation, and job services) to allow individuals to select work over benefits. For others still, the outcomes observed during the 1990s are simply evidence of the law of unintended consequences in policy-making, where policies to promote economic well-being (in the case of benefits) and work (in the case of the ADA) actually increased the disability benefit rolls and reduced employment.

DISABILITY POLICY TRADE-OFFS

Equity and the definitions of disability

The passage of the ADA challenged the conventional policy wisdom that working-age people with disabilities could not and hence should not be expected to work. Proponents of the ADA argued that unequal access to jobs rather than a worker's disability was the primary barrier to employment. In the extreme version of this view, there are no disabled workers, only a society that does not fully accommodate its citizens. If all citizens were fully accommodated, there would be no need for transfers specifically related to disabilities (although persons with disabilities would of course still sometimes receive unemployment or welfare benefits just like other citizens). This argument raises basic questions about the rights and responsibilities of people with disabilities. Most fundamentally, should people with disabilities categorically be expected to work?

A positive answer to this question would shift the boundaries of the population expected to work in our society and would help define our idea of equitable treatment for those with and without disabilities. On the one hand, an expectation that all persons with disabilities will work suggests that nonproductivity resulting from discrimination with regard to access to work should be stopped. It also suggests that eligibility criteria for permanent earnings replacement (SSDI) or for a categorical guaranteed income floor (SSI) based on disability should be re-evaluated, since disability should no longer be viewed as preventing work.

But a blanket expectation that all those with disabilities will work is too crude an approach. Disability is a more complex concept to define or measure than age, race, or gender, and thus targeting policies towards those with disabilities is more complicated as well. Disability is a dynamic process rather than a static classification. The way in which a worker responds to the onset of health conditions depends not only on the severity of the impairment as measured in a clinical sense, but also on the social environment: the availability of employment, the availability of accommodation, rehabilitation and retraining; the presence of legal supports or protections; and the accessibility and generosity of SSDI, SSI, and other government transfer programs.

Operationalizing a definition of disability for policy purposes is very difficult. Mashaw and Reno (1996) document over 20 definitions of disability used for purposes of entitlement to public and private transfers, government services, or statistical analysis. This problem is readily apparent for the three programs on which we focus in this chapter: the ADA, SSDI, and SSI. The definition of disability in the ADA is much broader than the definition of permanent and complete disability used in SSDI and SSI. There also are workers who would probably be eligible for SSDI or SSI benefits if they stopped working, but they keep working, and there are others who appear disabled and do not work, but are denied SSDI and SSI benefits. Thinking about the equity concerns of disability policy requires coming to grips with these definitional issues.

Limiting behavioral responses to disability policy rules

As we saw in our discussion of figures 9.3 and 9.4, disability income transfer programs, like all programs that involve income payments, contend with potential problems of moral hazard and work disincentives.[6] Estimates of the magnitude of these problems depend in large part on whether adults with disabilities are able or expected to work, since this determines the baseline level of work that would be expected in the absence of the programs, and on the precision of disability screening. If people with disabilities are unable or not expected to work, then disability benefits can be higher or lower with no efficiency cost since no work will occur (or was expected to occur) anyway. Moreover, if work disability is a clearly defined and immutable category, then participation in disability benefit programs would be purely a function of the prevalence of health limitations in the working-age population and unrelated to any specific characteristics of the program. However, our experience with SSDI and SSI suggests that disability eligibility is not well defined, and perhaps cannot be well defined, in a way that draws a bright line between those with disabilities who cannot work and all other workers. As a result, the population receiving disability benefits inevitably will be determined by a mix of social policies and how people with disabilities, employers, and frontline program administrators react to them.

Placing disability policy in the broader social welfare context

The typical working-age person with a disability experiences its onset during working life (Burkhauser and Daly, 1996). As a result, disability policy is always entangled with other policies related to job separations that occur before retirement. In the United States, workers may follow at least four paths following the onset of a health-related impairment.

The *work path* encompasses public programs that provide or encourage rehabilitation to overcome the work limitations caused by a disability. It also might include more direct labor market interventions, for example, the creation of specific government jobs for people with disabilities, subsidies to those who employ disabled workers, job quotas for the disabled, or legislation protecting workers with disabilities from discrimination or dismissal. The ADA clearly falls into this category. Private efforts to provide supported environments exist but on a small scale. Work path policies attempt to maintain those with disabilities on the job and in the labor market, either through the carrot of subsidies or the stick of mandates.

The *disability insurance path* encompasses traditional disability programs. These include short-term sickness programs, which mandate employers to replace lost wages during the first few weeks of sickness or directly provide such replacement through short-term social insurance. In the United States, these short-term sickness benefits and health care are typically provided through private contracts between employers and employees. After some point, workers are then eligible to move to a private long-term disability insurance program, which often has both health and employment criteria. This path eventually merges with the Social Security Disability Insurance program. For those with disabilities who drop out of the labor force, the disability insurance path is the most common way that individuals receive benefits.

The *unemployment path* recognizes that disentangling job exits because of a health condition from job exits due to economic forces is in practice a difficult and often controversial task, especially as these exits are influenced by the rules established by the social welfare system. A certain number of those who exit jobs for health reasons never end up on disability, but instead move from short-term unemployment insurance to longer-term unemployment insurance (typically at a lower level of payments). Eventually, this path merges with the Social Security retirement system. This is particularly likely for older persons who are close to retirement age.

The *welfare path* encompasses means-tested programs that serve as a safety net for workers without jobs who are not eligible for health- or unemployment-based social insurance. Welfare programs can be subject only to a means test or they can be linked to an inability to work either because of poor health, poor job skills, or child-rearing responsibilities.

When a health condition begins to affect the ability to work, important job-related decisions must be made by both the worker and the employer. These decisions will be influenced by the relative rewards provided by the disability insurance, unemployment, and welfare paths and by the carrots and sticks in the work path in deciding whether a worker will remain in the labor force or apply for transfer benefits. Thus, how easy it is to receive disability benefits and the size of such benefits affect how many people choose the disability path, rather than the work, unemployment, or welfare paths. Conversely, policy changes in other programs such as unemployment insurance, health care benefits, retirement benefits, and welfare likely will also affect SSDI and SSI caseloads.

In the United States, where welfare benefits are low and difficult to obtain for households without children, unemployment insurance benefits are of relatively short duration, and little is available in terms of rehabilitation and job protection or accommodation, the number of applicants for disability transfers will be relatively high. Numbers of disability applicants will increase as replacement rates increase, as the period over which benefits can be received lengthens, and as the probability of acceptance onto the disability rolls grows. On the other hand, numbers of disability applicants should decrease as access to the relative rewards in the labor market improves.

CONCLUSION

Using the criteria discussed above, one can discuss policy issues related to the US disability policy. Not surprisingly, the high and rising costs of federal disability programs are a concern, but policy-makers also are troubled by falling employment among those with disabilities, especially during an economic boom dominated by growth in less physically demanding jobs and after the passage of the ADA.

Box 9.3   *The Interaction of Retirement and Disability Programs on Employment Age*

Both the United States and the Netherlands have a mixture of public and private programs to ameliorate the loss of income associated with exit from the labor force due to disability or retirement. But the Netherlands disability program is much more generous and has a lower standard of eligibility. For instance, Dutch workers with partial disabilities are eligible for benefits. See Aarts et al. (1996) for a comparison of the two programs.

   Table 9.3 from Burkhauser et al. (1999) shows the employment rate of men from these two countries by age. For ages 51 through 53, the percentage of men working in the two countries is similar but thereafter, the decline in employment in the Netherlands is much more rapid than in the United States. By age 58, less than one half of Dutch men are employed. By age 61 (one year before the earliest age of eligibility for Social Security benefits in the United States), only 16.8 percent of Dutch men are employed. In contrast, in the United State 65.9 percent of men are still employed at age 61.

   The next three columns show the resources available to men not employed in the two countries at these ages. In the United States, some are receiving disability transfers and others are receiving private employer pensions. But a large share receives neither. In contrast, in the Netherlands, the great majority of men who don't work prior to age 55 receive disability transfers. Thereafter they receive either disability or employer pension benefits. Only a small percent of men receive neither.

   It is highly unlikely that differences in underlying medical conditions in the two countries can explain this dramatic difference in the use of disability transfers. Rather, public policies in the Netherlands are far more focused on providing alternative sources of income for those who do not work at "older" ages. In the United States, those who do not work before age 62 are much less likely to receive either disability transfers or a private employer pension. The result is that men work longer in the United States than in the Netherlands. But those who do not work at these ages are much less likely to receive either disability or private pensions in the United States than they are in the Netherlands. Clearly, the two countries have made difference choices on how they encourage workers to leave the labor forces and how much social protection they provide to those who do.

Table 9.3 Prevalence of work and transfer benefits for men by age in the Netherlands and the United States

| Age | United States Not working | | | | The Netherlands Not working | | | |
	Working[a]	Disability transfers[b]	Employer pension[c]	Other[d]	Working[a]	Disability transfers[b]	Employer pension[c]	Other[d]
51	82.6	4.1	0.9	12.4	83.3	13.7	0.0	3.0
52	84.9	3.0	2.4	9.9	87.5	8.1	1.9	2.5
53	82.8	3.5	0.5	13.2	81.9	14.1	1.7	2.3
54	84.6	2.9	2.7	9.8	74.6	17.2	1.9	6.2
55	78.5	4.5	1.8	15.3	72.2	16.7	3.5	7.5
56	76.9	5.0	6.3	11.8	59.0	23.9	10.2	6.8
57	80.3	4.6	7.0	8.0	58.7	17.4	15.6	8.3
58	71.5	7.5	9.2	12.0	49.0	25.0	19.0	7.0
59	68.9	6.5	9.3	15.3	44.1	23.2	27.5	5.2
60	67.9	6.1	12.6	13.3	20.9	33.3	42.3	3.5
61	65.9	5.6	16.0	12.5	16.8	26.9	50.5	5.8

[a] Those who are working at the time of the interview – 1993 in The Netherlands and 1992 in the United States.

[b] Those who are not working and are receiving disability transfers at the time of the interview.

[c] Those who are not working or receiving disability transfers but who are receiving private pension benefits at the time of interview.

[d] Those who are not working and receiving neither disability transfers nor private pension benefits at the time of interview.

Source: Burkhauser, Dwyer, Lindeboom, Theeuwes, and Woittiez (1999). Data from The Netherlands are weighted values of the 1993 Wave 1 CERRA Household Survey. Data from the United States are weighted values of the 1992 Wave 1 Gamma Release of the Health and Retirement Survey. pp. 233–65.

Looking forward, two other events in the next decade are likely to intensify disability policy discussion. As was shown in figure 9.5, applications for SSDI and SSI are sensitive to the business cycle. In the next recession, a downturn in the economy will boost disability applications and increase pressure to ease eligibility standards for disability transfers. This historical response likely will be intensified given that the welfare reforms of 1996 have made it more difficult for low-income people to be eligible for other programs.

Second, the percentage of the population aged 50 and over is increasing. Since the prevalence of disability rises sharply at age 50 and older, applications for both SSDI and SSI are likely to rise. Also, beginning in 2000 the age of eligibility for full Social Security retirement benefits began to rise from 65 to 67.[7] Although the rise will be gradual over a number of years, the increase in the normal retirement age will push up the relative value of SSDI and SSI benefits for workers considering exiting the labor market prior to age 67. Again, given the imprecise measurement of disability, some of these new applicants likely will be awarded benefits.

Finally, in the longer term, both SSDI and SSI will be impacted by the long-term fiscal problems discussed in chapter 8. For instance, any changes in the benefit formula that reduce AIME or PIA will also impact on those who exit the labor market via SSDI. For example, the Bush Commission proposal to shift from a wage index to a price index for AIME calculations will not only lower the replacement rate for future generations of older workers but also do so for future generations of younger workers coming onto the SSDI rolls. Unlike those who retire at older ages, those who come onto the SSDI rolls at younger ages will not have built up a stock of second-pillar defined contributions assets to offset this decline in first-pillar defined benefits. Policy-makers will either have to explicitly increase the "insurance" component of SSDI to offset this problem or younger workers will have to increase their private disability insurance to insure higher replacement rates following a disability.

If early or normal retirement ages are pushed back further to offset the increasing costs to OASI of future increase in life expectancy, the SSI-old age eligibility age of 65 will also have to be reconsidered. On the one hand, eligibility age for SSI-old age benefits could be pushed back with the normal OASI retirement age on the grounds that our society has pushed back the age when we are "no longer expected to work." This will leave the SSI disability to provide a safety net for workers below this older age who are not expected to work because of disability. Alternatively, SSI old age – which is funded by more progressive taxes than OASI – could be used to offset the declining redistributive goals of a smaller and more insurance-based OASI program by guaranteeing minimum income level for all persons age 65 or even age 62.

DISCUSSION QUESTIONS

Comment on the reasonableness of each of these statements:

1 All employers should be required to provide accommodations to workers with disabilities.

2   There is very little relationship between the DI and SSI disability programs and other government transfer programs since these two programs are specifically targeted on those who are unable to work based on their medical condition.

3   The dramatic differences in DI and SSI acceptance rates across states are evidence of the dramatic difference in medical conditions across states.

4   DI is a much more popular system than OASI because DI benefits are received at younger ages and in almost all cases beneficiaries will receive benefits that exceed their contributions into the system.

5   It is better to allow some working-age people with disabilities who could work onto the DI rolls than to deny someone who cannot work entrance to the DI program rolls.

6   Using figure 9.4, discuss the consequences of replacing the current SSDI system with a system that had a tax rate of 50 percent on labor earnings after a disregard of $780. What are the policy advantages and disadvantages associated with these changes? How much does your answer depend on the ability of those with severe disabilities to work?

Notes

1   Other disability transfer programs such as Workers' Compensation and Veterans' Disability benefits also provide income support, but these programs are targeted only to those whose disability occurred at work.

2   For a review of this literature, see Stapleton and Burkhauser (2003).

3   Workers aged 31 or older must have at least 20 quarters of coverage during a period of 40 calendar quarters ending with the quarter in which their disability began. Workers aged 24 through 30 must have quarters of coverage in one-half of the quarters of coverage elapsing after age 21, and workers under age 24 need 6 quarters of coverage in the period of 12 quarters ending with their quarter of disability onset.

4   Children of disabled workers are also eligible to receive monthly benefits equal to 50 percent of the worker's PIA, as are spouses under age 65 who are caring for at least one child of the worker under age 16 (or older but disabled). However, monthly benefits to the spouse and children are reduced so that total benefits do not exceed a "maximum family benefit" amount payable on the workers account. For disabled workers entitled after 1980, the maximum family amount is the smaller of: (1) 85 percent of the worker's AIME (or 100 percent of the PIA, if larger) or (2) 150 percent of the PIA.

5   The employment data come from Burkhauser, Daly, et al. (2002) and reflect the employment rates of CPS respondents who say they are limited in the amount or type of work they can perform. Data on SSDI and SSI beneficiaries come from the Social Security Administration (2000).

6   See Bound and Burkhauser (1999), Daly and Burkhauser (2003), and Hoynes and Moffitt (1996) for a review of these issues as they pertain to SSDI and SSI.

7   Beginning with individuals born in 1938, age 62 in 2000, the normal retirement age will rise 2 months per year for five years, to age 66. The normal retirement age will begin to rise again in 2017 (individuals born in 1955) and rise two years per year through 2021 to reach 67.

References

Aarts, L., Burkhauser, R. V., and de Jong, P. R. 1996: *Curing the Dutch Disease: An International Perspective on Disability Policy Reform.* Aldershot: Avebury.

Acemoglu, D. and Angrist, J. 2001: Consequences of employment protection? The case of the Americans with Disabilities Act. *Journal of Political Economy* 109 (5): 915–57.

Autor, David. and Duggan, Mark. 2003: The rise in disability and the decline in unemployment. Mimeo, *Quarterly Journal of Economics.* 118 (1): 157–206.

Berkowitz, Edward D. and Burkhauser, Richard V. 1996: A United States perspective on disability programs. In Leo J. M. Aarts, Richard V. Burkhauser, and Philip P. de Jong (eds.), *Curing the Dutch Disease: An International Perspective on Disability Policy Reform.* Aldershot: Avebury, 71–92.

Bound, J. and Burkhauser, R. V. 1999: Economic analysis of transfer programs targeted on people with disabilities. In O. Ashenfelter and D. Card (eds.), *Handbook of Labor Economics,* vol. 3(c). Amsterdam: Elsevier Science, 3417–528.

Bound, J., Cullen, J. B., Nichols, A., and Schmidt, L. 2002: *The Welfare Implications of Increasing DI Benefit Generosity.* (National Bureau of Economic Research working paper). Ann Arbor, MI: University of Michigan.

Bound, J. and Waidman, T. 2002: Accounting for recent declines in employment rates among the working-aged disabled. *Journal of Human Resources* 37 (2): 231–50.

Burkhauser, Richard V. and Daly, Mary C. 1996: The potential impact on the employment of people with disabilities. In Jane West (ed.), *Implementing the Americans with Disabilities Act.* Cambridge, MA: Blackwell Publishers, 153–92.

Burkhauser, Richard V. and Daly, Mary C. 2002: U.S. disability policy in a changing environment. *Journal of Economics Perspectives* 16 (1) (Winter): 213–24.

Burkhauser, Richard V., Daly, Mary C., and Houtenville, A. (2001): How working-age people with disabilities fared over the 1990s business cycle. In Peter P. Budetti, Richard V. Burkhauser, Janice M. Gregory, and H. Allan Hunt (eds.), Kalamazoo, MI, W. E. Upjohn Institute for Employment Research, pp. 291–346.

Burkhauser, Richard V., Butler, J. S., and Weathers, Robert R., II 2002: How policy variables influence the timing of Social Security Disability Insurance applications. *Social Security Bulletin* 64 (1): 52–83.

Burkhauser, Richard V., Daly, Mary C., Houtenville, A., and Nargis, N. 2002: Employment of working age people with disabilities in 1980s and 1990s: what current data can and cannot tell us. *Demography* 39 (3): 541–55.

Burkhauser, Richard V., Dwyer, Debra, Lindeboom, Maarten, Theeuwes, Jules, and Woittiez, Isolde, 1999: Health, work, and economic well-being of older workers aged 51 to 61: A cross-national comparison using the United States HRS and the Netherlands CERRA data sets. In James Smith and Robert Willis (eds.), *Wealth, Work, and Health: Innovations in Measurement in the Social Services.* Ann Arbor, MI: University of Michigan Press, pp. 233–65.

Burkhauser, Richard and Smeeding, Timothy 1981: The net impact of the Social Security system on the poor, *Public Policy* 29 (2): 150–78.

Daly, M. C. and Burkhauser, Richard V. 2003: The Supplemental Security Income Program. In Robert Moffitt (ed.), *Means-Tested Programs in the United States.* Chicago: University of Chicago Press; Cambridge, MA: NBER.

DeLeire, Thomas 2000: The wage and employment effects of the Americans with Disabilities Act. *Journal of Human Resources* 35 (4): 693–715.

Hoynes, H. and Moffitt, R. 1996: The effectiveness of financial work incentives in Social Security Disability Insurance and Supplemental Security Income: lessons from other transfer programs. In J. Mashaw et al. (eds.), *Disability, Work and Cash Benefits*. Kalamazoo, MI: Upjohn Institute for Employment Research.

Kaye, Steven 2001: Improved employment opportunities for people with disabilities. In David Stapleton and Richard Burkhauser (eds.) *The Decline in Employment of People with Disabilities: A Policy Puzzle*. Kalamazoo, MI: W. E. Upjohn Institute for Employment Research: 217–58.

Mashaw, Jerry and Reno, Virginia 1996: *Balancing Security and Opportunity: The Challenge of Disability Income Policy* (Report of the Disability Policy Panel). Washington, DC: National Academy of Social Insurance.

Mashaw, Jerry, Reno, Virginia, Berkowitz, Monroe, and Burkhauser, Richard V. (eds.) 1996: *Disability, Work, and Cash Benefits*. Kalamazoo, MI: Upjohn Institute for Employment Research.

Powers, Elizabeth and Neumark, David 2001: *The Supplemental Security Income Program and Incentives to Take up Social Security Early Retirement: Empirical Evidence from the SIPP and Social Security Administration Data*. Cambridge, MA: NBER Working Paper W 86970, December.

Social Security Administration 1975–2000: *Annual Statistical Supplements to the Social Security Bulletin, 1975–2000*. Washington, DC: US Government Printing Office.

Stapleton, David and Burkhauser, Richard 2003: *The Decline in Employment of People with Disabilities: A Policy Puzzle*. Kalamazoo, MI: W. E. Upjohn Institute for Employment Research: 1–22.

Stapleton, David C., Coleman, Kevin, Dietrich, Kimberly, and Livermore, Gina 1998: Empirical analysis of disability insurance and social security insurance application and award growth. In Kalman Rupp and David C. Stapleton (eds.), *Growth in Disability Benefits: Explanations and Policy Implications*. Kalamazoo, MI: Upjohn Institute for Employment Research, 31–72.

Ticket to Work and Work Incentives Advisory Panel 2002: *Advice Report to the Commissioner of Social Security: Statutory Requirement and Design Issues Related to SSDI $1 for $2 Benefit Offset Research (August)*. Washington, DC: Social Security Administration. http://www.ssa.gov/work/panel

West, Jane 1996: *Implementing the Americans with Disabilities Act*. Cambridge, MA: Blackwell Publishers, 153–92.

PART FOUR

Health and Long-term Care for Older Persons

CHAPTER TEN

The Financing and Delivery of Acute Health Care Services

LEARNING OBJECTIVES

After completing this chapter, you will be able to:

1   Explain the difference between acute and chronic health care needs.
2   Discuss how the aging of the population, advances in medical technology, and general economic conditions affect the projections of future costs for Medicare.
3   Describe the current benefits provided by Medicare and how coverage has changed over time.
4   Analyze current strengths and weaknesses of the Medicare system.
5   Explain why older persons still spend a higher proportion of their income on health care than younger households.
6   Discuss potential changes in Medicare to improve services and reduce costs.

CHAPTER OUTLINE

INTRODUCTION

Older Americans receive a substantial share of their health care coverage from government programs, setting them apart from the population as a whole. Enacted in 1965 as an addition to the Social Security Act, Medicare and Medicaid play crucial roles in the resources that individuals can rely upon in old age. Without these protections, few Americans could afford to retire. But Medicare and Medicaid do not cover all the health care needs of the population over 65, despite high levels of federal expenditures that leave many policy-makers concerned about the future. Thus, they need to be viewed in the context of both meeting health care needs and offering financial protections to older Americans.

Medicare is a federal health insurance program that serves over 97 percent of persons age 65 and older in the United States, providing basic protection for their acute-care needs.[1] Medicaid, which offers help for low-income and low-wealth Americans of all ages, is also important for older persons, filling in crucial gaps in Medicare coverage for this group. That is, Medicare does not offer a fully comprehensive set of acute care benefits, so Medicaid, which is a joint federal/state program, supplements that coverage for about one in every seven seniors.

Can these programs survive in an aging society when large infusions of revenues will be needed to keep them afloat? Should we retain Medicare essentially as it is today or change it dramatically over time, perhaps ceding responsibility to the private sector in hopes of holding down growth in health care spending? Greater financial responsibility on the elderly may reduce use of health care services. Is Medicare now a health care dinosaur that needs to be substantially revamped as some have suggested? Does it create incentives for overuse of care? Will Medicaid, which is currently under less scrutiny, become an issue as well? The most honest answer to these questions is likely to be equivocal since it is extremely difficult to look into the future some 30 or 40 years and have a sense of what our health care system will or should look like. Moreover, some of the economic incentives that work well elsewhere are often more problematic in health care, making policy pronouncements difficult. There are likely to be substantial changes both in how care will be provided to individuals and how systems of payment and oversight will be organized as we move further into the twenty-first century.

Most of the focus of this chapter is on acute care spending and Medicare, which forms the base for acute-care health insurance for seniors. Other programs, both public and private, wrap around or coordinate with the coverage that Medicare provides. In most cases, Medicare is the first payer, with other coverage only taking over where Medicare ends. We begin, however with an examination of specific health care issues facing the age 65 and above population.

SPECIAL CONCERNS REGARDING HEALTH CARE AND THE ELDERLY

As people age, they tend to spend more on health care services. Is such spending for the elderly as compared with the rest of the population inappropriate?

Table 10.1 Health spending and demographic structure in selected countries, 1997

	Per capita health spending			Health spending as a percentage of GDP		
	On all persons	On the elderly	Ratio aged 65+/Age 0–64	On all persons	On the elderly	Percent of population aged 65+
United States	$3,925	$12,090	4.4	13.5	5.0	12.5
Germany	$2,339	$4,993	2.8	10.4	3.5	16.8
Canada	$2,095	$6,764	4.8	9.3	3.6	12.9
France	$2,051	$4,717	3.0	9.6	3.4	16.0
Australia	$1,805	$5,348	4.1	8.3	3.0	12.2
Japan	$1,741	$5,258	5.3	7.3	3.4	17.5
United Kingdom	$1,347	$3,612	4.0	6.7	2.8	16.1

Expenditures expressed in US dollars, adjusted for purchasing power parities.
Source: Reinhardt (2000).

Comparisons from the 1980s indicate that average acute care spending for persons over age 65 was about 3.8 times as high as that for those under age 65 (Lefkowitz and Monheit, 1991). And in the 1990s, that share has risen to 4.4. Higher spending for the old also occurs in other countries – including those where individuals of all ages are in the same health insurance program (see table 10.1). The ratio is as high as 5.3 in Japan and 4.8 in Canada. The share is substantially lower in Germany and France, however (Reinhardt, 2000).

But as important as the level of spending may be, questions about affordability of health care in the future for seniors also depend upon the rate of growth in spending over time. Many of the factors affecting per capita spending for older Americans are the same as those affecting health care spending for all Americans. However, a number of critical factors may have a differential impact on spending for older persons: the higher acute and chronic care needs of older persons, demands on services at the end of life, the aging of the population, the role of technology, and the special needs of long-term care. In some cases, these differences affect rates of growth, while in other instances they influence the overall level of spending.

Acute and chronic care needs

Older persons are more likely to suffer chronic and acute care illnesses than are younger persons. The incidence of problems such as heart disease, cancer, arthritis, and diabetes rise with age. Rates of disability and the share of the population reporting poor or fair health status are positively correlated with aging (National Center for Health Statistics, 2000). International comparisons also show increasing

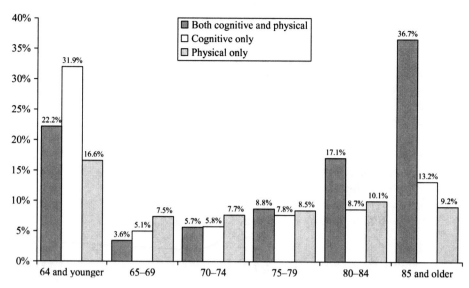

Figure 10.1 Percent of beneficiaries with health conditions, by type of condition and age, 1997

Source: 1997 Medicare Current Beneficiary Survey.

health problems by age and despite lengthening life expectancy, morbidity at older ages is still high (Miles and Brody, 1992). Not only does this mean that each condition is likely to be associated with high spending, but for those with multiple health limitations, treatment of any particular problem is more complicated when other health conditions need to be taken into account. Recovery from surgery may take longer for those with heart disease or diabetes, for example. All these factors contribute to higher levels of health care spending by age group, with particularly sharp rises after age 65. Figure 10.1 indicates rates of disability by age, focusing on summary measures aimed at capturing the population facing substantial physical and/or cognitive function limitations. These summary measures combine a number of physical measures such as multiple chronic conditions, and cognitive indicators such as having Alzheimer's disease or severe mental health problems (Moon and Storeygard, 2002).

There has been some good news, however, in the rates of disability facing the very old. A number of studies show a trend to lower rates of physical limitations at each age level, meaning that individuals are not only leading longer, but now also healthier, lives (Manton and Gu, 2001). These limitations are often measured as problems with Activities of Daily Living (ADLs) and their trends have been tracked for a long period of time.[2] Although life expectancy has increased over time, the number of persons with ADLs and their severity did not change much until the 1990s. This trend now suggests an improvement in functioning and mobility of older Americans.

What is less clear, however, is whether these lower disability rates will result in lower health care costs. The optimists suggest that this could be the start of a trend that will reduce health care spending as people's needs decline. They point out that there is a strong correlation between disability and health care spending. A more skeptical view, however, is that some of the reduced disability comes as a result of health expenditures such as cataract surgery, knee and hip replacements, and heart bypass surgery, for example. If so, this spending must be maintained to retain those improvements in ADLs. Moreover, a healthier and more mobile older population will likely demand more of certain types of acute care services. As the benefits rise relative to costs (and risks), demand for care will likely rise. Increasing physical mobility makes cataract surgery more important, for example. Finally, it may be more likely that reductions in rates of disability will help with long-term care costs rather than acute care spending. More study is needed in this area to determine how changes in disability and health status affect Medicare spending.

The end of life

Many casual observers of our health care system have suggested over the years that controlling use of services in the last year of life may be the magic bullet for reining in the level of health care spending. And since most of those who die each year are over the age of 65, this is particularly an issue for the Medicare program. Certainly, few statistics sound as compelling as the widely quoted statistic of 28 percent of Medicare spending concentrated on the 5 percent of enrollees in their last year of life (Lubitz and Prihoda, 1984). In 2002, this translates into approximately $72 billion in public expenditures.

But like most "magic bullets" for solving problems with the health care system, there is more to the story than just excessive spending on hopeless cases. First, if technology is being used extensively in futile cases involving the very old, the share of resources devoted to health care in the last year of life should be rising as technology has expanded. Anne Scitovsky (1984 and 1994) pursued this question and found that high expenditures were not a new phenomenon; they even preceded the introduction of Medicare in 1965. Lubitz (1990), updating an earlier study, found that between 1976 and 1985, a period of enormous cost growth in health care, there was no increase in the share of Medicare resources going to those in the last year of life. The proportion of decedents increased slightly, while the proportion of Medicare dollars fell slightly.

Further disaggregation of Medicare data also reinforces this analysis. While the fact that Medicare spending increases steadily by age seems to support claims about disproportionate spending on the very old, the data show exactly the opposite pattern for persons in their last year of life. Considerably more is spent on the 65 to 69 year olds who die in a given year than on decedents over age 85 (Lubitz and Riley, 1993). That is, more is spent on younger Medicare beneficiaries who are more likely to recover – a result consistent with reasonable health care policy. Since life expectancy at age 65 is now about 17 years, spending on the younger old is not necessarily just cheating death for a few months, but rather treating patients with many useful years left.

These findings suggest several things. First, physicians do not always know that death is imminent when making health care spending decisions. And since people often die after being ill or requiring medical treatment, it is only natural to see extraordinary spending in the last year of life (as well as on those who survive major illnesses). The issue more appropriately is whether it appears that we disproportionately spend on those with no chance of survival and whether that contributes substantially to the problem of the growth in health care spending. Here the evidence is much weaker. As noted above, there is a drop off in spending on the very old as compared to the young in their last year of life, suggesting that at least, on average, decisions are being made to resist heavy acute care expenditures. Moreover, while the 5 percent who die each year account for about a quarter of Medicare spending, the top 5 percent of all spenders under Medicare (only some of whom die during the year), account for just under half of all expenditures (HCFA, 2000). Certainly, end of life care is not the only source of high levels of Medicare spending.

The problem of excessive use of medical care near death by the elderly, thus, is likely overstated. Put in economic terms, a cost–benefit analysis is difficult to do with the uncertainty surrounding illness, although casual evidence suggests that some calculations about the likely benefits do take place. It does mean, however, that Medicare faces some unique challenges in addressing the problems of assessing inappropriate care and in needing to find ways to manage a disproportionate number of high cost cases.

The aging of the population

It is not just spending on the end of life or higher average costs compared to the young that leads to higher costs for Medicare than for the rest of the population. Medicare is a program in which the number of enrollees is growing more rapidly than the size of the rest of the population. At present, the number of enrollees is growing by about 1.1 percent per year, but that rate will increase to about 3 percent per year at the end of this decade as baby boomers begin to reach eligibility age for Medicare. Much of the current growth is occurring among the very old who have higher than average levels of expenditure. The longer life expectancies of older Americans mean that each person will remain on the Medicare rolls for a longer period of time. Since Medicare was enacted in 1965, life expectancy at age 65 has grown about three years.

As a result, we should expect not only that Medicare spending overall should grow more rapidly than health care spending for the population as a whole because of increases in the number of Medicare beneficiaries, but that growth should be higher on a per capita basis as well since the composition of the Medicare population is also changing. The share of beneficiaries with higher expenditure needs is rising as compared to those with lower average expenditures.

Spillman and Lubitz (2000) argue:

> if longevity increases because of reduced morbidity and mortality from diseases that
> are expensive to treat, then Medicare costs may be reduced. If longevity increases as
> the result of expensive treatments, Medicare costs may rise. The costs of both acute
> and long-term care increase with the level of disability. If increased longevity is accom-
> panied by declines in rates of disability, as suggested by recent studies, then the effect
> of increased longevity on health care expenditures may be moderated.

Crimmins (2001) expresses similar sentiments.

In practice, studies have indicated a positive but relatively small amount of
growth attributable to the changing composition of the population age 65 and older.
Several studies concluded that the aging of the population probably adds about
0.8 to 1.0 percentage point to the growth of Medicare spending each year relative
to the rest of the population (US Congress, 1994; Mayhew, 2000). Another recent
study found a lower 0.2 percentage point increase annually in Medicare spending
from population aging (Moon, 1999). None of these figures represent very great
amounts in any one year, but it means that just to keep Medicare on an even foot-
ing with the rest of the health care system, we should expect spending growth per
capita to be somewhat higher for Medicare than for younger age groups.

The role of technology

One of the important pressures on health care spending for everyone arises from
use of new technology, but these pressures may be disproportionately large for the
Medicare population. Technology has given us new tools such as CT scans and
magnetic resonance imagers (MRIs) and new procedures such as endoscopies
and arthroscopies. These new testing technologies are often less invasive and hence
less risky than earlier means for detecting illness. For example, subjecting older or
disabled patients to exploratory surgery might not be feasible, but giving them MRIs
does not carry the same risks. Thus, it is not surprising that these new tests are
particularly important for high risk Medicare patients. Although the costs of such
activities have increased, so have the benefits. These tests constitute the fastest
rising categories of services under Medicare (Berenson and Holahan, 1992). And
when used, they are likely to increase detection of problems and lead to more
procedures being undertaken.

Surgery and other technical procedures also continue to grow, while becoming
increasingly more complex and expensive over time. For example, cardiac bypass
surgery rates for men over the age of 75 rose from 3.0 per 1,000 in 1985 to 8.1 per
1,000 in 1990 and to 21.2 per 1,000 in 2000 (NCHS, 2002). What has not happened,
however, is any reduction in what we pay for such services. The improved success
of procedures such as hip replacements and cataract surgery means that outcomes
have improved relative to their risks. Thus, higher rates of use would certainly be
expected and appropriate, with the increases disproportionately benefiting older

and disabled patients (Fuchs, 1999). While certain surgeries in the past would have been performed routinely on younger patients, these advances mean that those who previously were poor candidates for treatment because of age or frailty are now undergoing treatments. The benefit–cost ratio improvements are greater for the Medicare population than for others. But the prices charged for these procedures do not seem to come down over time, so technological advances in medical care tend to increase, not decrease, costs.

Research on the benefits of technological advances in medical care, medical research, and medical advances more generally is still in its infancy. Yet recent work by Cutler and McClellan (2001), Cutler (1995), Lichtenberg (2001a, 2001b, 2002) and Topel and Murphy (forthcoming) suggest that the net benefits of public health expenditures for research, new treatments, and increasing access to high quality health care have been gains in longevity in the United States that are very cost-effective. And many of these gains accrue to the elderly. Moreover, the income elasticity of demand for health care in the United States is about 1.4 and 1.2 in most other nations (Freund and Smeeding, 2002).[3] While these issues are pervasive in the overall US health care system, the role of technology may have an even greater impact on spending for the Medicare population, helping to explain high rates of growth of service use within this age group.

The combination of an aging population and the special benefits of new technology for frail populations underscores that Medicare will have difficulty in holding down its rate of growth both absolutely and relative to the rest of the population in the foreseeable future. This does not signal inappropriate use, but rather the increased effectiveness of various tests and procedures. Nonetheless, a number of researchers, policy-makers and others have suggested that access to this type of care be limited to exclude the very old on the grounds that it is inappropriate to use aggressive techniques on the very old even if they are not dying (Lamm, 1993). Their arguments are not based on issues about effectiveness, but rather about how scarce dollars should be allocated.

The challenges posed by the need for long-term care

Long-term care expenditures represent an extremely large source of health care costs for seniors. While long-term care services used by this group are likely to be more supportive and hence less expensive than services for some of the younger disabled groups, the elderly disproportionately require such care. Aside from any acute care differences, burdens on older Americans will be high because of these long-term care needs. These issues will be discussed in more detail in the next chapter.

However, needs for long-term care can also affect acute care spending. Because of the inadequacy of financing of long-term care, available acute care services are sometimes used as a substitute for long-term care. Medicare is the major insurer affected by this use and likely has higher costs because of it. For example, Medicare offers a home health benefit intended to provide rehabilitation and other medical services to qualifying persons in their homes. But it is also helpful to those in need of long-term care who are residing at home because this home health benefit can also include supportive services as long as the need remains for skilled care. Restricting unskilled aide services in Medicare is controversial. These services certainly fill an important need for many older Americans, but providing them through a "medical model" may make them more expensive than if funded elsewhere. From the beneficiaries' point of view, however, this is a fully subsidized benefit and hence their costs are zero.

Rapid growth in home health care from 1990 to 1997 (since regulations on eligibility were eased in 1989) is attributable to its increasing use as a chronic care as well as an acute care benefit (Kenney and Moon, 1993). Legislation in 1997 tried to limit such use, resulting in an actual decline in home health spending at the end of the 1990s. But it is now beginning to rise again. Pressures to use skilled nursing facility beds to meet long-term care needs also have helped raise Medicare spending, particularly since 1988.

Further, when patients' long-term care needs are neglected, they may escalate into acute medical crises which raise the costs of care. For example, when nursing homes allow patients to develop bed sores, pneumonia or other conditions, rates of hospitalization can go up. The large amount of unmet need for those in the community also leads to higher but preventable acute care costs. No careful studies have been undertaken that can fully answer the question of how to appropriately balance these two types of services to achieve the most efficient outcome (see chapter 11).

It follows that if little expansion of affordable long-term care occurs, the pressures to use Medicare for this purpose will remain strong and likely continue to provide an upward bias in spending on this part of the program.

THE BASICS OF MEDICARE

Medicare was established by legislation in 1965 as Title XVIII of the Social Security Act and first went into effect on July 1, 1966. The overriding goal of the program was to provide mainstream acute health care – that is, hospital, physician and related services – for persons over the age of 65. This age group had been underserved by the health care system, largely because many older persons could not afford insurance. Further, insurance coverage as part of retirement benefits was relatively rare and insurance companies had been reluctant to offer coverage to older persons even for those seniors who could afford it. Consequently, Medicare has contributed substantially to the well-being of America's oldest citizens. It is the largest payer of acute health care services in the United States, providing the major source of insurance for the elderly (and, since 1974, the disabled). Medicare today has given a whole generation of people access to care beyond what they had before. One of Medicare's important accomplishments is that the very old and the very sick have access to the same basic benefits as younger, healthier beneficiaries. While there is certainly room for improvement, Medicare is insurance that is never rescinded because of the poor health of the individual.

When Medicare was instituted in 1966, it revolutionized health care coverage for all persons aged 65 and older. It almost immediately doubled the share of seniors with health insurance. Only about half of persons in this age group had insurance before Medicare (Andersen et al., 1976). By 1970, 97 percent of older Americans were covered by the program, and that proportion has remained about the same ever since (Moon, 1996). For the elderly portion of the program, anyone aged 65 or over who is eligible for any type of Social Security benefit (e.g., as a worker or a dependant), receives Part A, Hospital Insurance. Hospital Insurance covers hospital, skilled nursing and hospice care and is funded by payroll tax contributions from workers and employers. Supplementary Medical Insurance (Part B) covers physician services, hospital outpatient services, and other ambulatory care and is funded by a combination of general revenues and premium contributions from beneficiaries. Home health care benefits are covered by both Parts A and B.

When Medicare began, it was dominated by inpatient hospital care, which accounted for about two-thirds of all spending. Indeed, most of the focus of debate before Medicare's passage was on Part A (Hospital Insurance). But as care has moved out of the inpatient setting, Part B (Supplementary Medical Insurance) has become a much larger share of the program (see figure 10.2). Care in hospital outpatient departments and in physicians' offices now replaces many surgeries and treatments formerly performed in inpatient settings. In addition, skilled nursing facility care and home health – referred to as post-acute care – have also increased in importance over time as hospital stays have been shortened. When individuals leave a hospital after only a few days, post-acute care is often needed as a transition, either in a nursing facility or at home with visits from nurses or other skilled technicians. Further, some of these benefits, particularly home health, have been used for supportive or long-term care purposes as well as the skilled care aspects of home health care. The financial incentives established by payment to health providers and by coverage of benefits have affected the mix of services used.

Although Medicare's benefit package has changed little since 1965, in those areas where services are covered, the program has kept up with the times. Many surgeries that would have mean a hospital stay of a week or longer are now performed on an outpatient basis, for example. Moreover, even the oldest-old have access to mainstream medical care (National Center for Health Statistics, 2000). New technology is available to beneficiaries and in some cases, the dissemination of new procedures occurs at a faster pace for the old than for the young (Moon, 1999). A basic concern, described in more detail below, is the comprehensiveness of the benefit package, however. For services, such as prescription drugs, that have never been covered, Medicare is now inadequate. Moreover, Medicare requires high amounts of cost sharing from beneficiaries as compared to most group insurance, leaving seniors with potentially open-ended liabilities. (Potential reforms in these areas are discussed below.)

Medicare offers its beneficiaries the choice between two different types of insurance programs. The first is the traditional fee-for-service program in which the government essentially serves as the insurer. Doctors, hospitals and other providers of

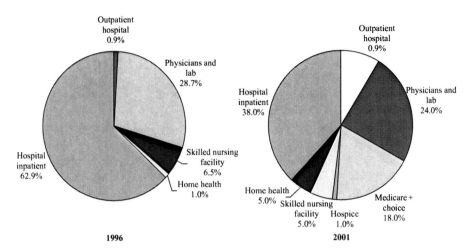

Figure 10.2   Medicare expenditures by type of service 1966 and 2001
Source: Health Care Financing Administration, 2000 and Gluck and Hanson, 2001.

care submit claims to Medicare. The federal government essentially bears the risk for the costs of this care.

The second type of coverage is referred to as Medicare + Choice. If a beneficiary chooses this option, she will rely on a private insurance plan to cover the costs of her care. These private insurers – usually health maintenance organizations (HMOs) – cover all Medicare benefits in exchange for a fixed monthly payment from the federal government. The insurer thus bears the risks of paying for all necessary care.

Medicare + Choice was established in 1997 and replaces the HMO risk option plan that had been a steadily growing share of the program since the 1980s. The intent of this change was to move Medicare further away from its traditional role as an insurer and expand its role as a purchaser of private insurance. This was consistent with the general move in the employer-based insurance world which was adopting managed care in the hope of saving costs. By making the private insurer live within a monthly budget, the goal is to lead them to seek efficiencies in the organization and delivery of care. Additional types of plans, such as privately offered fee-for-service or managed care organizations run by physician or hospital groups, are now also allowed to participate in Medicare + Choice, although so far only a few such plans have been offered to Medicare beneficiaries. About 14 percent of beneficiaries were in Medicare + Choice in early 2001, while the remaining 86 percent of beneficiaries remain in the traditional part of the program (Gold and Mittler, 2001).

Initially, when the HMO option began, private plans attracted only a very small share of Medicare beneficiaries because HMOs require participants to use only plan-approved doctors and hospitals as a condition of coverage. Medicare differs from the rest of the health care system in part because beneficiaries can choose to remain

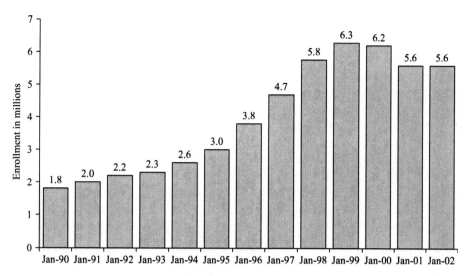

Figure 10.3 Medicare enrollment in HMOs
Total Coordinated Care Plans.
Source: Health Care Financing Administration.

in fee-for-service with no penalties attached. Consequently, HMOs need an "edge" to attract beneficiaries away from fee for service. To be more competitive, many of these plans offered beneficiaries services in addition to those covered by Medicare – particularly prescription drugs. This strategy became more successful as the cost of private supplemental insurance elsewhere in the system rose rapidly. Enrollment increased substantially from 1990 to 1997. Figure 10.3 shows the pattern of enrollment growth over this period.

Plans are able to offer more benefits in part because beneficiaries agree to abide by a stricter set of rules for participation, such as using only doctors, hospitals and other health care providers who are on a prescribed list. In exchange, beneficiaries usually face lower cost-sharing requirements and sometimes have access to benefits such as prescription drugs or dental care. But many of the HMOs offering further benefits do so in those parts of the country where Medicare's monthly contribution to HMOs is high.

Most studies of the private plan option have suggested that payments are more generous than what it actually costs to provide services – particularly in a few areas of the country – so that Medicare's monthly payments to plans effectively subsidize additional benefits for those in private plans. This is largely because plans were paid monthly amounts calculated to cover the costs of average beneficiaries. They quickly learned that the easiest way to make a profit was to attract healthier-than-average patients. This is an easier task than changing the delivery of care – an activity that is often opposed by patients. As a result, this option fails to save money for the government. Moreover, overly-generous payments have led both

HMOs and those enrolled in them to come to expect these extra benefits although they are not guaranteed by law.

Changes made in 1997 as part of the Balanced Budget Act (BBA) were intended to reduce these overpayments, but these changes have been controversial and have contributed to a number of plans withdrawing from the Medicare + Choice system. Consequently, the BBA did not accelerate the move to more private coverage of Medicare beneficiaries as some had hoped. In fact, as shown in figure 10.3, the numbers fell over this period. And despite some increases in payments from legislation in 1999 and 2000, Medicare + Choice remains a troubled program.

The viability of the Medicare + Choice plan is one of the most important problems facing Medicare, and raises concerns about some of the broader reform options now under consideration as will be discussed below.

SUPPLEMENTAL COVERAGE FOR ACUTE CARE

Because of Medicare's limited benefits, private and public markets have developed to meet the additional need for health insurance. Four kinds of supplemental policies have evolved. Medicaid, a public benefit established at the same time as Medicare, subsidizes many low-income beneficiaries through several different arrangements. Employer-based retiree insurance and individual supplemental coverage are provided by private insurers. A fourth option is essentially a hybrid, in which Medicare + Choice plans offer at least some additional services. These supplemental coverages vary in quality, beneficiaries' ability to access them, and the degree to which they relieve financial burdens. A good understanding of how these supplemental plans operate and the contributions they make is essential in any analysis of the health care system facing older Americans. Figure 10.4 shows the extent and type of supplemental coverage for Medicare beneficiaries.

Medicaid

Medicaid offers generous fill-in benefits for persons with low incomes. It is a joint federal/state program in which states have latitude in establishing eligibility and coverage. As a result there is considerable variation in the quality and quantity of services provided across the states. For example, spending on persons over the age of 65 ranged from $5,565 in Tennessee to $23,611 per person in the District of Columbia in 1995. Today, four separate programs provide some benefits under the Medicaid umbrella. Basic Medicaid coverage is limited to those with the lowest incomes, generally well below the federal poverty level. For those who get these benefits, coverage is comprehensive. In addition to paying the Part B premium and relieving beneficiaries of the responsibility for copayments and deductibles, these state-based programs all offer some type of prescription drug coverage, long-term care, and a range of other services as well.

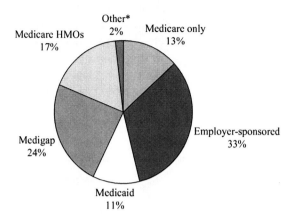

Figure 10.4 Sources of supplemental coverage among non-institutionalized Medicare beneficiaries, 1999
*Includes those receiving coverage from other public programs as well as those in an-risk HMOs
Source: Gluck and Hanson, 2001.

Those who use Medicaid also have to meet an assets test. This is even more stringent than the income requirements and results in a number of individuals who would qualify on the basis of income being excluded from the program (Moon et al., 2002). While income limits have been increased over time, most states have asset tests that have been in place since 1987, often restricting benefits to persons with assets below $2,000 or $4,000 and couples with assets below $3,000 or $6,000. A key policy issue here is how to balance the desire to appropriately target benefits to those most in need with the goal of encouraging older Americans to save for their future needs.

The remaining programs under Medicaid have been added since 1988 to provide some additional relief for low-income Medicare beneficiaries. Together, they are referred to as the Medicare Savings Programs. The Qualified Medicare Beneficiary Program (QMB), covers Part B premiums, deductibles and coinsurance for those whose incomes fall below 100 percent of the poverty level ($8,980 in 2003 for a single person). The Specified Low Income Medicare Beneficiary (SLMB) program provides Part B premium subsidies for those with incomes between 100 and 120 percent of the poverty level. Finally, the 1997 Balanced Budget Act created the Qualified Individuals (QI) program to cover the full premium costs for people with incomes between 120 and 135 percent poverty and a small portion of premium costs for those up to 175 percent of the poverty level (Moon et al., 1998; House Ways and Means Committee, 1998).

In practice, all these programs cover only some of the people who qualify for them. Participation rates remain low because of individuals' reluctance to seek help from a "welfare program," substantial enrollment burdens, and sometimes lack of awareness of potential eligibility. Traditional Medicaid, for example, has never covered more than half of all persons below the poverty line. Moreover, in 1996, only 55 percent of those eligible participated in QMB and just 16 percent of those eligible participate in SLMB (Barents Group, 1999). Thus, Medicaid is only partially successful in assuring comprehensive coverage to low income seniors.

Finally, a few states offer prescription drug plans to seniors at somewhat higher income levels. Such programs are usually quite small, however, except in New York, New Jersey and Pennsylvania (GAO, 2000). They also often have limitations on the kind of drugs covered.

Employer-sponsored plans

Employer-based plans normally offer comprehensive supplemental insurance for their retirees. Employers usually subsidize the premiums that their retirees are asked to pay and establish benefits comparable to what their working population receives by filling in gaps left by Medicare. A large share of these plans, for example, cover prescription drugs. Thus, these plans both reduce out-of-pocket expenses and increase access to services, often without limiting provider choice. Beneficiaries in these plans have among the lowest out-of-pocket costs (MedPAC, 2000), even though they are heavy users of care. They are thus among the best protected of all seniors.

But such plans are limited to workers and dependants whose former employer offers generous retiree benefits. As a consequence, these benefits accrue mainly to high-income retirees. This privileged group does not need improvements in Medicare to assure them access to care since they are covered very well at present. In fact, this group of seniors complicates making changes in the Medicare program since they may be opposed to anything that raises their costs and many policy-makers do not want to devote public dollars to essentially replacing benefits this group already has.

The strength of resistance to change by those with retiree insurance may decline substantially in the future, however, since many employers are beginning to cut back benefits: placing more controls on the use of care, raising contributions in the form of premiums or cost sharing, and even changing the benefit package. A number of studies have tracked changes in employer behavior in this area, with each focusing on different combinations of firms. Nonetheless the results all show the same downward trend. For example, in a study of large firms (with 200 or more workers who are most likely to offer such benefits), the percentage offering retiree health benefits declined from 66 percent in 1988 to 34 percent in 2002 (Kaiser Family Foundation and Health Research and Educational Trust, 2002). Another study by Mercer found similar declines from 40 percent to 24 percent for post-65 retirees from 1993 to 2000 (William Mercer, 2001). Although these reductions have not shown up yet in survey data on beneficiaries, they will likely start to have an impact on that coverage in the next several years. Moreover, the share of those with coverage who are required to pay the full premium costs rose from 27 percent in 1997 to 40 percent in 1999. Another approach to reducing liabilities is to raise the requirements for qualifying for coverage, for example, by adding more years of employment as a condition of participation.

Medigap

A traditional form of private supplemental coverage, commonly referred to as Medigap, offers only limited protections since the individual must pay the full costs of the coverage. The ten standardized plans that insurance companies are allowed to offer cover a basic package of Medicare's required cost sharing and in some cases include a limited prescription drug benefit. Even the limited drug coverage allowed in Medigap is becoming more difficult to obtain, however. Many insurers have dropped the options with drug coverage or set prices at such a high level that few can afford them. In 1998, only about 500,000 of such policies were issued (MedPAC, 2000).

Further, such insurance does not, on average, lower costs for beneficiaries since the premium is fully paid by the beneficiary and includes substantial administrative and marketing charges, and often, profits for the insurer. Thus, many beneficiaries have higher, not lower, financial burdens when they buy Medigap. Medigap is most useful for reducing potential catastrophic expenses for those who have high costs in a particular year. This form of supplemental insurance provides the least protection for beneficiaries, yet it remains popular with beneficiaries seeking to keep their out-of-pocket costs under control.

Another issue is that Medigap premiums have risen dramatically over the 1990s. Between 1992 and 1996, premium rates in Arizona, Ohio, and Virginia rose 18 percent, 41 percent, and 19 percent respectively, though the majority of those rate increases took place between 1995 and 1996 (Alecxih et al., 1997). National estimates for rate increases in 1999–2000 according to insurance experts were for 8 to 10 percent increases (MedPAC, 2000).

Over time, Medigap plans have changed the way they price policies, also contributing to access problems. Medigap providers can sell policies that are rated by community, issue age, or attained age. Companies have moved away from "community-rated" plans where the premium is the same for everyone, regardless of age. Most providers have moved to an attained age structure in which policies increase in cost rapidly as people age. This puts greater burdens on beneficiaries just as their incomes are declining. For the unwary buyer at age 65, these plans appear less costly than community-rated options (Alecxih et al., 1997). But since most beneficiaries cannot change their mind after the six-month period of open enrollment at age 65, they may lock themselves into a very bad deal over time. The premiums in these age-rated plans can get to be so high that older persons cannot afford them. This raises issues about access to care and reduces some of the protection by traditional Medicare which does a good job of pooling risks across a large group. Moreover, as will be discussed in more detail below, premiums for those options with prescription drug coverage have risen even more rapidly since those options attract sicker beneficiaries (resulting in adverse risk selection).

Medicare + Choice

As noted above, beneficiaries also can obtain additional benefits to supplement Medicare's basic package by enrolling in Medicare + Choice. Cost sharing is almost always lower and some additional benefits are usually offered for less than the price of a Medigap plan. But these plans also are becoming more expensive and less comprehensive over time. They are beginning to charge premiums for the additional benefits they offer. While these premiums are still likely to be lower than Medigap premiums, Medicare + Choice may result in high out-of-pocket costs when beneficiaries choose to get some of their care from out-of-network providers.

No coverage

Finally, an increasing number of beneficiaries cannot afford any supplemental policy. As of 1999, 15 percent of Medicare beneficiaries had no extra policy to cover what Medicare's benefit package does not (MedPAC, 2000). Beneficiaries who cannot afford to purchase supplemental coverage and who are not eligible for Medicaid are among the most vulnerable beneficiaries. Since they are likely to be older and poorer, high Medicare out-of-pocket costs likely prevent them from getting needed care.

Lack of supplemental coverage is associated with problems of access to care. Those who have no supplemental coverage, for example, are less likely to see a doctor in any given year, less likely to have a usual source of care, and more likely to postpone getting care in a timely fashion. For example, 21 percent of beneficiaries who rely on Medicare alone reported delaying care due to its cost while only 5 percent of beneficiaries with private coverage report delaying care (Gluck and Hanson, 2001).

PROBLEMS WITH AND STRENGTHS OF THE MEDICARE SYSTEM

One basic issue for Medicare is how well it meets the needs of older Americans. To assess this issue, it is important to focus on the adequacy of Medicare, its viability as part of our health care system, and the special role it plays for older Americans. Moreover, there are pressures on Medicare in its role as a public program to hold down costs as much as possible. For example, a number of critics of the Medicare program blame it not only for the high costs of health care for the elderly, but for aggravating health care inflation in general. The rapid growth in the program in its early years – expanding well beyond predicted spending levels – is often cited as an example of why no government program can be trusted. The needs of seniors and taxpayers are, thus, to some extent in conflict. Both areas of concern need to be considered.

The costs of health care to the beneficiary

Financial burdens for Medicare participants fell by nearly half as a result of Medicare's introduction. Over time, the share of income that seniors spend on

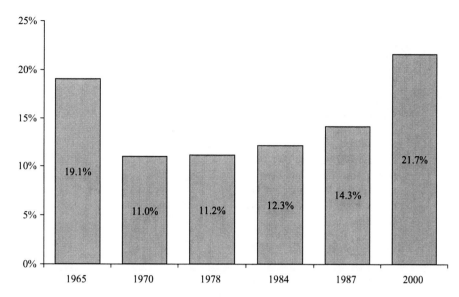

Figure 10.5 Out-of-pocket spending as a share of income among elderly beneficiaries
Source: The Urban Institute Calculations Using NHE, CPI, CPS, and Trustees Reports.

health care has crept back up, although the burdens would be much greater if Medicare was not there (see figure 10.5). In 1965, the typical elderly person spent about 19 percent of her income on health care. That share fell to about 11 percent in 1970. Today it is over 21 percent. This does not mean that Medicare is unimportant, however. Its contribution to the costs of health care for seniors totaled over $5,200 in 2000, or more than a third of the median income of persons aged 65 and older.

Several factors account for the high level of spending by Medicare beneficiaries. First, as has already been noted, Medicare is not a very comprehensive program. Traditional fee-for-service Medicare contains high levels of deductibles and coinsurance that individuals must pay. Further, the Part B premium totals $58.70 per month in 2003. Both Parts A and B have deductibles and most of the services are subject to some type of coinsurance. The Part A deductible – $840 in 2003 – is particularly high. Other cost-sharing requirements are shown in table 10.2. Overall, there is no limit on the total that any one beneficiary might have to pay. As a consequence, beneficiaries are liable for more than 20 percent of the overall costs of Medicare covered services (Maxwell et al., 2001).

And, finally, even though many beneficiaries have some supplemental insurance to cover these other expenses (as noted above), they often pay a substantial amount for such insurance. The combination of direct expenses paid by beneficiaries and their premium contributions to a supplemental plan make up their "out-of-pocket" costs, which are estimated to have averaged $3,100 in 2000. There is a great deal of diversity among beneficiaries in these out-of-pocket costs, however, largely

Table 10.2 Cost-sharing requirements in traditional Medicare, 2003

Requirement	2003 amounts
Part A	
Inpatient	
Deductible	$840 per illness spell
Co-payment for days 61–90	$210 per day
Co-payment for lifetime reserve days 91–150	$420 per day
Co-payment beyond day 150	100% of costs
Skilled nursing facility care	
Co-payment for days 21–100	Up to $105 per day
Co-payment beyond 100 days	100% of costs
Home health care	
Co-insurance for durable medical equipment	At least 20% of approved amount
Hospice	
Co-payment for outpatient drugs	$5
Co-insurance for inpatient respite care	5% of payment amount
Blood	
First 3 pints	100% of costs
Part B	
Premium	$58.70 per month
Deductible	$100 per year
Co-insurance	20% of charges

Source: Health Care Financing Administration.

based on the type of supplemental coverage they have. And frequently, it is those with low and moderate incomes who have the highest costs, making it difficult for them to obtain needed care. Figure 10.6, for example, indicates that older women with incomes below $20,000 and health problems (and who do not get Medicaid coverage) spend, on average, over half their income on health care expenses including premiums and care not covered by insurance. In contrast, individuals with incomes above $20,000 in the 65 to 69 age range spend much less.

The consequences of an inadequate benefit package

Medicare's required cost sharing and the exclusion of some benefits (such as prescription drugs, vision and dental care) from coverage have resulted in a less comprehensive benefit package than what is available to many younger families.[4] One study, for example, indicated that 82 percent of all private group insurance plans for younger persons are more generous than Medicare (Hewitt Associates, 2000).

One of the most important missing pieces of the benefit package is prescription drugs. Drugs have become an integral part of acute health care and their omission

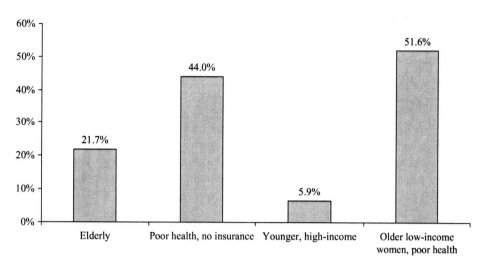

Figure 10.6 Projected out-of-pocket spending as a share of income among cohorts, 2000
Source: The Urban Institute's 1999 Medicare Projections' Model.

from Medicare raises costs to beneficiaries and likely to the program as a whole over time. Beneficiaries have a hard time getting coverage if they are not eligible for traditional Medicaid or employer-sponsored insurance. Consequently, those without coverage and who have limited resources may forego drugs or underuse them. This can not only harm their health, but lead to later higher costs of hospitalization and other use of Medicare-covered services. The problem is that such drug coverage would represent a very expensive addition to the benefit package. Although promised by both Presidential candidates in 2000 and stalled in the Congress in 2001 and 2002, the 2003 debate offers some promise of a new, although limited, benefit. The issues of cost and control over any new benefit have been major stumbling blocks to compromise. Moreover, the benefits from drug coverage are likely to occur sometime in the future while the costs are immediate. The uncertainty of the value of future benefits makes it difficult to assess whether adding a drug benefit will pay for itself over time.

Another concern with an inadequate benefit package is that it can lead to inefficient use of supplemental insurance. Because many of the supplemental plans held by seniors fill in all the gaps raised by cost sharing, this results in effectively "first-dollar" coverage. That is, the beneficiary does not feel the direct effects of most deductibles or coinsurance. For them, healthcare costs are of little direct concern. As a consequence, many analysts believe that spending on health care is higher than it would otherwise be if the users of services had to pay at least something for their care. Further, having two insurance plans creates unnecessary and duplicative administrative costs.

Overall restructuring of Medicare cost sharing could improve the Medicare program by shifting cost sharing to those areas where the incentives might be more effective. Some of this could be done in a relatively budget-neutral way with increases in some areas offsetting changes in others, simplifying the program and making it more consistent with insurance coverage held by the under-65 population (Moon, 1996).

If cost-sharing changes overall become too expensive to provide – for example, in the case of placing a limit on total cost-sharing owed (stop loss) – one way to offer at least partial relief would be to expand the QMB program. At least in theory, the QMB program now provides stop loss for those with the lowest incomes. And although participation is low (Barents, 1999), about 10 to 12 percent of Medicare enrollees now potentially have this protection. Thus, one less expensive way to provide some protection for the most vulnerable beneficiaries would be to expand the QMB program, say, to 150 percent of the poverty level (a move consistent with low income protections often proposed in other health reforms) and seek ways to increase participation in it.

Is Medicare a source of higher growth in spending?

The original goal of the legislation creating Medicare was to offer mainstream medical care to older persons and early fears for the program were that it would not be accepted by doctors and hospitals. Thus, there was a conscious decision not to undertake cost containment efforts initially (Feder, 1977). Medicare likely did contribute to some inflation as it expanded demand for additional services, while the supply of such services was not increased to cover this new demand.

When cost containment efforts were undertaken in the 1980s, Medicare's track record improved substantially (Moon, 1999). In fact, between 1970 and 1998, Medicare's per capita growth was below that of private insurance (Boccuti and Moon, 2003). Only between 1994 and 1996 has the private sector been able to point to lower per capita growth rates than Medicare. And in the late 1990s, Medicare growth was actually negative for two years. Figure 10.7 illustrates the differences in rates of growth of health care spending by Medicare and private insurance.

In general, the patterns of growth look similar between the two sectors. Any health insurance program must deal with the three drivers of health care cost growth: the price charged for services, the basic efficiency of the delivery system, and the number of services delivered. But even though the difference between Medicare and private insurance is relatively small over the full period, that difference eventually amounts to billions of dollars in lower growth.

Medicare has always been competitive in terms of holding down the price it is willing to pay for services, particularly in the key areas of hospital and physician services. Studies have consistently indicated that Medicare pays hospitals below their costs on average, and the fees that Medicare pays for physician services tend to be below even what insurers who demand discounts pay (PPRC, 1997; Zuckerman and Verrilli, 1996). In fact, many private sector plans have adopted the reforms that Medicare pioneered for hospital and physician payment. In other areas,

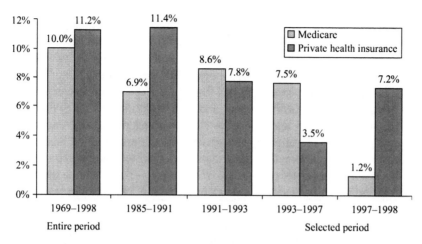

Figure 10.7 Average growth in per enrollee Medicare and private health insurance spending: selected periods, 1969–98
Source: Health Care Financing Administration, Office of the Actuary.

such as home health and skilled nursing facilities, Medicare held down spending growth with strict regulations in the 1980s, but rapid growth in the 1990s occurred after several lawsuits led to a slackening of the regulations. Legislation as part of the Balanced Budget Act of 1997 particularly focused on these services, again slowing their growth. In fact, the impact has been so strong that subsequent legislation has provided some "givebacks" to various provider groups, with more likely to follow. These price controls can become a problem when they are substantially below prices paid by other healthcare consumers. Care providers may shift their practices to serve younger patients, for example.

In the second area affecting growth, administrative costs which average about 2 percent of the costs of providing care, Medicare scores very well (Board of Trustees, 2001). Its costs are held down by law and largely kept separate from the trust funds that have been established to pay benefits. This track record is substantially better than achievements in the private sector where group insurance administrative costs run at about 8 percent and managed care plans often average 15 percent or more (CRS, 1989). But administrative costs are not the only issue, and indeed, it is likely that too little has been spent on oversight and management of Medicare, resulting in other inefficiencies.

This is particularly a danger with regard to fraud and abuse in the program. Until 1996, Medicare had few resources to devote to such activities. After legislation, the program can now use trust fund monies to finance investigations that promise to save money for the federal government. Some highly publicized crackdowns in the area of home health and hospitals in the late 1990s stem in part from increased vigilance.

However, while fraud and abuse are very popular ways to save money, many analysts are skeptical that this alone can make major inroads in reducing the growth in health care spending. Often what gets reported as fraud and abuse reflects the difficulty of knowing when care is appropriate and necessary, or whether required paperwork certifying its necessity has been filed. For example, one study by the Inspector General of the Department of Health and Human Services examined problems in Medicare's home health benefit and suggested that over 40 percent of such services represented fraud and abuse. A close reading of the document, however, indicated that these were after-the-fact reviews that found missing signatures, poor documentation and questionable judgments about when care was needed (Grob, 1997). This is considerably less dramatic that many lay persons believe when they hear about fraud and abuse in health care. And, in fact, many beneficiaries getting care that might not meet the technical definition of necessity value those services highly.

Costs imposed by insurers on the providers of care can also contribute to inefficiency, as can rules that lead to redundant activities or provision of services. Medicare has been criticized in these areas, both for overly rigid rules in certain cases and poor oversight leading to fraud and abuse in others. One of the early pledges from the Bush Administration was to improve the way the program operates in these areas. Moreover, boundaries between programs like Medicare and Medicaid encourage gaming where one program seeks to shift the burden onto the other, leading to poor coordination and likely inappropriate care. Poor coordination of care may mean both provision of too many services (to be discussed next), but also unnecessary reporting and other requirements that result in burdens on health care providers and patients. The development of managed care organizations (MCOs) ideally should address some of these issues by allowing the MCO the freedom to coordinate care with less direct oversight by government. However, many loosely organized MCOs focus more on managing costs than on managing care, and Medicare's experience with private plans has been a troubled one. As profit-making entities, they appropriately seek to hold down costs in the easiest and most effective ways. Getting discounts from doctors and hospitals has traditionally been much easier than finding new and innovative ways to coordinate care. Poorly managed care can mean under-service and undesirable rigidities in allowing access to care.

The most important source of growth in health care costs, however, arises from the increased use of services, both in numbers of services used but particularly in terms of using sophisticated new technology. This is often referred to as "intensity" of service use, that is when use of care shifts from a lower-level service to a more technologically intensive one. Truly reducing health care spending growth means tackling issues such as who will have access to new technology and judgments about whether care is improved – a challenging and controversial area of oversight that will affect all Americans and that no system can easily resolve.

Such controls have been difficult for Medicare and the rest of our health care system to introduce. There is little research to help sort out appropriate and inappropriate care. Often, promising new treatments or procedures are examined only in the context of initial trials and not when they become more widely used in less controlled settings. Studies that have looked at these issues have concluded that there is a substantial amount of overuse of care (for example, Winslow et al., 1988). But difficulty arises in pinpointing where it is occurring and how to control it. Even the development of general guidelines for treatment of certain conditions has proved to be controversial. For example, controversy over how often to give mammograms and what levels of cholesterol require medication have spilled over into the media in recent years. Absent good effectiveness and quality studies, many Americans (both providers and patients) view access to unlimited tests and procedures as a major way to assure quality. Particularly when services are noninvasive and hence not harmful, the path of least resistance is to do more tests and procedures rather than taking a wait-and-see stance in treatment of problems. Americans have a strong belief in and taste for high technology. And there is little reason to believe that new technologies now under development will be substantially cost saving (Schwartz, 1994; Cutler and McClellan, 2001).

Making the private sector work better for Medicare beneficiaries

The entrance of private plans, particularly HMOs, into Medicare marked a new era by introducing competition into many areas of the country. Of primary concern for both the program as a whole and for beneficiaries are cost, quality and access. Policy-makers hoped that HMOs could help the program hold down rising medical care costs. Many believed, and continue to believe, that HMOs can reduce costs through greater efficiency, thus achieving fiscal goals without compromising care for the elderly.

In general, studies indicate that HMOs have achieved modest cost efficiencies through management strategies, particularly those HMOs that are more tightly controlled. This is why they were attractive to Medicare policy-makers. In theory, these managed care organizations can use strong management techniques to control service use, negotiate discounts with providers, keep only those who are "efficient" in their network, and financially reward providers who keep costs down (Langwell and Esslinger, 1997).

In addition, most beneficiaries in HMOs indicate that they are satisfied with the quality of care, because they receive better benefits at lower costs. Only about 1 to 5 percent of beneficiaries disenroll due to quality or access issues (ibid.). Thus, those who choose to enroll largely seem to be satisfied with these private plans, perhaps reflecting a predilection for this type of care delivery since participation is voluntary. And there is evidence that low-income beneficiaries who would not qualify for Medicaid are seeking out HMOs to reduce their out-of-pocket costs (Blustein and Hoy, 2000).

But Medicare's experience with HMOs also has generated a number of concerns. Home health care and physical therapy can be harder for Medicare HMO beneficiaries to receive. There is also concern that the chronically ill fare worse in HMOs than traditional Medicare. In studies on this issue, the chronically ill experienced a

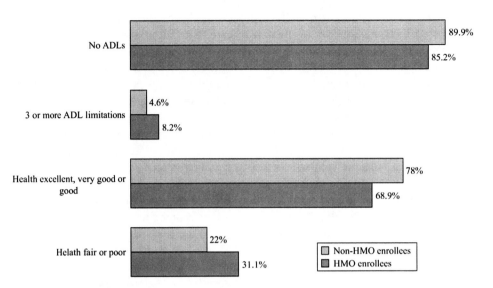

Figure 10.8   Relative health status of HMO enrollees, 1998
Source: HCFA/Office of Strategic Planning: Data from MCBS, 1998.

decline in physical and health outcomes in HMOs. Moreover, HMOs seem to skimp on care in areas most critical for those with chronic or severe health conditions. This is a major limitation for HMOs in Medicare; they serve a healthier population quite well, but fall short when beneficiaries have more serious needs.

In addition to potential problems for beneficiaries, Medicare has not achieved savings for the federal government through its private plan option. The combination of serving a healthier population and an inadequate structure for establishing payments has led Medicare to overpay its private plans for the cost of Medicare-covered services (GAO, 2000). As figure 10.8 indicates, persons enrolled in HMOs tend to be in better health, on average, than the rest of the Medicare population. But payments to private plans have been based on the "average" person. This gives an extra boost to HMOs in offering services. And when there are savings from greater efficiencies, Medicare rules result in some of the savings being shifted to beneficiaries in the form of added benefits. This allows plans to continue to attract enrollees since these overpayments effectively subsidize additional benefits. Consequently, both plans and beneficiaries have an economic stake in continuing this flawed payment system.

The Balanced Budget Act of 1997 recognized this problem and, along with a number of other changes, created a new Medicare + Choice program replacing (and presumably expanding) the managed care option for Medicare. These changes were intended to both stimulate further private plan participation in Medicare and to modify payments so that the program could achieve some savings for the federal government. These goals are at odds with each other, however, and thus far, at least, the tighter payments have had more of an impact, discouraging plans from participating. Between 1999 and 2001, plans withdrew from some areas, affecting nearly 1.7 million enrollees (Gold and Achman, 2001). Many plans that do not withdraw reduced the benefits they offered, and/or raised premiums for participating in their plans.

These changes have caused a great deal of concern in Congress and led to increases in payments to Medicare + Choice plans, delays in the implementation of risk adjustment (which would pay plans more for sicker enrollees), and some regulatory relief. Plans have claimed that they cannot provide services at the same levels to beneficiaries without these increases – or potentially even higher adjustments in the future. The outcome thus far is essentially dissatisfaction among all parties. Medicare still does not generate any federal savings from Medicare + Choice, while beneficiaries and plans claim they need even more federal support. Further, the impacts of these various changes are felt differently across the country due to the wide variation in payment levels by county (Cassidy and Gold, 2000).

The primary hindrance to a larger role for private plans in Medicare is *risk selection*. Not only does risk selection increase costs for traditional Medicare, it produces incentives that are not socially productive. Those who are considered "bad risks" may have more difficulty accessing care. The economic issue here is straightforward – if a plan is paid the same amount for a sick beneficiary as for one who is healthy, the insurer has no economic incentive to take the sicker patient. If it is able to concentrate on the healthy, it can provide extra benefits and good service. This is fine for those it enrolls, but excludes sicker patients from such enhanced care. Consequently, financial resources that could be spent on beneficiaries or in savings to Medicare are used for marketing purposes to recruit the healthiest beneficiaries (Buntin and Newhouse, 1998). While most analysts and policy-makers reiterate the need for good risk adjustment mechanisms – paying plans more to take sicker patients – to make the current Medicare + Choice program and any future reliance on private plans work well, there is a tendency to simply *assume* that such a risk adjuster can be developed and implemented.

Although not all analysts agree that such a risk adjuster is likely to be developed soon, there is considerable agreement that without it, expansion of private plan options will always be problematic. Twenty different studies show that the pre-1997 system of paying plans led to overpayment for HMOs (Kronick and de Beyer, 1997; Newhouse et al., 1999). There would not be a problem if HCFA's reimbursement formula could adjust for health differences that necessitated more or less spending. But prior to 1997, the formula was only adjusted for demographic differences, not health status differences. HMOs were reimbursed based on the average beneficiary cost adjusted for demographic characteristics including the beneficiaries' sex, age, institutional status, geographic cost differences, and eligibility for Medicaid. The problem was compounded by the fact that healthier HMO beneficiaries were not included when calculating the average rate. The formula uses fee-for-service beneficiaries to calculate the reimbursement for HMOs. Overpayment is estimated at between 6 and 37 percent (GAO, 2000). A new system of risk adjustment is being slowly introduced, although under considerable protest from private plans (Newhouse, 2001).

The special pressures on a public program

Although relative to total health care costs Medicare performed rather well in the 1980s and 1990s, Medicare is often portrayed as a runaway item in the federal budget based on the overall growth in spending on the program as compared to the rest of the budget. Further, since Medicare is funded with tax dollars in an era of anti-tax sentiment, it gets more scrutiny than health expenditures paid for by individuals or by businesses. Its absolute size and rate of growth cause Medicare to stand out from most other domestic programs.

Medicare began the 1970s as 3.5 percent of the federal budget and by 1990 accounted for 8.6 percent. Even after major cuts in 1997, Medicare's share totals nearly 13 percent of the 2002 federal budget (US CBO, 2002). In the view of many policy-makers, Medicare may be crowding out expenditures on other domestic programs. Critics often argue that Americans will only accept a certain level of public spending, so if Medicare grows rapidly, it hurts other spending even if it has its own revenue source. This alone makes it a potential focus of efforts to reduce government spending. Although Medicare, on a per capita basis, has not grown faster than the costs of private health insurance (Boccuti and Moon, 2003), critics of Medicare refer to this growth as unsustainable, but do not make the same claims for the rest of the health care system. Society will have to make some hard choices about our willingness to support Medicare in the future.

Until very recently, a second fiscal pressure faced by Medicare arose from the status of the Hospital Insurance (HI) Trust Fund. Current law provides a fixed source of funding for HI – and these revenues typically have not grown as fast as the level of spending, creating periodic crises when the date of trust fund exhaustion is close at hand. So far that day of reckoning has been postponed several times, by major cost-cutting efforts and an increase in the wage base subject to taxation. The strong economy and the slow growth in Medicare spending in 1998 and 1999 have pushed that date to 2026, based on the 2003 Trustees Report. As shown in figure 10.9, the date of exhaustion of the Part A trust fund is further off than ever (Moon, 2002). There is now less urgency attached to making changes, but eventually there will be a need for further changes in spending on or financing of the program.

Gaps for early retirees

As noted in chapter 6, many older Americans retire before the age of 65, leaving a potential period between having employer-provided insurance as a worker and age of eligibility at 65. Some of those who retire early do so in very poor health; they may qualify for Medicare as disability beneficiaries, but they will only get those benefits after a 29-month waiting period (five months to qualify for Social Security and two years more to qualify for Medicare). Thus, for anyone retiring at about age 62, this is not a viable option for filling in the gap. That leaves many individuals to rely upon private insurance – either from a former employer or the individual insurance market.

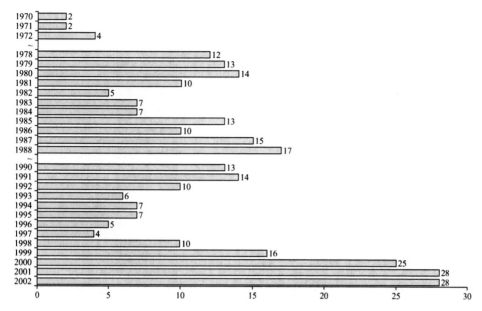

Figure 10.9 Number of years before HI Trust Fund projected to be exhausted
~Data Not Available for 1973–1977 and 1989
Source: CRS 1995 and 2002 Trustees Report.

The most desirable situation for early retirees is to have employer-subsidized retiree insurance. Such coverage not only allows individuals to keep the comprehensive coverage they had as workers, but usually subsidizes at least part of the premiums for the plan. The downside, however, is that employers in general are reducing, not increasing such benefits. A number of studies of such coverage find that costs are rising rapidly for retirees as employers pass higher cost sharing and/or higher premiums onto the retiree. Further, promises of future benefits for those who have not yet reached the age of retirement are being reduced as well.

A study by Mercer found declines from 46 percent to 31 percent for early retirees from 1993 to 2000 (William Mercer, 2001). Moreover, the share of those with coverage who are required to pay the full costs of coverage rose from 31 percent in 1997 to 42 percent in 1999. Again, these numbers are for early retirees. The world of retiree health insurance is changing rapidly.

Early retirees may also be able to continue employer-sponsored insurance after leaving employment even if no formal retiree coverage is offered. That is, federal law (referred to as COBRA provisions – a term that refers to the law under which the protection was established) requires that employers who offer insurance coverage must offer it to those who leave employment for various reasons for a period of time. For early retirees, this would normally be 18 months; the catch is that the individual must pay 102 percent of the costs of such coverage, often making it quite expensive.

Even the high costs of COBRA, however, are likely to be a better deal than purchasing insurance through the private individual market for persons in their sixties. The availability and premium costs for individual coverage vary substantially across the United States. State insurance regulations dictate how private insurance plans operate. But overall, such plans tend to be inadequate and very expensive, particularly for anyone with a health problem (Pollitz et al., 2001). The great irony is that insurance is least available to those who need it most.

As a consequence, about 14 percent of all persons aged 55 to 64 lack insurance, and 8 percent are paying substantial premiums for individual coverage (Boccuti et al., 2002). These numbers would rise if reported for persons out of the labor force or with lower incomes. These are the individuals most in need of some help to fill in the insurance gaps before Medicare eligibility.

Consequently, a number of policy-makers have proposed allowing individuals to buy into the Medicare program, giving them access to at least a basic policy. For example, the Clinton Administration proposed such an expansion several times in the 1990s. The difficulty is that if there is no subsidy, this type of proposal would mainly help those with substantial incomes but health problems that keep them out of the private individual market (or who are now paying very high premiums in that market). But to subsidize enrollment in Medicare would be quite expensive; most policy-makers have resisted adding to Medicare's burdens in this way.

REFORM OPTIONS TO IMPROVE BENEFICIARY PROTECTIONS

Along with ways to hold down the growth in spending on Medicare, discussed below, many analysts and policy-makers have raised concerns about the lack of comprehensive benefits in the program. In the 2000 Presidential campaign, for example, both candidates offered plans for adding a prescription drug benefit, filling in one important gap. After fruitless debate over such a benefit in 2001 and 2002 the Congress finally appears ready to act in 2003. But in addition to prescription drug coverage, a limit on the out-of-pocket costs that any individual beneficiary must pay is needed. Both are essential to achieving a strong basic health insurance plan. When Medicare was passed in 1965, the benefit package was reasonable as compared to other available private insurance. But over time, private insurance has expanded upon what is covered, while Medicare has changed little. Most private plans, for example, offer both prescription drugs and a limit on what the insured person will have to pay out of pocket.

Critics of Medicare rightly point out that the inadequacy of the benefit package has led to the development of a variety of supplemental insurance arrangements, which in turn creates an inefficient system with most beneficiaries relying on two sources of insurance to meet their needs. Medicaid and employer-sponsored retiree benefits do a pretty good job of comprehensively filling in the gaps. But private supplemental (Medigap) plans – which serve about one-fourth of all beneficiaries – are becoming unaffordable for those with average incomes. This is particularly true of older women whose incomes are low and whose premium costs are at their highest – because of the way premiums are set by insurers.

Prescription drugs are the primary acute care benefit excluded from Medicare coverage. Only in the hospital, a nursing home, or in a hospice will Medicare cover drugs. But drugs are now, more than ever, a critical part of a comprehensive health care delivery system. Lack of compliance with prescribed medications can raise health care costs over time. And for many who need multiple prescriptions, the costs can be beyond their reach. While a substantial number of beneficiaries now have drug coverage, the share with reliable coverage (employer-based or Medicaid) is considerably smaller. Only 39 percent of Medicare beneficiaries have reliable coverage. Further, states and former employers who now support good coverage may pull back as prescription drugs become even more expensive, intensifying demand for a Medicare drug benefit. But since Medicare beneficiaries are expected to spend nearly $1.8 trillion on prescription drugs over the period 2003 to 2012 (US CBO, 2002), designing a good drug benefit in a period of deficits in the federal budget is extremely difficult. Even if a law is passed, it is likely to cover only $400 million of those costs.

Adding prescription drug coverage would reduce the need for other supplemental insurance, but probably not by enough to encourage beneficiaries to drop their supplemental plans. Other changes in cost sharing would be needed, such as reducing the very high Part A deductible and limiting the total amount of cost sharing that any beneficiary would owe. A more rational Medicare cost-sharing package would not have to be an expensive addition, but some adjustments are needed. Increases in cost sharing in some areas could help defray higher costs elsewhere. It could be used to specifically discourage certain types of health care use – such as emergency room services for routine care, helping to improve efficiency. If the basic Medicare benefit could be made to look more like the insurance coverage that most working families have, the traditional Medicare program could satisfy both beneficiaries and those worried about costs. Many of those who now buy extra insurance policies could forego them, improving the overall efficiency of Medicare, see table 10.2.

REFORM OPTIONS TO REDUCE MEDICARE COSTS

Despite rhetoric on "protecting Medicare" for beneficiaries, much of the attention on program reform has been devoted to cost-saving measures to slow the rate of growth of what has often been the fastest rising major part of the federal budget. Some of the enthusiasm for change of the mid-1990s has declined because the 1997 Balanced Budget Act (BBA) and earlier efforts to curb fraud and abuse resulted in dramatically slower rates of growth in Medicare at the end of the 1990s. Medicare spending actually declined in 1999 even though the program was covering more people. Nonetheless, the BBA proved to be controversial and there have been several subsequent pieces of legislation that mitigate the changes, restoring payments to many of the providers and private plans that were cut under the BBA. And, in 2000 and 2001, health care costs began rising again in the private sector, suggesting that Medicare spending growth may also begin to accelerate. In conjunction with the aging of the baby boomers, proposals to reduce Medicare spending once again are likely to generate an important debate on Medicare's future.

Reforms under discussion in the last few years can generally be slotted into five categories: voucher plans, premium support plans, incremental reforms, changes in eligibility, and expanded financing options. Voucher and premium support plans entail structural and fundamental changes to Medicare, expanding economic incentives to beneficiaries as a means of generating savings. The philosophy that underlies them is also that competition makes the private sector more efficient than the government. Incremental approaches lean towards more limited structural changes that deal with pressing issues, but that maintain Medicare as a government-run social insurance program that covers a particular set of benefits. Private initiatives would still be used, but on a smaller scale. The battleground on structural reform centers on premium support versus more incremental change, with vouchers considered by many to be too extreme a change.

Unlike the first three strategies which seek to reduce per capita Medicare spending, the fourth, changes in eligibility, would decrease the number of beneficiaries as a way of lowering costs of the program. Finally, and often in conjunction with some of the other options, higher beneficiary contributions or tax increases have also been proposed to help meet future needs.

Vouchers

Voucher plans would most dramatically alter Medicare. And although there are a number of different approaches possible under this heading, the goal that unites most of these plans is to reduce substantially the government's control over health care. Essentially, Medicare beneficiaries would be given a voucher to help pay the costs of the plan of their choice, presumably in a market much like the one that individuals under age 65 now face if they do not have employer-based coverage. Thus, the program would assure a defined *contribution* for services instead of a defined set of *benefits* (Moon, 1996). If the contribution were not high enough to purchase a good insurance policy, beneficiaries would have to pay more. Second, the federal government would no longer act in the role of an insurer; traditional fee-for-service would be disbanded and all beneficiaries would be required to choose among private plans.

Supporters of this approach believe that vouchers would make beneficiaries and insurers more conscious of costs. The advantages, from the perspective of voucher plan supporters, are the resulting increased choice and competition that the market can foster, presumably resulting in higher quality benefits at lower costs for beneficiaries. This would apply economic principles in their purest form.

For example, individuals might be able to opt for larger deductibles or coinsurance in return for coverage of other services such as drugs or long-term care. Since many

Medicare enrollees now choose to supplement Medicare with private insurance, this approach would allow beneficiaries to combine the voucher with their own funds and buy one comprehensive plan. No longer would they have to worry about coordinating coverage between Medicare and their private supplemental plan. Moreover, persons with employer-provided supplemental coverage could remain in the health care plans they had as employees. To the government, this option would have the appeal of enabling a predictable rate of growth in the program (Scandlen, 2000).

But there are also potential disadvantages for beneficiaries as well. Over time, the risks of higher costs of health care are borne by the beneficiary and not the government; the government's contribution presumably would be tied to a formula that may not be associated with actual care costs. For example, it might be set to grow at the rate of growth of the economy, even if health care costs are rising faster (as is often the case). In fact, the purpose of a voucher approach is to make the government's share a more predictable, stable amount, placing the beneficiary at risk for rising costs.

Thus, it is likely that a voucher system would reduce Medicare's social insurance role of pooling and redistributing the risks associated with poor health in old age. Traditional Medicare places a large group of both the sickest and the healthiest beneficiaries under a single umbrella. This accomplishes two things. The larger the group, the lower the individual cost of insurance because risks are shared evenly. Second, benefits are redistributed between beneficiaries. The sickest beneficiaries with the most needs receive more benefits (or services) than do healthier beneficiaries. Vouchers can only accomplish these goals if there is an effective (and likely complicated) system for adjusting the voucher payments across individuals for differences in health status and risk. Thus far, such adjusters are crude and still being refined (as described above).

How successful is the private sector likely to be? First, private insurers will almost surely have higher administrative overhead costs than does Medicare. Insurers need to advertise and promote their plans. They would face a smaller risk pool that may require them to make more conservative decisions regarding reserves and other protections against losses over time. These plans expect to return a profit to shareholders. All of these factors cumulate and work against private companies performing better than Medicare. In addition, problems with the current Medicare + Choice program underscore some of the complications that arise in a market-based approach. As argued in this chapter thus far, the health care market is not as functional as many other markets for a number of reasons, including lack of good information, concentrations of market power, and geographic variability.

On balance, vouchers offer less in the way of guarantees for continued protection under Medicare. They are most appealing as a way to substantially cut the federal government's contributions to the plan indirectly through erosion of the comprehensiveness of coverage that the private sector offers rather than as stated policy. The risks under such a plan would be borne by beneficiaries.

Premium support

Like voucher options, premium support plans place an emphasis on the positive outcomes of competition and choice. But premium support plans limit the shifting of risks to beneficiaries as compared to a strict voucher approach and maintain a more active role for government in managing the program. They are thus a more controlled version of vouchers, recognizing some of the problems in the health care market. In premium support, plans would likely be subject to considerable oversight and the government contribution would be linked to some share of the costs of participating plans. For example, one approach is to pay a set percentage of the average plan's premium. Those who want more expensive plans would have to pay more, making beneficiaries more sensitive to the costs of care but not to the full risks of higher costs over time (Aaron and Reischauer, 1995). For example, if the average plan cost $5,000 and Medicare agreed to pay 80 percent of that cost, individuals in an average plan would pay a premium of $1,000. But those who choose a $6,000 plan would pay $2,000 in premiums – both a higher dollar amount and a larger share of the total costs of the insurance. Both government and beneficiaries would share the risks of growth in spending over time, but beneficiaries would face a substantial increase in premiums for even moderately more expensive plans.

Most premium support plans would retain traditional fee-for-service Medicare as one option – addressing one major concern of those worried about relying on the private sector. But the expectation is that traditional Medicare would be expensive and since that would translate into substantially higher premiums for beneficiaries, over time it would decline as a share of the market. This is a major concern of many who see this approach as putting the most vulnerable – who generally remain in traditional Medicare fee for service – at risk. On the other hand, if traditional Medicare did not turn out to be more expensive, this would be because the expected benefits from private plan competition did not materialize. When premium support was first proposed in the mid-1990s, it appeared that private plans could slow growth as compared to Medicare. But since then, growth in private insurance (and in programs such as the federal employees health system that many cited as a model) have again exceeded Medicare's per capita growth (Boccuti and Moon, 2003). Thus, it is not known whether such a plan could generate substantial savings.

Regulation would be needed to require insurers to take all comers and to guard against problems of adverse risk selection where one plan may be able to compete by choosing carefully what persons to cover. In practice, achieving this goal may be difficult. That is, if Medicare enrollees are free to supplement the basic Medicare program to enhance coverage, insurers may find that those with the most to spend on certain types of supplemental coverage may be the best risks. For example, covering the "extras" such as private rooms and specialized nursing care may appeal to enrollees who are relatively healthy and well-off as compared to enrollees attracted to a supplemental package that mainly offers coverage of prescription drugs or those who can only afford the bare minimum package. If the risk pool is broken up in that way, many Medicare enrollees who now have reasonable coverage for acute care costs, but who are the less desirable risks, would not be able to affordably obtain even a minimal level of protection.

Both vouchers and premium support assume that savings arise from two different sources: competition among plans that will cause them to be more sensitive to holding down the costs of care, and the flexibility and innovation from managed care or other types of insurance that will reduce the use of health care services over time. If plans compete on price and beneficiaries are responsive to joining less expensive plans, then competition can make inroads in the costs of care. But this also assumes that plans have tools for reducing costs; the unpopularity of managed care and its techniques to reduce use suggest this may be more of an uphill battle than many assume. Thus far, the flexibility plans have in Medicare + Choice sometimes result in arbitrary limits on access to care, sometimes even for services that are "covered" by Medicare. The problems with this limited private option for Medicare need to be carefully studied for lessons for options that would rely more heavily on the private sector.

Incremental reforms

The goal of incremental reforms is usually to modernize Medicare fee-for-service and the present Medicare + Choice plans, while not dramatically altering the program (Moon, 2000; GAO, 2000). These reform proposals attempt to draw on some market-based strategies, while maintaining strong government protections for beneficiaries. Such reforms would generally make changes in the way that private plans are paid by the federal government in Medicare + Choice, seeking ways to pay plans fairly and to adjust for differences in the health status of those who choose to enroll. Medicare fee-for-service would remain in place, but a number of changes emphasizing controls over use of services might be added. Case management strategies, improvements in contracting policies, and steering beneficiaries to efficient providers of care are possible examples. Some of these efforts are now being studied in demonstrations sponsored by the government.

Another aspect of proposed incremental reforms is often an improvement in Medicare's basic benefit package to help reduce reliance on supplemental plans that are both expensive and create inefficiencies in care delivery. Supporters of this approach argue that it is a way to test new ideas on a slower time schedule while offering maximum protection to the sickest beneficiaries who remain in traditional fee-for-service Medicare. This could seek to save costs – or to be a mechanism for improving benefits as described above. Opponents of incremental change argue that this is code for making no changes and that reliance on the private market is the only way to achieve major savings for Medicare without cutting benefits or eligibility.

Eligibility

A fourth category of reform is eligibility changes. This is a way to shrink the pool of Medicare beneficiaries and therefore total program costs. Increasing eligibility age from 65 to 67 is one commonly proposed option. Advocates argue this change would bring Medicare in line with Social Security and recognize that people live years longer and are healthier than when Medicare was created and the eligibility age was established (NCHS, 2000). It would enhance incentives for workers to post-pone retirement.

But the details are considerably more complicated for Medicare than for Social Security. Social Security allows partial eligibility at age 62. Moreover, many of those denied Medicare would face an imperfect private market for insurance that would require considerable reforms if the needs of those in their mid-60s are to be met. But such reforms have proven difficult to establish even after years of effort. Consequently, insurance costs in the individual market can be too high for even moderate income persons to afford (Pollitz et al., 2001). Without assuring individuals the ability to obtain reasonable insurance, the number of uninsured persons would likely rise, exacerbating an important overall health care problem. Further, employers that now often offer insurance to fill in the gaps between retirement and eligibility for Medicare might drop that coverage since this proposal would increase their costs substantially. Moreover, because this group is the healthiest among all beneficiaries, removing them from the risk pool produces only modest savings (Moon et al., 1997; Waidmann, 1998). One alternative that some analysts have suggested would be to raise the age of full eligibility, but offer coverage at a reduced premium for those who wish to buy into the Medicare program.

Making Medicare eligibility subject to a means test is another possible approach for reducing the number of persons eligible. Individuals would have to meet income and perhaps asset guidelines to qualify, significantly reducing the number of beneficiaries. Less clear is where to set eligibility limits. If the means testing requirements were set low, this would exclude many beneficiaries and effectively blend in with the Medicaid program. Asset tests, in particular, in means tested programs have been very restrictive, reducing eligibility substantially. And since many older persons rely on savings to supplement their retirement incomes, even assets in the range of $50,000 and higher may still not make individuals very well off if they are spreading these resources over the rest of their lives (Moon et al., 2002).

Alternatively, a high eligibility limit would include a substantially greater share of the population, but would pose challenges for administration. For a higher income cut-off, the simplest approach would be to use the Internal Revenue Service to determine eligibility at the time that people pay taxes, but this tends to be a very unpopular strategy. Excluded individuals would also have to find coverage in the private market, and unless the limits where coverage ends were high, even modest-income persons would have difficulty obtaining coverage. Further, means-tested programs tend to be unpopular, under-funded, and have high administrative costs. This is likely to be one of the least popular options for saving costs, although taxing or otherwise charging high-income beneficiaries more for participation could be seriously considered. These latter approaches deal less with eligibility and more with financing issues.

Financing

Regardless of whether broad structural or incremental approaches to change are adopted, it is unlikely that Medicare can be maintained in its current form without more revenues (Gluck and Moon, 2000). Figure 10.10 illustrates the long-term projections in income and expenditures if there are no policy changes. A further complicating policy issue arises over the desirability of improving the comprehensiveness of the benefit package. It is difficult to imagine achieving greater efficiency in the delivery of health care if major pieces of that care, such as prescription drugs, are not included in the basic benefit package, resulting in costly substitution of care. But new benefits inevitably mean higher costs, putting further pressure on the need for new revenues and/or reforms in the current system. The contentious debate on the prescription drug issue is illustrative of the difficulty in finding common ground for reforms that require a commitment of substantial federal dollars.

Technically, new revenues would not have to be raised for a number of years, but doing so soon would likely increase taxes most on baby boomers who will be drawing heavily on Medicare in the future. Issues of fairness raise important considerations about how much beneficiaries can be asked to pay and, if broader revenue sources are tapped, how they will affect different groups of the population. For example, payroll taxes remain relatively popular with the general public,

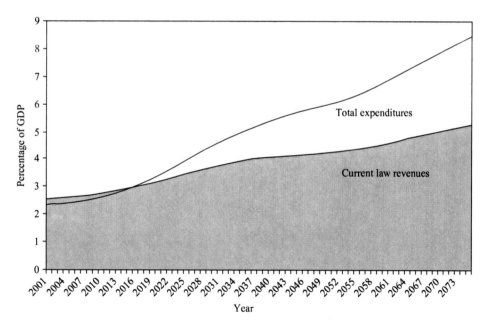

Figure 10.10 Medicare expenditures under revenue projections
Source: 2001 OASDI and Medicare Trustees Reports.

likely because they know where the revenues raised are supposed to go. But economists criticize these taxes as raising the costs of workers to employers, discouraging employment. General revenues, the other major source of income for Medicare, are more progressively distributed and require that older persons as well as the young contribute. Other taxes – such as those on alcohol and tobacco – often do not bring in enough revenue to resolve the financing issues. Whatever choices are made, this is likely to be a last resort approach given the political costs often associated with raising taxes. But it is also the case that someone will need to pay more to provide care for an aging population. The key issue will be how to share that burden, not whether it will increase over time as it surely will.

PROSPECTS FOR THE FUTURE

The status quo for Medicare will likely change dramatically even in the absence of major health reforms. Many of the problems that continue to plague both Medicare and the health care system at large will worsen and a patchwork response from government, largely to help hold down the costs of health care, will be painful. Medicare will likely be subjected to further stringent cost cutting of the type we have seen in recent years, lowering payments to providers and requiring beneficiaries of the Medicare program to pay more for their services through increases in the Part B premium and/or new copayments for home health care, for example. And further, more sweeping reforms to change the delivery of care and/or to move the elderly into a very different insurance system that were not seriously discussed before will now take center stage in future debates. But these reforms are based more on theoretical promises than proven approaches. The risk to beneficiaries from such reforms will thus be a crucial issue. There is little that legislators and politicians like less than having to choose among unpleasant options, so it is likely that the issue of Medicare will be around for some time to come.

The basic assumption in the financing of Medicare has traditionally been that a substantial share of the costs for such coverage must be borne by the young and not the old through the implicit subsidies that Medicare provides. The pressures of an aging society are likely to strongly test this assumption.

CONCLUSION

Older Americans have a number of health problems that result in higher spending on care than younger groups and potentially higher rates of growth over time as well. Each year, about 5 percent of all persons aged 65 and older die, often resulting in high levels of health care spending in the last months of their lives. In addition, as new technology comes on line, it often means that procedures that previously were too risky for frail individuals with multiple health care problems can now be safely performed. Thus, while all Americans face higher costs and benefits from new technology, it is particularly likely to raise costs for older Americans.

The Medicare program serves nearly all persons aged 65 and older, covering a basic set of their acute care needs. But the program has changed little since it was implemented in 1966, meaning that it has fallen behind coverage that younger families often have. Consequently, although Medicare is an expensive federal program, it covers only about half of the health care expenses faced by older Americans. As a consequence, a patchwork quilt of public and private supplemental health care benefits has grown up to fill in some of the gaps in the program. These supplemental programs complicate the health care system and tend to make it less efficient than if Medicare were a more comprehensive program.

One of the major areas of proposed changes in Medicare is improvement in the benefit package, particularly expansion of prescription drug coverage for this group. But drug coverage and other improvements in the benefit package would be expensive. Many of the other reforms that have been suggested for Medicare would seek to hold down cost growth over time through greater efficiency or limitations on the benefits or number of persons eligible. These two different goals have often led to stalemate in the Congress.

To absorb the baby boom generation and keep up with rising health care costs likely requires more than minor efficiency improvements in Medicare. Rather, tough decisions on who will pay for the program will also need to be made in the near future.

DISCUSSION QUESTIONS

Comment on the reasonableness of these statements:

1 Medicare was intended to provide complete health care for all older Americans.
2 The projected cost of Medicare is rising primarily due to the aging of the population.
3 Reductions in Medicare benefits over the past two decades have resulted in older households paying an increasing share of their income to health care.
4 The biggest shortcoming in the current Medicare program is its lack of a prescription drug benefit.
5 A key problem with providing comprehensive health coverage is that it drives up the cost of health care for all Americans.
6 Changing Medicare so that older persons must consider the cost of their health care would make the system more efficient.

Notes

1 By acute care we mean physicians, doctors, and related medical care. Medicare does not cover non-hospital-related prescription drugs or the expenses of long-term care related to chronic health conditions.

2   These ADLs include eating, dressing, bathing, toileting, and transferring (e.g., from bed to chair). Critics of these results argue that they do not focus on dementia (such as Alzheimer's disease) and loss of mental acuity which is much higher at older ages.

3   The income elasticity gives the percentage change in the quantity of health care expenses relative to the percentage change in income. Thus, an income elasticity of demand of 1.4 means that for every 1.0 percent increase in income, health care expenses rise by 1.4 percent.

4   Meeting the long-term care needs of the elderly – that is, social and supportive services for those with disabilities and the frailties of old age – is also neglected by the Medicare program. Changes that would make the coverage more responsive to the actual needs of older Americans would, however, be very expensive.

References

Aaron, Henry J. and Reischauer, Robert D. 1995: The Medicare reform debate: What is the next step? *Health Affairs* 14 (Winter): 8–30.

AARP 2000: *Across the States 2000: Profiles of Long-Term Care Systems*, 4th edn. Washington, DC: AARP Public Policy Institute.

AARP 2002: *Beyond 50: A Report to the Nation on Trends in Health Security.* Washington, DC: AARP, May.

Achman, Lori and Gold, Marsha 2002: *Out-of-Pocket Health Care Expenses for Medicare HMO Beneficiaries: Estimates By Health Status, 1999–2001.* New York: The Commonwealth Fund, February.

Alecxih, Lisa Maria B., Lutzky, Steven, Sevak, Purvi, and Claxton, Gary 1997: *Key Issues Affecting Accessibility to Medigap Insurance.* Report prepared for the Commonwealth Fund.

Andersen, Ronald, Lion, Joanna, and Anderson, Odin W. 1976: *Two Decades of Health Services: Social Survey Trends in Use and Expenditure.* Cambridge, MA: Ballinger Publishing Company.

Barents Group 1999: *A Profile of QMB-Eligible and SLMB-Eligible Medicare Beneficiaries. Contract #500-95-0057.* Baltimore, MD: Health Care Financing Administration.

Berenson, Robert and Holahan, John 1992: Sources of growth in Medicare physician expenditures. *Journal of the American Medical Association* 267 (February): 687–91.

Bishop, Christine 2002: Chronic and long-term care needs of elders and persons with disabilities, presentation at the National Academy of Social Insurance, January 24.

Blustein, Jan and Hoy, Ema 2000: Who is enrolled in for-profit vs. non-profit Medicare HMOs? *Health Affairs* 19 (1): 210–20.

Board of Trustees, Federal Hospital Insurance Trust Fund 2001: *2001 Annual Report of the Board of Trustees of the Federal Hospital Insurance Trust Fund.* Washington DC: US Government Printing Office.

Boccuti, Cristina and Moon, Marilyn 2003: Comparing Medicare and private insurance: growth rates in spending over three decades, *Health Affairs*, 22 March (April): 230–237.

Boccuti, Cristina, Moon, Marilyn, and Pollitz, Karen 2002: Prime Agers (55- to 64-year olds): Health Insurance Coverage and Trends. Report prepared for the Robert Wood Johnson Foundation, April.

Buntin, Melinda B. and Newhouse, Joseph 1998: Paying Managed Care Plans, *Generations* 22 (2): 37–42.

Cassidy, Amanda and Gold, Marsha 2000: *Medicare + Choice in 2000: Will Enrollees Spend More and Receive Less?* The Commonwealth Fund, August.

Cohen, Marc A., Miller, Jessica, and Weinrobe, Maurice 2001: Patterns of informal and formal caregiving among elders with private long-term care insurance. *The Gerontologist* 41 (2): 180–7.

Committee on Nursing Home Regulation, Institute of Medicine 1986: *Improving the Quality of Care in Nursing Homes*. Washington, DC: National Academy Press.

Congressional Research Service 1989: *Health Insurance and the Uninsured: Background Data and Analysis*. US Senate Committee on Education and Labor, Committee Print 100–2, pp. 122–3.

Coughlin, Terri, Holahan, John, and Ku, Leighton 1994: *Medicaid Since 1980*. Washington, DC: Urban Institute Press.

Crimmins, Eileen M. 2001: Americans living longer, not necessarily healthier, lives. *Population Today* 29 (2) (February/March): 5–8. http://www.prb.org/pt/2001/FebMarch2001/longer.html.

Cutler, David M. 1995: Technology, health costs and the NIH. Cambridge, MA: Harvard University and NBER. (September). Unpublished manuscript.

Cutler, David M. 2001: Declining disability among the elderly, *Health Affairs* 20 (6): 11–27.

Cutler, David M. and McClellan, Mark 2001: Is technological change in medicine worth it? *Health Affairs* 20 (5) (September/October): 11–29. www.healthaffairs.org.

Dawson, Steven L. and Surpin, Rick 2001: *Direct-Care Health Workers: The Unnecessary Crisis in Long-Term Care*. Domestic Strategy Group.

Desai, Mayur, Lentzer, Harold R., and Dawson Weeks, Julie 2001: Unmet need for personal assistance with activities of daily living among older adults. *The Gerontologist* 41 (1): 82–8.

Feder, Judith 1977: *Medicare: The Politics of Federal Hospital Insurance*. Lexington, MA: DC Heath and Company.

Feder, Judith 2001: Long-term care: a public responsibility. *Health Affairs* 20 (6): 112–13.

Federal Interagency Forum on Aging-Related Statistics 2000: *Older Americans 2000: Key Indicators of Well-Being. Federal Interagency Forum on Aging-Related Statistics*, Washington, DC: US Government Printing Office.

Freund, Deborah and Smeeding, Timothy M. 2002: The future costs of health care in aging societies: is the glass half full or half empty? Unpublished manuscript. Center for Policy Research, Syracuse University, Syracuse, NY.

Fuchs, Victor R. 1999: Health care for the elderly: How much? Who will pay for it? *Health Affairs*, (January/February): 11–21.

General Accounting Office (2000): Medicare reform: Leading proposals lay groundwork while design decisions lie ahead. Testimony of David Walker before the Committee on Finance, US Senate, February 24.

General Accounting Office 2002: *Long-Term Care: Aging Baby Boom Generation Will Increase Demand and Burden on Federal and State Budgets*, testimony of David Walker before the Special Committee on Aging, US Senate.

Gluck, Michael and Hanson, Kristina 2001: *Medicare Chartbook*, Menlo Park: The Henry J. Kaiser Family Foundation, Fall.

Gluck, Michael and Moon, Marilyn 2000: *Final Report of the Study Panel on Medicare's Long-term care Financing – Financing Medicare's Future*. Washington, DC: National Academy of Social Insurance, September.

Gold, Marsha and Achman, Lori 2001: *Trends in Premiums, Cost-Sharing, and Benefits in Medicare + Choice Health Plans, 1999–2001*. Commonwealth Fund Issue Brief, April.

Gold, Marsha and Mittler, Jessica 2001: *The Structure of Supplemental Insurance for Medicare Beneficiaries*. Washington, DC: Mathematica Policy Research, Inc.

Grob, George F. 1997: Medicare: home health benefit, testimony before the special committee on aging, US Senate 105th Congress, 1st Session, July 28.

Hagen, Stuart 1999: Projections of expenditures for long-term care services for the elderly. Washington, DC: Congressional Budget Office. http://www.cbo.gov/showdoc.cfm?index=1123&sequence=0. (Accessed on 3/12/99).

Health Care Financing Administration 2000: *Health Care Financing Review Medicare and Medicaid Statistical Supplement, 2000*. Baltimore, MD: US Department of Health and Human Services.

Hetzel, Lisa and Smith, Annetta 2001: *The 65 Years and Over Population: 2000*. Washington, DC: US Census Bureau. Census 2000 Brief.

Hewitt Associates LLC 2000: *The Implications of Medicare Prescription Drug Proposals for Employers and Retirees*. The Henry J. Kaiser Family Foundation, July.

Hewitt Associates LLC 2002: *The Implications of Medicare Prescription Drug Proposals for Employers and Retirees*. The Henry J. Kaiser Family Foundation, July.

Kaiser Family Foundation and Health Research and Educational Trust 2002: *Employer Health Benefits, 2002 Annual Survey*. Washington, DC: Kaiser Family Foundation.

Keenan, Maryanne P. 1988: *Changing Needs for Long-Term Care: A Chartbook*. Washington, DC: AARP Public Policy Institute.

Kenney, Genevieve and Moon, Marilyn 1993: *Supply Changes in Medicare Home Health Care*. Washington, DC: Urban Institute Working Paper, July.

Krauss, Nancy A. and Altman, Barbara M. 1998: Characteristics of Nursing Home Residents – 1996. Rockville, MD: Agency for Health Care Policy and Research. *MEPS Research Findings, No. 5*. AHCPR Pub. No. 99-0006.

Kronick, Richard and de Beyer, Joy 1997: *Risk Adjustment is Not Enough: Strategies to Limit Risk Selection in the Medicare Program*. The Commonwealth Fund, May.

Krout, John A., Oggins, Jean, and Holmes, Heidi H. 2000: Patterns of service use in a continuing care retirement community. *The Gerontologist* 40 (6): 698–705.

Lamm, Richard D. 1993: Intergenerational equity in an age of limits: confessions of a prodigal parent. In Gerald Winslow and James Walters (eds.) *Facing Limits: Ethics and Health Care for the Elderly*. Boulder, CO: Westview Press, Inc. pp. 15–28.

Langwell, Kathryn M. and Esslinger, Laura A. 1997: Medicare Managed Care: Evidence on Use, Costs, and Quality of Care. Report prepared for the Commonwealth Fund, May.

Lefkowitz, Doris and Monheit, Alan 1991: *Health Insurance, Use of Health Services, and Health Care Expenditures*. AHCPR Pub. No. 92–0017, National Medical Expenditure Survey Research Findings 12. Rockville, MD: US Public Health Service, Agency for Health Care Policy and Research.

Lichtenberg, Frank R. 2001a: *Benefits and Costs of Newer Drugs: Evidence from the MEPS*. NBER Working Paper No. 8147. Cambridge, MA: National Bureau of Economic Research. (March). papers.nber.org/papers.

Lichtenberg, Frank R. 2001b: The effect of medicine on life expectancy. Columbia University. January. Unpublished manuscript.

Lichtenberg, Frank R. 2002: *Sources of U. S. Longevity Increase, 1960–1997*. NBER Working Paper No. 8755. Cambridge, MA: National Bureau of Economic Research. (February). papers.nber.org/papers.

Lubitz, James 1990: *Use and Costs of Medicare Services in the Last Year of Life, 1976 and 1985*. Health Care Financing Administration, photocopy, May 11.

Lubitz, James and Prihoda, Ronald 1984: The use and costs of Medicare services in the last 2 years of Life. *Health Care Financing Review* 5 (3): 117–31.

Lubitz, James D. and Riley, Gerald F. 1993: Trends in Medicare Payments in the Last Year of Life. *New England Journal of Medicine* 328 (15): 1092–6.

Lui, Hongj and Sharma, Ravi 2002: *Health and Health Care of the Medicare Population: Data from the 1998 Medicare Current Beneficiary Survey*. Rockville, MD: Westat.

Manton, Kenneth 1982: Changing concepts of morbidity and mortality in the elderly population. *Milbank Quarterly* 60: 183–244.

Manton, Kenneth and Gu, X. 2001: Changes in the prevalence of chronic disability in the United States black and nonblack population above age sixty-five from 1982 to 1999. *Proceedings of the National Academy of Sciences of the United States of America* 98 (11): 6354–9.

Maxwell, Stephanie, Moon, Marilyn, and Segal, Misha 2001: *Growth in Medicare and Out-of-Pocket Spending: Impact on Vulnerable Beneficiaries*. Report prepared for the Commonwealth Fund.

Mayhew, Leslie 2000: *Health and Elderly Care Expenditure in an Aging World*. IIASA Working Paper RR-00-21. Laxenberg, Austria: Institute for Applied Systems Analysis. September. http://www.iiasa.ac.at/Publications/Documents/RR-00-021.pdf.

McCall, Nelda 2001: Long-term care: definition, demand, cost, and financing. In Nelda McCall (ed.) *Who Will Pay for Long-term Care?* Chicago: Health Administration Press. pp. 3–31.

Medicare Payment Advisory Commission 2000: *Report to Congress: Medicare Payment Policy*. Washington, DC.

Mercer, William M., Inc. 2001: *Mercer/Foster Higgins National Survey of Employer-Sponsored Health Plans, 1999*. William M. Mercer, Inc.

Miles, Toni P., and Brody, Jacob 1992: International Aging. In *Health Data on Older Americans: United States, 1992, Vital and Health Statistics* 3 (27). Hyattsville, MD: National Center for Health Statistics.

Moon, Marilyn 1996: *Medicare Now and in the Future*, 2nd edn. Washington, DC: Urban Institute Press.

Moon, Marilyn 1999: *Beneath the Averages: An Analysis of Medicare and Private Expenditures*. Washington, DC: The Henry J. Kaiser Family Foundation.

Moon, Marilyn 2000: Medicare matters: building on a record of accomplishments, *Health Care Financing Review* 22 (1): 9–22.

Moon, Marilyn and Mulvey, Janemarie 1996: *Entitlements and the Elderly: Protecting Promises, Recognizing Realities*. Washington, DC: Urban Institute Press.

Moon, Marilyn and Storeygard, Matthew 2001: *One-Third at Risk: The Special Circumstances of Medicare Beneficiaries with Health Problems*. New York: The Commonwealth Fund.

Moon, Marilyn, Brennan, Niall, and Segal, Misha 1998: Options for aiding low-income Medicare beneficiaries, *Inquiry* 35 (3): 346–56.

Moon, Marilyn, Friedland, Robert, and Shirey, Lee 2002: Medicare beneficiaries and their assets: implications for low-income programs. Prepared for the Henry J. Kaiser Foundation, Washington, DC.

Moon, Marilyn, Gage, Barbara, and Evans, Alison 1997: An examination of key Medicare provisions in the Balanced Budget Act of 1997. Report prepared for the Commonwealth Fund, September.

National Center for Health Statistics 2000: *Health, United States, 2000 with Chartbook on Trends in the Health of Americans*. Hyattsville, MD: National Center for Health Statistics.

National Center for Health Statistics 2002: *Health, United States, 2002 With Chartbook on Trends in the Health of Americans*. Hyattsville, MD: National Center for Health Statistics.

Newhouse, Joseph P. 2001: *Medicare Policy in the 1990s.* NBER Working Paper No. 8531. Cambridge, MA: National Bureau of Economic Research.

Newhouse, Joseph, Buntin, Melinda B., and Chapman, John 1999: *Risk Adjustment and Medicare.* The Commonwealth Fund, June.

Pauly, Mark 1990: The rational nonpurchase of long-term-care insurance. *Journal of Political Economy* 98: 153–68.

Penning, Margaret J. 2002: Hydra revisited: substitution formal for self- and informal in-home care among older adults with disabilities. *The Gerontologist,* 42 (1): 4–16.

Pollitz, Karen, Sorian, Richard, and Thomas, Kathy 2001: *How Accessible is Individual Health Insurance for Consumers in Less-Than-Perfect Health?* The Henry J. Kaiser Family Foundation, June.

Physician Payment Review Commission 1997: *Annual Report to Congress.* Washington, DC: US Government Printing Organization.

Prospective Payment Assessment Commission 1997: *Report and Recommendations to the Congress.* Washington, DC: US Government Printing Office.

Reinhardt, Uwe 2000: Health care for the aging baby boom: lessons from abroad, *Journal of Economic Perspectives* 14 (2): 71–83.

Rice, Thomas, Thomas, Kathleen, and Weissert, William 1991: The effect of owning private long-term care insurance policies on out-of-pocket costs. *Health Services Research* 25 (February): 907–34.

Scandlen, Greg 2000: *Defined Contribution Health Insurance,* Policy Backgrounder No. 154, National Center for Policy Analysis, October 26.

Schwartz, William 1994: In the pipeline: a wave of valuable medical technology. *Health Affairs* 13 (Summer): 70–9.

Scitovsky, Anne 1984: The high cost of dying: what do the data show? *Milbank Memorial Fund Quarterly* 62: 610–15.

Scitovsky, Anne 1994: The high cost of dying revisited. *The Milbank Quarterly* 72 (4): 561–91.

Spillman, Brenda C. 2002: *Changes in Elderly Disability Rates and the Implications for Health Care Utilization and Cost.* Washington, DC: Office of Disability, Aging, and Long-Term Care Policy, ASPE.

Spillman, Brenda C. and Lubitz, James 2000: The effect of longevity on spending for acute and long-term care. *New England Journal of Medicine* 342 (19) (May 11): 1409–15.

Tilly, Jane, Goldenson, Susan, and Kasten, Jessica 2001: *Long-Term Care: Consumers, Providers and Financing: A Chart Book.* Washington, DC: The Urban Institute Press, March.

Topel, Robert, and Murphy, Kevin forthcoming: The Economic Value of Medical Research. In *The Economic Value of Medical Research.* Chicago: University of Chicago Press.

US Congress, House Committee on Ways and Means 1994: *1994 Green Book: Background Material and Data on Programs Within the Jurisdiction of the Committee on Ways and Means.* Washington, DC: US Government Printing Office.

US Congress, House Committee on Ways and Means 1998: *1998 Green Book: Background Material and Data on Programs Within the Jurisdiction of the Committee on Ways and Means.* Washington, DC: US Government Printing Office.

US Congressional Budget Office 2002: *The Budget and Economic Outlook: Fiscal Years 2003–2012.* Washington, DC: US Government Printing Office.

US General Accounting Office 2000: *State Pharmacy Programs: Assistance Designed to Target Coverage and Stretch Budgets.* Pub. No. HEHS-00-162. Washington, DC: Government Printing Office, September.

US House of Representatives 1993: *1993 Green Book: Overview of Entitlement Programs.* Committee on Ways and Means. Washington, DC: US Government Printing Office.

Waidmann, Timothy A. 1998: potential effects of raising medicare's eligibility age. *Health Affairs*, 17, March/April: 156–64.

Waidmann, Timothy A. and Lui, Korbin 2000: Disability trends among elderly persons and implications for the future. *Journal of Gerontology* 55B (5): S298–S307.

Walker, David M. 2001: Long-term budget issues: moving from balancing the budget to balancing fiscal risk. Testimony before the Committee on the Budget, US Senate GAO-01-385T. Washington, DC: Government Printing Office. February 6. http://www.gao.gov/new.items/d01385t.pdf.

Weiner, Joshua M., Illston, Laurel, and Hanley, Raymond 1994: *Sharing the Burden: Strategies for Public and Private Long-Term Care Insurance.* Washington, DC: The Brookings Institution.

Winslow, Charles M. et al. 1988: The appropriateness of performing coronary artery bypass surgery, *Journal of the American Medical Association* 260: 505–9.

Wolf, Douglas A. 2001: Population change: friend or foe of the chronic care system? *Health Affairs* 20 (6): 28–42.

Zuckerman, Stephen and Verrilli, Diana 1995: *The Medicare Relative Value Scale and Private Payers: The Potential Impact on Physician Payments.* Report prepared under Health Care Financing Administration Contract no. 500-92-0024, D.O. #4. Photocopy.

CHAPTER ELEVEN

Additional Health Issues: Long-Term Care

LEARNING OBJECTIVES

After completing this chapter, you will be able to:

1 Describe the lack of coverage for long-term care under Medicare and how it influences the behavior of young and old households.
2 Discuss the role of privately purchased or employer-provided long-term care insurance.
3 Assess whether the long-term care needs of older Americans are being met.
4 Evaluate proposals for expanded long-term care programs.

CHAPTER OUTLINE

INTRODUCTION

Much of this book has documented the many aspects of American life that have improved for older persons in the last century, but improvements in the provision of long-term care services have lagged behind other changes. We have made enormous advances in meeting acute health care needs, for example, but we have done less to creatively deal with support and care for those with disabilities. Chronic disease and traumatic injuries leave individuals with medical and supportive service needs. Treatment requires a labor-intensive effort, the burdens of which fall on families – often wives and daughters – and some government-provided programs. And such care, when delivered in formal settings, can be very expensive. Too often these services fall short, leaving substantial unmet needs among the elderly population.

Yet as inadequate as long-term care services are at present, the aging of the population will lead to even greater future demand for long-term care. While long-term care is a problem for young as well as older persons, its prevalence increases dramatically for those over age 80 or 85. Need for expensive care rises as the ability to afford that care declines. And while men and women are both affected, particularly at the end of life, American women face a disproportionate risk of a loss of independence and a lower quality of life from the impact of chronic disease and disability.

Politically, long-term care has been a backburner issue in the US for more than a decade. The last serious discussion of a broad public program for long-term care occurred as part of the Pepper Commission in 1988 and 1989. Named after Claude Pepper, a legislative champion for long-term care, several options were examined that would have offered protections for people with need for supportive services. But, even though the Commission was established to consider long-term care issues, the additional charge of looking at health insurance for the whole population took center stage. Again in the 1992–94 debate over expanding health insurance coverage, long-term care issues were treated as nearly an afterthought. Only minor public expansions were proposed. Such support recognized the need for further help for the elderly and disabled and the problems of relying on the means-tested Medicaid program to meet these needs. However, only one proposal – the so-called single payer plan – offered a comprehensive long-term care benefit.

After the Congressional elections in 1994, the political landscape dramatically changed. Plans for health reform were dropped and a new focus on reducing government programs took over the political agenda. Establishing a block grant for Medicaid to control its growth over time was debated in 1995, but defeated. This would have been particularly important for long-term care since it is projected to grow substantially over time. If states had been made responsible for absorbing all of that growth, cuts in long-term care benefits would have been a likely response, and the cutbacks would not have occurred evenly across the states.

The only recent interest in long-term care has been in efforts to encourage private long-term care insurance, often through various tax benefits for those purchasing such coverage, and some interest in expanding home and community-based services under Medicaid, the public program providing the most long-term care support. Thus, at the start of the twenty-first century, there is little serious discussion of ways to extensively expand long-term care services by the public sector, although the demand for such care will likely grow rapidly over time.

The problem was and is essentially one of cost. Reluctance to raise new taxes or take on major new burdens through the public sector mean that few policy-makers have been willing to propose the more than $80 billion per year in new public spending that would be required to comprehensively cover long-term care services. When expansion has been considered, it tends to be limited in scope and phased in slowly over time. This chapter will examine long-term care issues in this context. But the first challenge is to define what long-term care is and how it is provided today.

DEFINING LONG-TERM CARE

Problems of poor health, disability or frailty give rise to the need for a group of disparate services referred to as "long-term care." There is little concrete agreement on what constitutes long-term care; it is something that people know when they see it, but it is also difficult to succinctly define. The term refers to the extended nature of care provided, but there is also no agreement on when acute (hospital and physician) services become long-term care services. Moreover, there is enormous variation in the types of care needed and received. Some services are more medical in nature and include, for example, rehabilitation and monitoring of medications, but many of the needs are supportive, helping the individual meet daily personal needs that range from housework to such basics as eating or bathing. Most of the care is labor-intensive, but assistive devices (such as walkers) and home modifications can also be used to meet long-term care needs.

Nor is there specific agreement on who should receive such services. Usually, recipients of care can trace their disabilities back to specific illnesses or medical problems, such as broken hips or strokes. Dementia, stemming from Alzheimer's disease or other causes, also contributes. In other cases, frailty results from the slow deterioration in functional status from minor chronic problems exacerbated by the aging process. The only common theme is that long-term care represents a critical area of concern for older persons when they become unable to meet basic needs without assistance.

Given the variability in needs, it is difficult to define exactly what an ideal long-term care system should look like. The differences in settings for long-term care add to this dilemma. Institutional (nursing home) services for those who cannot remain at home and community-based services that offer a variety of options for persons who remain in their homes are both crucial components of a long-term care system. Institutional care may be needed not just for the level of skill required, but the constancy of care, such as round-the-clock supervision for those with Alzheimer's disease or dementia. When needs are extensive, a residential setting is probably needed. But long-term care is *not* just nursing home care. Community-based services include skilled and unskilled services in the home and programs such as adult day care or congregate meal services. Moreover, other facilities, such as assisted living can often meet the needs of people with less extensive disabilities. Finally, a range of Social Services such as "meals on wheels" and senior centers also help meet the needs of persons with disabilities. These tend to be classified as "Social Services" (and hence are often not counted when people describe the scale of resources devoted to long-term care). An ideal system is thus likely to vary substantially in response to the desires of the recipients of such care.

Whatever the specific setting, such services are likely to represent relatively permanent arrangements, stretching over months, if not years. Thus, they need to reflect quality of life concerns and the living environment of the disabled as well as providing needed technical services. In this way, long-term care differs substantially from the acute care setting, which is designed for the convenience of the providers and to which patients are only briefly exposed. Actually, this distinction is more a wish than a reality, since too often institutional settings take on an air of sterility and discomfort rather than incorporating the housing, services and other needs of residents into facility design (Committee on Nursing Home Regulation, 1986). Some alternative arrangements, such as assisted living and continuing care retirement communities (CCRCs) have helped to improve living environments, at least for those who can afford such arrangements. Assisted living often puts individuals into their own apartments while providing meal service, housekeeping help, and some personal care. Such facilities may not be able to provide care to those with very extensive needs, however. CCRCs, on the other hand, are often developments that offer a variety of living arrangements from fully independent apartments or houses to assisted living to nursing home care. One of the advantages of CCRCs is that residents whose functioning deteriorates do not have to move away from a spouse or friends. Both of these types of living arrangements tend to be quite expensive, however, and hence have not reached a broad cross-section of the elderly population.

An important part of any ideal long-term care setting should also be the presence of informal care provided by relatives and friends. Again it is essential to distinguish between medical needs that require highly skilled personnel and supportive services that are most effective if they are part of a normal routine involving other family members. Such informal support has always been a crucial element in helping persons with disabilities and frailties; model systems seek to find ways to supplement rather than replace the informal care offered. And in some cases, there is resistance to providing care that may ultimately substitute for the informal support that many elder persons receive.

Informal support is not costless. It often takes a toll on the caregiver in terms of lost earnings, delayed careers and emotional stress. Even when "hands on" care is not required, the need for an aware and able adult to monitor the behavior of an aging and semi-demented loved one can cause great disruptions in market work and other normal activities. Establishing the right balance between formal and informal care needs to include the wishes of family caregivers as well as the long-term care recipient.

Who needs long-term care?

Among persons aged 65 and over, the need for long-term care grows consistently with the age of the individual. Since the frailty associated with aging itself can be a factor in generating need for supportive services, this should not be a surprising finding. But in addition, many chronic diseases such as arthritis, diabetes, and pulmonary disease also are associated with aging. Thus, disability and need for long-term care services become a major problem for the very old.

The usual indicator used to capture long-term care needs relates to problems with Activities of Daily Living (ADLs, as defined in chapter 10). Although through the years the number of specific categories that make up this measure have changed, it has remained the principal way in which long-term care needs are established. Often, the measure used for establishing need is at least two or three limitations in the areas of bathing, dressing, eating, toileting, or transferring (that is, moving from a bed to a chair). Disability is then referred to as either "inability to perform" or "needs help with a certain number of" ADLs. Alternative ways of phrasing questions about ADLs lead to disparities in the number of persons defined as disabled at any one point in time.

Moreover, ADLs capture only physical limitations. Dementia, Alzheimer's disease, and other cognitive problems may also place an individual in need of long-term care services. Measures of these types of needs are usually captured by Instrumental Activities of Daily Living (IADLs), which refer to difficulty in performing activities such as handling money, or talking on the telephone. Together, limitations in ADLs and IADLs are often used to qualify for public or private assistance. The number of limitations that help people qualify vary; it is believed that the number of ADL limitations capture severity of disability, for example (see figure 11.1).

Using these indicators as a measure, a substantial number of older persons are in need of some long-term care assistance. For example, if a cut-off is set at three or

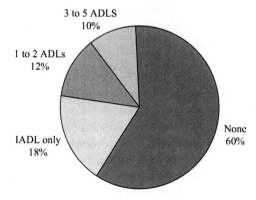

Figure 11.1 Percent of ADLs and IADLs for Medicare beneficiaries, 1998

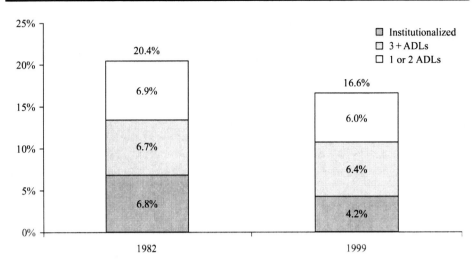

Figure 11.2 Declining disability rates
Source: Manton and Gu 2001.

more ADLs to establish need for a benefit, 2.2 million Medicare beneficiaries over
the age of 65 and living in the community – including over 700,000 beneficiaries
over the age of 85 – would have been categorized as in need of care in 1998
(Lui and Sharma, 2002). If a less stringent measure of at least one ADL or IADL
limitation is used to indicate disability, the numbers of persons in need rises to six
million. Even when limited to three or more ADLs, the number of people classified
in need is much in excess of the number of people who actually receive formal
services from either the public or private sector.

Hence, long-term care is an area where discussions about unmet need often take
place. For example, one recent study of unmet need focused on persons aged 70
and above, finding that 6.2 million people in this age group had at least one ADL
limitation (Desai et al., 2001). And among that group nearly half – three million
people – reported needing assistance and one in every five of that group (629,000)
had unmet needs for care. Among those with unmet needs 47.6 percent had negative consequences from the lack of assistance. It is important to note, however, that
most of the care received by those who did get help was informal care provided
by relatives or friends.

Why is there unmet need? The demand for care outstrips individuals' ability to
pay for such care. And this problem has been getting worse over time. For example, in 1970, average Social Security income could cover about 20.5 percent of the
costs of nursing homes in that year. The outlook improved modestly through 1980,
but by 1997, Social Security payments averaged only 15.3 percent of nursing home
expenditures (McCall, 2001). Costs have grown faster than income and as a consequence, the costs of long-term care are beyond the ability to pay of those in need
of it with only modest exceptions.

One emerging area of research does suggest some relief from rising health care expenditures, however. In addition to improvements in mortality, morbidity among the elderly now also seems to be declining, particularly in relation to levels of disability (Manton et al., 1997; Waidmann and Liu, 2000). As figure 11.2 indicates, by 1999 the share of elderly persons with 1 or more ADLs or in an institution has fallen from 20.4 percent in 1982 to 16.6 percent in 1999. (IADL declines are even greater over this period, but some recent analysis suggests that one of the IADL measures has become unnecessary, resulting in a decline in reported IADL limitations.[1]) If these improvements hold over time and if they translate into lower health care spending, then the task of slowing the rate of growth in health spending may be eased, particularly with regard to costs of Medicaid long-term care.

It is too early to assume, however, that this alone can solve the problems facing Medicare and Medicaid (Waidmann and Liu, 2000). For example, are some of the improvements due to greater reliance on acute care services such as hip replacement surgery, cataract surgery or other procedures? And, if people live longer, will they demand more services at age 80 than they did in the past? If the answer to these questions is positive, then costs might actually rise over time rather than decline in concert with declines in disability. This represents a difficult research question which will require more research before the claims of greater or lower spending on healthcare can be demonstrated.[2]

THE CURRENT LONG-TERM CARE "SYSTEM"

Despite the fact that a great deal of care is delivered informally and hence is not measured in terms of spending, long-term care expenditures for the elderly were estimated at $123 billion in 2000 and are expected to rise to $207 billion (even after controlling for inflation) by 2020 (US CBO, 1999).

Delivery of care

While the options for disabled persons are changing rapidly in the United States, care for the most disabled persons in our society continues to occur in traditional institutional settings. The CBO estimates for 2000 indicated expenditures of about $85 billion on nursing home care, or nearly 70 percent of the formal spending on long-term care.

Despite these very large amounts of expenditures, however, the proportion of persons in nursing homes has actually fallen over time. For example, data from the National Nursing Home Survey found that the rate of nursing home residence among persons age 65 or older dropped from 54 per 1,000 in 1985 to 45.3 per 1,000 in 1997 (Federal Interagency Forum on Aging-Related Statistics, 2000). Numbers from the 1990 and 2000 Censuses also show similar results: in 1990, the Census found that 5.1 percent of persons 65 and over were living in nursing homes, but by 2000, the number declined to 4.5 percent (US Census Bureau, 2001). This drop

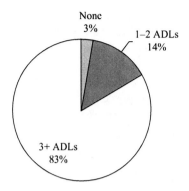

Figure 11.3 Percent of nursing home residents, by number of ADLs
Source: Urban Institute Analysis of the 1998 Medicare Current Beneficiary Survey, unpublished.

occurred for men and women at all ages. But the actual numbers of persons in nursing homes grew slightly over the same period, reflecting the growing numbers of people over the age of 65. In 1997, 1.47 million persons were nursing home residents as compared to 1.32 million in 1985 (Federal Interagency Forum, 2000).

Moreover, those who are in formal nursing home settings tend to be more disabled than ever before, in part because of the development of less intensive residential environments. People seem to be able to delay moving to nursing homes as compared to the past, so when they do go they tend to be very frail or disabled. Over half (50.6 percent) of older persons in nursing homes have dementia, 48.3 percent have heart disease and 37.7 percent have hypertension (Krauss and Altman, 1998). And when examined in terms of ADLs, 83.8 percent of elderly nursing home residents receive care for 3 or more ADLs (figure 11.3). These individuals are largely in a nursing home because of the multiple conditions they face.

A number of older Americans also live in some type of residential setting that provides at least some services such as meals and housekeeping help. But these congregate facilities are relatively new and not well defined, making it hard to estimate exactly how many people now reside in such facilities. According to the National Center for Assisted Living (2001), more than 1 million people reside in one of 28,000 assisted living residences in the US. While a little over a third of all residents have no ADL limitations, on average, residents need help with 1.7 ADLs. This is less than half the average (3.75) of those in nursing homes. But even this level of care is expensive, with the typical resident paying approximately $21,700 per year and staying in a facility for 35 months. The majority of assisted living facilities contract with a home health agency to provide nursing care as needed, usually at additional cost to the resident unless the services are covered by Medicare or Medicaid. CCRCs offer yet another option, and because individuals who choose this setting are encouraged to move while they are independent and in good health, they tend to be even less in need of care (Krout et al., 2000).

At the same time, use of formal home and community-based services has grown substantially. These expanding areas of service use may be home-delivered services where nurses and/or aides come to the patient's home, or adult day care and other activities in settings outside the home. The level of services provided can also vary substantially, with some visits provided by nurses and rehabilitation specialists that are medical in nature (and often paid for by Medicare) and others relying on much less well trained aides who perform personal and household tasks to enable the individual to remain at home. Data from 1984 indicated that just 30 percent of all persons with at least one ADL limitation used home and community-based services (Keenan, 1988). In just three years, that figure rose to 41 percent (AHCPR, 1992). Service use in the early 1990s showed further dramatic expansions especially in benefits from Medicare. For example, home care use grew from 17 percent of spending on long-term care to 26 percent between 1988 and 1997 – or in dollar terms, a 287 percent rise (McCall, 2001).

Demand for long-term care services is expected to continue to rise dramatically over time, even after assuming improvements in disability. Projections suggest that 10 million people will have ADL or IADL limitations by 2040 as compared to about 5.5 million today (Tilly et al., 2001). By 2050, the same model indicates 10.5 million adults aged 85 and over will receive home care services (compared to 5.4 million today) and 4.5 million over age 85 will receive institutional care (compared to 2.0 million today).

Funding sources

At present, long-term care is funded mainly by the federal/state Medicaid program and by individuals and their families. Medicaid steps in for those with limited resources, although even then individuals continue to contribute what they can to the costs of care. Other public programs, such as Medicare, play only a limited role. Over the last decade, private insurance has emerged as another means for spreading the risk of long-term care. The contributions from various sources are summarized in figure 11.4. Medicaid paid for about 45 percent of measured long-term care spending in 2000 (GAO, 2002), with the lion's share going to nursing homes. In contrast, Medicare only picks up about 14 percent of the costs. Out-of-pocket spending occurs both by persons who fully privately pay for their care and by those receiving Medicaid and other support. But it is also important to note that this measure is based on formal services, and does not capture the substantial informal market where individuals rely on relatives, friends and neighbors for a large portion of the actual long-term care delivered in the US. Finally, private insurance coverage has been growing since the late 1980s and now accounts for about 11 percent of the funding.

Since costs often exceed $55,000 per year for nursing home services (AARP, 2002) and can be well over $20,000 per year for extensive home care services, these expenses can be devastating to families who lack private insurance. For that reason many Americans ultimately turn for help to the Medicaid program.

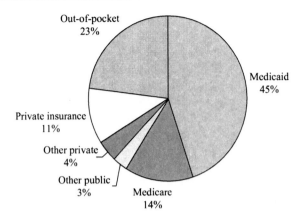

Figure 11.4   Funding sources for long-term care
Source: GAO 2002.

MEDICAID. The Medicaid program, which was originally established to help low income families meet acute care needs, has become the most important public program providing long-term care. And since originally it was not designed to play such a role, it is not surprising that almost no one expresses satisfaction with the long-term care benefits provided by Medicaid. Despite current public expenditures of nearly $43 billion on that part of Medicaid, many gaps and inequities remain (US CBO, 1999).

Medicaid provides mostly nursing home coverage and eligibility is limited to individuals who have spent down their income and assets to very low levels.[3] Middle-income people benefit from the program but only once they have already devoted most of their resources to paying for care. Thus, Medicaid essentially offers protection after catastrophe has already occurred. Medicaid has been characterized as insurance where the deductible is your lifetime savings and the coinsurance is your annual income. Nonetheless, since it is the only public program to offer substantial coverage to the disabled population, Medicaid has been used more and more by middle-class families who find the costs of long-term care prohibitively expensive. It is no longer confined to a minority of persons with low incomes.

For many American families, the spend-down requirements represent a very unpalatable option, and have led to systematic efforts to subvert these requirements. Policy-makers have become alarmed at the resulting growth and perceived manipulation of the system – for example, by those who have substantial resources but choose to give them to relatives or make other arrangements in order to qualify under Medicaid. This makes them eligible sooner than if they used those resources to pay for care. While this abuse may not be widespread, it is substantial enough to create considerable concern about fairness. And, in some areas of the country, such as New York, the feeling is that the abuses are large and come from those with very high incomes. Recent changes in the law to limit transfers of assets reflected a direct response to these perceived abuses. But these new state activities in areas such as estate recovery programs may penalize most those who are least sophisticated while failing to curb abuses by those able to afford sophisticated legal advice. Thus, the welfare nature of the program creates problems for both government and the public. The bottom line issue is whether enough is saved through these stringent spend-down requirements to justify the dissatisfaction and abuse that have developed around Medicaid.

The rapid growth in the costs of long-term care have also led states to focus on holding down the number of nursing home beds, to limit reimbursement for nursing homes, and to restrict their programs to institutional settings as additional ways to hold down spending. For example, limits on home care programs reflect the fact that placing bounds on services is more difficult in a setting where individuals remain comfortably at home. Such individuals would see government-provided services as a benefit with few costs and hence seek more services whenever possible. In contrast, having to make a major decision to move to an institutional environment is itself an impediment to demanding such care. This, perhaps more than any other reason, is why Medicaid policy continues to be dominated by nursing home care. For example, in 1992, almost 90 percent of all Medicaid long-term care dollars for the elderly were for nursing home services (Coughlin et al., 1994), and in 1998 the share was still 85 percent (unpublished Urban Institute calculations, 2002).

MEDICARE AND OTHER PUBLIC SOURCES. Although Medicaid is by far the dominant public program contributing to long-term care spending for the elderly, Medicare and other public programs also offer some support. Medicare, which focuses on acute care services, often overlaps into long-term care. In addition, the Veteran's Administration is active in providing a range of long-term care services to those who qualify for its services. In fact, the VA is often viewed as an innovative leader in this area. Social Services Block Grants and elderly nutrition programs of the Administration on Aging also offer limited benefits to those in need. But these are appropriated programs, and not very generously funded. Moreover, the Social Services Block Grants cover a variety of services and long-term care must compete for a share of the total. Finally, some states provide community services on a small scale to persons in need when they do not wish to seek to qualify under the Medicaid rubric.

While Medicare is supposed to be restricted to acute care needs, it is difficult to firmly distinguish when care has passed from acute to long-term care status. For example, an elderly woman who breaks her hip is likely to receive skilled nursing facility care or home health services (or perhaps both) following hospitalization to treat the broken hip. But at what point does that woman's need shift from rehabilitation services for the hip to meeting other needs that she has for supportive care? Particularly if she has other health problems, such as diabetes or high blood pressure, for example, her recovery may be slow and complicated. At what point should benefits cease to be viewed as stabilizing or improving the patient? These are the types of decisions that are required of those who oversee Medicare services. And over time, those judgments have shifted, resulting in rapid growth through the early 1990s, for example, and then declining after legislative changes in 1997.

LONG-TERM CARE INSURANCE. By the end of 1999, about 6.8 million Americans had purchased private insurance policies, although some of those do not remain in force. As yet, they only cover a small share of long-term care spending, although this should increase over time. Moreover, policies that promise adequate protection against likely costs (a standard some do not meet) are not affordable by those senior citizens most in need of protection. Indeed, these policies are held disproportionately by those with higher incomes; in 2000, 42 percent of all policies were held by people with annual incomes above $50,000.

The Health Insurance Association of America (2000) estimated the average annual premium for such a policy as $1,677, although the number would be higher for anyone who purchases insurance at an older age. And part of the "cost" of making such insurance affordable is precluding anyone with a long list of health problems from purchasing policies. Further, acceptance of the purchase of this new type of private insurance is bound to be slow. It will be many years before companies can point to a successful track record in this area since there is likely to be a long lag between purchase of insurance and payment of benefits. Indeed, a number of analysts have argued that the public is responding rationally by not purchasing private long-term care insurance (Pauly, 1990).

Efforts to encourage employers to offer such coverage to employees, even without subsidies, may help in the growth of such policies. When purchased by individuals in their working years, policies are less expensive. There is more of a problem with individuals dropping the policies at some point, and thus losing protection. Efforts by the federal government to encourage take-up of long-term care policies that began in 2002 will be closely watched. (See Box 11.1 on federal workers' LTC insurance.)

INFORMAL CARE. By its very nature, informal care is difficult to define and measure. It may be as simple as doing grocery shopping for an older person or taking them to the doctor. Or, it may be intensive care by a relative living with the disabled person, meeting a wide range of supportive needs. Since most of this care is delivered by a friend or relative, payments are not usually made for the services. In terms of lost wages or the value of leisure time lost, however, caregiving can represent a major sacrifice by the individual providing such services. Because of these implicit high costs, many policy-makers fear that if services become available through the private sector, provision of informal care will decline. A number of studies, however, have concluded that caregivers continue to play an important role in the lives of those they are helping even when other services become available (Cohen et al., 2001; Penning, 2002). Other types of informal care may include arrangements such as paying a neighbor to do grocery shopping; although

---

Box 11.1 *Private Long-term Care Insurance and the Federal Government*

Although private long-term care insurance has been offered in the United States for about twenty years, it has been slow to develop. The number of policies sold in the United States is still quite small and only a few individuals have actually drawn benefits from this insurance. This is difficult insurance to price: insurers must calculate the likelihood that those who sign up will continue in the program for many years before receiving benefits, the numbers of individuals who will eventually draw on those benefits and the average cost of the benefits for those who receive them. Since this takes place over a long period of time, insurers need to be cautious. If they price the product too high, no one will buy, but if they price it too low, the insurer will not have enough resources to pay benefits when the time comes.

Many believe that its future growth depends upon employers offering this coverage to their employees (even if all or most of the costs are borne by the employees). Group coverage has the advantage of getting the policies before individuals in their prime working years. Costs of marketing are low and, if purchased by persons in their thirties and forties, premiums are not very high.

The federal government has taken a major step in this direction, setting an example for other employers, by offering long-term care insurance coverage to federal workers. Open enrollment for workers began in early 2002 and extended through December 31, 2002. During that period, substantial educational efforts were undertaken and those who signed up during this period were allowed to do so with little required underwriting. That is, the number of conditions that could preclude an individual from obtaining coverage were relatively limited (as compared to individual long-term care insurance enrollment). And even for those who are declined by the screening process, more limited insurance will be made available.

The benefit offered by a consortium of two insurance companies is an "indemnity product." That is, a person will become entitled to a daily benefit amount times a certain number of years of coverage from which he or she can draw resources as needed. The amount of coverage can vary depending upon what the individual chooses.

This experiment will be closely watched to see what share of workers take up the offer of insurance – and at what level and at what age. In the constantly evolving process of offering this insurance, insurers, employers and potential clients all remain cautious about the future.

---

payments are occurring, they are unlikely to be captured well in most formal measures of long-term care.

PROBLEMS WITH THE CURRENT SYSTEM

Almost no one expresses satisfaction with the long-term care benefits provided by Medicaid, the primary payer of long-term care – apart from individuals' own resources. Despite current public expenditures of over $43 billion on long-term care by the Medicaid program, many gaps and inequities remain. Most experts agree that further efforts to expand the availability of long-term care services are desirable, but there is little consensus on how any expansion should take place or how it would be financed.

Moreover, expansions that seemed possible in the context of broader health care reform are likely to be much less feasible in an environment in which Medicaid will be more likely to be contracted than expanded. Nonetheless, improvements in the public provision of long-term care will remain an important goal of those who recognize the following concerns associated with the existing Medicaid program.

Lack of home and community-based services

One of the most commonly cited problems with long-term care is the strong emphasis on institutional benefits and the exclusion of other services. For many years, nursing home services were about all that Medicaid covered in long-term care. Program rules encouraged this emphasis in the beginning and institutional care is a required federal benefit. Although the federal government now allows greater flexibility in services that can be offered, many states have been reluctant to expand substantially into home and community-based services.[4] Despite rapid growth in the home and community-based services area of over 20 percent per year since 1984, Medicaid remains primarily a nursing home program.

Again, this problem is largely a financial one. At present, states are often reluctant to expand their Medicaid programs, recognizing that new benefits, even if cost saving for some, are likely to be additive to their existing expenditures. Once people are in nursing homes, it is difficult to move them back into the community. And a new home and community-based benefit program could rapidly expand, resulting in very high expenditures unless other types of controls are put in place.

If states are relieved of some of the required benefits they now must provide under the program in exchange for greater state efforts in long-term care, some states might opt to shift more dollars from the institutional side of the program into home and community-based services. The balance of services might improve, but perhaps at the expense of provision of nursing home services for those who do not have the option of remaining in the community. Whenever interest arises in expansions of these services, it is often because policy-makers hope to reduce nursing home costs elsewhere. For example, the Bush Administration, and the Clinton Administration, before it proposed making it easier for states to offer non-institutional care. In practice, however, there has never been strong evidence that such changes would save money since many more individuals are likely to seek care in the home. States have moved cautiously in this area, fearing cost increases in their program. Particularly in an environment where states are likely to be in straightened financial circumstances for some time to come, this is unlikely to change.

The welfare nature of Medicaid

Unlike insurance, which protects people against financial catastrophe, our current system mainly provides protection *after* catastrophe occurs. Medicaid is thus not an insurance program; it is a welfare program for those who have impoverished themselves. To be eligible for Medicaid, individuals must either initially be poor or spend enough on acute or long-term health care so that their incomes minus health care spending are low enough to qualify. Further, they must not have substantial assets.

Since long-term care is so expensive, many people qualify by "spending down" either their income, their assets, or both. A number of economists have pointed out how these requirements run contrary to the goals of encouraging older Americans to save for retirement. And even after becoming eligible, families must devote much of their income toward the cost of that care; that is, Medicaid only picks up the amounts not paid by the family or individual. In the case of a single person, this will amount to *all* income above a personal needs allowance – usually $30 per month. Moreover, the special rules for nursing home asset protections that help couples avoid spending down all their assets do not apply for home and community-based services.

The welfare aspect of a long-term care program leads to a number of problems. First, much of the public's dislike of Medicaid centers on the requirement that individuals impoverish themselves or at least lower substantially their standards of living in order to receive help from the government. The relaxation of requirements on couples where one spouse enters a nursing home has eased the problem, but certainly has not solved it. Particularly for older persons who have saved all their lives, the limits are often viewed as punitive. And when a spouse is left in straitened economic circumstances, it may make dependence on Medicaid more likely in the future for the surviving member of the couple.

The harsh eligibility requirements also create problems with compliance. In part because Medicaid spend-down requirements are viewed as unfair, organized efforts to circumvent the law have sprung up. An entire legal industry for "estate planning" built around Medicaid eligibility determination and tax avoidance has been part of this effort. Divestiture of assets to children or other relatives offers a means for protecting resources, while becoming eligible for help from Medicaid. Such responses tap state budgets to pay for middle-class beneficiaries. It also means that people who do not engage in such activities do not get help, leading to resentment that people in the same circumstances are not treated equally. To reduce gaming of the system, states are required to look back three years or longer for asset transfers that appear to take place solely to qualify for Medicaid.

On the other hand, many older persons fear most having to depend upon Medicaid and seek to avoid it, if possible. The stigma Americans associate with welfare operates as a powerful disincentive to obtaining care. Moreover, private pay patients have advantages in nursing homes not usually available to Medicaid beneficiaries, resulting in a two-tier system.

Variability in programs across states

State Medicaid programs vary enormously across a number of dimensions (AARP, 2000). For example, total Medicaid spending on long-term care per person aged 65 and above ranged from $5,086 in New York to $599 in Nevada in 1999.[5] Spending on home and community-based services varied from $1,710 in New York to $62 in Mississippi. These disparate levels of effort in part reflect differences in states' abilities to contribute to the program. But in addition, they capture states' willingness to expend resources on these particular programs. If we believe as a society that there should be a minimum level of protection for the costs of long-term care for those of modest means, it makes little sense to have the level of variation that now exists. Thus, expansion that builds on Medicaid would need to deal with this variability. New benefit programs should be cognizant of the pitfalls of creating new joint federal/state programs that could replicate this problem. Solutions are often difficult, however, since bringing up the low states with greater federal contributions effectively penalizes the more generous states. To avoid this problem, solutions often become much more costly, offering enhanced benefits to everyone.

Lack of coordination with acute care

Since acute care services for the elderly mainly occur under Medicare and long-term care services are under the purview of Medicaid, there is a natural tendency for each program to seek to shift the burdens off onto the other. This is exacerbated by the fact that states must pay a substantial share of the costs of Medicaid, but none of Medicare's costs. For example, a nursing home patient covered by Medicaid who develops an acute problem will often be sent to a hospital for Medicare to pay, even if it might be both feasible and less disruptive to keep the patient in the nursing home. Moreover, providers are almost always better reimbursed by Medicare than by Medicaid, leading to group of physicians who do not take Medicaid patients and thus to some discontinuities in care. Any well-designed program for improving long-term care ought to seek better integration of care between the two programs, or at the very least, a reduction in the incentives for gaming that currently exist. But many of the approaches to health care reform thus undertaken treat long-term care as a very separate piece.

Disincentives to purchase long-term care insurance

Many advocates of long-term care insurance as a solution to the problem of meeting the needs of the elderly cite barriers that discourage individuals from purchasing this coverage. Even among those who could afford to obtain such coverage, take-up has been quite low.

The problem for the private sector is to guess what costs and needs will be in 20 years. Insurance companies face the dilemma of either pricing conservatively and thus discouraging sales, or later canceling policies if costs rise faster than anticipated. And if policies do not sufficiently keep up with the costs of long-term care, they may not protect even those who do buy insurance. There is some anecdotal evidence that people who have insurance cannot afford the cost sharing and extra costs beyond what the insurance is offering. Modest-income individuals may see Medicaid as a reasonable safety net and hence find no reason to buy coverage. And those with very high incomes can "self insure." For these and other reasons, many Americans have hesitated to buy policies. Consequently, it seems unlikely that long-term care insurance will expand sufficiently to address this unmet need, even with the recent changes in tax policy intended to stimulate sales (Wiener, 1997). The range will likely always be limited.

Usually it is better to spread the risk of such an expense. It is both difficult to predict who will need care and when that happens the costs are substantial – characteristics of a situation that lends itself well to insurance. However, the uncertainty about future costs requires insurers to build up large reserves and protect themselves against the potential for much higher than anticipated losses. This uncertainty thus reduces some of the advantages from risk pooling.

On the other hand, sales of such insurance have grown over time and early experience with claims indicates that ADL measures have worked reasonably well in allowing individuals to qualify for help. Premiums are less expensive if people purchase coverage long before it will be needed, and the willingness of employers to offer (often at full cost) such insurance to their employees has also helped with the expansion of this insurance. Nearly a quarter of policies written now are done so through employers (GAO, 2000).

Personnel issues

Work in the area of long-term care is challenging. It requires strength and patience in dealing with people who are frail and sometimes very unhappy about their situations. Persons with Alzheimer's disease, for example, can become aggressive and violent in some instances. Further, long-term care must rely on the goodwill and careful observance of patients' needs by workers when the patient cannot advocate for herself. On the other hand, individuals who are physically very frail may be very mentally alert and only too aware of the limitations that their bodies present. High rates of depression in nursing homes also present challenges to workers. Thus, long-term care workers must deal with many unpleasant situations.

It is no surprise then that personnel issues are a commonly cited problem for long-term care today and expected in the future. Nationwide, there are over 2 million paraprofessionals providing long-term care services (Paraprofessional Healthcare Institute, 2001). These workers are disproportionately women and persons of color, and often wages are lower than for less demanding jobs elsewhere in the economy. Such low pay can lead to a less than desirable population serving the needs of older persons and high rates of turnover.

Public policy concerns about payment of aide workers has often centered on requirements that increases in payments be passed through to workers in the form of higher wages. As of 2000, 26 states had some type of legislation seeking to raise pay for long-term care workers, but that has as yet done little to ease the problems. Under a less robust economic picture, jobs in long-term care may become more attractive.

Quality issues

A wide range of quality issues are raised for long-term care. Patients with dementia or severe physical limitations are vulnerable to abuse or neglect. And in the case of home care, it is difficult to provide oversight. Thus, personnel issues often come to the fore. It is important not only to have competent workers but also workers who are sensitive to the needs of this population.

In 1986, a path-breaking study of nursing homes found many quality problems and unmet needs (Committee on Nursing Home Regulation, 1986). This led to the establishment of sweeping new regulations, but as yet little has been done to implement those regulations. The greater expense that improvements would require has been an obstacle to change. Consequently, when the General Accounting Office went to nursing homes in California in 2000, investigators found many problems and procedures that have long since been denounced. But even when the situations are sub-par, state officials are often reluctant to close homes because of the disruptions caused and often because of a lack of beds available elsewhere.

Nonetheless, some states have moved aggressively to improve oversight and quality of nursing home operations. There is also a federal ombudsman program which funds individuals in each state to serve as patients' representatives. But in an area where appropriate care is not well defined and where few norms or standards have been set, it is difficult to measure quality. Much of the effort in this area focuses on appropriate inputs, not on the outcomes that ideally would be measured.

For example, one of the challenges in the provision of long-term care rests with the amount of specific services needed. In the institutional area, recommendations on hours per day of direct or total care per resident have been discussed. Studies have shown that time spent with patients does improve the quality of care. One conference of experts in 1998 recommended at least 4.13 hours of direct care per day – a standard not met by about half of all facilities. Other studies have focused on registered nurses and also found inadequate amounts of time being devoted to patient care in many facilities.

APPROACHES TO IMPROVE COVERAGE AND MEET OTHER NEEDS

As recently as the mid-1980s, serious discussions of a comprehensive program of social insurance for long-term care took place. Such a program would guarantee to all disabled persons access to nursing home, and home and community-based services as needed. But the high and escalating price tags for long-term care, coupled with the enormous growth in the acute care portions of Medicare and Medicaid, moved the discussion away from such solutions to more modest initial steps. The Clinton approach was to offer a new home and community-based services program outside of Medicaid, phased in gradually over time, and to require improvement in the nursing home portion of Medicaid (US Congress, 1993). Democratic attempts to build consensus in 1994 generally kept the basic outline of a new home and community-based services program, but stretched out the phase-in period. The Bush administration has eased restrictions on providing home and community-based services under Medicaid, but has not provided additional federal resources.

Reforms to the financing of care

The limited home and community-based block grant approach proposed by the Clinton administration as part of its overall health care package now likely represents an upper bound on possible expansion of long-term care services in the public sector. Another approach would be to encourage purchase of private long-term care insurance, supplemented by modest expansions in Medicaid for those with the lowest incomes. The least inclusive proposals now under discussion would only provide tax relief for those purchasing insurance or providing caregiving.

The biggest policy issue over time is likely to be whether the problems of affordability of long-term care are best handled through the public or the private sector. Some form of insurance is likely to be needed, but the question is whether this should be privately run and managed on a voluntary basis (perhaps with subsidies) or publicly run as a social insurance program. Protections will undoubtedly be needed for those with low incomes, but how should we handle the needs of the rest of the elderly population?

Even if proposals to expand publicly-supported long-term care are again seriously debated in the next few years, it is likely that any long-term care piece will be modest, at least initially. Options likely to receive the most attention would likely limit both eligibility and benefits to keep the scope of any new program manageable. But even a private sector approach relying on insurance would likely need to be spurred on with either subsidies, tax benefits, or both.

LIMITED PUBLIC EXPANSION. Any effort to improve public provision of long-term care is likely to take place in incremental steps. The first way to limit how much is spent on expanded long-term care coverage would be to rely upon the welfare-based approach of Medicaid and means test access to any program, restricting eligibility based on the financial situation of disabled persons, usually in terms of both income and assets. While this approach concentrates eligibility on those least able to pay, it may result in making persons ineligible who still could not afford the costs of long-term care. That is, if income and asset limits are low enough to substantially limit the number of disabled persons who qualify, many who need services would be excluded. In most states, Medicaid deals with this problem by establishing eligibility on the basis of income after health care spending has been subtracted.[6] In other words, persons will ultimately get government help but only after they have "spent down" their incomes and assets. And as discussed above, this is extremely unpopular with potential beneficiaries, in part because of its punitive character. It seems inconsistent with other goals of aging that stress saving for future needs. For those who ultimately go onto Medicaid, having to spend down assets just postpones receipt of benefits.

Moreover, the level where these limits are set will determine how well a combined public/private approach would fill in the gaps for those with moderate incomes. If set too low, it would be unlikely that private purchase of insurance could attract most of those ineligible for the means-tested program.

Another way to expand Medicaid would be to reduce the spend down requirements, allowing people to become eligible sooner, but continuing to require substantial annual contributions toward the cost of care. Thus, eligibility could extend further up the income scale, but higher income persons would have to contribute to the costs of care. This cuts costs directly through the sharing of expenses and may limit demand for care when recipients must pay something for the care. It is less burdensome than a full spend down requirement and hence may be somewhat less subject to the gaming which often occurs under the traditional Medicaid approach. Those with short-term needs could get help without having to divest all their assets. Long stayers would ultimately tap many of their resources, but on a more gradual basis and where public contributions would be apparent. It may be possible to achieve much the same goal as means testing but in a less demeaning fashion. If viewed as a fairer system, efforts to avoid the rules might go down.

Costs may also be limited by restricting eligibility to those with severe disabilities. This may satisfy concerns of policy-makers about mildly disabled persons taking advantage of homemaker and personal care services that they do not need. It is easier to make a case for needs for the severely disabled population. At the same time, however, this precludes early intervention for disabled persons whose functional limitations might be reduced or eliminated. Critics of limited long-term care coverage often make the analogy to preventive services for acute care. Moreover, many of the exciting innovations in long-term care are occurring for the less severely disabled who are still able to retain considerable independence. But if severity is the strategy for limiting eligibility, the program would not be able to take advantage of these innovations.

A fourth way to reduce the costs of new coverage would be to limit benefits offered – often by expanding just home and community based services, for example. While home and community-based services are the most undeveloped part of long-term care, what people fear most are the crippling costs of institutional care. Moreover, any strategy that places arbitrary limits on how care may be delivered will likely distort choices and lead to inefficiency.

A fifth strategy would focus on controlling payments to care providers. This could be done by price controls or fee schedules for services to limit the rate of growth

---

Box 11.2 *On Lok and PACE*

One innovative program coordinating acute and long-term care needs has been formally adopted as part of the Medicare program. The acronym, PACE, for Program for All-inclusive Care for the Elderly was created as part of 1997 legislation and can now be established anywhere in the US. Largely serving the very frail dual-eligible population, PACE seeks to provide an interdisciplinary team approach to providing intensive care while keeping most of its clients in the community. It includes more than just medical services, however, incorporating adult day care activities, therapy, counseling, meals and transportation services to assure that clients get the services they need.

PACE evolved from one program started in 1971 in San Francisco's Chinatown called On Lok. On Lok began as a day health center where seniors could receive supervision, health care and other services. On Lok launched a Medicare-funded demonstration in 1979 to demonstrate that it could provide services in a cost-effective manner even though it covered much more than the basic services. Since 1983, On Lok has had waivers from both Medicare and Medicaid allowing the organization to receive a capitated payment to provide care.

Viewed as a successful model, PACE demonstrations were established around the country before achieving a permanent place as a Medicare option. While there has been great interest and a number of programs that have begun to replicate On Lok, this program remains a very small part of Medicare and Medicaid. In 2002, just 8,000 people participated in the program. A key question for the future of PACE is whether it can and should expand to encompass a larger share of the Medicare population.

---

of payments. Moreover, allowing less formal care to be provided, thus avoiding expensive certified agencies, is another way to potentially limit provider reimbursements. Critics of this strategy claim that we likely get what we pay for and if payments are too restrictive, quality of care received will likely suffer. In fact, as discussed above, shortages of workers in this field have already caused problems for long-term care providers of all sorts.

Finally, some proposals place fixed limits on the amount of dollars allowed for the program. For example, the federal government could either give grants to states or offer a matching program with an upper bound on what the federal government is willing to contribute. This is in contrast to the open-ended nature of Medicaid, which expands automatically when eligibility and service needs rise. A variation on this approach is to combine broad eligibility standards with fixed appropriations. These so-called "capped entitlements" are intended to avoid the problem of expenses going up directly in response to beneficiary demand, while assuring open-ended eligibility to the disabled. If states or other entities are left to administer such a program, they must find ways to live within budgets (or bear the risks of higher costs themselves).

Each of these options for limiting the scope of any long-term care expansion thus has advantages and disadvantages. Any program that seeks to hold down the costs of long-term care must adopt several of these strategies. If means testing is a major strategy, it makes sense to build on the Medicaid program (or at least take the existing Medicaid program and combine it with any newly named long-term care system).

But if means testing is ruled out as a mechanism for limiting public liability, the other strategies could be combined to create a complimentary long-term care program. This was the strategy of the Clinton proposal and others. They would have used all of the techniques aside from means testing to lower costs. However, full implementation would still have meant new federal spending of about $40 billion per year in 1990. Consequently, these proposals sought to limit the initial costs of the new long-term care benefit by phasing in the system very slowly over time. Few details were offered on how to accomplish this feat, however, suggesting that it would have been very difficult to develop such a plan. Instead, the burdens of deciding how to limit spending would have fallen to the states since they would have been liable for any promised benefits beyond the "capped" federal payments. It is not clear in retrospect whether states would have been willing to gamble on such a program.

FACILITATING PUBLIC/PRIVATE PARTNERSHIPS. In an effort to help expand coverage for long-term care beyond what a public expansion would offer, there might be efforts to encourage families and individuals to purchase long-term care insurance. Currently, over 6 million persons hold such coverage and it is likely that more policies will be sold in the future. But what will it take to expand this line of business enough to provide serious relief? If substantial tax benefits or offering those with insurance some expedited eligibility for Medicaid as a back-up are considered, new federal resources will be needed as well for this part of the effort.

Americans thus far have shown a healthy skepticism about policies that is well-founded. A first step for making insurance a more viable option would be to establish federal standards to protect consumers. These would include outlawing high pressure tactics in marketing, and requiring inflation adjustments so that the benefits would provide adequate protection when the services are needed. If products are to be made attractive to younger persons, some type of nonforfeiture benefit is needed to guarantee that someone who pays in for 20 years but then lapses can withdraw some portion of the payments. (Insurance companies now price insurance premiums low for those in their 40s, for example, precisely because they build into their calculations that many will fail to keep their premiums current until they need the care.) All these changes would add to the costs and reduce the number of persons who would buy such coverage. The National Association of Insurance Commissioners have developed guidelines, but they lack the teeth necessary to enforce standards.

Estimates prepared for the Pepper Commission (1990) indicated that only 6 percent of today's elderly population could afford such a policy without spending more than 5 percent of their income – and even then, they would not be fully protected against the costs of care.[7] Many older Americans wishing to protect themselves from the costs of long-term care would have to lower their standards of living for many years in order to obtain partial protection. Rice, Thomas and Weissert (1991) also found that the insurance policies they studied failed to provide much protection against the possibility of high out of pocket costs from long-term care expenses. High deductibles and relatively low daily payment rates may leave policy holders vulnerable to spending down their assets even if they have insurance, for example. At the end of the 1990s, the picture was not that much improved.

Thus, private insurance, with the addition of consumer protection standards, can offer a minority of Americans some security against the financial risks of long-term care. As policies improve, at least some expansion of this market can be expected. But for the vast majority of the elderly, anyone who already has a disabling condition, and the younger population with a small but real risk of long-term care needs, the emerging market provides little prospect of protection. Major expansion of the private sector would require new public spending or tax benefits.

New ways of organizing and delivering care

Long-term care changes will likely occur very slowly because of funding limitations. The Medicaid program will continue to feel the strains of enormous expenditures and face pressures to reduce rather than expand. Any greater flexibility in terms of benefits and eligibility would undoubtedly lead to greater costs, so it will be tempting to freeze the current system in place. But, again, even without reform a number of things will change. Burdens on Medicaid will likely increase precipitously as the population continues to age (Wiener et al., 1994), even if benefits are not made more generous. As health care costs rise faster than the incomes of older Americans, the likelihood of their spending down and becoming eligible for Medicaid rises over time.

Nonetheless, there have been efforts to improve care. For many years, states have been encouraged to develop their own home and community-based services through a waiver program in Medicaid. These programs have allowed innovation that a number of states have used to their advantage. Further, Oregon has focused on moving people out of nursing homes and into less institutionally-oriented settings such as group homes.

In addition, there have been a number of experiments aimed at improving care, particularly through better coordination of acute and long-term care services. In particular, the Program of All Inclusive Care for the Elderly (PACE) has grown from one model (On Lok) in California to a nationally-sanctioned program that combines Medicare and Medicaid funding. This program, however, aims to aid the extremely frail and disabled and remains a very small part of the picture. (See Box 11.2 on On Lok.)

Finally, the hospice movement, which seeks to help patients with terminal illnesses, may also be considered a model for long-term care. Medicare is the largest funder of hospice; in that case, individuals with a terminal illness may choose to go into hospice, foregoing curative care for their terminal illness. In exchange, the hospice offers more intensive home care, counseling services, and some prescription drugs. Patients usually remain at home. Some of the lessons learned in this area could be important for providing expanded services to those not in the last six months of life, but who nonetheless have a combination of medical and supportive needs.

CONCLUSION

Will things get better in the future? The answer is likely to be yes, at least for some older Americans. Disability does seem to be coming later for many Americans as they age, postponing at least the problems of multiple health care needs. But as described above, this is not likely to be a magic elixir that eliminates the need for long-term care services.

As a society, we will likely be wealthier over time, even counting the costs of an aging society. Older persons and their families who have considerable resources can undoubtedly cobble together a reasonable set of long-term care services – although even there the lack of coordination and the complexity of needs make this a burdensome task. Private insurance may continue to expand and evolve, further aiding those who have the means to purchase such coverage. For those with more modest resources, however, the question of how generous we choose to be as a society will be a major factor (e.g. see Feder, 2001). Improvements can certainly be made in the provision of long-term care services, but that will require a commitment of taxpayer resources.

Long-term care problems that arise from poor health and frailty often result in the need for supportive care for long periods of time. In addition to medical needs to treat conditions such as stroke, broken bones, or heart disease, patients with these chronic needs also need help to improve functioning and quality of life. And without such help, the medical costs can rise when conditions worsen.

The current long-term care "system" is based on informal home care for many and formal care at home, in nursing homes and other residential settings. Expenditures for long-term care, not counting the informal support of families and friends, are high ($123 billion in 2000) and growing rapidly. But private insurance aid is limited and public programs focus mainly on those with low incomes or who have "spent down" to effectively become poor. The Medicaid program – using both federal and state funds – is the primary formal payer of long-term care services. For many older persons, long-term care expenses weigh heavily on even those with substantial incomes, putting the healthier spouse at financial risk as well as making demands on the spouse as a caregiver.

Without systematic help for families needing long-term care and with great variations across the US in the quality and quantity of services available, there are a lot of shortcomings in the current "system." It is difficult, for example, to reach individuals with resources too low to allow them to use some of the innovative facilities that are now available (such as Continuing Care Retirement Communities). And although the very poor can rely on Medicaid, it heavily emphasizes institutional care, sometimes of dubious quality. Thus, a considerable amount of unmet need remains. It is also important to find ways to improve the coordination of acute and long-term care.

Despite the strong case that can be made for doing more in this area, the costs of any expansion of long-term care services and its status as a less urgent need than financial and acute care support for older Americans have resulted in inaction for many years. This is an important area for assessing how many resources society is willing to devote to this population.

DISCUSSION QUESTIONS

Comment on the reasonableness of these statements:

1 Long-term care is not covered by Medicare because relatively few older persons need this type of assistance.
2 In the future as health continues to improve, even fewer people will need long-term care as part of Medicare.
3 Because everyone is at risk of needing long-term care, the government should provide this type of assistance.
4 Medicaid provides long-term care assistance to the truly needy and this insures that everyone who needs to be in a nursing home is provided with a room in an appropriate facility.
5 Individuals who are concerned about their future needs can purchase long-term care insurance in the private market.
6 Our system of long-term care involves federal and state governments and the private sector. The coordination across these groups is working well and should be continued.

Notes

1 Interestingly, this measure is ability to handle money. There seems to be a very close correlation between a reported decline in this as a problem and the required shift of Social Security payments from checks to direct deposits (Spillman, 2002).
2 For instance, see the differing viewpoints of Cutler (2001) and Wolf (2001) on this issue.
3 "Spend down" is a term used to refer to the requirement that before becoming eligible, an individual must use all of his assets above a certain cut-off to pay for care. And then after becoming asset eligible, he must spend essentially most of his income each period before Medicaid will pay the balance.
4 Personal care, which is an optional service under Medicaid, has become a major new way to expand services for some states, such as New York. Several waiver programs are now in place and restrictions on them have been eased. The 1915 (c) waiver programs used to be limited to those at risk of institutionalization and now can be used for certain persons with chronic conditions as well. Moreover, the 1915 (d) program for the elderly no longer has to meet the budget-neutrality requirements that restricted its use originally.
5 Arizona is a special case since its program is run as a federal demonstration grant outside Medicaid. Hence, although its averages are even lower they are not shown here.
6 But there are some states that do not offer a medically needy option. In those states, eligibility is very limited.
7 Although 5 percent does not seem to be an exorbitant amount, it would be an addition to any insurance purchased for acute care. Moreover, as a premium that must be consistently paid for many years, most analysts believe that the annual cost needs to be quite low.

References

AARP 2000: *Across the States 2000: Profiles of Long-Term Care Systems*, 4th edn. Washington, DC: AARP Public Policy Institute.

AARP 2002: *Beyond 50: A Report to the Nation on Trends in Health Security* (May). Washington, DC: AARP.

Agency for Health Care Policy and Research 1992: Unpublished data from the National Medical Expenditure Survey, US Department of Health and Human Services.

Bishop, Christine 2002: Chronic and long-term care needs of elders and persons with disabilities. Presentation at the National Academy of Social Insurance, January 24.

Cohen, Marc A., Miller, Jessica, and Weinrobe, Maurice 2001: Patterns of informal and formal caregiving among elders with private long-term care insurance. *The Gerontologist* 41 (2) (April): 180–7.

Committee on Nursing Home Regulation, Institute of Medicine 1986: *Improving the Quality of Care in Nursing Homes*. Washington, DC: National Academy Press.

Coughlin, Terri, Holahan, John, and Ku, Leighton 1994: *Medicaid Since 1980*. Washington, DC: Urban Institute Press.

Cutler, David M. 2001: Declining disability among the elderly. *Health Affairs* 20 (6): 11–27.

Dawson, Steven L. and Surpin, Rick 2001: *Direct-Care Health Workers: The Unnecessary Crisis in Long-Term Care* (January). Queenstown, MD: Aspen Institute, Domestic Strategy Group.

Desai, Mayur, Lentzer, Harold R., and Dawson Weeks, Julie 2001: Unmet need for personal assistance with activities of daily living among older adults. *The Gerontologist* 41 (1) (February): 82–8.

Feder, Judith 2001: Long-term care: a public responsibility. *Health Affairs* 20 (6): 112–13.

Federal Interagency Forum on Aging-Related Statistics 2000: *Older Americans 2000: Key Indicators of Well-Being (Federal Interagency Forum on Aging-Related Statistics)* (August). Washington, DC: US Government Printing Office.

General Accounting Office 1998: *California Nursing Homes: Care Problems Persist Despite Federal and State Oversight*. Pub. No. HEHS-98-202. Washington, DC: Government Printing Office, July 27.

General Accounting Office 2000: *State Pharmacy Programs: Assistance Designed to Target Coverage and Stretch Budgets* (Pub. No. HEHS-00-162, September). Washington, DC: US Government Printing Office.

General Accounting Office 2002: Long-term care: aging baby boom generation will increase demand and burden on federal and state budgets. Testimony of David Walker before the Special Committee on Aging, US Senate.

Hagen, Stuart 1999: *Projections of Expenditures for Long-Term Care Services for the Elderly*. Washington, DC: Congressional Budget Office. http://www.cbo.gov/showdoc.cfm?index=1123&sequence=0 (accessed March 12, 1999).

Health Insurance Association of America 2000: *Who Buys Long-Term Care Insurance in 2000? A Decade of Study of Buyers and Nonbuyers* (October). Washington, DC: Health Insurance Association of America.

Hetzel, Lisa and Smith, Annetta 2001: *The 65 Years and Over Population: 2000* (Census 2000 Brief, October). Washington, DC: US Census Bureau.

Keenan, Maryanne P. 1988: *Changing Needs for Long-Term Care: A Chartbook*. Washington, DC: AARP Public Policy Institute.

Krauss, Nancy A. and Altman, Barbara M. 1998: *Characteristics of Nursing Home Residents, 1996* (MEPS Research Findings, No. 5. AHCPR Pub. No. 99–0006). Rockville, MD: Agency for Health Care Policy and Research.

Krout, John A., Oggins, Jean, and Holmes, Heidi H. 2000: Patterns of service use in a continuing care retirement community. *The Gerontologist* 40 (6) (December): 698–705.

Lui, Hongj and Sharma, Ravi 2002: *Health and Health Care of the Medicare Population* (data from the 1998 Medicare Current Beneficiary Survey, March). Rockville, MD: Westat.

Manton, Kenneth 1982: Changing concepts of morbidity and mortality in the elderly population. *Milbank Quarterly* 60: 183–244.

Manton, Kenneth G. et al. 1997: Chronic disability trends in elderly United States populations: 1982–1994. *Proceeding of the National Academy of Sciences* 94 (March): 2593–8.

McCall, Nelda 2001: Long-term care: definition, demand, cost, and financing. In Nelda McCall (ed.), *Who Will Pay for Long-term care?* Chicago: Health Administration Press, 3–31.

Moon, Marilyn and Mulvey, Janemarie 1996: *Entitlements and the Elderly: Protecting Promises, Recognizing Realities.* Washington, DC: Urban Institute Press.

National Center for Assisted Living 1998: *1998 Facts and Trends: The Assisted Living Sourcebook.* Washington, DC: National Center for Assisted Living.

National Center for Assisted Living 2001: *2001 Facts and Trends: The Assisted Living Sourcebook.* Washington, DC: National Center for Assisted Living.

Paraprofessional Healthcare Institute 2001: *Direct-Care Health Workers: The Unnecessary Crisis in Long-Term Care* (January). Washington, DC: Aspen Institute, Domestic Strategy Group.

Pauly, Mark 1990: The rational nonpurchase of long-term-care insurance. *Journal of Political Economy* 98: 153–68.

Penning, Margaret J. 2002: Hydra revisited: substitution formal for self- and informal in-home care among older adults with disabilities. *The Gerontologist* 42 (1) (February): 4–16.

Pepper Commission 1990: *A Call for Action* (US Bipartisan Commission on Comprehensive Health Care, September). Washington, DC: US Government Printing Office.

Rice, Thomas, Thomas, Kathleen, and Weissert, William 1991: The effect of owning private long-term care insurance policies on out-of-pocket costs. *Health Services Research* 25 (February): 907–34.

Spillman, Brenda C. 2002: *Changes in Elderly Disability Rates and the Implications for Health Care Utilization and Cost.* Washington, DC: Office of Disability, Aging, and Long-Term Care Policy, ASPE.

Tilly, Jane, Goldenson, Susan, and Kasten, Jessica 2001: *Long-Term Care: Consumers, Providers and Financing, A Chart Book* (March). Washington, DC: Urban Institute Press.

US Census Bureau 2001: *The 65 and Over Population: 2000* (Census 2000 Brief, October). Washington, DC: US Government Printing Office.

US Congressional Budget Office 1999: *Maintaining Budgetary Discipline: Spending and Revenue Options* (April). Washington, DC: US Government Printing Office.

US House of Representatives 1993: *1993 Green Book: Overview of Entitlement Programs.* (Committee on Ways and Means). Washington, DC: US Government Printing Office.

Waidmann, Timothy A. and Liu, Korbin 2000: Disability trends among elderly persons and implications for the future. *Journal of Gerontology* 55B (5) (September): S298–S307.

Wiener, Joshua M. 1997: How to pay for long-term care. *Washington Post*, April 21.

Wiener, Joshua M., Illston, Laurel, and Hanley, Raymond 1994: *Sharing the Burden: Strategies for Public and Private Long-Term Care Insurance.* Washington, DC: Brookings Institution.

Wolf, Douglas A. 2001: Population change: friend or foe of the chronic care system? *Health Affairs* 20 (6): 28–42.

CPSIA information can be obtained at www.ICGtesting.com
Printed in the USA
LVOW11s0601040813

346063LV00006B/126/P